LIVING PLANTS
OF THE WORLD

LIVING PLANTS OF THE WORLD

The Random House Illustrated Science Library

by Lorus and Margery Milne

Photographs by

Josef Muench
E. Javorsky
E. S. Ross
Ernst Peterson
Lorus and Margery Milne
E. Aubert de La Rue
Ingmar Holmasen
Wilhelm Schacht
Grant Heilman
Vinton Richards
and others

A Chanticleer Press Edition

Random House, New York

*In fond remembrance of Dr. David Fairchild
who taught us how to get the delicious milk
out of a green coconut.*

Preface to the Second Edition

Since the appearance of the first edition of this book and of
translations of it into other languages, we have appreciated
letters from plant admirers in many lands. They have added
to our knowledge and our enjoyment of the green world. A
broadening familiarity with living plants adds to the pleasure
in travel, because peculiar vegetation is recognized in new
settings. In the British Channel Islands, we met luxuriant
hedges of New Zealand daisy bush *(Olearia)* and magnificent
spires of a giant bugloss *(Echium)* from the Canary Islands,
both introduced among native European vegetation and all
favored by warmth from the Gulf of Mexico carried across
the ocean by the Gulf Stream. And, through the generosity
of Mrs. Edward C. Sweeney and stimulating assignments
from Florida International University, we have been able to
live for a while on The Kampong (see pp. 279–280) amid a
fascinating community of tropical trees introduced by our
one-time mentor Dr. David Fairchild.

L. J. M. and M. M.

Durham, New Hampshire

Planned and produced by Chanticleer Press, New York

Library of Congress Catalog Card Number 67-22637

*Manufactured in Zurich, Switzerland:
Color separations by Cliché + Litho
Color printing by Offset + Buchdruck
Black and white gravure printing by Conzett + Huber AG
Bound in USA*

Contents

1

Plants Over the Land

As we look about our world today, we see plants growing almost everywhere on land. In country after country they form great forests. In the wet tropics they lace together into dense jungles. They fill shallow lakes with swamps, and clog the slow reaches of the biggest rivers with vast marshes. Over the arid plains they grow root by root in seemingly endless prairies. In the Arctic, the Antarctic, and high on lofty mountains, they tolerate some of the planet's coldest weather, its harshest winds, its most severe extremes. Even in the driest deserts they find places to thrive. Yet not one of these areas on the continents was clad in vegetation until long after the oceans teemed with life.

Now that plants have colonized the land so thoroughly, we can wonder why it took them (and animals) so long to become tolerant of dry air, intense light, rapid changes in temperature, and other features of terrestrial existence. It seems almost incredible that for 275 million years, plants and animals of conspicuous aquatic kinds should have lived, died, and been preserved as fossils in sedimentary rocks before any of them got a roothold or a foothold in the soil or unfiltered sun. For all those millenia no plant had a root. The earth had no soil. Over its bare continents the sun beat down, with no leaf anywhere to cast a spot of shade.

Of all the plants we can see alive with the naked eye, only the seaweeds, the pond scums and the fungi suggest the types of vegetation to which the world was restricted for so long. Some of the seaweeds are giant kelps, which cling to the bottom along our coasts in as much as sixty feet of water, while displaying great blades supported at the surface by gas-filled floats. They are the nearest approach to trees in the sea. But they cannot survive on land. They die if exposed to air and sun for longer than it takes the tide to ebb and flow over them again. For all their size and rubbery covering, they are almost as dependent upon a constant abundance of water as are their minute green relatives drifting in the upper levels of the open ocean.

Algae of all sizes are the "grass of the sea," upon which ocean-going fishes, sea birds, and whales depend ultimately for food. Drifting algae in fresh waters serve a similar role, and are believed to have nourished the first animals to invade the estuaries, the rivers, and lakes from the sea.

Toward the end of the Ordovician period, some five hundred million years ago, plants began growing flat on the muddy shores of estuaries and lagoons. Fossils of these earliest land plants, named *Foerstia* and *Parka,* resemble in many ways the pioneering lichens that now find places to grow on bare rock, on old stone walls, on tree bark, and on the ground. Possibly the earliest land plants resembled lichens also in consisting of a partnership between an alga and a fungus. In each lichen, the green alga makes food for both partners whenever water and light are available, while the nongreen fungus keeps moisture from evaporating quickly and holds the partners in place upon the land. This cooperative arrangement has allowed lichens to develop immense tolerance for prolonged drought and intense cold, and to grow from the tropics to mountain peaks, from the Arctic to the Antarctic.

According to the fossil record, the Ordovician period had already given way to the Devonian—called the "Age of Fishes"—before any momentous change took place in the inherited nature of plants along the fringe of the desolate land. The alteration had to wait for millions of years, perhaps because the change was statistically so improbable. It involved the simultaneous appearance of several new features, each possibly detrimental alone, but in combination producing a new and auspicious pattern for life. The outcome was the world's first stem as a green structure that could stand erect in the sun and cast a shadow on the ground.

The feature most responsible for letting these Devonian plants grow upright into air was a system of special cells of unusual length. Located near the center of each stem, some of these long cells transported water upward from the wet ground rapidly and efficiently; they kept the stem tip well supplied. Other long cells conducted foodstuffs downward to parts of the plant that were buried in the mud, giving the anchorage needed by an upright stem by being remote from life-giving light. No alga or fungus possesses such elongated conducting cells as a vascular tissue serving all parts of the plant.

Conducting cells are the distinctive mark of just one subdivision of the plant kingdom: the tracheophytes or "vascular plants," which appeared so suddenly in the early Devonian. At first they were few. Today, more than seventy per cent of all the known kinds of vegetation are tracheophytes, so named in reference to the tubelike cells (tracheids) that conduct water and foodstuffs in their stems. They are the familiar trees, shrubs, herbs, and grasses of the land, and include a few (such as water lilies and eelgrass) that are at home in shallow water.

THE DISCOVERY OF PSILOPHYTON

The earliest of all vascular plants that have been found as fossils once grew close to the sea near Rhynie, in Aberdeenshire, Scotland. A Dr. Mackie collected some of them in the rocks there, and sent them to the distinguished botanist Sir William Dawson. Sir William recognized their uniqueness, and named them *Psilophyton* in 1858. He could scarcely have invented a more appropriate name, for the Greek *phyton,* meaning plant, and *psiloun,* meaning to lay bare, describe this bare plant perfectly. It never had any roots or leaves, flowers or fruits. Its firm stem grew horizontally in the wet mud, and sent up erect woody branches at intervals. Like the stem, the branches had near their center long cells of vascular tissue.

The actual center of each stem was occupied by a pith composed of small, almost spherical cells, grouped loosely like a handful of green peas, with air in between. Similar loose cells, bright green with chlorophyll, surrounded the vascular tissue like a thick sheath; in them, the plant made its food in daylight.

As raw materials these cells needed chiefly water from the vascular tissue and carbon dioxide from the air between the cells. In darkness these same spherical cells used up some of their store of food to get energy for life. They exchanged carbon dioxide for oxygen, and in turn released water into the intercellular air.

Covering the earliest stems and branches was an epidermis, consisting of flat cells fitted together tightly. They formed a sheath one cell thick, covered by a thin waterproof cuticle. But here again was novelty, for the epidermis was pierced at many points by breathing pores to which the name *stomata* (Greek for "mouths") has been given. Each stoma was a mouth-shaped hole communicating between the outside world and the intercellular air spaces within the stem. It allowed exchange of oxygen and carbon dioxide. Yet a stoma is more than a pore, for its size can be controlled. It is flanked by two guard cells whose shape often suggests lips. They can part and open the stoma, or press together and close it. They close whenever too much water escapes from the intercellular spaces and the plant begins to wilt. None of the alga or fungus has stomata through its epidermis.

Later in Devonian times, the bare plant *Psilophyton* had shrubby neighbors on the land. They were discovered during the 1920's when two botanists, R. Kidston and W. H. Lang, went to the same Rhynie rocks of Scotland and began to explore them more thoroughly. Among the sedimentary deposits that had accumulated in Devonian times, they found more specimens of *Psiliphyton* and also representatives of hitherto-unknown relatives to which they gave the names *Rhynia, Hornea* and *Asteroxylon.* All of them were rootless, leafless stems that once had been green. They differed in fine details, such as where on their upright branches they bore small spore cases from which their microscopic reproductive cells (spores) escaped and were distributed by the Devonian winds.

The same sedimentary deposits at Rhynie yielded fossils of a few animals—some sea scorpions (eurypterids), a spider, and enough parts of a primitive insect to be given the distinctive name of *Rhyniella praecursor.*

LIVING FOSSILS

Also no fossils of closely similar plants have been found among the sedimentary rocks that accumulated in the 335 million years since the end of the

Devonian period, these earliest of vascular plants did not die out completely. Three small relatives of *Psilophyton* survive today. One is the "whisk fern" (*Psilotum nudum*) of Florida and Bermuda, where it grows both in the soil of shady woodlands and from decaying matter in the leaf bases of palms or the bark crevices of hardwood trees. In Hawaii, *Psilotum triquetrum* has a similar habit. Australia, New Guinea and islands to the north as far as the Philippines have *Tmesipteris tannensis,* whose graceful green stems curve out and down from the soggy bark of tree ferns. They bear several ranks of flattened branches that resemble leaves.

Botanists recognize all of these plants as "living fossils," which descended with little change from the ancient vascular plants of the early Devonian. *Psilophyton* and its kin seem to have been ancestral also to all of the plants that composed the great forests of Carboniferous times—the famous "Coal Ages"— and to all of the familiar vegetation on the land today. It is remarkable only that *Psilotum* and *Tmesipteris* found a way of life and a style of growth that required so little change over the eons, while all about them the other vascular plants diversified in so many different directions.

Much of this diversification can be recognized near its very beginning, during the 100 million years of the Devonian period. It was then that the "bare plants," such as *Psilophyton,* gave rise to tall trees, anchored in the soil by a new plant structure—roots. Probably a soil had to develop, by addition of decaying plants and the agents of decay to the previously sterile muds and sands and gravels, before a root became important. Certainly the rooted plants towered over *Psilophyton* and its kin, none of which grew more than nine feet tall.

Today, most kinds of land plants are not woody trees, but low-growing herbs. Instead of having life spans measured in centuries or thousands of years, they mature in fewer seasons, die, and are replaced. Yet the first plants with conducting tissue were woody shrubs. Their descendants were forest trees that formed great swamp forests in Carboniferous times. But there were no corresponding marshes and no prairie grasses waving in the wind.

The low-growing herbs came later. Nor have these changes ceased. Even without man's influence, the vegetation on the continents continues to shift in emphasis. Its trend is toward shorter lives and less reliance upon a continuous supply of water. Plants that could change as their future unfolded have spread over the lands we know.

CHAPTER 1

The First Forests, Flowers and Prairies

THE FORESTS

For only about a century has anyone realized how incredibly vast were the swamp forests of the Coal Ages—the first forests in the world. Yet only a fraction of those communities of ancient trees was preserved in the form of coal. Just those forests that grew where the sea flowed in every thousand years or so, killing them and covering their partly-decayed remains with salty mud, were transformed into carbon of such purity.

Most of the world's coal dates from this period, and shows the locations of coastal forests. Despite the enormous amount of it hidden among the sedimentary rocks, coal remained a curiosity long after man had found a use for it. Shore dwellers sometimes died from noxious gases liberated by black lumps of "sea coal" they found on the beaches and burned in fireplaces built for wood smoke. Laws were passed, banning the perilous stuff. As late as 1295, Europeans discredited Marco Polo's story, when the Venetian traveler told of the Chinese digging into a mountain for rocks to burn as fuel. Until the 17th century, European coal was little used. Then, because most of the forests had been felled, coal became an essential substitute for the charcoal that had been used in smelting iron ever since the days of Solomon in the 10th century B.C.

The true origin of so much rocklike combustible material remained a mystery until after 1815, when scientists began to puzzle over the imprints of bark and leaves in the shales of coal seams. Virtually all of these patterns impressed on the salty muds of the early Carboniferous period were of tree-sized

Ferns, which bear spores, were once the dominant plants on land. Now they grow chiefly in the shade of seed-bearing trees. (E. Javorsky)

8

clubmosses, horsetails, and ferns. No plant had yet produced a flower. No herbs or grasses grew. All of the vascular plants were of types that today are represented by much lower-growing kinds of vegetation.

Many of the giant clubmosses of the late Devonian and early Carboniferous reached a height of more than a hundred feet. The giant horsetails, known as calamites, included some that ranged from sixty to ninety feet tall. Tree ferns competed with them for light in the great swamp forests. In this contest the ferns had an advantage. From their green buds they uncoiled feathery leaves that caught the sunlight more efficiently than the small stiff projections from branches of clubmosses or the flat scalelike branches that arose in whorls around the upright green stems of horsetails.

THE COMING OF THE SEED-FERNS

Inconspicuous changes pointed the way to the future, and the avenues toward colonization of drier land. Among the tree ferns of the late Devonian, a few seed-ferns appeared. They were the first plants to produce seeds, and started a tremendous revolution in the green world. A seed is an embryo plant, with diminutive root and stem, with leaves and a supply of food upon which to live until it can germinate and become independent. Seeds made possible the spread of tall plants beyond the swamps, and the progressive replacement of the forests of tree ferns, giant clubmosses and horsetails by forests of seed plants.

Animals in the swamps changed rapidly too as the Devonian became the Carboniferous period. Insects, in particular, diversified spectacularly. They fed on the forest trees and were, in turn, eaten by many other kinds of animals. Insects chewed the foliage and sucked plant juices. Other insects in the swamp water caught and ate small crustaceans and worms. Dragonflies as much as twenty-nine inches in wingspan flitted among the trees, hawking for

Far left: Across the Northern Hemisphere from east to west, and on many mountain slopes, forests of ancient forms of coniferous evergreen trees grade into stands of the newer, flowering deciduous trees. (Bill Ratcliffe) Left: Birch trees grow rapidly where light reaches the ground among the spruces and pines in southern Finland, but die out when shaded by the slower-growing evergreens. (Teuvo Suominen)

smaller insects that flew there. Spiders and scorpions caught insects. So did the fishes and ponderous amphibians that swam in the more open water. Most of the amphibians were heavily armored, with bony plates under their thin slippery skins. They had to stay close to water to keep their skins moist enough to assist their lungs in taking oxygen from the air.

Together the seed-ferns, the insects, and the descendants of some of the amphibians spread toward drier land. Spiders and scorpions went along. These were the kinds of life that had developed a new tolerance for drought, a new freedom from swamp water and humid air.

Seed-ferns differed from true ferns, and from the clubmosses, horsetails and other descendants of Devonian plants, in the site of their sexual stages. Those of a fern ordinarily are found on moist soil, where a fern spore has grown into a tiny, heart-shaped green plant upon which sex organs appear. In a film of dew or rain, the male cells swim to fertilize the female eggs. That film of moisture is essential. The plant can reproduce only if the liquid is there, and hence only if the weather is propitious on the critical day. By contrast, a seed-fern produced its female sex organs and eggs on a part of its upright stem. To this part the wind brought spores (pollen grains) carrying the male sex organ. If the weather did not provide a film of moisture in which the male cells could swim to the waiting eggs, the parent plant secreted the watery solution. The fertilized eggs grew into seeds, each wrapped up neatly in a seed coat provided by the parent. For a while it remained attached to the parent plant, drawing nourishment until a diminutive plantlet grew within the seed. The fertilized egg that can become a fern has no such protection or source of food. If the weather is unsuitable for immediate growth, it dies. A seed can usually wait for weeks or months or years, until conditions are right for germination.

As the first seeds spread to drier land and germinated there in wet weather, the insects followed, feeding on the seed-ferns. Protected in its thin, waterproof skin, an insect could move freely beyond the swamps. Chasing or stalking after the insects came the first reptiles. These descendants of the amphibians differed in having better lungs, better ways of breathing and routing their blood, and a scaly skin that held in the precious moisture. Reptiles, moreover, had no need to return to the swamps, as amphibians did to reproduce and start a new generation of swimming tadpoles. Reptiles laid eggs with

Fifteen-foot fronds of Cyathea *in New Zealand's fern forests on the South Island suggest a Carboniferous forest of long ago. (New Zealand National Publicity)*

strong shells that enclosed an imitation aquarium. Surrounded by this substitute for swamp water, the reptile embryo could develop directly into an air-breathing miniature of the adult form. Some of the reptiles even replaced insects in their diet, and ate plants. On this reliable green food they could grow to larger sizes.

Among the fossilized remains left to represent the animals and plants of the first forests, it is often difficult to decide whether a specimen is an amphibian or an early reptile, whether it is a true fern or a seed-fern. The earliest known seed-fern, *Eospermatopteris,* was a tree about thirty feet high, having a trunk as much as three feet in diameter. From its green crown, it uncoiled great fronds—just as ferns do and always have. In fact, only recently have scientists learned to distinguish between the feathery leaves of tree ferns and those of seed-ferns. Many of the fronds preserved in the slate layers of coal deposits from late Carboniferous days are from seed-ferns,

rather than tree ferns, as was formerly believed. It was not just the "Age of Ferns" but the "Age of Seed-Ferns" too.

Soon after the end of the Paleozoic era some 200 million years ago, the trees and woody vines that are clearly seed-ferns vanished from the fossil record. In the forests their places were taken by descendants of distinctively different types. These newer trees spread widely during the Mesozoic era, the "Age of Reptiles," forming diverse forests that today are represented by only the 750 kinds of woody vegetation we call the "softwoods." After the giant dinosaurs of the Mesozoic became extinct, the softwoods were replaced as the dominant vegetation of the land by the later, flowering plants.

Nearly a hundred of the surviving softwoods are cycads, which are palmlike trees and shrubs of warm countries. They grow very slowly and unfold leaves that are coarse and stiff. In this respect and in the prominent role they held in the forests of the Mesozoic era, they resemble an extinct group (the Bennettitales) from which the flowering plants may have arisen.

One more kind of modern softwood, the beautiful ginkgo tree *(Ginkgo biloba),* shows in its fan-shaped leaves the repeated forking of the fine veins that was so characteristic of the ancient *Cordaites*—tall trees of the late Devonian whose similar descendants became extinct during the Mesozoic. Both the ginkgoes and the trees so widely known as "conifers" seem to have arisen from the *Cordaites* line.

The softwoods bear their seeds in exposed positions. They are the "naked-seeded" plants—the Gymnosperms. All of them are woody. Today they include the tallest trees and the oldest living things. Nearly all of them are evergreen. Many of them still rely upon fungus strands instead of hairlike extensions of their own root cells to reach moisture among the particles of soil, much as did the bare stems of *Psilophyton* so long ago. But by comparison with the flowering plants, they provide almost no food for birds, for mammals, or for man. The 575 modern kinds of conifers do furnish three-quarters of our lumber and nine-tenths of our pulpwood for paper products. They are our largest crop, even if we prefer other things to eat.

THE FLOWERS

Until about a century ago, it was possible to regard all living things as being of the same kinds that had existed since the beginnings of life on earth. A

Tree ferns of the genus Cibotium *form a feathery understory in the Hawaiian Islands. They grow also in tropical Asia and Central America. (V. R. Johnston: National Audubon)*

careful reading of the fossil record dispelled this idea and showed that changes have been progressive. The plants and animals of modern times are the elite descendants of earlier, different ancestors. In a host of ways they escaped extinction. Those that continue to elude destruction will be the ancestors of all the living things we can expect on earth.

Doors to the future rarely open automatically. Instead, each species of plant or animal must compete for its energy and space as though it had its back to the wall. A few linger on for millenia by being conservative, and by staying in some corner where the main stream of life passes them without pressing hard. Other species find a key to a door in the wall, and escape through it when an urgent need arises. Until they reach the next insurmountable obstacle, they may have an opportunity to express their inherent versatility—and to find new keys to doors that will prolong their future.

The cycads and conifers, described in the previous section, today are the dwindling conservatives among seed plants. They rely upon harsh foliage, upon sticky resins, and upon woody cone scales to protect the vital seeds that are their bids for posterity. As individuals some of these gymnosperms live on for thousands of years, producing annual batches of seeds from which a few may take root and eventually replace the parents. For the most part these plants grow slowly, benefiting few other kinds of life, and needing only to be left alone among members of their own species.

The flowering plants, by contrast, are generally more sociable. They tend to protect their seeds, but at the same time to make use of animals instead of warding them off. To the great majority of flowering plants, certain animals are valued partners. Botanists now suspect that the development of partnerships with animals was the key to the future for land plants. Mutual adaptations made flowering types of vegetation the dominant terrestrial kinds during the last 55 million years. The Cenozoic era became the "Age of Flowering Plants," as well as the age of mammals, of birds, and of countless insects.

At first, the changes that led to flowering plants

during the Age of Reptiles may have been mostly through adaptations that provided protection for the plant egg cells. The softwoods had found two ways toward success; most produced their eggs in the narrow spaces between fleshy, resinous bracts that became woody, arrayed in a compact cone; others formed eggs in isolated groups. In none of these were the nutritious grains of pollen borne by the plant anywhere near the centers of egg-production. The ancestors of flowering plants were somewhat more vulnerable, since they bore their pollen and the ovules in which their eggs developed in the same spiral cluster at the end of a short stem. If an insect came to feed on the abundant pollen or to sip the droplets of secretion with which the plants caught pollen from the wind, the insect might also bite into the ovules and destroy the eggs. Pollen could be spared, for it was produced in vast quantities which compensated for the wastefulness of wind distribution. Pollination droplets could be renewed by further secretion. But for reproduction, eggs were indispensable.

The abrupt change that distinguished the first flowering plants from the softwoods was a simple wall between the ovules and the hungry insects. It came into being when each spore-bearing leaf on which ovules developed became folded to form a closed chamber (a carpel) around its ovules. Inside the carpel wall was a cavity containing the ovules, and the eggs from which seeds might form. This swollen portion (the ovary) narrowed to an extension (the style), which ended in a sticky tip (the stigma) to which the pollen grains could adhere. Gland cells that might have produced pollination droplets kept the stigma sticky, at least until suitable pollen grains were caught in the secretion and had extended long pollen tubes to the ovules, bringing sperm cells to each egg.

The fertilized egg that began at once to develop into a seed was still covered by the wall of the ovary portion of its carpel. It was a covered seed, and the plant that bore it an Angiosperm *(angeion* meaning a cover, *sperma* meaning a seed), instead of a Gymnosperm *(gymnos* meaning naked).

Additional spore-bearing leaves in each spiral seem to have shrunk to the point where only their glandular parts remained. Around the spiral of carpels at the center of the flower they became nectaries, providing a sugary reward for an animal that would go from flower to flower, picking up pollen in each and scattering a little in the next. Ready to brush pollen on the animal stood an indefi-

nite number of stamens, each consisting of a slender stalk (the filament) supporting a cluster of four pollen sacs (together known as the anther). The sacs split open to release their pollen grains.

Even without special advertising, a flower that has nectar and pollen to offer will attract insects. But success seems to have come most quickly to the seed plants in which the reproductive organs (carpels and stamens) were surrounded by showy sterile leaves that an animal could see from far away. These showy parts constitute a perianth (literally, around the anthers), perhaps composed of distinctive petals forming a corolla above a series of sepals forming a calyx. In some flowers, the sepals are petal-like. In others, they remain green and leaflike, protecting the petals and reproductive parts in the bud until the whole advertising display is ready to unfold and make use of animals. Insects and birds and bats can all carry pollen from flower to flower, visiting mostly a single variety, far more reliably than any wandering breeze.

Flowers show many interesting adaptations that increase the chance that their most consistent pollinators will pick up pollen and deposit it where it will serve the plant, and thereby decrease the chance that other animals will raid the plant for its pollen and nectar. Snapdragons stay closed until a strong bumblebee comes along and forces its way into the site of the pollen, to the pollen-catching stigma, and the rewarding nectaries. Flowers that are pollinated by bees are rarely red, since most bees cannot see this part of the spectrum. Or they reflect the ultraviolet of sunlight (which we cannot see but an insect can). The nectar of a zinnia is hidden deep in the flower where bees have difficulty reaching it, although a butterfly can probe for it with an uncoiled "tongue" and the slender beak of a hummingbird finds it easily. Flowers that open at night are usually white, odorous, large, bell-shaped, and appeal to hawk-moths, for which they are easy to find. Tropical plants, such as the cannonball tree of South America and the sausage tree of Africa, often rely for pollination upon fruit-eating bats. Both of these trees extend their flowers on long stalks, where the bats can find them readily in darkness without colliding with trunk or foliage. The cannonball tree and several others even provide small landing platforms upon which a bat can rest while it nibbles on the flower, transferring the pollen that clings to its hair.

Pollination of the flower, fertilization of the eggs, and growth of the embryo in each seed to the state of dormancy, are all preparations for distributing

Trumpet trees (Cecropia, *left foreground) rise quickly in clearings in the rain forests of tropical America, but are shaded to death by slower-growing hardwoods. (E. Aubert de La Rue)*

Clumps of hardy fescue grass (Festuca) *bend with winds that whip across the steppe country of Patagonia, in southernmost Chile. (E. Aubert de La Rue)*

new dormant plants. These steps do not differ markedly in flowering plants from the corresponding ones in the life of a gymnosperm, such as a pine. But the seeds of a flowering plant are still enclosed within the carpel (ovary) wall. A majority of flowering plants gain from this extra layer. It ripens to become a fruit, which may aid mechanically in seed dispersal, or may serve as a reward to an animal that carries the enclosed seeds some distance from the parent plant.

Many fruits are dry when ripe. A few kinds, such as those of the touch-me-not, develop tensions as they dry, and release the stored energy when they rupture, hurling the seeds for many yards. Others continue to cover the seeds with thin walls but, as in the dandelion, spread a floss of short glistening hairs that catch the breeze and carry the seed for miles on a windy day. The many kinds of burrs hitch rides on animals that brush against the ripe fruits. Still other dry fruits open little pores, as a poppy capsule does, and shake out the tiny seeds like a pepper caster whenever the wind blows vigorously.

Fruits that are fleshy when ripe usually show special development of the carpel wall. The outer epidermis of the wall becomes the "skin" over the peach. The inner epidermis of the wall becomes thick with stone cells that convert it into the "pit"

around the seed. Between the two epidermises is the flesh of the fruit, which is juicy and sweet enough to induce many animals to eat it and perhaps carry the whole fruit away from the parent plant. The inner epidermis of the fruit wall is often impervious to digestive juices. If an animal swallows the fruit whole, the seed passes unharmed through the alimentary canal and emerges ready for germination far from the parent plant. The number of seeds that birds distribute in this way can be appreciated from the rate at which chokecherry trees, mountain ash, and brambles spring up from the scorched earth of a burned-over woodland. The fire may have been hot enough to kill all of the trees and the undergrowth. But soon a ring of seedlings begins to grow around each dead stub; upon these stubs passing birds can perch.

In some cases, the animal that carries the fruit away from the plant and devours the flesh before discarding or burying the armored seed, is discouraged from cracking the armor and eating the seed as well. The seed may contain a poison. Peach seeds contain cyanides in quantities great enough to sicken or kill a small animal that eats many of them one after another.

A quick examination of a fruit may reveal neither whether it is safe to eat nor how it developed from

15

the flower that preceded it. A raspberry or a mulberry is composed of units each with a single seed surrounded by a fleshy pulp; each unit develops from a separate carpel—a simple pistil—from the many that are attached to the center of each flower. A pineapple is composed of units too, but each unit represents the fruit of a separate flower in a cluster. A strawberry, so juicy and fragrant and bright red when ripe, is the enlarged end of the flower stalk (the receptacle) on which minute indigestible fruits are borne in slight depressions of the surface; each of these fruits contains one seed. An apple or a pear gains its fleshy, edible portions through remarkable enlargement of both the carpel wall and of the calyx which is fused to it; the five little points at the opposite end from the stalk that supports the fruit are the calyx tips; sometimes the single style of the compound pistil can be seen too at the center of a depression which once was the center of the flower.

The fruit matches the flower from which it develops, far better than either of these corresponds to any particular style of root or stem or leaf. But in trying to simplify the recognition of interesting and important plants, the botanist must make use of all the distinctive features he can find. By relying upon all of his senses, particularly sight and touch and smell, he can often identify a plant in winter or at some time of year when neither flowers nor fruits are visible. Only when he knows the plant under all conditions, including its habits of growth, can he feel that he understands its place in the living community of which it is a part.

Among the small details that have proved important among flowering plants is the number of leaves an embryo produces in the seed before it goes into dormancy. One group (eighty-three per cent of the species of flowering plants) produce two of these leaves, called cotyledons. They are the "dicotyledonous flowering plants" or dicots, which have profusely branching veins in their leaves (forming a network) and generally show reduction of their flower parts to fours or fives (or multiples of these). The other group (seventeen per cent) have only a single cotyledon on each embryo in the seed. They are "monocotyledonous," or monocots, and possess leaves with veins extending unbranched from base to tip, and flower parts regularly in threes or multiples of three.

The dicots are the hardwood trees, the familiar shrubs, the wealth of flowering herbs with which so much of the tropics and temperate lands are clad. The monocots are the tropical palms, the grasses of arid prairies and some well-watered areas from which man has removed the woody vegetation. Historically, the dicots antedate the monocots by many millions of years. Flowering trees resembling today's magnolias appeared during the last years of the dinosaurs—the Cretaceous period of the Age of Reptiles. The first grass seeds in the fossil record are of Miocene age, less than 20 million years ago as compared with 70 million. Together, the dicots and monocots established the green world that led to the present, to mankind, and to the future.

THE PRAIRIES

For millions of years after the flowering plants began displacing the more conservative softwoods in the forests, the land beyond the trees consisted of bald, windy, dusty plains. There were no prairies because no grasses had yet appeared and colonized those dry uplands. For a very long time, the forested areas continued to be almost the exclusive roothold of vascular plants upon the land. All of the early flowering plants (angiosperms) were woody shrubs and trees. In this they resembled and merely took the place of the previous vegetation of the forests, the softwoods (gymnosperms). This style of growth— the tree habit—is virtually limited to regions of the earth where the annual rainfall is at least thirty inches and where the water is available to roots all through the growing season.

During the summer, a tree cannot go dormant. If its supply of water fails then, it dies. Consequently, only some lichens and a few hardy mosses were able to invade the arid plains until new styles of life without the tree habit appeared among the flowering plants. The new plants placed less emphasis upon building woody stems above ground, and more upon producing leaves, flowers, seeds, and fruits. These angiosperms died down to ground level each year, in the herbaceous habit of herbs. Some of them lived year after year as roots and horizontal stems

Right above: Limited rainfall and a long dry season in late summer restrict the plants of this Russian steppe to grasses, such as feathergrasses (Stipa species), and low, flowering herbs such as buttercups and thistles. (Kai Curry-Lindahl) Right: Among the grasses on the high slopes of the Bitterroot Valley in Montana, Indians dug out the edible roots of golden-flowered balsam root. Cattle are often poisoned by eating the blue larkspur. (Ernst Peterson)

below ground. Each spring they spread upward a fresh crop of greenery with leaves at intervals and flower buds in the branch tips. These plants ripened their seeds, died back to ground level, and waited in dormant safety through a severe drought and perhaps a cold winter as well.

Change in this direction seemingly was encouraged by the same drier, colder weather on the continents that made the world unfit for dinosaurs. As the monsters died out and the Age of Reptiles ended, these new types of vegetation became more noticeable. Even the dependence of plants upon a good growing season year after year seems to have been partly abandoned. Many of the herbs did remain perennial, like the shrubs and trees. Others fitted their lives into two consecutive years as biennials. They developed no flower buds until they had stored away in their roots the starches and oils and proteins from a whole season's active growth. Their flowering and fruiting came in their second year, using up the stored food, transferring it into seeds and fruits. After reproducing once, each biennial died. Still other angiosperms became annual plants, reaching full size, flowering, fruiting, and dying all in a single summer.

As the herbaceous vegetation spread over the drier uplands and the central plains, it was followed by a host of appreciative animals that ate the leaves, the fruits, and the seeds, and attacked the exposed stems. But no longer did the plant kingdom need to support the hordes of herbivorous dinosaurs, for dinosaurs had become extinct. Instead, some new types of mammals were becoming adapted to a diet of plants that were green in wet seasons and dry "hay" on the ground at other times of the year. Most of them were the ancestors of antelopes and cattle. Others were on their way toward becoming horses. Although neither type of animal could digest the cellulose

Far left: The Mexican cycad Dioon edule *may be 1000 years old by the time it is six feet tall. The starchy seeds in the large papery cone can be ground into an edible meal.   Left above: A separate seed is ripening below each of the upturned points on this two-foot cone of* Cycas revoluta, *an Oriental cycad introduced to Coconut Island, off Oahu, Hawaii. (Both by Lorus and Margery Milne)   Left: Resembling short palms with coarse evergreen fronds, the cycads of Thailand and adjacent countries are often felled to obtain sago starch from the pith of the woody trunk. (E. S. Ross)*

that formed the principal constituent of dried herbaceous plants, both had already acquired as internal partners some microbes that could use cellulose as food.

With herds of grazing animals wandering over the arid plains, able to nourish themselves (and their microbial partners) on herbaceous plants at any time of year, the vegetation there was in continual danger of attack. During summer droughts and winter, this did not matter because only the dead parts of the herbs were exposed above ground. But if a plant lost its fresh green foliage to a large hungry animal early in the short growing season, it might not be able to replace it and get use from another set of leaves before summer's drought arrived. To survive under these conditions, still another habit of growth was needed. The monocot angiosperms already possessed the key that would open this door to survival. Those that used it most became the plants we know today as grasses and sedges. They are now the largest and most successful group of monocots, and the principal plants of prairies from the tropics almost to the poles.

THE MONOCOT WAY TO THE FUTURE

The special feature that aided monocots so much lay in the nature of their leaves and way of growth. Unlike a dicot leaf, which unfolds from a bud to final size and cannot repair itself if partly eaten, a monocot leaf on a grass or sedge can continue to grow from its base at the stem and compensate for destruction at the tip. When the netted vein system of a dicot leaf expands to full size, it can do no more than close a break from which valuable juices would escape. A monocot leaf can do this too, but its parallel veins can be added to indefinitely, pushing up more leaf blade into the light as the exposed parts are grazed away. Man makes use of this same feature in matching grassy lawns to grazing lawnmowers.

Just as the animals that came to plants for pollen and nectar increased the efficiency of reproduction in plants that developed attractive flowers, and just as different animals aided many plants in distribution of their fruits and seeds, so also the grazing herds on the plains led to a change in the vegetation there. Among the plants that had colonized these areas of lesser rainfall and long summer drought, the monocots survived grazing better. Grasses and sedges came to dominate the scene. Tall or short, perennial or annual, they waved in the winds above the prairies and became adapted for pollination by air currents. Perhaps reduction in flower parts also aided in survival, by drawing less attention to the plant that had reached maturity and was ready to store energy in seeds for the future.

As grasses and sedges spread their roots, they interwove and formed a turf above the mineral matter of the plains. This mat of vegetation protected the land from the winds that could drive it as dust or as dunes of sand. The vegetation stabilized a soil, and let it accumulate organic matter, improving the area as a place for plants and animals alike. It captured the rain and the meltwater from winter snow, prolonging the period of greenness more than seemed possible where annual rainfall was so scanty.

To the fringes of the deserts that remained, the grasses and sedges spread. But few of them could invade this most arid of the earth's land. The annual dicots did better at compressing all of a lifetime's growth into a few weeks after germination of the seed. As "ephemerals" they rushed into action after each heavy storm, reached flowering and fruiting and faded away, all on an average of five inches or less of rain a year that might come in a great downpour at intervals of two years or more. Animals could scarcely migrate fast enough into a rained-on area to take advantage of this sudden bounty. Those that arrived too late found only withered little plants and tiny seeds. Or they met other dicots, such as the perennial cacti and creosote bushes, which had barbs, thorns, chemical repellents, and other adaptations to protect the stores of storm water they soaked up and lived on until once more the rain came down.

With the prairies clothed in grasses and sedges, with other monocots (such as orchids and bromeliads) growing atop the outstretched branches of dicot trees in the wet tropics, with specialized cacti and other dicots clinging to life in the deserts of the world, and with the bulk of land plants retaining the tree habit or growing as herbs along the fringes of forests, the long past of land plants has become the present. Except for the lowly mosses and liverworts, and the remnants of psilopsids, clubmosses, horsetails, and ferns, it is a terrestrial world of seed plants, unfolding leaves and stems and roots into a fruitful future.

2

The Softwoods

On a coffee plantation in Guatemala, while we were being shown the remaining areas of rain forest, our host and his handyman asked if we could explain the difference between wood, timber, and lumber. In Spanish, *madera* seemed to them to include all three. We added to their list: woods or woodland, and timbers. Wood, to us, is the solid material of a tree, just as meat *(carne)* is the main part of an animal. A woods or woodland is a natural community of trees, equivalent to the Spanish *bosque*—a forested area. We were going into and out of the woods each time we reached another steep valley filled with rain forest.

Timber, we told the men, was wood of dimensions and types useful for construction work. A woodcutter might go through a forested area and estimate the quantity of valuable wood in trees of large size. Men who did this in commercial forests were *timber cruising*. They calculated the amount and the kinds of timber to be cut. After the big trees were felled, all large units of their material (wood) might still be referred to as timbers, if these were long, wide and thick. Timbers were used for the beams to support a roof, or to give strength to the hull of a wooden ship. To break so heavy a piece of wood requires tremendous force, such as that of a hurricane. Hence the sailor's exclamation "Shiver my timbers!"

When timber goes to the sawmill and is cut into boards, it becomes lumber. The wood in flat strips of uniform thickness is stacked in a lumber yard, to be sold by the board-foot. It is still wood, and has been this material ever since the plant produced it. In any situation, wood is the tissue in which vascular plants conduct watery solutions from their roots up their stems to their leaves. Strands of wood are often found even within the stalk (petiole) that broadens out to become the blade of a leaf, or within the heavy veins of a big leaf.

The long slender cells that serve as water pipes in wood have reinforcement in their walls that prevents them from bursting under pressure or from collapsing under tension. The cells die in readying themselves to serve as conductive tissue. But among them are other cells of more nearly cubic shape, which remain alive and have several roles. These live cells provide avenues for the radial movement of water and nutrients, between the center of a stem or root and the outermost sheath of living cells. They are used as storage centers. They may help the plant in controlling the upward movement of liquid in the dead, pipelike cells.

For countless years, wood has been valuable to primitive people as a fuel and a building material. Women and children have used their nimble fingers to separate the woody strands in stems and leaves, and to weave these durable strands into mats, baskets, hats, and other useful articles. All of their products are actually wood. Often the plants from which these strands came were of kinds in which the dead conducting cells and the live cubic cells are accompanied by other dead cells of great length, correctly known as "fibers." A fiber cell has a wall so thick that almost no space remains at its center. It gives lengthwise strength to the wood, since fibers run parallel to the dead conducting cells.

Various woods differ greatly in strength. Lumber merchants have long recognized this in referring to pines and other coniferous trees as "softwoods," and to oaks, hickories and other flowering trees as "hardwoods." The softwoods are gymnosperms, the hardwoods all angiosperms. Generally the softwoods have needle-shaped leaves that persist on the tree for more than one year before being dropped. Leaves of a new year expand and reach full size before the old ones fall, making the tree an evergreen. Most commercial hardwoods shed all of their broad leaves and remain bare for a month or more before expanding a new set of foliage. But some conifers, such as the larch and the bald cypress, are deciduous—dropping all of their needles at the approach of winter. And in tropical or subtropical lands, many hardwoods are evergreen, as are magnolias and the shrubby trees in the coffee orchards.

The botanist relies upon other features to distinguish the gymnosperms from the angiosperms, and avoids the jargon of the lumbermen. So long as he guides himself according to the details of reproduction and of plant structure, he can separate the seed plants easily into their natural groups. Then it makes no difference that the gymnosperms—the "softwoods"—include some with wood of outstanding hardness, or that the angiosperms—the "hardwoods" and the herbaceous plants—include the tropical balsa tree whose wood is the softest known.

In all living gymnosperms, the pollen-producing organs are remote from the seed-producing ones (the ovules). Sometimes they are restricted to separate plants. By contrast, angiosperms usually bear their stamens and carpels in the same flower. Among those that do not, other evidence shows that one set or the other of their reproductive organs has been lost. The double set is normal in flowering plants.

Under a microscope, just one pollen grain is needed to show whether a plant is a gymnosperm or an angiosperm. Gymnosperm pollen contains one or two sterile cells in each grain, as vestigial remains that are comparable to the useless human appendix or to other structures that have lost the significance they once had among remote ancestors. Angiosperm pollen contains no nonfuctional cells.

The seed-producing ovules of any gymnosperm differ from those of angiosperms in ways that help a botanist tell one group of seed plants from the other. The gymnosperm ovule lies exposed, "naked," shielded from the elements and from animals only by a thin integument that is destined to become the seed coat, and by any overhanging parts of the parent plant, such as adjacent scales of a woody cone. Unlike an angiosperm ovule, which is covered by a carpel wall and produces no more than seven cells during its development, a gymnosperm ovule divides itself repeatedly into hundreds of cells. At several points these cells become organized into minute sex organs, each containing a single egg cell.

Days or weeks or months before the egg cells are ready for fertilization, the site of each one can be discovered. At the point nearest to each egg cell, the integument over it turns to liquid and projects as a shining drop—a pollination droplet. It serves to cap-

ture pollen from the wind, and to hold each grain by surface tension. As the wind evaporates the droplet, its surface film pulls the pollen through the minute hole in the integument, close against the ovule. Consequently the pollen tube has almost no distance to grow to bring the male cells inside it to a maturing egg. As soon as one male cell has fertilized the egg, the rest of the living material in the pollen grain dies and shrivels. Unused pollen grains have the same fate, and the wind carries away the remains.

Several eggs in a gymnosperm ovule may be fertilized by male cells from as many pollen grains. But soon one embryo becomes dominant, and takes over all of the resources in the developing seed. By the time it is ripe the embryo is fully formed and dormant, with a miniature root, a short stem, and at least two embryonic leaves (the cotyledons). It is ready to travel, surrounded by food-filled cells of ovule tissue, and by the seed coat—nothing more. At the end of its journey it can awaken and germinate, to grow as an independent plant.

These seemingly inconsequential details of reproduction, upon which a botanist bases his ultimate decision in separating the gymnosperms from the flowering plants, provide a good example of nature's real secrets. For years the scientists overlooked the significance of the steps by which a male cell reaches an egg, and a seed is prepared for travel. Yet these details are almost unique in having remained unchanged for hundreds of millions of years. They were protected from the competitive world by the small size and concealed position of the sexual parts. None of the conspicuous features has remained so conservative, so meaningful in relating the present softwoods to the past or in considering their future.

CHAPTER 2

The Living Cycads

People who live where severe frost never comes have a good chance to know cycads among the native vegetation around them. Distributed widely in the tropics and subtropics of the world, almost ninety varieties of cycads survive today. Their ancestry antedates present boundaries of the continents and explains their occurrence in all warm lands. Many are raised for their handsome foliage, as ornamental palmlike plants that tolerate life in a tub of earth in a greenhouse or a hotel lobby. Outdoors in the tropics, some grow slowly to a height of sixty feet, with a trunk a foot in diameter. Others show only their coarse leaves and reproductive parts above ground, while the heavy stem remains hidden in the soil.

Curiously, any cycad is clearly unlike its near-relatives among the gymnosperms, but it may fool even a botanist because of a remarkable resemblance to a tree fern or to a palm (a flowering plant). In fact, the South African cycad now known as *Stangeria paradoxa* was described first as a tree fern. And the name *Cycas* was coined originally to indicate a similarity to the doum palm *(Hyphaene thebaica)* of Egypt and the Sudan. Almost the only real correspondence between this particular genus of cycads and the doum palm is that both sometimes have branching trunks, which is a feature virtually unheard-of in any other cycad or palm tree.

On five continents, people seem to have discovered independently a practical similarity between some cycads and some palms. In the upright trunks or the underground stems of both, starch is stored in a fibrous pith. If these parts of the plant are ground up and washed with water, both the fibers and a dangerous poison are rinsed away, leaving an insoluble starch in crude grains that can be dried and stored. They are "sago," used for making puddings and as a starch for stiffening cloth. This source of sago has never achieved much economic importance since the plant must be killed to obtain its starchy pith and since cycads grow so slowly. As soon as demand exceeds the rate at which the wild cycads grow and reproduce, the home industry based upon them dwindles away.

The trunk of the tree-sized cycads, like the trunk of so many palms, is rough where the dead leaves have broken away. The glossy green leaves themselves might well be called "fronds," just as are those

Right above: The Seminole Indians of southern Florida discovered that bread could be made from the underground stem of the native cycad Zamia floridana. *(Lorus and Margery Milne) Right: Adding a few fronds to its crown each year as old ones die, the Mexican cycad* Dioon *changes little with time. (Walter Dawn: National Audubon)*

of palms and ferns. Each cycad leaf actually resembles the coarsely divided frond of a "feather palm" in having its leaf stalk (petiole) continue as a strong central shaft bearing stiff leaflets on each side. In the cycad genus *Bowenia* of Australia, the leaflets too are divided on this same plan. Its fronds are said to be "twice-pinnately compound," instead of just pinnately compound, using words that indicate the resemblance to the leaflets (pinnae) along each side of the main shaft of a fern leaf. In *Cycas,* each new leaf unrolls from a fiddlehead like that of a fern, but in *Dioon* and other cycad genera the young leaf lies straight in its bud scales and emerges like a fluted spear. As it extends more and more from the center of the whorl of foliage at the end of the stem, the spear opens into the double row of leaflets, each facing the sun.

Poison in the tissues of its leaves gives a cycad an immunity from attack by most animals. But in Australia, where domestic cattle seem unable to learn to go hungry rather than eat the green foliage of *Macrozamia,* the government has felt obliged to come to the aid of the ranchers in exterminating this palmlike cycad over large areas of the dry, overgrazed pasture land. Similar poisoning of cattle is common in Mexico, between San Luis Potosi and Tampico, where the animals are often starved into eating the leaves of *Dioon edule,* which grows abundantly there. In each area, a paralysis develops in the stricken beast and it starves to death from being unable to reach more food. Elsewhere in the warm world where cycads live, fewer domestic animals have found their evergreen leaves so attractive and fatal.

Man has profited from collecting cycad foliage and selling it, either as leaves to be crossed in pairs upon a coffin or as "palms" to be carried on Palm Sunday. These uses depend upon another feature of cycad leaves: their resistance to wilting, even when exposed to dry air and hot sun. Over all outer surfaces, each leaf is coated with a thick, waterproof cuticle, which gives it a glossy, waxy appearance. In addition, its "breathing pores" (stomata) are all sunken in pits in the under side of the leaflets, and a system of mucilage ducts in the petiole provides an efficient sealing compound for the conducting cells through which water might be lost when a leaf is detached from the plant.

Both man and animals are attracted to the seeds of cycads for food. Indeed, cycads are unique among the gymnosperms in actually drawing attention to their seeds. They benefit when animals devour the outer fleshy layer of the seed coat and stop at the inner stony layer, while carrying the seed to some other place—perhaps one suitable for germination of the embryo plant hidden inside the armor. The seed coat itself provides the lure for animals. It gives the naked seed of the cycad the visual appeal of a fruit, such as a cherry or apricot or plum, and protects the dormant embryo almost effectively. Each kind of cycad seems to have its characteristic color of fleshy covering: bright red in *Encephalartos caffer,* orange red in *Zamia floridana,* salmon pink in *Microcycas,* and an off-white in *Dioon* and *Ceratozamia.*

This interplay between plants and animals began about 200 million years ago, during the Age of Reptiles, when cycads held a dominant position among the vegetation of the land. It arose before the insignificant mammals of the day had grown versatile enough to use plant food, rather than reptile eggs, insects, and other small animals. The cycads became adapted to the feeding habits of dinosaurs, not to those of warm-blooded creatures. The earliest birds, such as *Archaeopteryx,* may have picked up bright cycad seeds in their tooth-studded beaks and flown off with them to peck at the fleshy covering and to drop the rest of the seed in its armor. Today's birds and mammals have simply inherited these reproductive products of the cycads by replacing the ancient reptiles where cycads grow.

So intent are African baboons and monkeys on getting the seeds of the Natal "bread palm" *Encephalartos caffer* that the native people have difficulty harvesting enough to make a starchy meal and then bread. The baboons raid the cycads before the cone-shaped reproductive clusters have reached full development, and often tear off the whole structure to get the ripening seeds. In this particular cycad the "cones" are huge—the largest reproductive bodies in the plant kingdom. Large plants sometimes bear more than one at a time. If allowed to ripen fully, a single "cone" may hold enough seeds to weigh ninety pounds. Three "cones" that matured on one plant in a botanic garden reached a combined weight of 140 pounds.

The "cones" that produce pollen or that bear seeds on a cycad are its most distinctive feature. Yet they are too unlike the woody cones of a pine or a spruce to make the cycad a conifer. Among many cycads the reproductive clusters are far more obviously a close-set spiral of special leaves, in which the leaflets are replaced by clusters of two or more pollen sacs or by the corresponding parts in which seeds can develop. No cycad produces both pollen and seeds on the same individual plant, and it has become common to speak of "male" cycads and of "females." The botanist realizes that the pollen grains in which sperms form, like the ovules that produce eggs and then seeds, are actually spores within which the sexual stages develop. He is likely to avoid any confusion between the "cone" of a cycad and the cone of a conifer by calling these reproductive structures *strobiles,* each a spiral of *sporophylls* ("spore-bearing leaves"). Rather than use the accurate jargon of a strobile composed of microsporophylls (bearing microspores that become pollen) or one composed of megasporophylls (bearing megaspores, which are ovules inside their integuments), he may still speak of "male" strobiles and "female" ones. Even the quotation marks may be dropped without forgetting that the mature cycad and its strobiles have no sexual nature themselves. By asexual methods they bear inconspicuous products in which sexual features develop.

The largest of "male" strobiles among cycads are found on the Australian *Macrozamia denisonii,* which has been known to raise single reproductive clusters measuring $31\frac{1}{2}$ inches tall and nearly eight inches in diameter. Such a strobile almost doubles its length during the final day when its pollen is ready for dispersal. Its central stalk elongates and the hundreds of sporophylls separate a little. From the under surface of each sporophyll, where the pollen sacs are grouped, dry pollen falls gently to the upper surface of the next sporophyll in the spiral. Breezes carry away the golden dust, some of it to be captured by pollination droplets extruded by ripening ovules on the sporophylls of "female" strobiles. On *Macrozamia denisonii,* the "female" strobile may be thirty-seven inches high when its seeds are ripe, and weigh eighty-five pounds.

Relying upon the conservative features to be found in the strobiles of cycads, the botanists have distinguished nine different genera among the living species. None is represented in both the Old World and the New. *Cycas,* with about sixteen species, includes the handsome *C. revoluta* of southernmost Japan and *C. circinalis* which is the "sago palm" of Indonesia and the Philippines. Both have been popular as a source of cheap starch and as handsome "palms" for so long that botanists cannot be sure how much of their present wide distribution is natural and how much caused by man's introductions. Other species live in Madagascar, on the mainland of southeastern India and southwestern China, along the island chain of the East Indies, as far as Australia's southeast

corner. *Cycas* not only gives its name to all cycads, but seems to be the most primitive group of species surviving to the present time. At intervals of a few years, a mature *Cycas* produces from its terminal bud a crown of sporophylls that are more leaflike than in other genera. After their reproductive role has been fulfilled, the bud starts to grow again and expands a new crop of foliage leaves while the sporophylls wither and eventually drop. The buds of *Cycas,* moreover, are tightly rolled. Both the central shaft (rachis) of each leaf and the individual leaflets unroll from base to tip. No other cycad shows these fernlike features.

Australia is home also to about fifteen species of *Macrozamia* and two of *Bowenia.* The sporophylls of *Macrozamia* are tipped with a long stiff spine, but the tree-sized species include those regarded as the tallest *(M. hopei,* to sixty feet) and the most beautiful *(M. denisoni)* of all cycads.

South Africa has about fifteen species of *Encephalartos,* in many of which the foliage leaflets have spiny edges or tips. This name is most appropriate, for it comes from the Greek for "bread within the head," which describes well the giant reproductive clusters full of seeds that have given *E. caffer* the nontechnical names Kaffir-bread and Hottentot breadfruit. *Stangeria,* with two species, is a fernlike inhabitant of Zululand, where its thick stems remain hidden in the dry soils of the grassvelt and bushvelt alike.

In the Western Hemisphere only *Zamia,* with about thirty species, is distributed widely and represented in the United States. *Zamia floridana,* whose stems are all subterranean, is the coontie or Seminole bread plant of southern Florida. Observant tourists sometimes notice its colorful seeds in compact strobiles close to the ground along the carefully tended streets of Daytona Beach. *Z. pygmea* of Cuba is the smallest cycad, but other species of this genus resemble palms of moderate height, with fronds as much as three feet long. They range through the West Indies, Mexico, Central America, and into South America along the slopes of the Andes as far as Chile. *Microcycas,* which belies its name by growing to a height of ten feet, is restricted to one species in western Cuba. Its leaflets hang downward so vertically that those of one side of the leaf are constantly brushing against those of the opposite side.

Mexico alone is the native home to *Dioon* and to *Ceratozamia.* Both genera are represented by four species in various parts of the country. They are easy to distinguish, for in *Dioon* (literally "two eggs," referring to the two ovules on each sporophyll) the leaflets are widest where they join the central shaft of the leaf, whereas in *Ceratozamia* (whose sporophylls end in a pair of divergent spines) the leaflets are narrowed both at the base and tip. *Dioon edule,* whose pithy stems yield sago starch rather easily, is among the commonest cycads used to decorate a patio. It vies with the Old World *Cycas revoluta* as the most frequent "palm" in the hotel lobbies of the world.

In the open, a cycad may produce a new crown of leaves every year or two, at a rate that seems fairly constant over the decades. As old leaves die, they seldom break off cleanly. Instead, they fragment and only gradually expose a scar on the trunk that shows how tight is the spiral in which the foliage grows. From records of the number of leaves added in each new crown and these measures that show the rate of growth to be so steady, it is possible to count the exposed scars on a cycad trunk and estimate the age of the individual plant. Totals close to one thousand years are common, even in plants no more than six feet tall. A similar longevity seems indicated among the fossil cycads from the Age of Reptiles. In many extinct kinds, moreover, the formation of reproductive organs is so often limited to individuals of great age that these plants may well have gone far beyond the habit that in usually credited to century plants. For ten centuries they may have grown without reproducing, then raised one giant strobilus, set seeds, and died. So deliberate a way of life simply did not keep up with modern times.

CHAPTER 3

The Cultured Maidenhair Tree

Spreading its roots under cement sidewalks and its leaves into the shade of tall buildings, the maidenhair tree has become familiar to city people as one of the few that can survive despite soot and auto-

mobile exhausts. Its sturdy trunks, clad in gray bark with irregular furrows, rise one after another along the streets and avenues, often set in little more than a square foot of earth. Early in spring the many branches leaf out in fresh foliage of a clear green that dulls very little during the summer. In autumn the leaves turn golden, and flutter down, letting the tree stand bare throughout the winter. Yet few people realize that this tree is a "living fossil," one seemingly extinct in the wild condition, and the sole representative of an ancient group of softwoods that once grew over much of the Northern Hemisphere.

Lone survivor of an ancient order, the maidenhair tree (Ginkgo biloba) *from the Orient is a "living fossil." (J. H. Gerard: National Audubon)*

The leaves (right) of the maidenhair tree (left) spring from short side spurs growing directly from the branches. Each leaf is fan-shaped, with fine veins that fork repeatedly as they progress toward the notched outer edge. (Both by Lorus and Margery Milne)

For about 150 million years, the maidenhair tree *(Ginkgo biloba)* has remained virtually unchanged, despite the rise and fall of the dinosaurs and the later arrival of mankind.

The ginkgo may have been rare as far back as the 10th century. A.D., when priests in China began growing it in their temple grounds. From China the practice spread to Japan, where European travelers "discovered" the tree and asked its name. The Japanese called it *gingko.* But by the time some seeds of it germinated in Occidental gardens, the name had been altered to ginkgo. Horticulturalists have recently voted it to be one of the eleven most beautiful kinds of trees in the world. Nowhere is it known for sure to be a native member of a natural forest.

Those among the rich woodlands of the upper Yangtse Valley in western China may be escaped from cultivation, rather than truly wild trees.

Planted by itself, a ginkgo grows tall and straight, like a steep pyramid reaching as much as eighty feet above the ground. Its branches rise steeply and bear along their length short side spurs about an inch long and a quarter of an inch in diameter. From these most of the leaves arise in clusters of three to five, on flexible petioles that let the thin green blades flutter in the breeze. Each leaf has the shape of an Oriental folding fan. Many are notched near the middle of the outer curve, hence the name *biloba.* All of them have the same pattern of radiating veins that branch repeatedly, yet run almost parallel. No other tree alive today has leaves shaped and veined in this way. Perhaps a two-inch to five-inch ginkgo leaf is most similar to the half-inch leaflets of the maidenhair fern. This is the resemblance suggested in the name maidenhair tree.

In early spring, before the new leaves reach full size, a mature ginkgo makes its annual attempt to reproduce its kind. But along man's streets, this seldom adds more than some pollen as yellow dust to the city air. It cascades gently from loose, catkin-like clusters of stamens which droop gracefully from the thick spurs on the tree's branches. The horticulturalists in Public Works Departments are careful not to plant ginkgoes that would bear seeds, for when the seeds ripen they drop off, each clad in a fleshy seed coat like that on a cycad seed. To many people the fleshy part is poisonous, even to touch, and it rots quickly with a nauseating odor. Yet the Orientals have celebrated ginkgo seeds in poetry as "silver apricots," referring to the waxy bloom that covers them when first they ripen. Orientals know how to gather the seeds, to let fermentation remove the fleshy part, to boil and dry (or roast) the mildly poisonous remainder in its stony covering to get delicious "ginkgonuts" to eat.

Although the ginkgo is like the cycads in producing seeds that resemble true fruits, and also in following the ancient habit of having a spiral band of hairlike cilia on each male sex cell to propel it through a watery medium to an egg cell, the tree's trunk and sturdy branches are far more like those of a pine or other conifer. The wood is useful for lumber, and burns well as a fuel. The woody part expands year after year, a sheath at a time, producing a pattern of annual rings from which the age of a felled tree can be learned. Unlike cycads and like many conifers, the ginkgo can tolerate very cold weather—to thirty degrees Fahrenheit below zero. Uniquely among softwood trees, it can be grown from cuttings. This makes easier the horticulturalist's task of setting out no ginkgoes that will later produce seeds where youngsters can get them or oldsters be offended by the rotting flesh. Despite the forbidden seeds, the city planners have succeeded in brightening New York City, Washington, and other cities where millions of people live and work, with a handsome tree that survived extinction only because it was so "cultured."

Kauri "pines" (Agathis australis) *of New Zealand are among the largest of the world's commercial trees. Lichens and perching lilies* (Astelia *and* Collospermum) *cling to the bark. (John Johns)*

CHAPTER 4

Cone-Bearing Trees

The oldest, the tallest, and the heaviest of living things are all conifers. All the ultimate forests, whether toward the treeless Arctic or the perpetual snows on high mountains around the world, are coniferous. The most extensive and most valuable timberlands are composed almost exclusively of cone-bearing evergreens. Yet these records are held by less than a quarter of one per cent of the known kinds of seed plants—actually by only some of the 575 species of softwoods. These same trees supply three-quarters of the world's commercial lumber and virtually all of the pulpwood that is used for making paper.

If the sites of these important softwood forests are marked on a map of the world, they show as a rough figure-of-eight, one ring of which rides the mountain tops around the great Pacific Ocean while the other encircles the cold water and ice of the Arctic. It might

Stone pines (Pinus cembra) *have a silhouette that is familiar around the Mediterranean coast from Italy to Spain. The seeds are edible and much sought after.* (*Julius Behnke*)

be claimed that conifers grow best where the weather is cool, whether at high latitudes or high elevations. They do survive on poor, shallow, rocky soils such as were left by the retreating glaciers at the end of the long Ice Ages. In the tropics they occur mostly at high elevations where the soil and the climate are more challenging than near sea level. But it can be argued convincingly that in these areas they meet less competition from hardwoods, most of which are the forest trees of the warm tropics and kinds intolerant of frost.

Since people enjoy living in the temperate and cool climates that suit conifers, almost everyone recognizes the cone-bearing trees and can distinguish them from the common hardwoods. In the Northern Hemisphere, most conifers have evergreen leaves in the form of slender needles or green scales, which droop with the small branches when loaded with wet snow, and let it fall harmlessly from their waxy surfaces. As conifers we think of pines and "Christmas trees" (such as spruce or balsam fir); or of hemlock, cedar, or juniper. In the Southern Hemisphere, people may visualize, instead, various of the resinous conifers to which they give the name "pine" (such as an *Araucaria* or an *Agathis*), or a *Podocarpus* (despite its flat, elliptical leaves and plumlike seeds), or one of the strange phylloclads whose flattened side branches take the place of real foliage.

Of the world's softwood forests, more than half are in Asia, forming the native vegetation over vast areas of Siberia, adjacent China into the Himalayas and Korea, and much of Japan. For the most part they are inaccessible and untouched, growing on muskegs and steep mountains. Some day they may become important sources of pulpwood and timber. The commercial forests of conifers are in Canada, the northern and southeastern United States, Scandinavia, and countries bordering on the Baltic Sea. The remaining continents and islands account for less than eight per cent of the total.

The most spectacular display of conifers in the world is in the western United States. Yet these great trees, which are still the dominant forest-makers there, are slowly dwindling toward extinction. Giant size, whether in a redwood or a Douglas fir or a dinosaur, seems to indicate the end of a line. Among conifers, many lines seem near the end, with only a single species left to represent a genus that once was large. Many species are severely limited in their geographic range. Between Carmel and Monterey in California, for example, a person can walk in an hour to visit two different cypresses *(Cupressus macrocarpa,* the Monterey cypress, and *C. goweniana)* and two kinds of pine *(Pinus radiata,* the Monterey pine, and *P. muricata)* each of which is now restricted to a few acres on a once-broad range. To the north along the coast is a similar small remnant of the pygmy cypress *(Cupressus pygmaea),* while to the south are the last small stands of the Torrey pine *(Pinus torreyana).*

The conifers are not doomed by any inner inability to grow. They simply lack the means to reach new regions where the climate and soil match their needs, or where the flowering plants do not offer intolerable competition. The Monterey pine is flourishing in New Zealand, where it has been introduced. Many of the American and Mediterranean conifers are being planted successfully in the Southern Hemisphere in reforestation and afforestation programs aimed at developing a reliable source of lumber and firewood. They offer a quicker return than the slow-growing native hardwoods wherever these have been cut or have failed to spread into higher, cooler regions.

In all conifers, the pollen is produced in small cones each consisting of a cluster of papery scales in a short spiral. Many of the scales bear on their under sides two or more pollen sacs, which open in order to dust the pollen into the wind. The seed cones to which the pollen travels, however, show less uniformity.

In the plant families to which the araucarias, the pines, the bald-cypress, and the true cypresses belong (Araucariaceae, Pinaceae, Taxodiaceae, and Cupressaceae), the production of pollen and of seeds usually occurs on the same plant, and the seed cones are composed of fleshy resinous scales. Ordinarily they dry out and become woody as the seeds mature. "Juniper berries" on junipers (genus *Juniperus,* family Cupressaceae) are the exception, for the small cones remain fleshy. In all of these conifers the cone conceals the seeds until they are ready for dispersal.

In the yews, the podocarps and phylloclads (families Taxaceae, Podocarpaceae, and Phyllocladaceae), the seeds commonly develop on one tree or shrub, and the pollen on another. The ovules arise singly, protected only by four green bracts that suggest the sepals of a flower rather than the parts of a cone. As the seeds ripen, they project in a conspicuous way, usually made more eye-catching by a colorful cup-shaped enlargement of the stalk that supports them or by a similarly bright fleshy outer layer to the seed coat.

THE ARAUCARIANS (Family Araucariaceae)

In the Petrified Forest National Monument near Holbrook, Arizona, the main exhibit is an impressive array of gigantic tree trunks lying scattered on the desert. These fossilized logs, many with the remains of roots in place, grew during the early days of the dinosaurs. Floods swept the trees down from the forests and left them stranded in lowland swamps where massive reptiles lived. Branches and bark were torn off. But the mud that finally buried them was rich in volcanic ash, from which silica, iron, and manganese seeped into the buried wood. Delicately the silica filled the dead cells, preserving the inner structure and coloring it with the other minerals. Only during the past few thousands of years have the winds eroded and blown away the sediments that entombed the trees and petrified them. Enough of the structure remains for botanists to recognize the trees as araucarians. No cones have yet been found attached to the battered remains of the trunks. Some of these trunks are two hundred feet long, a length attained by many araucarians during the Mesozoic, both in the Americas and in much of the Old World too.

Today only two genera survive: *Araucaria,* with about twenty-five species of trees and shrubs, and *Agathis* with twelve. Most live in the Southern Hemisphere. Their leaves rise in a spiral around the branch, no leaf ever opposite another. Each cone scale bears no more than a single seed. Species of *Araucaria* dominate the coniferous forests of southern Brazil, and many mountain slopes in Chile. Others are found in New Guinea and eastern Australia. Most widely known is the Norfolk Island "pine" *(A. excelsa)* from north of New Zealand; where winters are severe, it is raised for its symmetrical beauty indoors, and outside around the Mediterranean Sea,

Adapted to shed snow, resist wind, and grow when frost and sun allow, spruces and firs spread close to glaciers and meltwater lakes in mountain country. (Julius Behnke)

in Florida and California. The monkey-puzzle tree *(A. araucana)* of Chile is often introduced as a curiosity because its branches offer no handholds; each is covered by short, stiff, prickly leaves. *Agathis* trees furnish lumber and the valuable resin known as copal, harvested in southeastern India, Malaya, up the Asiatic coast to the Philippines, in Australia, New Zealand, and some of the Pacific islands. The kauri "pine" *(A. australis)* of New Zealand is one of the largest timber trees in the world.

THE PINES AND THEIR KIN (Family Pinaceae)

Better than any other family of softwoods that outlived the dinosaurs and survived the Ice Ages, the pines and their kin have become well adapted to cold dry climates. In almost pure stands they form dense forests from which man gets for his construction work more lumber than from members of any other family of trees. Pines were among the most valuable of the resources discovered in the New World. For the countries of western Europe the finding of tall timber on the other side of the Atlantic Ocean came just in time, for logging operations to get fuel for iron smelting had almost exhausted Europe's western forests—forcing a conversion to use of coal despite its noxious smoke.

While northeastern America was still a British colony, the parliament of Queen Anne passed an act (1711) forbidding "any Person or Persons" from Maine to New Jersey "to Cut, Fell or Destroy any White or other sort of Pine-Tree." Every one of these tall

Far left: Nourished by fog from the sea off California and southern Oregon, redwoods (Sequoia sempervirens), *the tallest trees in the world, attain ages of 3000 and 4000 years. (M. Woodbridge Williams) Left above: With needles five to seven inches long, two to three in a cluster, and small robust cones, western yellow pines* (Pinus ponderosa) *form open forests with trunks to four feet in diameter and 180 high. (Ernst Peterson) Left center: In their second year, the seed cones of white pine* (Pinus strobus) *enlarge and hang downward. When the two winged seeds under each cone scale are ripe, the cone dries, opens and releases them. Left: A scarlet, fleshy enlargement of the stalk that holds the seed on low-growing American yew* (Taxus canadensis) *gives the appearance of an edible fruit, but is highly resinous. (Both by Lorus and Margery Milne)*

straight trunks was reserved to provide a strong mast for the British Royal Navy. Sixty years later, when the colonists freed themselves from the irritation of this (and other) restrictive legislation, the exploitation of white pine forests led colonization westward as far as the Wisconsin territory. This one species provided "the most cut, most used, and most prized timber in the New World" until 1900. Only when eastern forests of white pine gave out did attention swing by necessity to the western resources of Douglas fir.

Today, the Douglas fir *(Pseudotsuga taxifolia)* provides more than a quarter of all the saw timber cut in the United States, more than twice as much as any other tree. Symmetrical young Douglas firs serve in the West as "Christmas trees." The name commemorates David Douglas, a Scottish botanist in America, who described in detail this giant of the forest, which reaches a height of 221 feet, and bears flattened needles on short stalks. When the needles fall off, they leave the stem smooth or nearly so. The pendant cones attain a length of two to four inches when dry and mature. Each is unique in that every cone scale is accompanied by a three-pronged bract that projects half an inch or so beyond the scale. No other conifer produces cones with this feature.

As settlers from little European countries spread over the vast area of North America, they sought for distinctive features in different regions and found many among the trees. From these observations arose the custom of naming an official tree for each state, comparable to the national emblems of other countries. Often the tree chosen by one state is found native in many others too, as with the Douglas fir (emblem of Oregon), which grows wild in western Canada and all of the states from the Pacific coast to Montana, Wyoming, Colorado and New Mexico. More than a third of America's fifty states are now represented by a pine, a spruce, or a hemlock; no other family of plants has provided so many honored emblems.

True pines (genus *Pinus*) constitute almost half of the species in the pine family. Most bear their leaves in little clusters of two to five, each cluster wrapped at the base by a short sheath. All of the "white pines" have five needles in a cluster, and the sheath falls off early. These trees produce a white sapwood that darkens or reddens as it becomes the heartwood of a trunk or bough. It is uniformly close-grained, softer and easier to work than the wood of other pines. Eastern white pine *(P. strobus)* sometimes attains a height of 200 feet, whereas western white pine *(P.*

The noble fir (Abies procera) *grows from California northward into western Canada, its lower needles flat but those of its upper branches four-angled. (Jack Dermid: National Audubon)*

monticola) and sugar pine *(P. lambertiana)* vie with one another at 219 and 220 feet as the tallest of all pines. Sugar pine, which is restricted to Oregon and northern California, yields a sugary exudate from its heartwood; it excels all other pines in the length of its cones, which reach eighteen inches in length when they expand to release their seeds. Bristlecone pine *(P. aristata)* near timber line in the White Mountains of California attains spectacular age; more than eighteen trees of this species are known to be older than four thousand years, and to have been seedlings when the Great Pyramid was built in Egypt.

Of the three-needle pines, the most valuable are those called "yellow pines" because their sapwood is yellowish. It is also harder and coarser in grain than that of white pines. Western yellow pine *(P. ponderosa)* is second only to Douglas fir in yielding saw timber today. It is a handsome tree of the Rocky Mountains and of the Pacific coast north into Canada. On old trees the bark becomes a rich yellow brown, marked by irregular fissures into flat plates which

slowly scale away. In the southeastern United States, "yellow pine" forests contribute a slightly greater volume of lumber annually than does western yellow (ponderosa) pine. But four different species contribute to this total: *P. palustris,* the longleaf pine, with needles twelve to fourteen inches long, is the most valuable; *P. caribaea,* the slash pine of the southern Atlantic and Gulf states and the West Indies; *P. taeda,* the loblolly pine, growing from Maryland to Texas; and *P. rigida,* the eastern pitch pine, found from Maine to Florida. In the southeastern forests, many of these trees are tapped for turpentine, from which tar, pitch, and other so-called "naval stores" can be made. Western pitch pine *(P. coulteri)* is also a three-needle pine, but too much restricted to a relatively few mountain slopes in California to be much used for lumber or gum. It is outstanding for the size of its cones which, although no more than ten to fourteen inches long, weigh more than those of any other pine.

Blobs of gum often drop into the litter of fallen needles below pines that have been damaged by storms. The gum hardens as volatile, fragrant oils evaporate. This natural aging process may continue for millions of years, yielding amber. Some of the fossilized gum contains whole insects and spiders that were trapped and covered over when the resin was fresh and sticky. Bits of plant debris too have been preserved in this way. From them it has been possible to learn more reliably what lived in the pine forests of Eocene times, when Baltic amber originated, than during periods much nearer the present. Amber was known in classical Greece as a hard, gem-like material that would attract particles of lint when rubbed on cloth. The Greek word for amber, *electron,* later became the name for the unit of electrical charge. Germans call the material *Bernstein*—the stone that will burn. For centuries it has been valued for jewelry and as a material from which high-grade varnish can be prepared. Possibly amber represents the gum from many different pines, although an extinct one *(P. succinifera)* is often regarded as the chief source of amber washed up on beaches of the Baltic Sea.

Two-needle pines produce gum too, but other values are rated higher. Red pine *(P. resinosa)* of

Winds through the fertile valleys among the Karwendel Mountains near Kalis, Austria, distribute the winged seeds of the coniferous trees and the winged fruits of birch. (Gerhard Klammet)

eastern North America and lodgepole pine *(P. contorta)* of western North America are major sources of lumber.

Scotch pine *(P. sylvestris)* of northern Europe is one of the most important timber trees in the Old World. Known as a "fir" in old Norse sagas and also in Britain, it forms the forests that clothe the Scottish Highlands. Its short needles curve and often twist, and its branches in maturity grow gnarled and irregular until the tree attains a dense, mushroom silhouette. The stone pine *(P. pinea)* of Italy develops a similar shape; its hard pyramidal cones have been collected and stored since Roman days, to provide pignolia "nuts," which are still used for food. In the American Southwest, the Indians similarly hoarded the seeds of the piñon pine *(P. edulis).*

Edible seeds are produced also by the singleleaf pine *(P. monophylla),* which is native to the Great Basin states of the United States, to California and Baja California. Perhaps the Indians did not distinguish it from the piñon pine. The seeds of both, known as "pine nuts," "pinyon nuts," or "Indian nuts," are about sixty per cent fat, rich also in protein and carbohydrate, and easy to eat since each is clad in only a thin seed coat. In former times, all members of each Indian tribe in the Southwest hunted through the scrubby pinelands, gathering seeds from the ground, knocking them from the hard cones, or robbing them from the underground caches of squirrels. Working diligently all day, one person may still collect twenty pounds of seeds. Today the reproduction of these pines is threatened, and the native animals of the pinelands are hard pressed for food because as many as three thousand tons a year are taken away for sale to the nut-and-candy industry. Only the fact that seed production is irregular, rising to a high point every five years or so and then decreasing sharply, may save the trees.

The conifers known as spruces *(Picea*—approximately forty-five species) and true firs *(Abies—*about forty species) get confused in many parts of the world where people recognize as pines any of the ninety-odd species of *Pinus.* Often spruces and firs grow side by side, forming a solid coniferous belt

Baldcypress (Taxodium distichum) *forms swamp forests, thrusting up "knees" through the water to get air for submerged roots. Festoons of Spanish moss* (Tillandsia usneoides) *are often more conspicuous than the needles of this deciduous tree. (J. C. Allen & Son)*

that diagonals across Canada, and from Scandinavia to eastern Siberia. In America, red, white and black spruce *(P. rubens, glauca,* and *mariana,* respectively) and balsam fir *(A. balsamea)* are the principal species cut for pulpwood and Christmas trees. In the vast taiga country of northern Eurasia, the corresponding evergreens are the Siberian fir *(A. sibirica)* and spruce *(P. obovata).* Young trees maintain a uniform pyramidal shape as their successive whorls of branches lengthen progressively. For Christmas decoration, balsam fir is preferred because its needles stay on longer after the tree is cut than do those on spruces. Anyone who buys or decides to make a fragrant "pine pillow" should be sure that it is filled with fir needles, not spruce, and never pine (which soon lose their scent). Spruce needles are stiff and sharp at the tip, often penetrating the cloth of the pillow, whereas those of fir are softer and blunter.

Spruce needles each grow atop a short woody peg on the side of the stem, whereas fir needles arise at full width from the stem directly. When spruce needles fall off, the pegs remain as conspicuous roughness on the stem. A fir stem is smooth, marked only by inconspicuous scars. Spruce seed cones turn downward as they ripen, and drop their seeds a month or more before the whole cone separates as a unit from the tree. Fir seed cones remain upright,

Cedars of Lebanon (Cedrus libanotica) *survive principally in remote forests of Turkey, near the Taurus Mountains. (Wilhelm Schacht)*

and release their seeds by disintegrating altogether. Cone scales and dry seeds tumble into the breeze, leaving only the cone axis to mark its place. In a Douglas fir *(Pseudotsuga),* by contrast, each needle arises from the stem by a short, slender leaf stalk, and the mature cones are pendant. They remain whole until they drop off, after their seeds have been dispersed.

With the exception of the noble fir *(Abies nobilis)* of the northwestern states, whose wood is strong and of high quality, the firs are less valuable than the spruces for lumber, but more productive of resins. The silver fir *(A. alba)* of Europe yields Strasbourg turpentine, Burgundy pitch, rosin, and other similar materials. The balsam fir *(A. balsamea),* which is widespread in North America from the Yukon to the mountains of Virginia, develops great blisters of resin in its bark. These are "Canada balsam." White fir *(A. concolor)* of the Rocky Mountains and Pacific coastal states to Baja California, is one of several used for making plywood, rough boxes and crates, and is also grown to ornament fine estates.

Spruce wood is generally stronger, more elastic, and lighter in weight than fir wood. It is used in air-craft construction and, because of its resonant quali-ties, for the bodies of violins and the sounding boards of pianos. For lumber, the most valuable spruce is the one honoring the American botanist, G. Engel-mann of St. Louis *(Picea engelmanni).* Forests of it grow between 1500 and 12,000 feet elevation in the Rocky Mountains. The runner-up is the Sitka spruce *(P. sitchensis),* which is harvested from near tide-water all the way from northern California to Alaska. Both Engelmann and Sitka spruce reach a height of 180 feet, the tallest of their genus in America.

The dwarfed potted trees ("bonsai") that are the pride of Japanese horticulturalists are usually the yeddo spruce *(P. jezoensis)* of Japan and Manchuria. The most confusingly named of all is the Norway spruce *(Picea abies*—combining both generic names!), which is a valuable timber tree of Europe and is now introduced widely in America.

The name "cedar" is even more loosely used.

Left above: Spires of alpine fir (Abies lasiocarpa) *are familiar landmarks in mountain meadows of the western United States and Canada. (Bill Stackhouse) Left: Siberian larch* (Larix sibirica) *is common in the northern coniferous forest that extends from eastern Europe through Siberia. (Jeanne White: National Audubon)*

Properly it belongs to four species of *Cedrus,* in the pine family. Most famous of them is the cedar of Lebanon *(C. libanotica),* from which Solomon built his temple and palace. The original forests, in which "fourscore thousand hewers" cut trees for Solomon alone, have dwindled to a few hundred trees in one small park—and a tree on the Lebanese flag. Fortunately, Turkey has a few forests of cedar of Lebanon, but lumbering is excessive in almost every one. The Atlantic cedar *(C. atlantica),* which once was immensely valuable in Algeria and Morocco, is becoming rare. Goats, fires, and woodcutters are eliminating the Cyprus cedar *(C. brevifolia),* mostly as seedlings and young trees. Only the deodar *(C. deodara),* a handsome large tree of the Himalayas, is not yet seriously threatened. Its name is the Hindu for "timber of the gods."

Hemlocks *(Tsuga)* include about a dozen species, all with flattened needles marked with white lengthwise below, on short stalks. Western hemlock *(T. heterophylla)* is one of the principal timber trees of the Pacific Northwest. The eastern hemlock *(T. canadensis)* grows commonly as an understory in hardwood forests of beech, oak and hickory. Other hemlocks grow in Japan, China and Korea, but none are native to Europe or other continents.

The larches *(Larix)* are more widely distributed in the north temperate zone. All ten species yield useful wood, but the uninitiated often think the trees to be dead when they are first encountered in winter. Larch needles, which arise in clusters of ten or more, turn a glorious golden yellow in autumn and then drop to the ground. This deciduous habit, so strange in a conifer, is indicated in the name of the European larch, *L. decidua,* which is common in the Alps and the Carpathians. It is the source of Venice turpentine—a yellow resin used in lithographic work. Cold bogs, such as are inhabited by spruces and firs, are suitable also for the Siberian larch *(L. sibirica)* of northern Russia to Alaska, and the tamarack *(L. laricina)* of boreal Canada and as far south as the Pocono Mountains of Pennsylvania. The western *L. occidentalis* is among the largest of larches, for it attains a height of 210 feet in the northern Rocky Mountains, where it is cut to get lumber. Its gum, called galactin, can be used in making baking powder.

THE BALDCYPRESS FAMILY (Taxodiaceae)

The world's most enormous trees are among the sixteen kinds in nine genera that remain today to represent this group of conifers. Unlike the members of the pine family, their pollen grains bear no balloon-like wings, and their woody seed cones often bear three to eight seeds atop each scale instead of only two or one. Some species, such as the dawn redwood *(Metasequoia)* and the baldcypresses *(Taxodium),* are deciduous in a strange way, for in winter they drop off the slender branches along which their green needles arise.

The baldcypress itself *(T. distichum)* produces important wood in coastal swamps from Virginia to Texas, where its roots gain extra oxygen and nourishment from strange upward projections called "knees," which extend into the sun and air above the water. Another *Taxodium (T. mucronatum)* is the famous "big cypress" of Mexico. One massive giant that grows beside the cathedral at Santa Maria del Tule, near Oaxaca, is 112 feet in circumference at its base. Known as the "Tule tree," it may actually represent a dozen or more trees that sprang up as "suckers" from the roots of a fallen ancestor, and later grew into a single inseparable edifice. If so, the estimates that place the seedling stage of the original tree at five thousand years ago may be close to the truth. So large a tree requires enormous amounts of water. Recently, the people of Oaxaca took heroic measures to insure an adequate supply for their famous landmark, which was showing signs of trouble whenever the annual dry season lasted longer than usual.

The bulkiest trees from a single root are the giant *Sequoia (S. gigantea),* of which more than three hundred are in Sequoia National Park, near San Francisco, California. One is 101 feet six inches in circumference at the base, 272 feet tall, like a lofty pyramid of wood from which spreading branches hold out small scalelike needles as much as forty-five feet to each side. The tallest trees are coastal redwoods *(S. sempervirens),* in the fog belt near the Pacific coast north of San Francisco. One measured recently was three hundred feet high, and sixty-five feet nine inches in circumference at the base. Any of these massive trunks contain enough wood to build a dozen frame houses, with plenty left over to make shingles for the roof, crates for all the furniture they could hold, panelling for every room, and thermal insulation (made from the bark) to keep them snug in the coldest winter. The needles on a coastal redwood are as much as an inch long; its cones may measure the same both in length and diameter. Each seed from the tallest tree would fit on the top of a pinhead.

Sequoia, named for Chief Sequoya of the Cherokee

Indian tribe, is now native only in California and Oregon. Once the genus was widespread both in America and Europe. The same is true of its nearest surviving relative, the dawn redwood *(Metasequoia glyptostrobioides),* which was discovered in 1944 forming a small forest near the Yangtse River in central China. If the maximum recorded age for a redwood (about 3500 years) is typical, and if seedlings have found a place to grow in the forest chiefly when a patriarch toppled from natural causes, then it is not so many generations ago that ancestral redwoods shaded the giant dinosaurs and other reptiles now long extinct. Fossils of these trees are found in sedimentary rocks of the Mesozoic.

Lesser relatives of bald-cypresses and *Sequoia* live in the Orient, where they provide timber and add beauty to the landscape: the parasol-pine or umbrella-fir *(Sciadopitys verticillata)* and the "cedar" *(Cryptomeria japonica)* of Japan and a few kinds each of *Cunninghamia* and *Glyptostrobus* along the coast of China, Korea and Formosa. Three species of *Arthro-*

Bishop pine (Pinus muricata) *often grows so close to rocky coasts in California that it is distorted by storms and salt spray. (M. Woodbridge Williams)*

Loblolly pines (Pinus taeda) *grow on sandy soil in the southeastern United States. The reddish-brown bark clings in flat, scaly plates. (Georgia Forestry Commission)*

taxis in Tasmania are the sole representatives in the Southern Hemisphere.

THE CYPRESS FAMILY (Cupressaceae)

It is far easier to recognize any member of the cypress family by its structure than to know whether to call it a cypress, a cedar, or an arbor vitae. All of them are unique among cone-bearing trees and shrubs in having small needles in pairs of threes or fours, often so tightly applied to the stems that the points of attachment cannot be seen. Other conifers bear their needles singly or in clusters, as in pine and larch.

Almost half of the 140 kinds in the cypress family are junipers, native to the north temperate regions, where they bear their seeds concealed within a fleshy coating that resembles a berry. Both in America and the Old World, the blue "juniper berries" from *Juniperus communis* are gathered by hand as the source of an aromatic oil which gives gin its distinctive character. *Juniperus virginiana* is known from Georgia to Texas, the Dakotas to Maine as "eastern redcedar" —once the principal wood for fence posts, lead pencils, cedar chests and closet lining. Whether the distintive odor of cedarwood oil repels clothes moths or conceals from them the scent of woolen garments on which their caterpillars might feed, has never been proved scientifically. Branches of the tree yield

Bristlecone pines (Pinus aristata) *produce new needles and cones after many branches have succumbed to harsh conditions in the White Mountains of California. (L. B. Graham: National Audubon)*

Foxtail pines (Pinus balfouriana) *in the High Sierra wilderness of California gained this name because of the dense masses formed by their needles. (U. S. Forest Service)*

"cedarleaf oil" with a slightly different aromatic pungency. Because this juniper is known to serve as the alternate host for apple rust, it has been eliminated in may regions where apple orchards are set out. Elsewhere the fungus can be admired on the tree after any summer rain, when the hard, inconspicuous "cedar apples" extend bright orange steamers from whose soft surfaces spores are freed into the breeze.

All other members of the cypress family have woody seed cones. Western redcedar is *Thuja plicata,* the chief source of wooden shingles in America today. In pioneer days it was known as canoe cedar, because the Indians along broad rivers leading to the Pacific Ocean used its tall trunks for their dugouts. Like northern whitecedar *(T. occidentalis)* of northeastern America, it bears pale green blunt needles in pairs. They fit together so compactly on flat sprays that individual leaves are scarcely noticed. Whitecedar is often called arborvitae, literally "tree of life," because it is so similar to *Thuja orientalis* of northeastern China and Korea, which was introduced to Europe along with its symbolic meaning about the time of Marco Polo. Its natural pyramidal form can be modified radically by selective pruning, allowing artists to create with it geometric figures such as cones and spheres, or to trim it to contours matching the shape of buildings or the curve of roadways.

The symbolism of life, death and the hereafter are particularly bound up in the cypress family. All over the Christian world, the slim spire-shaped trees most commonly planted in cemetaries are the Chinese cypress *(Cupressus funebris),* of which the branches droop and are said to be weeping. Beside the cemetary, the church may be fragrant with smoke from smoldering incense. Most incense wood comes from some one of the nine different kinds of *Libocedrus,* the incense-cedar. This genus is found all around the Pacific Ocean, along coasts of the Americas, New Zealand, the Asiatic mainland, and into the East Indies. In California and Oregon, large trees of the California incense-cedar *(L. decurrens)* are cut as the principal wood for making lead pencils. This tree, and also the yellow-cedar *(Chamaecyparis lawsoniana)* of the same region, also provides the favorite wood to be cut into thin slats for Venetian blinds. *C. lawsoniana,* known also as the Port-Oxford cedar because it was common around this city in Oregon, has long been used also for the wooden "separators" that keep the metal plates apart in the corrosive acid of a storage battery.

Yellow-cedar or falsecypress are among the names given to members of the genus *Chamaecyparis.* One of these, *C. nootkatensis,* is an important timber tree of Alaska. Another, *C. thyoides,* lives in the swamps along the Atlantic and Gulf coasts from Cape Cod to

Occasional fires among the undergrowth of coastal redwoods (Sequoia sempervirens) *make room for redwood seedlings. (U. S. Forest Service)*

In the soggy ground in which baldcypress trees grow, their trunks expand into buttresses, the roots extending outward and downward. (American Forest Products)

Louisiana; called Atlantic cedar, it is highly regarded for making small boats, watertight tanks, wooden-ware, and water-shedding siding or shingles for homes.

In the Southern Hemisphere, the cypress family is represented too. Cedar Mountain in the Cape Province of South Africa is named for a juniper-like "cedar" *(Widdringtonia juniperoides)* that grows there as well as in scattered other remnants from a once-broad distribution. In southern Chile and Patagonia, one of the few important timber trees is the handsome cypress-like *Fitzroya cupressoides,* which honors Captain Robert Fitzroy who commanded H. M. S. *Beagle* around the world in 1831–1836 with naturalist Charles Darwin aboard.

THE YEWS *(Family Taxaceae)*

Robin Hood's bow was almost certainly made from the strong, flexible wood of the English yew *(Taxus baccata)* of Europe; *taxus* is the Latin word for a bow. Eight more species of this genus are found in

the Northern Hemisphere as shrubs and small trees with handsome shining needles and, in season, hard dry seeds each almost surrounded by a fleshy red cup. In each case, the cup (an aril) is formed by enlargement of the end on the short stalk that supports the solitary ovule before it is pollinated. Children who sample the attractive red cups on the Canada yew *(T. canadensis),* which is grown as low evergreen shrubbery around many homes, discover that it is too resinous to be palatable. Birds, however, enjoy the arils as they would a true fruit, and distribute the indigestible seeds of the yew which they swallow at the same time.

Most of the yew family live near the coasts of the North Pacific Ocean. One, *Austrotaxus,* is found only in New Caledonia in the South Pacific. Another, *Torreya,* named for the American botanist John Torrey, has three species in the Orient, but is well known in America from the "nutmeg" *(T. californica)* along the Pacific coast and the "stinking cedar" *(T. taxifolia)* of Florida. The Chinese plum-yew *(Cephalotaxus fortunei),* planted widely as an ornamental,

Monterey cypress (Cupressus macrocarpa) *lives precariously on storm-swept shores of California. (Gladys Diesing: National Audubon)*

Americas as Mexico and the West Indies, as well as in Africa south of the great deserts. On many of its species, the evergreen leaves are shaped like the narrow head of a lance, suggesting perhaps a thick-leaved willow. They provide dense shade under the tropical sun, and might not be suspected of being conifers if not for the cones in which winged pollen is produced in prodigious quantities. The smallest conifer in the world belongs to a related genus *(Dacrydium)* of about twenty species, found from Malaya to Tasmania, New Zealand, and Chile. The "pygmy pine" *(D. laxifolium)* of New Zealand produces tiny cones when only about three inches high.

THE PHYLLOCLADS (Family Phyllocladaceae)

Among the strangest conifers of far places are the six kinds of *Phyllocladus* found in Tasmania, New Zealand, Borneo, and the Philippine Islands. These timber trees quickly shed the tiny leaves they form, and depend upon photosynthesis in their evergreen, flat, leaflike branches which are often lobed so deeply as to suggest heads of celery. Celery-pine is a common name for these trees. They seem to represent an experiment in architecture that went no further. But they do provide an exception to the popular idea that all conifers are needle-leaved trees.

represents a genus which is found from Japan to the Himalayas.

THE PODOCARPS AND THEIR KIN (Family Podocarpaceae)

Among conifers, only the true pines outnumber in variety the members of the genus *Podocarpus*. But most of the sixty species in this genus live in remote parts of the Southern Hemisphere, where they form forests and scrub vegetation in many different climatic zones. Australians call some of their species "blackpine." New Zealanders rely upon the brown timber from *P. ferruginea,* which the Mauri people call miro-miro. Kahikatea there is *P. dacrydioides,* which yields tough wood, resin, and a sweet edible aril that could be mistaken for a plum. Chileans, in fact, call *Podocarpus andina* of the whole Andean chain the "plum-fir"; the fruitlike covering of the seed is yellowish white and delicious.

Podocarpus grows also in the East Indies, southeastern Asia and Japan, and as far north in the

CHAPTER 5

The Frilled Ones

Three utterly different kinds of vegetation, that fit nowhere else in the whole plant kingdom, form a separate order of softwoods. Once they were called the Chlamydospermae—"the frilled ones with seeds." Now the order is Gnetales, referring to a plant of Indomalaysia and its close kin. With no common name other than the word gnemon on the island of Ternate in the South Pacific where it was discovered, the plant *(Gnetum gnemon)* is cultivated for its fiber and the edible fleshy covering of its seeds.

Some fifteen kinds of *Gnetum* grow as shrubs and woody vines in the tropical and subtropical forests

While its two leathery leaves erode, the huge tuberous root of Welwitschia mirabilis, *a most unusual plant, stores water in the desert of South West Africa. (R. J. Rodin)*

from Australia to the Himalayas, in Central and South America, and in West Africa. At conspicuous swellings along the stem they bear pairs of oval leaves as much as three inches long. They are net-veined, and could easily be mistaken for those of many flowering plants. But when *Gnetum* readies itself for reproduction, it produces clusters of peculiar organs that are neither flowers nor cones although the cylindrical group in each case may suggest a catkin. In a cluster that releases pollen, as many as three thousand of these strange organs are present. In a cluster that yields seeds, the total may not exceed one hundred. The strange or peculiar feature of these organs is the pair or two pairs of crescent-shaped bracts that rise up around them as a frill almost like the petals of a flower. Those around the pollen sacs drop off, but the bracts beside the developing seed first help guide the pollen tube to the ovule and then grow fleshy, attracting animals and men who may help disperse the ripe seeds unharmed.

A somewhat similar reproductive structure is produced by *Welwitschia mirabilis,* which is one of the world's most unusual plants. Found only in the deserts of Southwest Africa, it produces just two long leaves during its lifetime of a century or more. The huge tuberous root of *Welwitschia* projects slightly above the surface of the gravelly soil. Its low crown adds to the length of the broad strap-shaped leaves, which continue to grow although their tips become twisted, torn and dried. No more leaves ever develop, but each mature plant sends up new reproductive organs every year or two.

The third and largest genus among the plants with frill-like bracts is *Ephedra,* of which more than forty species inhabit arid regions of the New World and the Old. In the American Southwest, *Ephedra nevadensis* is known as Mormon tea bush (or Brigham tea, after Brigham Young), or as jointfir. It is a densely branching shrub, growing to a height of five feet, often forming, along with creosote bush, almost impenetrable thickets called chaparral—vegetation too dense to ride a horse through.

No *Ephedra* produces conspicuous leaves on its green twigs. Instead, it bears only whorl after whorl of persistent bracts at intervals around each stem, the bracts from an eighth to a quarter of an inch in length. Two Oriental species, *E. equisetina* (referring to its resemblance to a horsetail) and *E. sinica* (known as mahuang), were for many years the principal source of the medicinal alkaloid ephedrine. The drug is still used in nose drops to reduce the inflammation and congestion of a head cold. But synthetic ephedrine has now replaced the natural product.

For nearly a century, botanists puzzled over the nature of *Gnetum* and *Ephedra,* and then over *Welwitschia* when it was discovered. The reproductive catkins of these plants show so many similarities to flowers that it was tempting to regard them in that way. In details of the anatomy in stems and roots, they resemble the flowering plants. None of them possesses the resin canals that are so customary among softwoods. The conducting cells in the wood of these three genera also include the open-ended pipes known as vessels, as well as the closed-ended tubular cells called tracheids. No other softwoods possess vessels. But when the plant anatomists traced the steps by which vessels arise in Gnetales, they learned that the process is unlike that in a flowering plant. Presumably these larger tubes, which carry watery solutions upward more efficiently than tracheids can, evolved independently. Members of the three genera show in their inner bark only the same kind of conducting cells (sieve cells) for sugary solutions as are found in other softwoods. None of them possesses the more advanced sieve tubes and companion cells that serve this role in the inner bark of flowering plants.

It seems unlikely that the Gnetales and the flowering plants had a common ancestor much later than the Coal Ages, when softwoods were not yet the dominant vegetation of the land and real flowers were millions of years in the future. Almost certainly the flowering plants arose from extinct softwoods whose reproductive parts included the ovule-producing and the pollen-producing kinds in the same spiral. In all of the softwoods, including the "frilled ones," they are on separate branches if not on separate plants.

3

Hardwoods and Herbs

So often it is the small things in life that have the largest consequences. It was not the giant dinosaurs that changed the direction in which the world's vegetation evolved during the Age of Reptiles, but the insignificant insects. Probably it was the beetles, already established in a life cycle and body form that was to make them the most successful, versatile style of creature on earth, that provided the chief stimulus toward success in flowering plants. They enhanced the chance of reproduction for plants that could benefit at second hand from an insect's senses, brain, and ability to get around.

Unlike the wind, which learns nothing as it carries pollen wherever it blows, a beetle can remember and recognize again a kind of plant upon which it finds a rewarding meal. The insect can use its keen sense of smell to locate the next plant from afar. Its eyes may help. At close range, taste and touch become important aids. But for the plant, these consistent visits bring opportunity: pollen grains by special delivery, to the address the flower spells out in ways an insect's senses can interpret.

For the flowering plant, the benefits to be gained from pollinating animals go far beyond any economy in the amount of pollen that is required. They include one of the most important features of evolution: the isolation of breeding populations, which allows adaptation to be added to adaptation until the descendants of one ancestral type can survive in two or more unlike situations. The distinguished botanist Dr. Verne Grant of Santa Ana Botanic Garden in California found a fine example of this recently among the columbines of the Rocky Mountains. At one elevation, a red-flowered columbine came into bloom each springtime, and its pendant blossoms attracted the hummingbirds that flitted up the mountain slopes on sunny afternoons. At a higher elevation, later in the season, a white-flowered columbine grew in comparable abundance. Its blooms faced the sky, and were tended by hawkmoths on warm summer nights.

At an intermediate elevation, Dr. Grant found a few of these two kinds of columbines growing side by side. In some years their flowering seasons overlapped. The red flowers attracted hummingbirds but not hawkmoths, which could neither see them at night nor easily aim their uncoiled tongues to reach the nectar from below at dusk or dawn. Hummingbirds, however, not only pollinated the red-flowered columbines as usual, but also hovered over the white species to probe for nectar. Pollen traveled between white and red. No longer did color, time of flowering, or the directions the blossoms faced serve to isolate the two types where they grew at the same elevation. Hybrids developed, for the two kinds of columbines had not yet evolved far enough apart to be incompatible. Until that further step is made, the white columbines are vulnerable to the red, which presumably are closer to their common ancestor. By being white, tilting their flowers upward, and blossoming at a slightly different season, the white columbines have a chance to consolidate their position upon the high slopes without having their special heritage diluted by lesser adaptations that suffice for the reds at lower levels.

More than any other organ of a flowering plant, its flowers serve to isolate it from all closely-related species until hybridization becomes unlikely or impossible. Consequently, it is the flower that botanists look to most regularly for features that will distinguish the 285,000 different varieties of flowering plants.

Flowers are more conservative, more related to the past and to the future, than are other organs of a flowering plant. They correspond to changes that can be discovered in the fossil record. They match similarities and differences in chemical composition, in features of inheritance, and in geographical distribution. Generally there are far fewer meaningful patterns in the roots, stems and leaves of plants than in their reproductive parts. Roots, stems and leaves are too subject to modification in perfecting the fit of a plant into its present way of life. They match the type of soil and amount of moisture or of nutrients there. They correspond to the usual intensity of light, of wind, of animal attack, and perhaps the range in relative humidity where the plant grows. But the features that are passed on from one generation to the next are those that lie hidden in a pollen grain and deep in each ovary of the flower. It is the flowers that protect and project this heritage from age to age.

In comparing modern flowers with one another and with those of extinct flowering plants, a number of trends can be recognized as simplifications of the original pattern. One trend is a reduction in the number of parts that compose a flower. The number of carpels decreases. So does the number of stamens. Not only may the number of parts in the perianth become fixed, but their relative positions show regularity, such as stamens alternating with petals around the cycling spiral of the flower.

Another trend is toward fusion of flower parts. Two or more carpels may join to form one compound "pistil" at the center of the flower. The filaments of the stamens may join with the ovary wall for part of their length, so that they appear to arise from it and the botanist describes them as *epigynous* ("on the ovary") instead of *perigynous* ("around the ovary"). The petals may be joined together, making the flower *gamopetalous* instead of *polypetalous* (with separate petals). The whole corolla may fuse with the ovary for a short distance, making the ovary "inferior" to it, instead of "superior" to the corolla. The whole symmetry of the flower may even be changed from a perfect radial plan in which the spiral nature can be traced easily to one that shows bilateral symmetry, as is seen in snapdragons and in members of the pea family.

Still another trend is toward elimination of flower parts. In an oak tree or a fig, the carpels have vanished from some flowers, leaving them staminate (pollen-producing); disappearance of stamens from other flowers of the same species leaves them carpel-

late (egg-producing). Or the showy parts may be greatly reduced, removing obstructions to wind, which brings these particular plants more pollen than insects do. The alders and birches, oaks and elms excel in this direction.

With growing appreciation for these several trends it becomes easier to understand why a waterlily, a buttercup and a magnolia tree are regarded as more alike than any of these is to a watercress, a yellow daisy or an apple tree. Often one close look at a flower, or a brief inspection of bark and branching on a tree, or a few features of an herb suffice to place it in its correct family of plants—perhaps to identify it positively. Seldom is this skill as hard-won as to distinguish a Scotsman from an Australian by his speech, or to recognize each of a hundred friends no matter how they are dressed. The plant world is identifiable into its wonderful variety in all parts of the world by features that are far easier to describe in words than those by which we tell apart the friends (or the music) we have come to know.

CHAPTER 6

Modern Plants With Old-Style Flowers

CUES: *A dicot plant that has all of its perianth parts separate from one another, all of its stamens and all of its carpels separate and distinct, is a member of the Order Ranales. It may be a magnolia tree, a buttercup, a waterlily, a tropical custard apple, a prickly barberry, a nutmeg, or an honored laurel.*

Of all the flowering plants in the modern world, these seem to have changed least from their primitive, fossilized ancestors. Many of them have an indefinite number of carpels, of stamens, and of perianth parts that may show no clear distinction into sepals and petals. Some petal-like parts bear an anther at the tip, and are actually functional stamens. Perhaps the reproductive parts of the extinct Bennettitales were similarly indefinite, although grouped in a tight spiral bearing both carpels and stamens. All other flowering plants are suspected of evolving from this same ancestral line.

THE MAGNOLIA FAMILY *(Magnoliaceae)*

The North Temperate Zone is still hospitable to some of the most ancient types of flowering trees. Magnolias *(Magnolia),* with about twenty living species, and tulip-poplars *(Liriodendron),* with two, are represented in eastern Asia and in North America. Both are represented by fossils in Greenland, Scandinavia, Alaska and other northern lands where they are now extinct but to which they once spread after their appearance during the Cretaceous period.

The evergreen magnolia *(M. grandiflora),* with its large shining leaves and handsome cream-white flowers, has become a gracious symbol of the Deep South of the United States. When its petals, which vary in number from six to a dozen, open widely, they form a soft, yielding cup as much as six inches across, fragrant with a suggestion of lemon. Above a fringe of stamens, the conical cluster of carpels rises at the center of the flower. As the fruits begin to form, the stamens and petals drop, and the receptacle enlarges until it resembles a small green cucumber. Later, the scarlet fruits bulge from its surface, which blackens and dries. Eventually, each is freed on a long slender thread which breaks when the wind is strong enough to propel the heavy seed some distance from the parent tree.

The tuliptree *(Liriodendron tulipifera)* of the eastern United States grows often to a height of a hundred feet and a trunk diameter of ten feet, impressively erect on dry hillsides and in dry woodlands where it is protected from strong winds. Its flowers appear artificial, with three sepals downturned and six stiff petals forming a cup two inches deep around a palisade of stamens and a tall conical cluster of carpels. As the carpels ripen, the central receptacle elongates until the mass resembles a dry cone, from which the winged fruits break off and are carried away by the breeze.

THE BUTTERCUP FAMILY *(Ranunculaceae)*

Four familiar plants—a peony, a buttercup, a virgin's bower *(Clematis)* and a columbine—provide a fair sample of the herbs and woody climbers of which

In springtime, before the leaves on trees shade the woodland floor, fragile anemones (Anemone) *display their white, starlike flowers. (J. Allen Cash)*

more than fifteen hundred different kinds constitute this big family. Most of them have leaves so deeply indented around the margins that they are palmately compound.

Even though horticulturalists have developed more than seven hundred named varieties of peonies, the handsome fragrant flowers still mostly show the multiplicity of petals and of stamens that are so evident in their wild ancestors—*Paeonia officinalis* of Europe (the "old-fashioned" single kind) and *P. albiflora* of China. When these two were crossed, their offspring proved remarkably variable. Hybrids with attractive features have been continued by vegetative propagation. Often the globular buds of peonies are better known than the large seeds that develop one to a carpel on a large fleshy disk after all of the stamens and petals have dropped.

Similarly, a majority of people recognize the three hundred different species of buttercups *(Ranunculus)* when the bright yellow, shining petals are cupped and will reflect the golden rays of sunshine against a person's face, as all of us did in childhood to reach the conclusion "You like butter." Buttercups thrive in the Arctic, all over the north temperate regions and far up on mountain slopes. They are found too

in New Zealand, and in subantarctic parts of South America.

One of the commonest of tall buttercups in fields of Eurasia and North America is *Ranunculus acris,* introduced accidentally to the New World during pioneer times. Like other members of its family, it has a colorless acrid juice. Despite the bitter flavor, cattle and horses that can find little else to eat will sometimes devour enough buttercups to be poisoned by them.

Marsh marigold *(Caltha palustris),* with butter-yellow flowers of larger size, is equally dangerous to livestock that eat it green. Yet the buds and handsome heart-shaped leaves are harmless when dried as hay, and delicious when cooked for human consumption. Marsh marigold flowers by mid-spring in wet places across Eurasia and in North America, known variously as cowslip, kingcup, and May blob.

Blossoming at about the same time in the woodlands of the Northern Hemisphere are delicate spring wildflowers which lack petals but display petal-like sepals of various shades from violet and blue to white. *Hepatica triloba,* the liverleaf, grows all across Eurasia and in cultivation, its three-lobed leaves shaped enough like a human liver that infusions of them were used formerly to treat liver ailments. American hepaticas bear similar foliage, which remains green all winter, only to be replaced by new leaves which unfold from hairy buds after the flowers have faded. *Anemone coronaria,* the poppy-anemone, grows all around the Mediterranean. It is almost certainly the plant referred to as "lilies of the field" (Matthew 6, 28), since it is common in the Holy Land, whereas true lilies are not. Pasque-flowers, which open their attractive flowers before their leaves and usually well in advance of both Easter and Passover—the religious events of the Pasch season—are anemones too: *A. pulsatilla* in Europe and many gardens, and *A. patens* in America. Most other anemones are known as windflowers. A

Left above: The first flowers, which evolved in Cretaceous times, were closely similar to the showy blossoms on the Japanese magnolia (Magnolia stellata). *(Lorus and Margery Milne) Left: Each flower of a magnolia* (Magnolia grandiflora) *drops its showy parts and stamens before it matures into a conelike fruit. (Jack Dermid) Right: Golden columbine* (Aquilegia chrysantha) *adds sparkle to springtime among the western yellow pines on Mogollon Rim, in Sitgreaves National Forest, Arizona. (Josef Muench)*

few of them are found high in the Andes Mountains.

Petals are lacking also in *Clematis,* whose flowers have many stamens and four large sepals that spread to form a conspicuous symmetrical cross. They are delicate white or greenish-white in virgin's bower *(C. virginiana)* of the eastern United States, which flowers all summer. By autumn each cluster of blossoms is represented by a great fluffy ball composed of the feathery tips on the long curved carpels in which the seeds are ripening. Then people know the plant as "devil's hair," or "old-man's beard." The intertwining woody stems in masses along riverbanks have often been misnamed woodbine. Some people are allergic to the foliage of all species of *Clematis,* of which about two hundred and thirty are known, mostly from regions with cool summers. An exception is traveler's-joy *(C. vitalba)* of southern Europe.

A hoodlike upper sepal tends to hide the petals in European wolfbane *(Aconitum napellus),* which has spread widely in America, and its native New World relatives of the same genus, generally known as monkshood. Wolfbane is the source of the drug aconite, which is used to calm a heart or an upset digestive tract. A Nepalese species *(A. ferox)* is the source of bikh, a deadly poison that has sometimes been used in crime. The foliage of most kinds of *Aconitum* is toxic to domesticated animals.

In the American West, stockmen refer to wild larkspurs *(Delphinium)* as "locoweed," because sheep and cattle that eat these plants develop a staggering gait and other symptoms which often lead to death. Larkspur is named for the long hollow extension from one of the five colored sepals. Close to it, the upper pair of petals have shorter spurs of their own. In these the nectar is secreted, attracting long-tongued butterflies, moths, and hummingbirds as pollinators. Horticulturalists often reserve the name larkspur for annual delphiniums and use *Delphinium* only for the perennial kinds.

In columbines *(Aquilegia)* the five sepals are colored, and may drop off early. Each of the five petals extends into a long spur, offering nectar to animals

Left above: Waterlilies grow in shallow freshwater all over the world. But the two horned frogs on the buoyant leaves identify this Brazilian scene as typical of northern South America. Left: The six-foot leaves of the giant waterlily (Victoria regia) *are reinforced below by heavy veins armed with prickles. (Both by James R. Simon)*

Flies and bumblebees come to the European anemone buttercup (Ranunculus anemoneus), *a common spring flower whose acrid juice warns of its poisonous nature. (A. B. Costin)*

with mouthparts to match. The European columbine *(A. vulgaris)* is widely cultivated, and has escaped cultivation to become wild over much of eastern North America. The large, open-faced, blue columbine *(A. coerulea)* of the Rocky Mountains is often raised in gardens all over the world.

THE WATERLILY FAMILY (Nymphaeaceae)

Anyone who has tried to transplant a waterlily from a pond to a garden pool knows what a tremendous rootlike underground stem it has, buried in the mud of the bottom. Each spring in northern lands, the lily leaves that have been held on coiled petioles well below the floating ice, begin to rise. In the water film they come to rest, their tops dry and waxy, providing landing platforms for dragonflies and perches for frogs and small turtles.

South American ponds and slow streams, especially

Giant among buttercups is the mountain buttercup (Ranunculus lyallii) *of New Zealand. Its waxy white flowers are two inches across. (New Zealand Information Service)*

in the backwaters and the basins of the great Amazon and Orinoco Rivers, float the six-foot leaves of the giant waterlily *(Victoria amazonica),* each with an upright rim like a circular pan. Drainage notches in the rim and peculiar holes let rain water drain off, while a trusswork of reinforcing veins give stiffness to the thin leaf. Sharp prickles protect the lower surface, but the top is smooth and buoyant enough to support a small child. The pink flowers open just above the surface, as do those of the fragrant white waterlily *(Nymphaea odorata)* in eastern North America. By contrast, the smaller golden flowers of the cow lily *(Nuphar advena),* which are composed of fewer, thicker petals, are held several inches above the water.

Both the flowers and the leaves of the lotus *(Nelumbo)* rise a foot or more into air, the waxy petals spreading like a decorative bowl around the broad receptacle within whose flat top the many carpels are embedded. A thick fringe of golden stamens surrounds the receptacle, which is actually the end of the stalk that bears the flower. When petals and stamens fall and the nutlike fruits ripen in their individual pockets, the whole receptacle breaks away from the stem and floats for weeks, face downward. Gradually the edge of each pocket rots, releasing the fruit within, letting it sink and germinate. Since the wind blows the floating fruit-carriers from place to place, the lotus becomes distributed easily around the shores of quite large lakes and along great rivers.

Man has helped too, for *Nelumbo nucifera,* the sacred lotus of China, Tibet, and India, is depicted on some of the oldest decorative drawings in the Nile Valley, where it grows in almost every marsh. The fruits have long been regarded highly there as "sacred beans," just as those of an American species became the "water chinquapins" of the Indians. The starchy rhizomes of a lotus may be fifty feet in length, and yield a wealth of food for man.

Lotus seeds have lived in dormancy for longer than any others known. A collection of them dug from an ancient lake bed in Manchuria was taken to Tokyo in 1951, where a distinguished Japanese botanist Dr. Ichiro Ohga succeeded in getting a few to germinate. Two seeds from this collection went indirectly to Washington, D. C., where American botanists followed the same technique—filing carefully through the flint-hard seed coats to admit water—and got both to grow. At first, an age of 50,000 years was put on these seeds. But careful studies with radioactive carbon-14 proved them to be only about a thousand years old. One of Ohga's plants is still alive, flowering regularly, in a botanic garden dedicated to him in Kemigawa, where he is affectionately known as "Doctor Lotus." The Washington plants produce pink flowers in the Kenilworth Aquatic Gardens, maintained by the National Park Service.

Another member of the waterlily family, *Cabomba caroliniana,* is grown all over the world by fish fanciers, since it provides food, oxygen, shelter, and ornament in aquaria for their pets. This plant is native to ponds and slow streams in the United States from the Great Lakes to Florida and Texas, where it produces two types of leaves. Most of them arise in whorls from the weak, branching underwater stem, and are so threadlike in their divisions that the

Right above: The shining green leaves and butter-yellow flowers of the cow lily (Nuphar advena) *commonly grow out of the water in ponds and swamps of eastern North America and the West Indies. (Vinton Richards) Right: Crimson poppy anemones* (Anemone coronaria) *and nodding cyclamens grow wild in the well-drained rocky soils around the Emeq Valley of Israel, close to Nazareth. Far right: Bright yellow blossoms attract bumblebees and other insects in early spring to marsh marigold* (Caltha palustris) *in wet meadows and woodlands of northern Eurasia and North America. (Both by Lorus and Margery Milne)*

plant appears feathery. Indoors, this seems to be the only type of foliage produced. Outdoors the second style of leaf is formed, on long slender petioles that let them float at the surface, each leaf a narrow oblong as much as an inch in length. The flowers also arise on long stems, break through the surface film into air, and open white or yellow, to three-quarters of an inch across.

THE CUSTARD-APPLE FAMILY (Annonaceae)

Most of the 850 species in this family live in the tropics, where they produce edible fruits that are highly regarded by native people. One of the few temperate-zone trees belonging to the family is the American pawpaw (Asimina triloba) which used to be common along streams from southwestern Ontario to Michigan, Texas, Florida, and New Jersey. Its dark purple flowers, which open to a width of 1½ inches at the same time as the leaves unfold in spring, produce a sweet berry-like fruit as much as seven inches long and two in thickness. Its brown color gives no hint of the creamy consistency that makes it so delicious when ripe. A similar softness prevents success in shipping to temperate-zone markets the custard apple (Annona reticulata), soursop (A. muricata) and sweetsop (A. squamosa) of the West Indies and tropical American mainland. These are typical of the one hundred different kinds of Annona, which yield some of the most delectable fruits in the

Far left above: Alpine hellebore (Helleborus niger) *blooms despite winter snow, and is often called Christmas rose. Its knotty underground stems are poisonous. (Wilhelm Schacht)   Far left: The three-sided fruits of peony* (Paeonia obovata) *split open when ripe to release bright-colored seeds. Because its seeds, flowers and roots were important in Greek medicine, the plant was dedicated to Paeon, the god of medicine. (John Markham)   Left above: The nodding flowers of the meadow windflower* (Anemone pratensis) *open briefly in the early dawn of warm spring days across much of northern Europe and Asia. (Ingmar Holmasen)   Left center: Close to the ground, the sagebrush buttercup* (Ranunculus glaberrimus) *flowers and sets its seeds before the dry winds of late spring take away the last of the winter's moisture. (James R. Simon)   Left: Handsome fruits ripen on a prickly-leaved barberry* (Berberis Darwinii) *introduced from Chile to the cool, moist climate near Edinburgh. (Lorus and Margery Milne)*

world, each with the texture of melting ice cream. In each of them, the fleshy walls of the ripening ovaries from all carpels in a flower join together with fleshy tissue of the central receptacle to produce the final composite fruit.

THE BARBERRY FAMILY (Berberidaceae)

Woody shrubs are the most widely known members of this family. Each of them produces decorative berries that appeal to birds in winter. Barberries (Berberis) grow principally in the Asiatic part of the North Temperate Zone, and in the Andes. But two of them have been introduced widely as ornamental shrubs. Japanese barberry (B. thunbergii) is often substituted for the European one (B. vulgaris) because it does not form an intermediate host for the parasitic fungus that causes stem rust of wheat. The European barberry is a more graceful shrub, bearing pendant clusters of yellow flowers in May and June, and corresponding clusters of scarlet berries from September on. Japanese barberry seems to hide its solitary flowers under the leaves, and exposes its scarlet fruits after the foliage drops for the winter. Sharp stiff spines protect both of these shrubs, those on European barberry in groups of three, those on the Japanese shrub as a single prominent needle at each place along a stem where a group of leaves arises.

Oregon grape (Mahonia aquifolium) belongs to a very similar genus with about fifty species in western North America and eastern Asia. Oregon grape is a native evergreen with pinnately compound, holly-like leaves bearing prickles around the margins. From northern California to British Columbia it grows on humid soil where it is somewhat protected from strong wind and sun. Its clusters of flowers spread upward, and there the small, dark blue berries mature. In the southeastern United States, where real holly grows too well for Oregon grape to be a popular competitor, horticulturalists often set out shrubs of the Japanese heavenly-bamboo (Nandina domestica), on which the lacy foliage of compound leaves persists all winter. The leaves are bronzy green from spring to fall, but change to coppery red just about the time when the brilliant clusters of scarlet berries reach their greatest intensity of color.

Anyone who has an eye for drama in miniature can find inexpensive entertainment in the quarter-inch flowers of a barberry, a *Mahonia* or a *Nandina*. In all of these the stamens are T-shaped, attached opposite each of the six concave petals, and will move suddenly if touched near its base. The crossbar

Notches in the rim of the giant waterlily (Victoria amazonica), *a native of the Guianas and lowland Brazil, allow rainwater to drain off. (J. H. Gerard: National Audubon)*

at the top of the stamen snaps abruptly against the rim of the stigma on the central pistil. Ordinarily this action smears the sticky pollen on the body of a small insect that is visiting the blossom. Few movements in the plant kingdom are so regular and rapid.

The barberry family includes also some herbs that are favorites among spring wildflowers. Of special interest is the mayapple *(Podophyllum peltatum)* whose erect, pale, rather brittle stem bears from one to three large umbrella-like leaves that are deeply lobed but supported at the middle. Where the leaf petioles arise, like branches from the upright stalk, a single white, waxy, saucer-shaped flower is borne in May. Unlike other members of its family, the mayapple has twelve to eighteen stamens, which outnumber the petals. The single pistil ripens into a golden-brown globular fruit as much as two inches in diameter. The American statesman De Witt Clinton once dreamed of harvesting and marketing mayapple fruits, which are edible and grew in abundance along the Erie Canal ("Clinton's Ditch"—opened in 1819), but his enterprise failed. While still even slightly green, mayapple fruits are poisonous, having a purgative alkaloid that can be fatal. The leaves and underground stems contain the same toxic substance.

THE NUTMEG FAMILY (Myristicaceae)

Among the curiosa for sale in an old-style country store we recently found a boxful of brand-new nutmeg graters of a pattern our grandmothers relied upon whenever they wanted to add this spice to a bowlful of rich eggnog or a pie such as deep apple, pumpkin or custard. Immediately we recalled how

whole nutmegs were bought at the grocery, each to be tested in the grocer's presence by prodding it with a hatpin to see if it was fresh. "Good" nutmegs promptly oozed a non-drying oil from the pinprick. If they were too dry the customer would charge that they were the famous imitations known as "wooden nutmegs." During the intervening years we have seen nutmegs growing on trees in the West Indies, where Grenada in the Lesser Antilles has come to be the nutmeg capital of the world. From this island the United States alone imports annually some two thousand tons. The tree itself *(Myristica fragrans),* with oily evergreen simple leaves like all members of its family, was introduced from the East Indies, where it grows wild from New Guinea to the Moluccas.

Nutmeg flowers are inconspicuous on a fifty- to sixty-foot tree, for their parts are greatly reduced. Some trees are staminate, others carpellate, but each flower is a pale little cup formed by three united sepals. Staminate ones contain a dozen stamens that are partly united into a central tube. A carpellate flower has a single pistil, which begins to ripen as soon as a bee or a fly has brought pollen to set the single central seed. The fruit resembles a small peach. But once the orange-colored carpel (ovary) wall is cut through, a brilliant red layer of fibrous flesh is found still covering the seed. The inner layer is an aril, produced by extraordinary growth of the short stalk that supported the ovule inside the carpel. The outer pulp is edible, although faintly resinous as well as sweet. At Christmas time, many islanders prepare from the fermented flesh a special festive brandy with a distinctive bouquet and taste. The red aril tissue, when dried, is the spice known as mace. The seed, when removed from its thin hard shell, is dried to become the nutmeg of commerce. Its fragrant oil is almost a pure fat, a compound that can be separated into glycerine and myristic acid, or nutmeg butter can be produced from it, to be used as a counterirritant in liniments and in the treatment of tropical rheumatisms. This is the spice our ancestors prepared for their cooking, flaking off just the amount they judged to be "to taste" when they rubbed a fresh nutmeg against the outside of the metal grater. The remainder of the "nut" went into the little chamber under the hinged lid.

THE HONORED LAURELS (Family Lauraceae)

According to Greek legend, the god Apollo obtained purification from the blood of the Python in the laurel groves at Tempe. The large evergreen shrub *(Laurus nobilis),* which is native to Greece, Italy and North Africa, became sacred to Apollo, and was used for many years as the source of garlands and crowns with which to adorn the victors in the Pythian games. Later the laurel became the symbol of triumph in Rome, the sign of truce, and a charm against being struck by lightning. Today, laurel wreaths are used ceremonially over much of the world, and the shrub itself is much cultivated in the warmer parts of the United States, often trimmed to a decorative shape while growing in a tubful of earth.

Laurel flowers are seldom noticed, for they are small, yellowish green, and last a very short time. Each cluster is either staminate or carpellate, with a four-part perianth almost enclosing either nine stamens or a single carpel. The fruit is a succulent berry, around which the base of the perianth forms a fleshy cup.

The laurel family includes more than a thousand tropical and subtropical kinds of shrubs and trees, all of which possess an aromatic bark and also many leaves that are rich in fragrant essential oils. *Cinnamomum* of Indomalaysia includes *C. zeylanicum* of Ceylon, whose bark provides the cinnamon of commerce, and *C. cassia* of southern China, yielding cassia bark either as a spice in its own right or as an adulterant for cinnamon. Camphor is distilled from the young shoots of *C. camphora* from Japan, Formosa and China, or from chips of the wood from old trees. In America, pioneers discovered how to extract oil of sassafras from *Sassafras albidum* of the eastern states and adjacent Canada. The pith of young stems and the bark of old roots are the best source of the oil. But a strong idea of its flavor can be obtained by chewing the mitten-shaped leaves before they turn orange or yellow in autumn. Sassafras grows only as a shrub in the northern states and Canada. Farther south, to Florida and Texas, it becomes a tree as much as 125 feet tall, growing usually on dry sandy soil.

Where sassafras grows, one the earliest shrubs to flower in spring is the spicebush *(Lindera benzoin),* a plant whose bark is so oily that its branches will burn well while still green. Except for one other species in the southern United States, the many members of *Lindera* are all Asiatic—from Japan to Java.

Tropical America has provided mankind with the avocado or alligator pear *(Persea americana),* which grows wild from Mexico to the Colombian Andes. It was cultivated for its fruit long before the Spanish conquest, but did not achieve popularity until the twentieth century when horticulturalists in Florida, California and South Africa began planting orchards and exporting fruit of high quality. Each tree produces dense clusters of small greenish flowers, in which six lobes of the perianth surround nine stamens and a single carpel. A fruit may grow as much as twelve inches in length and four in diameter, with a single large egg-shaped seed at the center. When ripe, a good avocado has a thick layer of greenish or yellowish flesh of a consistency like firm butter and as much as twenty per cent oil. Many people who enjoy avocadoes in a salad add a little lime or lemon to enhance the sweetness of the flesh. Avocado seeds grow readily if stood in a jar of water for the month or more they need to germinate.

Less well known in the Northern Hemisphere but of great importance in Africa and South America are the timber trees of the laurel family, particularly those of the large genus *Ocotea.* Some of the heaviest and most handsome furniture we saw in South Africa was made from the native trees of black stinkwood *(O. bullata).* This one genus, in fact, comprises nearly a quarter of the known species in the family. Many valuable kinds, however, grow so slowly that once the virgin timber has been cut, foresters replace *Ocotea* with more productive trees, such as pines and eucalypts.

CHAPTER 7

Plants With No Petals

CUES: *If a dicot plant lacks petals and has whatever carpels are present all fused into a united pistil, it belongs in a group of thirteen orders that seem to show a degenerate loss of their showy parts. It might be a pepper, an Australian "pine," a poplar, a birch, a walnut, an elm, a mulberry, a hop plant, an inconspicuous buckwheat, a spectacular protea, a mistletoe, or the largest known single flower,* Rafflesia.

Most petal-less (or "apetalous") flowers rely upon the wind to distribute their pollen. Many of them expose their blossoms early in the spring, before the leaves expand and interfere with the free flow of air through the branches. It is then that, as Mary Webb writes in her poem *Little Things*,

> *Among the purple buds, like laden censers,*
> *Careless upon the wind the catkins swing;*
> *They lay a golden spell upon the morning.*

Whether in a catkin or separately, these flowers appear to have become simplified through loss of petals. Some, such as the proteas and the members of the order to which the Dutchman's pipe belongs, make use of animals for pollination, but attract them with other parts of the flower.

THE PEPPER FAMILY
(Order Piperales, family Piperaceae)

Over much of the world, pepper and salt are on every table where meals are served. Yet to many people, the actual source of pepper remains a partial mystery. For such people both black pepper and

The eastern cottonwood tree (Populus deltoides) *grows in damp soil east of the 100th parallel in Canada and the United States. (J. C. Allen & Son)*

white appear magically in marked cans on the grocer's shelf. They come from the same plant *(Piper nigrum)* and enter the United States at the rate of 25.000 tons a year, as the most valuable spice in commerce.

Alexander the Great may have introduced pepper into Europe at the time of his campaign into northwest India, where the pepper vine is native. The spice became a medium of exchange under Greek and Roman conquerors, and the preferred form of the tributes they levied. In the 13th century, Marco Polo found pepper being used in China, and learned that its culture had spread to Java. He had a special interest in it, for already the Venetians and Genoese were competing for a monopoly of the overland route to get pepper, and for sea routes by which the condiment could be brought more easily to Europe.

Piper nigrum is a woody climber that clings by means of adventitious roots to trees or to poles erected to support it. Three large veins crease its broad ovate, shiny leaves lengthwise from petiole to tip. Its flowers appear in inconspicuous clusters of about fifty, along pendant slender supports that taper like a mouse's tail. Those that are pollinated may mature into small globular berries, each yellowish red, as much as one-quarter of an inch in diameter, with a thin pulp around a single seed. People harvest them by hand just before all of the green color disappears. Almost ripe, the individual fruits (called peppercorns) are dried quickly, which blackens them. When ground, the whole peppercorns are black pepper. To make white pepper, the outer skin and pulp are removed from the peppercorns before they are dried, and the seeds alone are ground up. White pepper is milder, less "hot," but easy to confuse with salt when the two are in transparent unlabeled shakers on the dining table.

Pepper is cultivated and prepared in Indonesia,

Right above: The native beech (Fagus sylvatica) *of central and southern Europe gives shade in summer and sheds three-cornered seeds in autumn. Deer, game birds, and domestic hogs have fattened on these for centuries. (Ingmar Holmasen) Right: The starchy breadfruit is an important food in Indomalaysia, where the tree* (Artocarpus altilis) *is native. It has been introduced in Africa and tropical America. (E. Javorsky) Far right: High in the mountains of Europe, dwarf willow* (Salix reticulata) *spreads close to the ground, raising its leaves and clustered catkins to the summer sun. (Ingmar Holmasen)*

India, and Thailand, and raised also in some tropical parts of Africa and South America. Often it is interplanted in tea or coffee plantations, and yields a supplementary crop. It is the outstanding member of a genus with more than seven hundred species in both the Old World and the New. A few others are important to some people. *P. cubeba* of the East Indies yields cubebs, which once were used as a condiment but now serve chiefly in medicine for treatment of respiratory diseases. *P. betle* provides the fresh pepper leaves that are chewed in the East Indian and South Pacific islands along with lime and dried slices of betel nuts, to produce a copious supply of brick-red saliva. The practice may have some value in protecting a person from parasitic worms.

People who enjoy tropical plants in their homes usually know *Peperomia*, a genus of about five hundred species, many of which have fleshy, glossy leaves and an ability to grow in a shady room if given a little earth and frequent watering. Sometimes they flower, developing slender pendant clusters that are so inconspicuous that they are overlooked.

THE AUSTRALIAN BEEFWOODS
(Order Casuarinales, family Casuarinaceae)

About fifty kinds of trees in the one genus *Casuarina* are all that represent this family today. Native to Australia, New Caledonia, Malaysia, and the Mascarine Islands in the Indian Ocean, they have now been introduced widely as timber trees and as evergreen windbreaks in lands to which frost seldom comes. Variously known as beefwood, South-Sea ironwood, Australian "pine," and horsetail tree, they are valued for their hard wood, which is commonly dark red like medium roast beef, hard enough to turn a nail, and so dense that it sinks in water or just barely floats. In Florida, *C. equisetifolia* is now naturalized. From a distance, its long slender green branches

Left: Quaking aspens (Populus tremuloides), *often mistaken for birch because the greenish bark is so pale, quickly colonize mountain slopes that have been burned over. (James R. Simon) Right above: This aspen frequently grows in dense stands on mountain slopes of the American West, and turns a golden color in autumn. (Grant Haist: National Audubon) Right: Until overshadowed by slower-growing trees, quaking aspen thrives in the high country of Yosemite National Park, across Canada and the northern United States. (Bill Stackhouse)*

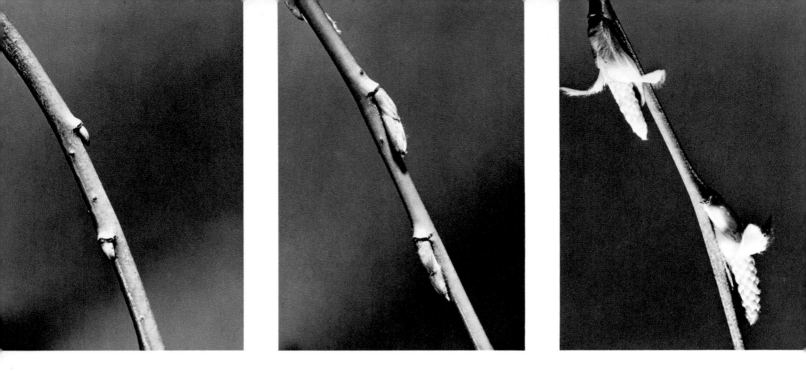

In spring the buds of a willow tree (Salix) *open rapidly. First to unfold are those that conceal the reproductive catkins, either pistillate* (center) *or staminate* (right). *(Otto Croy)*

suggest coarse pine needles. At close range each is seen to be grooved longitudinally and to bear whorls of small scalelike leaves at node after node, somewhat like the stem of a horsetail. Wind carries the pollen from long spikes of staminate flowers, each of which consists of a single stamen between a pair of perianth scales. The carpellate flowers are more noticeable, since they form almost spherical heads about one-half inch in diameter. Above each scale in the spiral of the head is a pistil between two bracts that represent the simplified perianth. Inside it are two ovules, one from each of the two carpels that fuse to form the pistil. As the seeds mature, the bracts join to provide a pair of woody valves unlike anything to be found elsewhere in the plant kingdom. By the time the fruit and its valves drop out of their cavity in the hard little head, the head itself has turned brown and appears more conelike than ever. It is no wonder that people talk of Australian "pine" as though it were a conifer. They also call it she-oak because of the shee-ing sound of wind through its branches.

THE WILLOWS AND POPLARS
(Order Salicales, family Salicaceae)

Just about everyone knows that some "pussy willows" expand into a fluffy mass of gold-tipped stamens, while others form a green head with projecting points, sticky enough to capture the golden pollen from the wind. Some people notice the staminate catkins on poplars. A few see similarity, as botanists do, in the staminate catkins on bayberries, hickories and birches, which led in the past to grouping of six different orders as "catkin-bearers." The willows and poplars are the most conspicuous of them.

The three hundred kinds of willow *(Salix)* and forty of poplar *(Populus)* are chiefly trees of the North Temperate Zone. Willow leaves are narrow and firmly attached to the branches, whereas poplar leaves tend to be triangular and to flutter on a flattened petiole that bends easily in the slightest breeze. European aspen *(P. tremula)* of Eurasia and the quaking aspen *(P. tremuloides)* of America produce a characteristic fluttering sound as their leaves strike against one another. In eastern North America, cottonwood *(P. deltoides)* attains a height of 175 feet, but the giant of the family is the black cottonwood *(P. trichocarpa)* of the West from California to Alaska, some of which measure 225 feet high.

The true "pussy willow" is *Salix discolor,* a tree of North American swamps that exposes long, shining hairs on its flower bracts as soon as the dark bud scales drop off in early spring. Weeping willow *(S. babylonica)* of China is planted as an ornamental in many cities. But other willows and poplars have lost most of their former popularity because their roots spread so quickly into sewer pipes and clog them.

Unlike most of the catkin-bearers, the willows and poplars produce nectar and attract pollinating insects. The sweet bait is available from a short nozzle-like projection from the glands, one of which

is located in each bract of a catkin, either where the pair of stamens is attached or where the single pistil (of two united carpels) arises. When the seeds ripen, the single chamber in each pistil splits open. The wind catches on the long silky hairs of each dry seed, and carries it away.

THE FRAGRANT BAYBERRIES
(Order Myricales, family Myricaceae)

Almost any plant with fragrant leaves was a *myrika* to the Greeks, perhaps from their similar verb meaning "to perfume." Certainly the word applies well to the forty members of this little family, all but two of them in the genus *Myrica.* Most of them can be identified by their pleasant scent if a leaf is crushed between the fingers and held to the nose.

Sweet gale *(M. gale)* is distributed widely as a shrub of bogs in northern Eurasia and in America, where it grows from Alaska and Labrador into the mountains of Tennessee. Better known are bayberry *(M. cerifera* and others), called also candleberry and wax-myrtle, and sweet fern *(Comptonia peregrina).* All are shrubs of thickets and poor soil, where they shelter rabbits and birds such as quail. In a few places, *M. cerifera* becomes a tree over thirty feet tall, with a trunk almost eight inches in diameter.

Bayberry fruits are still collected, as they were in colonial times, and boiled to release the fragrant wax that covers them. The wax is floated off and made into candles, which give out the odor as they burn. Nurseries sell bayberry shrubs as ornamentals, because the pale blue berries remain in conspicuous clumps on the bare branches all winter.

Some of our earliest memories relate to sweet fern, which grows in old pastures from the Maritime Provinces of Canada to Manitoba, and south to the higher parts of northern Georgia. As children we walked through it, where the three-foot shrubs of it were mixed with bracken (a true fern) and chest-high. We pinched the soft long leaves that are so fragrant, and so easy to recognize by the continuous row of small rounded lobes along each side. The leaves can be dried and put into little pillows that continue to yield their spicy odor all winter. During Revolutionary times, the American colonists used sweet-fern leaves to make a substitute for tea. They are harmless, pleasant, but never become habit-forming.

Bayberries and sweet ferns are catkin-bearers, although the catkins are inconspicuous, appearing in spring about the same time as the foliage. The staminate catkins of sweet fern are brown, cylindrical, about an inch long, and borne in clusters at the ends of the branches. The carpellate ones are concealed among the leaves back from the tip. They are globular and tend to be burlike as they mature. On bayberries the catkins are all found on stems of the previous year's growth, those with stamens being cylindrical and those with carpels being more or less globular.

THE BIRCHES AND BEECHES (Order Fagales)

One of the special pleasures in a visit to the North Woods, whether in America or Europe, is to see white birch trees gleaming "like a holy thought" among the dark trunks in a mixed forest, or reflected

River birch (Betula nigra) *is a tree of wet soil in eastern America. Its bark turns a silver-gray and curls back in papery scales. (J. H. Gerard: National Audubon)*

from the margin of a little lake. European white birch *(Betula alba)* is used for fuel since its wood is too soft for structural purposes. American Indians made more spectacular use of the paper birch *(B. papyrifera)* of Canada and New England, peeling off its bark to full thickness and fastening it over canoe frames, whence the tree gained its name of "canoe birch." Others of the forty kinds of birch, which are trees and shrubs in the temperate and arctic parts of the world, provide hard wood, often made today into handsome veneers.

Grouped with birches in the family Betulaceae are the alders *(Alnus)* and hazels *(Corylus),* which also bear their carpellate and staminate flowers in catkins. Black alder *(A. glutinosa)* of Eurasia is a favorite source of wood for making charcoal. Red alder *(A. rubra)* is the leading hardwood tree of the northwestern United States from California northward into British Columbia. It reaches a height of 130 feet, and provides wood that is a good imitation of mahogany for the construction of furniture. Most

other alders are trees of swamps and thickets, where they resist erosion and also add nitrogen to the soil from large nodules on their roots. In the Arctic, around each clump of alder, the wildflowers show a conspicuous gradation in size—tall and luxuriant where the soil nitrates are abundant near the alder roots, smaller and less thrifty as distance from the alder increases. Like birches, alders produce winged seeds that are carried by the wind.

Hazels yield edible nuts that are appreciated by squirrels and people wherever the eight different kinds grow in the North Temperate Zone. Commercial filberts come from the European *Corylus avellana,* which is cultivated in Italy, Turkey, Spain, and the state of Oregon. Although American orchards now produce as many as 2300 tons a year, most filberts eaten in the United States come from Europe. Usually they are larger than, but almost identical in shape, color and flavor with the nuts from native American hazelnuts *(C. rostrata* and *C. americana),* shrubs that grow to a height of about eight feet along the edge of woodlands from Florida and Kansas into Canada from coast to coast. Each of these kinds of *Corylus* produces pistillate flowers clustered in short catkins tight up against the branch, their long threadlike stigmas bright red while they are catching pollen from the winds of early spring. Short side spurs on the same branches generally support pendant pairs of bright yellow staminate catkins. The hard-shelled nuts, each with a single seed, ripen while concealed between two thick green bracts. These dry out and spread to drop the fruits in autumn.

The nuts of beech *(Fagus),* chestnut *(Castanea),* and oak *(Quercus)* come from hardwood trees that are members of a different family, the Fagaceae, because only their staminate flowers are borne in catkins. Their pistils arise two or three in a place, or singly. They seem to represent separate flowers, and for this reason the cup-shaped whorl of bracts associated with them is called an involucre instead of a calyx. The involucre becomes the prickly enclosure that opens to release three ripe chestnuts in each group, or the two forked lobes that spread apart when paired beechnuts are ready to drop to the ground, or the saucer-shaped support for the solitary acorns on an oak. The ripe fruits of these three genera have long been classed as "mast," and appreciated by bears, deer, wild turkeys, squirrels, native people, and their domesticated pigs. Today the trees are more appreciated for their timber.

Wood of the European beech *(Fagus sylvatica)* and of the similar tree *(F. grandifolia)* in America east of the Mississippi and north of Florida, is sought for use in furniture, tool handles, and old-fashioned clothespins. An ornamental variety of the European beech is often planted because of its purple or copper-colored leaves. In the Southern Hemisphere are large forests of rather similar trees: the sixteen kinds of antarctic beech *(Nothofagus)* in Chile, Patagonia and Tierra del Fuego, New Zealand, Tasmania, Australia and the East Indies. Australians call *N. cunninghami* their "myrtle tree."

In America, the word "chestnut" has no longer the same significance as it had fifty years ago. It still applies to the roasted nuts that are sold on street corners in New York and other big cities, or that are bought to add flavor and body to the stuffing in a Thanksgiving turkey. But of the once-common American chestnut trees *(Castanea dentata),* almost none remain. Previously they were an important component of the forests covering the Appalachian area from Maine to Ontario and south to Alabama. They grew to a height of over one hundred feet, providing annual showers of nutritious nuts and a hard wood that was greatly admired both for decorative interior trim and for heavy construction. In the early days, Indians and settlers alike harvested the dry nuts, storing them for roasting or boiling, or making them into meal.

Now the American chestnuts that remain are almost all slender trees rising as suckers from the surviving root of a former giant. They are doomed as soon as they lose their juvenile immunity. Spores reach them from trees (including oaks) infected by a fungus introduced accidentally from Asia in 1904. Perhaps even without the fatal fungus disease, American chestnuts would have been doomed by excessive cutting. A use still awaits the trunks of long-dead trees, for they are rich in tannins and do not deteriorate significantly. They are being salvaged and cut into chips from which an extract is made for use in the tanning of leather. No other native plant has been found to supply tannin so reliably. Yet no way has been discovered to rebuild the resource.

The European chestnut *(C. sativa)* provides almost all of the nuts roasted in the United States today. They are imported from Italy and other countries of the Mediterranean region. This tree is equally susceptible to the fungus blight that came from Asia. Only the less desirable Oriental chestnuts *(C. mollissima* of China, and *C. crenata* of Japan) and the shrubby chinquapin *(C. pumila)* of the southeastern United States seem to be immune to it. Their wood is much inferior to that of the threatened

By mid-May in southern Sweden, the European beech (Fagus sylvatica) *has opened its new leaves above a ground cover of wild flowers. (V. R. Johnston: National Audubon)*

species and of the one that is already almost extinct.

Chestnuts and beechnuts have always been more popular than acorns, but acorns (and the oaks on which they grow) are more widely familiar to people who walk through the parks of the world or read Western literature. Actually, acorns grow not only on the three hundred kinds of oaks in the North Temperate Zone and in Polynesia, but also on one hundred kinds of evergreen shrubs and trees in the genus *Lithocarpus,* for which there is no universal common name. Most *Lithocarpus* grow in southeast Asia and Malaysia, but *L. densiflora* is the tanoak of California and Oregon, where it furnishes lumber, fuel, and tannin. Unlike true oaks *(Quercus),* the species of *Lithocarpus* have erect staminate catkins and their acorns require two years (not just one) to mature.

Only in adversity did American pioneers turn to acorns from oaks as food, although they knew that the Indians around them gathered the fruits regularly, dried and ground the seeds, and extracted the bitter flavor with hot water. The famous American naturalist. John Muir insisted that flour cakes made from washed acorn meal were the best of all foods to take on hiking trips. His hearers were content to leave acorns for wild creatures, such as deer, bear, turkeys and woodpeckers, or for hogs.

Botanists now suspect that acorns for hogs were introduced to the British Isles along with Christianity, by missionary monks of monastic orders in which the keeping of pigs was traditional. Otherwise the

English oak (or brown oak, *Q. robur*) grows chiefly near the Mediterranean and in Asia Minor as far as the Caucausus Mountains. Its fine-grained, heavy heartwood became popular for construction of British merchant ships, and for durable wood carvings, such as the shrine of Edward the Confessor in Westminster Abbey. No other oaks are native to Britain and no introduced species of other kinds have attained such size there. One English oak, known for centuries as "the great oak" at Newland in Gloucestershire, was $47\frac{1}{2}$ feet in diameter at shoulder height when lightning struck it down.

Oaks still provide more hardwood timber than any other genus of trees in the world. Many kinds can be identified quickly from the shape of their leaves, the form of their acorns, and of the involucre cup that holds each nut until it is ripe. The deciduous oaks include red oak *(Q. rubra),* black oak *(Q. velutina),* and pin oak *(Q. palustris),* all of which have sharp points on each lobe around the margin of every leaf, and bur oak *(Q. macrocarpa)* and white oak *(Q. alba),* which have rounded lobes. All of these are fine shade trees, whose strong wood is durable in hardwood floors, watertight in barrel staves, unyielding in heavy construction, and used for many other purposes. Pin oak wood was cut into the slender wooden pins with which houses and furniture were fastened together before metal nails and screws became inexpensive. The dead leaves of some deciduous oaks stay on the tree all winter, but drop off before the new buds open in spring.

Left above: The smooth blue-gray bark of an American beech (Fagus grandifolia) *is more familiar to most people than the few edible seeds that drop from each spiny bur. (Pierre Berger: National Audubon) Left: The flowers of American beech appear in pendant clusters soon after the leaves unfold. (J. C. Allen & Son) Right above: Native markets, known as "banyans" in India and the East Indies, are so commonly held in the spreading shade of the giant fig tree* (Ficus benghalensis), *native to these regions, that it became known as the banyan tree. Right: As on all fig trees, the fruits of the banyan ripen inside a fleshy receptacle. The small hole through which insects enter, distributing pollen while getting a sip of nectar, closes in the mature fig. (Both by Lorus and Margery Milne) Far right: The acorns of the holly oak* (Quercus ilex), *a hardy evergreen of southern Europe, are held securely by scaly cups until they are ripe. (Weber and Hafner)*

The cork oak *(Q. suber)* of Mediterranean countries and the live oak *(Q. virginiana)* of the American Southeast, of Cuba, and of Mexico, are evergreens. Their leaves are comparatively small, thick and leathery, and show no lobing of the margins. Live oak has the heaviest wood of any tree in the United States, and formerly was much prized for timbers to be used in shipbuilding. Cork oaks are native to the Mediterranean region but are now also grown in the American Southwest. At intervals of nine or ten years, the thick bark is removed in large panels as the raw material for an important industry. The need for corks to stopper bottles has decreased over the decades, but the other uses of cork have multiplied—particularly for making linoleum, cork tiles, and insulating materials.

No such proliferation has taken place in the industry of Europe by which indelible ink is prepared from oak trees. This use of the Aleppo oak *(Q. infectoria)* of western Asia and Cyprus was mentioned by Pliny in the first century A.D. as a cosmetic aid—a dye with which to keep the hair black. The essential pigment is prepared from galls formed on the oak by a tiny wasp. An extract of these galls, which have been collected systematically for thousands of years, is specified in formulas for official inks used by the Bank of England, the United States Treasury, and the German Chancellery, to name a few.

The oldest dyestuff known is obtained from another oak *(Q. coccifera),* which is native to Turkey and many Mediterranean countries. The purplish-red juice is squeezed from small pea-shaped "kermes berries" found on the leaves and stems of the shrubby plant. Following a process of mordanting with alum that was discovered in India prior to 2000 B.C., the concentrated solution of the dye in cloth leaves an intense yellowish red color that withstands laundering and considerable exposure to the sun. Known at various times in the past as Turkey red, scarlet, and crimson, it appears to be the dye mentioned as "scarlet" in Genesis and other books of the Bible. It was not replaced in favor until the discovery of carmine from cochineal bugs on cacti in Mexico during the 16th century. Somewhat later, the "kermes berries" (which had been suspected of being galls) were identified correctly as hard-backed mealybugs

Around the Mediterranean Sea, people cut the thick dead outer bark from the cork oak (Quercus suber) *to obtain commercial cork. The tree is not harmed. (Wilhelm Schacht)*

Antarctic beech (Nothofagus antarctica) *is pruned by winds in wet parts of southern South America. Its close relatives grow in New Zealand, Tasmania, Australia, and the East Indies. (E. Aubert de la Rue)*

(Kermes), containing kermesic acid as the active ingredient. Since 1875, when synthetic dyes of greater reliability became available, Turkey red from the kermes oak has fallen into disuse, except among poor people in Europe who can collect the raw material from local shrubs and use the money thus saved for things they cannot get free.

THE NETTLES AND THEIR KIN
(Order Urticales)

Although only some of the plants that compose the families in this order produce catkins, many botanists believe that they all evolved from the same ancestral line as the birches and beeches. Their flowers are mostly inconspicuous, with four to eight sepals as a perianth around four to eight stamens, and a pistil of one or two fused carpels. Except in these and other details of their structure in reproductive parts, the members of the order show outstanding variation as herbs, climbing vines, and lofty hardwood trees.

Most conspicuous and well loved of the trees is the American elm *(Ulmus americana).* But today many people are wondering if it is as doomed as the American chestnut. A fungus disease carried by insects, known as the Dutch elm disease because it was discovered first in Holland, is spreading out from New England, killing the elms as it goes. No remedy

69

for it has been found, and attempts to slow its progress by use of insecticides on the susceptible trees have had disastrous side effects on bird life. The disease may eventually eliminate most of the elms in a great area where they have provided welcome shade from the summer sun—from the Dakotas to east Texas, to north Florida, and into Canada. American elms grow to a height of about 160 feet, their tops spreading like a great fountain to a radius of almost 75 feet. Their wood is so cross-grained as to be virtually unsplittable. It finds use in burial caskets, milking stools and other furniture, the inner frames of beehives, barrel staves, and woven wooden baskets.

Other kinds of elms in America have few of the features that have made the American elm such a favorite for planting along streets and avenues. Their wood is also not as valuable either. For these reasons, their relative immunity to the blighting fungus is of little consequence. The English elm *(U. campestris),* also a lesser tree, seems immune to the disease although it can carry infections of the fungus even in lumber that has been dried and cut into boards.

In elms and hackberries *(Celtis),* the base of the

Chinese chestnuts (Castanea mollissima) *are native to highlands up to 8000 feet in China and Korea. Varieties are now cultivated in temperate lands for the tasty seeds. (Grant Heilman)*

leaf is generally oblique where the blade meets the petiole. Hackberries are all shrubs and low trees in warm parts of the Northern Hemisphere. Unlike elms, whose lightweight fruits are encircled by a wing that catches the wind, hackberries produce small fleshy fruits resembling plums. Birds distribute the indigestible seeds. The elm family (Ulmaceae) includes both hackberries and elms.

The fruits of the members of the mulberry family (Moraceae) are completely different, each one a multiple structure developing through the combination of ripe parts from many flowers in a cluster. The luscious "berries" on a mulberry *(Morus),* for example, consist of more than a dozen little fruits butting together and supported on the central strand of fibers that once held the individual flowers in the cluster. Each part of the multiple fruit is derived from the fleshy calyx of a separate flower, surrounding its own central ovary in which a tiny armored seed ripens like a miniature cherry pit. Black mulberry *(M. nigra)* of western Asia is the kind raised for its fruits, which are larger and juicier but scarcely more delectable than those from the red mulberry *(M. rubra)* of the eastern United States. The white mulberry *(M. alba)* of China is cultivated mostly to provide leaves to feed silkworms.

The edible part of a fig *(Ficus)* has a different origin. It is the greatly enlarged end of the receptacle, which is so concave on the surface where it bears the abundant flowers that it is pursed together around them, and opens to the outside only through a small hole. Almost the only insects that will enter the hole and pollinate the commercial fig *(F. carica)* are minute wasps that produce galls and reproduce inside the inedible fruits of a horticultural variety known as a caprifig. This led to a strange ritual, which is depicted on monuments of ancient Egypt. Whenever the trees in an orchard of the edible fig (the Smyrna variety) come into flower, men carry in branches of the caprifig. The gall wasps, bearing pollen from inside the caprifigs, enter the pursed-up flower heads of the Smyrna figs and pollinate them while searching in vain for the short-styled pistils (such as a caprifig has) that alone are suitable for growth of gall-wasp larvae. If "caprification" is not carried out, the young receptacles of Smyrna-type figs drop off and there is no crop. Now hormone sprays can be used to induce maturation of the receptacle, or even to produce "seeded" edible fruit.

A newer horticultural variety, known as the common fig, will develop seedless fruits without being pollinated in the first crop each year, but may fail to

With so many adventitious roots of a banyan (Ficus benghalensis) *extending to the ground, it is difficult to find the original tree upon which this strangler grew. (Georges Bourdelon)*

produce any in the second crop if the gall wasps bring no pollen. All of these differences puzzled people before the details of reproduction in figs became known. Yet by following the ritual, fresh and dried figs became so cheap that they became "the poor man's food" in Mediterranean countries and, in some districts, were used for stock feed. The mature leaves are often harvested for fodder. The fig may well have been man's first domesticated plant.

Although commercial figs are propagated almost entirely from woody cuttings, other species of *Ficus* start from the minute indigestible seeds that have gone through the digestive tracts of birds, fruit-eating bats, monkeys, or squirrels. Often the seeds germinate high up in a palm or other native tree, and the young plant sends down roots around the trunk of its sup-

port. Commonly the fig roots interlace and join together until they appear to be "strangling" the tree on which the fig is growing. Fig leaves may actually shade it to death, after which the trunk of the supporting tree rots away, leaving a "strangler fig" in its place. This type of growth is particularly common in the sacred fig *(F. religiosa)* of southern Asia, which is planted for religious purposes in India and Ceylon. Called the bo tree, or the peepul, it is revered by both Brahmans and Buddhists who commemorate in this way the fig under which Gautama Buddha is believed to have received his divine powers in the 6th century B.C.

The banyan tree *(F. benghalensis)* of India, whose foliage is a favorite fodder for Indian elephants, often shows this same strangling habit. It is spectacular also for the number of aerial roots that grow down to the soil and provide sturdy props for the outspread branches. One banyan in its native province of West Benghal was found to have three hundred thick roots, each resembling a separate trunk, and to have a

The hemp plant (Cannabis indica) *from Asia is cultivated for its strong fibers in many temperate countries. Because resins in the plant have a narcotic action, countries such as the United States ban it. (J. H. Gerard: National Audubon)*

combined circumference of two thousand feet. India and Java are also the home of the India-rubber tree *(F. elastica),* which furnished most of the gum from which rubber was made prior to the cultivation of the very different Brazilian rubber trees. Small specimen plants of this tree have long been favorites for homes and greenhouses, where their glossy elliptical leaves and pink buds have been admired for a century or more.

The breadfruit tree *(Artocarpus altilis),* another member of the mulberry family, became the center of some romantic history because James Cook, the English admiral and explorer, observed that it provided the staple food of people in the South Pacific. He urged that Captain William Bligh, who had served well as the master on one of Cook's ships during Cook's last expedition, be sent to Tahiti for the express purpose of collecting young breadfruit trees.

He was to take them to the West Indies and introduce them there as food for the Negro slaves. In 1787, Bligh gathered his plant cargo from Tahiti aboard H. M. S. *Bounty,* only to be turned adrift in a long boat —the plants were thrown into the sea—when his mate Fletcher Christian, and many of the crew mutinied and sailed off with some native women to the seclusion of Pitcairn Island. Bligh managed to return to England, was reoutfitted, and successfully transported living breadfruit trees from Tahiti to Jamaica in 1792. Cook's plan met with little success, however, because the Negroes preferred bananas and plantains, no matter whether the starchy breadfruit was boiled, baked, or fried for them.

Only gradually did the tall handsome breadfruit trees become introduced widely in tropical America, and gain acceptance. Near the ends of their branches, which bear large glossy lobed leaves, they produce staminate flowers in club-shaped upright catkins, and pistillate flowers in large prickly heads. As the fruits ripen, they attain a diameter of five to eight inches. The solid mass is composed of the central receptacle, the fleshy perianths, and the ripened ovaries of all of the flowers in the head. Seedless varieties are the most valuable, and these have been cultivated since remote antiquity in Malaysia, where breadfruit appears to be native. A related tree, the jackfruit *(A. heterophyllus),* is found in the same areas, but is often regarded as the "poor man's breadfruit" since all but its large seeds ripen with an unpleasant odor and taste, and the seeds must be well washed before they can be eaten raw, boiled or baked for human food.

We sometimes wonder whether any of the strange tree sloths that clamber in slow motion in the rain forests of Central America and northern South America would have survived to the present day if not for the presence of another member of the mulberry family, the cecropia tree *(Cecropia peltata),*

Right above: Cushionflower and corkwood are among the names given to Australian trees (Hakea *species) that produce woody fruits from flower clusters as much as twelve inches long. (Michael Morcombe) Right: Low forests of Australian honeysuckle* (Banksia *species) clothe the highlands in New South Wales. The flower clusters, ten inches tall, suggest corncobs. (E. S. Ross) Far right: The Christmas tree* (Nuytsia floribunda) *of western Australia differs from other members of the mistletoe family* (Loranthaceae) *in never being a parasite. (Eric Lindgren)*

whose buds and foliage form almost the complete diet of all sloths. The cecropia is a fast-growing tree that succeeds as a pioneer in clearings. Its deeply lobed, umbrella-like leaves are gray-green, supported on long petioles. Fierce biting ants cut through where the petiole joins the hollow stem, and raise their young in the cavity. When a cecropia tree is jostled, the ants rush out and defend their brood, but somehow fail to disturb a sloth. Despite this interference, men of some tribes in tropical America cut the trunks of cecropia trees into six- or eight-foot lengths with a continuous cavity five or six inches in diameter, and use them for trumpets in communicating with distant neighbors. This practice has led to the name trumpetwood or trumpet tree for the cecropia.

Often it seems that man is resourceful enough to make use of almost anything that grows. The glandular hairs that sting a person or an animal brushing against a nettle *(Urtica,* of family *Urticaceae)* have not prevented people from gathering the young tops from two different kinds found in Eurasia to cook and eat them as a substitute for spinach. The roots of these plants *(U. urens* and *U. dioica)* can provide a yellow dye, their stems a fiber that could be used in place of flax to make fine linen.

Aptly, both *urtica* and *urens* are derived from the Latin verb meaning to burn. When the sharp stiff hairs penetrate one's skin, the tips break off under the surface and discharge small quantities of concentrated formic acid. Usually the pain lasts only a short time. Both *U. urens* and *U. dioica* were introduced to the New World and have become naturalized, as additions to the thirty different kinds of stinging nettles that were native to the Americas. A related genus *(Urera)* of the tropics makes travel on foot particularly miserable in the rain forests of America. Some Asiatic nettles are reported to be so virulent that an individual who happens to touch several plants one after another may die.

Left above: Shrubby water-dock (Rumex), *growing in the shallows of Lake Karla in the Thessalia region of Greece, is a close relative of the docks and sorrels on land. (Walter Fendrich)   Far left: Delicious Queensland-nuts mature on small trees* (Macadamia ternifolia) *native to eastern Australia. (Lorus and Margery Milne)   Left: A parasitic mistletoe* (Satyria) *of the mountain rain forests in Costa Rica produces large clusters of brilliant fruit after its orange-yellow flowers have faded. (Martin R. Brittan)*

The fibrous husk of English walnuts (Juglans regia) *cracks open to release the armored seed. The tree is found native from southern Europe to the Himalayas. (U.S.D.A.)*

Nonstinging members of the nettle family are also valued highly for their fibers. The toughest and most silky natural fiber discovered so far comes from ramie *(Boehmeria nivea),* a shrub or small tree of southeastern Asia. Unfortunately, the fibers are expensive to separate and free of gum for use.

Three species of plants that clearly belong to the Order Urticales are placed in the hemp family (Cannabinaceae) because they differ from members of the mulberry family in having a watery juice instead of a milky one, in keeping the stipules on each leaf instead of dropping them off, and in fine anatomical details.

Hemp *(Cannabis sativa),* an erect annual, has been raised since the 28th century B.C. to yield tough strands from which to make rope. In the Far East, Europe, Chile, and the United States, where hemp is raised as a crop, the hollow stems ordinarily reach a height of twelve to twenty feet before inconspicuous green flowers appear at the tips. Customarily the stems are cut as soon as the plant begins to shed pollen freely, in the belief that the fibers are then at their strongest. Usually the cut stems are laid out on the stubble in the field until the action of bacteria and fungi has rotted away the decomposable parts of the plant. If dew is heavy or if a light rain falls, the process may be complete in a week; otherwise it may require a month or more. The longest fibers remain as flat ribbons, sometimes eight feet in length. Shorter ones are raked up and used for such packing materials as tow.

The leaf hairs and the rottable tissues of the hemp plant contain a resinous mixture of organic substances that possess narcotic power. Although no alkaloid has been found in the mixture, it causes hallucinations. Known as marijuana in the New World, as hashish in Asia Minor and Egypt, as kif in Morocco, and as bhang or ghanga in India, it is either smoked or eaten. Usually the resins in marijuana induce a sensation of general happiness (euphoria), followed by a period of supernormal sensitivity to stimulation of all kinds. This is soon followed by hallucinations and mental confusion, leading to extended dullness or drowsiness, depression, and often prostration. Neither habit-forming nor producing withdrawal symptoms by itself, marijuana is commonly the first drug tried in a series that goes on to alkaloids and more dangerous and damaging drugs.

Deliberate use of marijuana to suppress inhibitions

was reported first by returning Crusaders, who found a sect of Muslim terrorists calling themselves the hashishin ("hemp-eaters"). Corrupting this word into the English term "Assassins," the Crusaders described the practices of the terrorists as beginning with a use of marijuana to induce hallucinations before setting out to murder the sect's enemies—generally Christians or other non-Muslims. The open history of the sect began in 1090 in Persia, and ended in 1273. But some followers remain in Asia Minor and Central Asia, with the largest group in Pakistan; they claim allegiance to the Aga Khan, spiritual leader of all Mohammedans.

Quite different values are found in one of the two species of plants in the related genus *Humulus*, which are coarse vines with perennial roots. The one is Eurasian hops *(H. lupulus),* now cultivated in many countries on trellises and poles as an important crop. Many people develop a severe irritation of the skin from contact with any part of the plant, but particularly its leaves. The saleable product is the ripe carpellate catkins, which are covered with glandular hairs containing an oleoresin that is used to

The opening of a terminal bud on a shagbark hickory (Carya ovata) *exposes a group of pinnately compound leaves. (J. Roche)*

Stiff flower clusters await bees of Australia on Banksia coccinea, *a shrub of the dry eucalyptus forests. (Australian News and Information Bureau)*

give the characteristic bitter flavor and sparkle to brewed beer.

THE WALNUTS AND HICKORIES
(Order Juglandales, family Juglandaceae)

The Persian, or English walnut *(Juglans regia)* has been cultivated for so many centuries that no one is sure where it originated. *Juglans* is a contraction for *Jove glans*—the nut of Jove, and *regia* means the royal one. It may have been introduced into England in Caesar's time, or not until the 16th century, when the first written records of it there turn up. Probably the first colonists brought it to America, but the tree had no suitable place to grow until Oregon and California were settled. Now these two states produce as many English walnuts as all the rest of the world combined, and still leave the need to import a few million pounds annually from Europe for confectionary use. When the valuable wood of this handsome tree is made into furniture, it usually is called Circassian, French, Italian, or Turkish walnut. It may well have come from the mountains of western and northern China, where it still grows wild.

In America east of the Rocky Mountains, the black walnut *(J. nigra)* and the butternut *(J. cinerea)* are almost as valuable. Their nut meats go into candy and ice cream, their wood into furniture, interior finishings, and gun stocks. Military needs have drained the supply of black walnut wood. In World War I, it was made into airplane propellers because it did not fragment under the vibration and violent forces produced when rotated rapidly. In World War II, an even larger volume was needed just to make gunstocks.

Hickories *(Carya)* differ from walnuts in having a solid pith in young stems, rather than one separated into a succession of thin crosswise diaphragms. The husks of hickories regularly open to release the nuts when they are ripe, whereas walnuts found in the New World remain tightly closed even when they dry out. In both, the husk is derived from a combination of involucre bracts, sepals, and the outer layers of the ovary wall from a single pistil that represents two carpels. Only one large seed develops in the single central cavity.

Except for one species of hickory in Southeast Asia, all members of *Carya* are native to central and eastern North America. Like walnuts, they are all trees with pinnately compound leaves, and stamens in pendant catkins. The most valuable for nut meats is the pecan *(C. pecan)*, which is raised commercially in Georgia and adjacent states, although its original home was the Mississippi Valley from Illinois and Indiana through Texas into Mexico. Some varieties of pecan are seventy per cent fat, more than in almost any other vegetable product.

THE BUCKWHEAT FAMILY
(Order Polygonales, family Polygonaceae)

Among the weeds that take over in neglected lawns and flower gardens are many members of the buckwheat family. Most of them show local swelling of the stem where a leaf arises, and the base of the petiole is enlarged to clasp the stem. Buckwheat *(Fagopyrum sagittatum)* produces grainlike seeds, each shaped like a beechnut, and was adopted long ago as one of man's valuable crop plants. It is planted in broad fields in many temperate parts of the world, where it supplies nectar from which domestic honeybees make a dark honey with a distinctive flavor. It matures as a forage crop that can be threshed when dry to yield the small starchy fruits.

A coarse relative of buckwheat is rhubarb *(Rheum rhaponticum)*, which is among the few vegetables in which the petiole is consumed. Its branching underground stem may be hollow, with conspicuously swollen joints, and dark brown roots. In spring, pink buds rise from its crown to the soil surface and open into large green leaves with petioles as much as two feet long and as thick as a woman's wrist. If left to grow, as it does wild in its probable original home, Asia Minor, the plant may attain a height of six feet and then produce an abundance of tiny white flowers in a loose branching cluster. The leaf blades are poisonous, probably because they contain so much oxalic acid, but the tissues of young petioles make a delicious salad, or can be crushed and sweetened as a beverage, or stewed as a dessert, or used to fill pies as though with a tart fruit. This leads to another name for rhubarb: pie plant.

About a quarter of the eight hundred species in the Polygonaceae are members of the largest genus, *Polygonum.* Many of them are almost cosmopolitan because they have followed man as noxious weeds. The smartweeds, knotweeds, bindweeds, and tear-thumb *(P. sagittatum,* which is armed with saw-toothed prickles), all grow where the native vegetation has been removed and sunlight reaches bare soil. Only the Eurasian *P. orientale,* which is known as princess-feather and "kiss-me-over-the-garden-gate," has been introduced as a decorative plant—

Wild ginger (Asarum canadense), *found in eastern North America, has an aromatic underground stem. (National Museum of Canada)*

and escaped from cultivation to become another weed. The various kinds of dock *(Rumex),* including sheep sorrel *(R. acetosella)* are often regarded as evidence that the soil is poor, acid, or badly neglected.

In south Florida, throughout the West Indies, and along the coasts of Central America, the seagrape *(Coccoloba uvifera)* grows as a small tree on almost pure sand. Its handsome heart-shaped leaves are large enough to serve as picnic plates, and somehow tolerate salt spray during storms. They grow on crooked branches, which send out small flowers on pendant slender spikes. They produce reddish, berry-like fruits as much as three-quarters of an inch in diameter, which are edible. Where the birds and land crabs do not devour the ripe fruits of seagrape before people can collect them, the pulp is made into a delicious red jelly.

THE WONDERFUL PROTEAS
(Order Proteales, family Proteaceae)

Merely the geographic distribution of this order of amazing plants in the Southern Hemisphere is enough to indicate their great antiquity. Their ancestors may have spread before the continents reached the present locations, for of the 1200 species, about 700 live in Australia, 475 in South Africa, and the rest in temperate South America. They are named for the Greek sea god Proteus, whose habit it was to change shape through an almost limitless gamut to avoid recognition. It is the flower clusters of proteas that exhibit this outstanding variety of forms. The plants themselves are all either trees or shrubs, and their individual flowers retain a pattern of four petal-like sepals, four stamens, and one pistil with a superior ovary.

In South Africa we were dazzled by the colorful variety of the proteas. Giant bouquets rise from the shrubby chaparral known as *maqui* atop Table Mountain behind Cape Town, and along the high slopes of the Drakensberg chain that parallels the coast of the Indian Ocean. Protea itself is represented by eighty species there, many of them flower heads just one of which makes an armful. The prize is *P. cynaroides,* whose flowerheads are eight inches in diameter, about the same in height, and almost as heavy as though their showy involucre and sepals were made of wood. *P. barbigera,* the wooly-bearded protea, is often called a sugarbush ("suikerbos" in Afrikaans) because its seven-inch heads can be bent over to drain out the nectar by the spoonful, to collect it for boiling down to a sweet syrup.

Proteas are well adapted to a dry climate, and regenerate so slowly after people cut the flowers that many kinds had to be protected by law. Even the famous silvertree *(Leucadendron argentum),* which grows atop Table Mountain, had to be conserved because tourists took away so many of its narrow gray leaves, each clad in silky silvery hairs, as a souvenir or a bookmark.

Even without petals, the proteas attract pollinators to their spectacular colorful bracts or to long slender pistils that extend out from the flower head to knob-shaped stigmas, like brilliant pins in a pincushion. The shrubby South African species of *Leucospermum* offer so many variants of the pincushion pattern that they have to be seen to be believed. In Australia, the silk-oak *(Grevillea robusta)* has somewhat similar flowers, but the vivid orange and yellow pistils project from only one side of each elongated cluster. The silk-oak is just one of the 170 species of *Grevillea* on that continent. Many of them are tall trees that provide both timber and welcome shade. The advantages of shade are particularly noticeable in Australia, where the principal forest trees are eucalypts rather than proteas, and cast almost no shadows. Among their sunny bases, Australians find about fifty species of *Banksia,* shrubs whose spectacular flowers with long extended pistils and stamens are known as "Australian honeysuckles."

Some of the proteas produce fruits that are attractive, but so woody as to be inedible. Exceptions are the Chilean "hazelnut" *(Guevina avellana),* which is appreciated in its native country, and the Queensland-nut *(Macadamia ternifolia)* of eastern Australia.

Macadamia seeds are freed from an extremely hard shell and sold as delicacies around the world. Horicultural varieties with a thinner shell are being sought to reduce the labor and hence the cost, until the price can be made competitive with other kinds of nuts.

THE SANDALWOODS AND MISTLETOES
(Order Santalales)

When the prime minister of India, Jawaharlal Nehru, died in 1964, his body was placed on a great funeral pyre of fragrant sandalwood and publicly cremated, and more than a million Buddhists came to pay their respects. Millions more witnessed the ceremonies by television and newsreel, without feeling the intense heat either of the sunny day in India or of the burning wood as it released the energy the trees had captured from the sun. Wherever Buddhism is practiced in India and China, the white sandalwood *(Santalum album)* is used in this way. Its wood, which dries to a creamy white, contains up to five per cent of an oil that continues for years to give off a pleasant odor. Although other species of the genus produce wood of similar fragrance and uniform texture, white sandalwood is in special demand for use in the manufacture of fine inlaid boxes, ornamental fans, and the powder or paste that is mixed with pigments and applied to the face in the distinguishing caste marks of Brahmans.

It was to obtain sandalwood, then in much demand, that sailing ships set out for the islands of the South Pacific in the late 18th and early 19th century. In 1821, while George IV was the reigning British monarch, it is recorded that "The king purchased Cleopatra's barge for 8,000 pickles of sandalwood, valued at Ten (10.00) Dollars a pickle." The wood used for this transaction came from a foggy, cold area at 2600 feet elevation on the Hawaiian island of Maui, where the particular type of tree *(S. haleakalae)* grew tall. Yankee traders attended to the shipment, taking a percentage of the $80,000 involved in the deal.

Sandalwoods, like most of the four hundred species in the sandalwood family (Santalaceae), are partially parasitic upon the roots of various kinds of trees. But this relationship is not one that can be established artificially with any ease. The white sandalwood that was introduced to Hawaii, planted close to *Casuarina* and to the native *Acacia koa,* which were to serve as host plants, did not thrive. Now the experiment is not worth repeating, for the demand for sandalwood in most parts of the world is dwindling rapidly.

Anyone in North America or Europe who is interested in meeting some of the half-parasitic relatives of sandalwoods can do so without a major expedition. Buffalo nut (or elk nut, or oil nut, *Pyrularia pubera),* which parasitizes a number of different deciduous trees and shrubs from Pennsylvania to Georgia and Alabama, produces inch-long fruits that are pear-shaped and, like the rest of the plant, full of an acrid, poisonous oil. Six kinds of *Comandra,* called "bastard toadflax," are native to Europe and North America. They get their water and minerals from the tree roots upon which they attach themselves and grow in clumps, but make most of their organic substances in their green leaves, which grow on the herbaceous upright stems. They are not very different from the 220 kinds of *Thesium* which are found in Africa, southeast Asia, Tasmania, and Brazil.

For most people, the first example of a parasite among flowering plants is almost sure to be a mistletoe. We hear about this peculiar rootless kind of vegetation in childhood, along with stories of its use in ceremonials of the Celtic druids—people who dyed themselves blue with woad, an extract from a plant of the mustard family. The supposed magic virtues of mistletoe are rededicated every Christmas season when branches of any mistletoe—preferably one bearing the characteristic white, sticky berries—are hung up where girls can stand under them, intentionally or otherwise, and be kissed.

Anyone who visits the American Southeast has a good chance to see mistletoe growing. It forms almost spherical masses of evergreen branchlets, some masses still small, others larger than a bushel basket, on high branches of many kinds of trees. To supply the demand at Christmas, boys and men go out with long poles ending in a metal hook, and wherever they can reach, break off mature mistletoe from live oaks, maples, black gum, and other trees in Florida, east Texas, New Jersey, Kansas, and states in between.

Properly, the member of the mistletoe family (Loranthaceae) sold so commonly in American markets should be called "false mistletoe." The plant that first received this Anglo-Saxon name is the European *Viscum album,* whose name refers to the viscid, sticky substances that exude from the fruits of most mistletoes, or that coat their small indigestible seeds even after these have gone through a bird's digestive tract. Because of the sticky coating, birds often have difficulty swallowing the berries, and scrape them off their beak on tree branches, where the fruits adhere until the two or three seeds inside them germinate. Mistletoes get the water and inorganic nutrients they need by sending highly specialized branches (called haustoria) into the tree branch, and sometimes do considerable damage to the conducting tissue of the host.

More than two-thirds of the known kinds of mistletoe belong to two genera: *Loranthus,* with about five hundred species in the tropics of the Old World; and *Phoradendron,* with three hundred in warmer parts of the Americas. The familiar species in the United States is *P. flavescens.* Only one member of the mistletoe family, a small forest tree *(Nuytsia floribunda)* of West Australia, seems able to live independently.

FLOWERS WITH A CALYX DISPLAY
(Order Aristolochiales)

A lack of petals has not kept the pipevine, or Dutchman's pipe *(Aristolochia durior)* or the largest single flower in the world, *Rafflesia arnoldi,* from being noticed. Long before scientific names were given to the parts of any blossom, the flower of *Aristolochia* caught the attention of primitive practitioners of medicine. Rather than see that the showy calyx is tubular and curved upon itself like a Dutchman's pipe, the herb-gatherers of Europe saw in the flower a similarity to a fetus curled up in the womb. Following the "doctrine of signatures" proposed by the Swiss alchemist and physician Paracelsus (1493–1541), they regarded this resemblance as a God-given sign that an extract from the plant should be used in the delivery of babies. From this use come both the name birthwort (or birthroot) for the Eurasian *A. clematitis,* and also the generic term, *Aristolochia,* meaning "best for delivery."

The three hundred different kinds of *Aristolochia* are mostly tropical woody climbers whose stamens are fused so intimately with the single central pistil that the six anthers appear to arise from the rim of the angular stigma. When not under cultivation as an ornamental vine, Dutchman's pipe twines in rich woods and along stream banks from southwestern Pennsylvania to higher parts of Georgia and Alabama. A related vine *(A. serpentaria),* which grows in many of these same areas and beyond them to Florida, Texas, and Kansas, is called snakeroot because the Indians of Virginia are supposed to have used it to cure snakebite.

A very different type of plant *(Asarum),* known in Europe as asarabacca and America as wild ginger, is grouped with *Aristolochia* in the family *Aristolochiaceae* because it too has three sepals joined together in its petalless flower, the sepals fused also for a short distance to the ovary of the central pistil. This relationship is described by botanists as an inferior ovary, meaning below the other flower parts because they are fused to it. In a wild ginger, however, the twelve stamens are all distinct, completely hidden within a globular, chocolate-covered flower that barely extends above ground. The stems of *Asarum* are all subterranean. They send up only the inconspicuous flowers and the attractive kidney-shaped or heart-shaped leaves, which have long petioles. When bruised, the leaves give off a pleasant aromatic scent. Botanists do not agree as to whether wild gingers are self-pollinated or attract small fungus gnats and other flies to their malodorous flowers. A fruit does form from each flower. It is a globular capsule that bursts when ripe, scattering the large thick seeds, which resemble gray pebbles.

In the other family (Rafflesiaceae) of this order, the flower is the only recognizable part of the plant. It has five spreading sepals, surrounding either a large number of stamens or a broad, inferior ovary of a compound pistil. The vegetative portions of the plant resemble the threads of a fungus, and reach into the roots of vines or trees in tropical forests for all of the nourishment required for production of flowers and fruits. The thirteen species of *Rafflesia,* which live in Indonesia, grow only on the roots of woody climbers known as possum-grapes. The genus is named in honor of Sir Thomas Stamford Raffles, who served as lieutenant-governor of Sumatra and founded the city of Singapore in 1819. *R. arnoldi* of Sumatra produces solitary flowers as much as thirty-seven inches across, weighing up to twenty pounds. They rest on the ground, and give off a strong odor that resembles decaying meat. Flies are attracted, and serve as pollinators. Malayan-born British traveler Stewart Wavell, who is active with the British Broadcasting Corporation, insists that people of the Kelantan district hunt out the *Rafflesia* buds while each still resembles a giant cabbage. Known as Pak Mak, the buds are sliced and steeped in water overnight by wives who wish to give their husbands a love potion in the morning, one claimed to confer on an older man all the vigor of a younger one. Wavell claims also that any buds missed by the keen-eyed searchers will open with an explosive sound. Neither of these features has been reported for the small flowers of a related genus *(Pilostyles),* of which twenty species can be found in Iran, North Africa, Mexico, and a few adjacent parts of the United States.

CHAPTER 8

The Domesticated Beets and Their Remarkable Relatives

CUES: *If the dicot plant produces several carpels in each flower and all of them join together in a circle around a common central cavity, into which rises a projection bearing the ovules at the middle, it is a member of the Order Centrospermales. It may be a spinach plant, a beet, a tumbleweed, a four-o'clock, a bougainvillea vine, an iceplant, or a carnation.*

Where the weather is uniformly propitious and the soil equally suitable, almost any kind of land plant should be able to grow. Tolerances for adverse conditions are the really distinctive features of plants. Some kinds are able to thrive despite waterlogged or salty soil, or chronic drought, or extremes of temperature, or the repeated baring of the soil by men who wish to raise a crop. A plant that tolerates drought well enough to colonize a desert is a xerophyte. Plants that grow on a salt flat or a sea shore are halophytes. Those that move in quickly and thrive on bared earth in the hot sun are weeds.

A wealth of weeds, xerophytes and halophytes are met in the Order Centrospermales. Through their extra tolerances, the plants escape from the competition that is so furious (although silent) wherever living conditions are ideal. For a while each tolerant plant gains a chance to diversify. Special tolerances

When its seeds are ripe, a tumbleweed (Amaranthus) *curls its dry branches into a ball, breaks from the earth, and rolls away, dropping seeds as it goes. (Grant Heilman)*

mark the six thousand different kinds of plants in Order Centrospermales, fitting them into challenging ways of life on every continent from the Arctic to the Antarctic, and on many an island so remote that few men are willing to call it home.

Outstanding diversity in tolerances, in structure of root and stem and leaf is a feature of the goosefoot family *(Chenopodiaceae),* despite the close similarity among all members in their flowers and fruits. These plants find places in the rainless scrubland that Australians call the *mulga,* on the dry steppes of Central Asia, the karroo country of South Africa, the semi-arid pampas of Argentina, as well as along the sea-swept shores of the Caspian, the Mediterranean, and the Red Sea, and in the alkali plains of the American Southwest where broad lakes dried up and left the soil supercharged with salts.

The weed species are more familiar than their relatives that grow in inhospitable places. Lamb's quarters (or pigweed, *Chenopodium album*) has followed man from its native Eurasia into virtually every agricultural area of the world. With hoe and harrow, herbicide and plastic strips, he tries to prevent its tap roots from taking water from his crops, its quick-growing tops from shading his seedlings or serving as a host for insects that transmit harmful crop diseases. Its useful relative is quinoa *(C. quinoa),* which grows twice as tall and produces grainlike heads of edible seeds in the high Andes. Long before the Spanish destroyed the Inca Empire, the Indians in Peru, Chile and Bolivia were raising as much as half a ton of quinoa seeds to the acre. It provided them with a starchy food second only to the tiny potatoes that will grow in the poor shallow soil on the same mountain slopes. Quinoa seeds became porridge, or a base for thick soups, or a flour from which tortillas could be made. It sustained poultry at a higher elevation than most places in the world, and furnished the raw material for a warming alcoholic beverage. The Incas revered the quinoa, and ritually used a golden tool each autumn to open the first furrow in which the quinoa crop was to be planted.

Gardeners in temperate regions all over the world set out a relative called belvedere (or summer-cypress, *Kochia trichophylla),* which forms a handsome pyramidal shrub whose slender leaves retain a fresh green color until autumn, when they turn a brilliant red. Fewer people meet the white sage *(K. vestita)* of salt deserts in the American Southwest or the several kinds of *Kochia* known as bluebush in the mulga scrubland of Australia. Fictional accounts of frontier days in these areas often mention the characteristic vegetation, which includes also the greasewood *(Sarcobatus vermiculatus)*—a low dense shrub now widely distributed in deserts of California, Nevada and Utah, where its thick leaves and strong spiny branches provide browse for cattle in fall and spring. Readers of Westerns become familiar with the name of winter fat *(Eurotia lanata),* one of the most valued forage plants available during the cold months in the Great Basin States. Less often do they encounter mention of Russian thistle *(Salsola kali),* although this native of Asia is now established from California to New York State, as a noxious prickly weed. Often it is the last conspicuous survivor on arid lands after a long drought. A single Russian thistle may produce 100,000 seeds, which are blown for miles by the prairie winds; they start new plants and also nourish birds, rodents, and countless colonies of ants. True-breeding races of the same plant are known as saltwort where they grow along the world's sandy seashores.

For a family named from a fancied resemblance of its foliage to the imprint of a goose's foot, the Chenopodiaceae show a spectacular range in leaf form in relation to living conditions. Leaves are lacking altogether on the shrubby little glassworts *(Salicornia)* that grow in salt marshes. Their turgid, branching, jointed stems absorb moisture from the sea air, allowing the plant to grow on land too salty for any agricultural crop. The stems burst with a crackling sound, like breaking glass, when stepped on. In autumn they often turn a vivid red, for which the plants are known also as samphire. Somewhat similar plants, which have an even more tenacious hold on the water they capture from dew and rare rains, are the desert-cauliflowers *(Anabasis)* that are so characteristic of the Sahara Desert, and the small leafless saxuals *(Haloxylon persicum)*—trees in the deserts from Turkestan to Mongolia.

At the other extreme, with large green crisp leaves, are spinach *(Spinacia oleracea),* a native of southwestern Asia, and beets *(Beta vulgaris),* which originated in northern Europe. Texas and California produce nearly 200,000 tons of spinach annually as a green vegetable, to be cooked as a potherb. Many people in America prefer it to the foliage of beets ("beet tops") prepared in the same way. This use of beets in Europe antedates the Christian era, and led to the isolation of Swiss chard as a preferred variety. Centuries ago, the coarse mangel beet (mangel-wurzel) made its appearance among European crops being raised for their tops. Its bulbous tap root suggested that of a turnip, being equally pale yellow in color, and could be stored easily in a root cellar for use in winter or for feeding to cattle. Red beets seem to have been unknown until the 16th century, and are still little appreciated except in Britain and Anglo-America, where thousands of tons of them are diced fresh into salads, or boiled as a vegetable, or made into pickles.

Recognition that some varieties of beets contain an abundance of sugar (sucrose) in their roots came in the late 18th century. Napoleon encouraged the first development of a true sugar-beet industry while he was at war with Britain and his usual sources of cane sugar were cut off. Gradually through selection, beets containing fifteen to twenty per cent of sugar were bred. Improved methods for raising and extracting the beets allowed a decrease in the price of beet sugar until it became competitive with sugar from cane. Now beets are raised for sugar in the Temperate Zones of all continents except Africa. Beets

Right: Matching the worn pebbles of rocky deserts, the "living stones" (Mesembryanthemum *species) of South Africa reveal their true nature as they open blossoms soon after a rain. (E. Javorsky) Far right: A bitterroot* (Lewisia species) *hoards water in its fleshy leaves, thick buried stems and enlarged roots, letting it produce beautiful flowers in arid parts of northwestern America. (Ray Atkeson)*

from the western United States yield more than two million tons of sugar a year, and leave a residue of pulp and tops to be processed into livestock feed, fertilizer, and pectin.

Among the other families in Order Centrospermales are plants with more conspicuous and familiar flowers than any of the goosefoot family. Largest of these plant groups with similar structure of flowers and fruits is the pink family *(Caryophyllaceae)*, which includes the most popular of boutonnieres— the carnation *(Dianthus caryophyllus)*—as well as old-fashioned garden flowers of Eurasian origin, such as sweet william *(D. barbatus)*, Chinese pinks *(D. chinensis)*, and baby's-breath *(Gypsophila paniculata)*. A few add color to the roadsides of the Temperate Zone, as does bouncing bet *(Saponaria officinalis)*, a weed from the shores of the Mediterranean. Others hide in the grass of the world's lawns, among them the chickweeds *Cerastium* and *Stellaria,* whose tiny white star-shaped flowers delighted us as children. Still others of the pink family surprise the venturesome naturalists who land on the Falkland Islands, or South Georgia, or other bits of land close to the ice of Antarctica. There *Colobanthus crassifolia,* as one of the southernmost seed plants on earth, survives and flowers with no common name.

Most members of the four-o'clock family (Nyctaginaceae) live in the tropics. The showy parts of their flowers are not petals but other colored parts. Flaring tips of sepals, which otherwise form a cup at the bottom of the flower, open with amazing regularity at 4 P.M. in four-o'clocks *(Mirabilis jalapa)*, which were introduced from the highlands of Latin America into the gardens of the temperate world and then escaped from cultivation. In the Brazilian vine *Bougainvillea spectabilis,* which is grown as an ornamental in many warm countries, the three flowers in each cluster are scarcely noticed because they

Lambs'-tails (Ptilotus exaltatus), *a member of the amaranth family, is widespread in Australia. (Australian News and Information Bureau)*

are so surrounded by three colorful bracts which have the shape of leaves but the role of petals.

The thin, leaflike bracts scarcely show on the diminutive individual flowers of familiar plants in the tropical amaranth family (Amaranthaceae). Instead, it is the distinctive habit of seed dispersal for which many are famous. Best known of these tumbleweeds is one *(Amaranthus graecizans)* in the western United States, which has spread as far as eastern Quebec and grows well on disturbed soil or neglected land until the native trees can recolonize the area. Another *(A. albus)*, which was discovered originally in Virginia, has the same way of drying into the shape of a ball, breaking loose from the soil, and rolling with the wind, dropping its small fruits as it goes. It has spread widely in America and also to Europe, riding on ships among more useful seeds of New World plants.

Occasionally, man is able to take to a new region an exotic form of vegetation that seems exactly adapted to a place where few native plants will grow. Exposed coasts of California remained largely bare until the introduction of South African members of the huge genus *Mesembryanthemum,* of the carpet-weed family (Aizoaceae). The name iceplant is applied properly to just one *M. crystallinum,* whose fleshy flat leaves are coated densely with minute bladder-shaped hairs that glisten like ice in the sun. Actually several other species are given the same name, including the favored *M. multiradiatum,* which produces handsome pink or golden flowers as much as three inches across, each with an upflaring circle of many yellow stamens.

Fleshy leaves and attractive flowers that open only

Left above: Carpets of daisy-like flowers open in springtime on the low-growing succulent (Mesembryanthemum crenifolium) *that grows so widely over arid areas of Namaqualand, South Africa. Far left: With the first touch of autumn frost, glasswort (Salicornia europaea) reddens the salt marshes of the Northern Hemisphere with leafless succulent stems that appear jointed. (Both by Lorus and Margery Milne) Left: Sepal-like bracts and a petal-like calyx provide all the color in a cascade of* Bougainvillea. *The flowers themselves, in groups of three, are inconspicuous. (E. Javorsky)*

while the sun is on them, only to close forever after a single day, are common on plants of the purslane family (Portulacaceae). Purslane itself *(Portulaca oleracea)* is a widespread weed that sprawls on the ground, radiating in all directions from a central point where all of its stems arise from the deep taproot. Eradicating it is difficult, both because its many seeds are scarcely larger than dust particles and ride the wind easily, and also because any piece of stem or plump leaf that is dropped when the plant itself is weeded out can take root and thrive. A saving grace of purslane is that it is edible. It is sold regularly in native markets of Mexico, France, India, China, and many other countries. A near relative, the showy portulaca *(P. grandiflora)* from the Argentine, grows well in rock gardens and produces large flowers so long as the soil is loose and it has no real competition from other plants. An even larger flower and much smaller leaves, spreading from a low crown atop a large taproot, marks the bitterroot *(Lewisia rediviva)*. Indians in Montana collect bitterroots, chip off the bitter bark, dry the starchy and mucilaginous inner portions, and boil them in winter as a favorite food.

It is possible to eat the starchy bulblike underground stems of spring-beauty *(Claytonia virginica* and *C. caroliniana)* too, as the Indians did in the eastern United States. But it is better to leave this delicate little plant to signal the departure of winter. It sends up starlike flowers with five white petals, each streaked with pink, to twinkle above the first fresh vegetation in the moist woodlands as early as March—and often gets buried again under a late snowstorm.

CHAPTER 9

The Gay Poppies and Many Mustards

CUES: *If the dicot plant has both its sepals and petals separate, but its two or more carpels fuse to form one pistil with a superior ovary, and if its* *leaves are not adapted for catching insects, it is a member of the Order Papaverales. It may be a poppy, a bleeding heart, a mustard, a horseradish, or an ordinary cabbage.*

Among plants of this order, the members of the poppy family (Papaveraceae) stand out because of their colorful or milky juice. As a poppy bud opens, its two or three large thick sepals drop off, exposing at least four paper-thin, colorful petals. Quickly they unfurl, and soon drop off, leaving the central pistil surrounded for a day or more by a fringe of stamens. The pistil matures into a capsule that opens to release the tiny seeds when they are ripe.

The true poppies *(Papaver)* have a milky white juice, and the capsule resembles a pepper caster, opening by a series of small holes around the rim of the flat top. For more years than historical records show, Europeans have been collecting the black seeds of the common poppy *(P. somniferum)* and using them to add a slight tang to rolls and breads, especially since they are able to withstand the baking process. If pressed cold, these seeds yield thirty to forty per cent of their volume as a mild-flavored, colorless oil that is preferred to olive oil for salad use in Germany, since it does not quickly become rancid.

The raising of the European poppy to obtain poppy seeds and poppy-seed oil spread eastward to India in ancient times. There, perhaps in the first century A.D., peasants discovered how to scratch the surface of the ripening capsule and to collect the gummy drops of juice that oozed out and dried. The exudate is raw opium, which could be saved without deteriorating until wanted. Most of this material was chewed or eaten in very small quantities to relieve pain. Only after the habit of smoking tobacco was brought from America to Europe in the 17th century did anyone try inhaling the smoke from an opium pipe. Only then did addiction become serious—particularly in India and China where alcoholic beverages are less popular than in Europe. The famous book *Confessions of an English Opium-Eater* by Thomas De Quincey (1822) actually deals with an addiction to the drinking of laudanum, which is an alcoholic extract of opium, rich in its derivative alkaloid, morphine.

Since 1946 it has been illegal to grow the European (opium) poppy in the United States. All seeds of it that are imported for any purpose must first be sterilized by heat. Curiously, the seeds of the poppy contain none of the dangerous alkaloids. But young seedlings, grown from unsterilized seeds, produce enough morphine before they are an inch high to enable narcotics agents to identify them.

None of the other species of *Papaver* seem to produce usable amounts of narcotic alkaloids, and their cultivation is unregulated. These plants include the decorative Oriental poppy *(P. orientale),* which is native to the Middle East but grown widely for its large orange flowers, and the Iceland poppy *(P. nudicale),* which ranges in color from white or yellow to orange-red in the Arctic and Subarctic, and on alpine meadows on all sides of the North Pole.

The California poppy *(Eschscholtzia californica)* has only four petals, which spread widely open in the sun, then fall off on the second day. Its capsule becomes slenderly pear-shaped, splitting into two to free the many seeds within. Native to Oregon as well as to California, where it sometimes seems to paint the landscape a glorious golden yellow, the plant has spread through Utah, Arizona, New Mexico, and escaped in Europe.

A similar capsule follows the flower of the bloodroot *(Sanguinaria canadensis),* a beautiful little woodland poppy of early spring in the eastern United States and Canada. The plant is named for its orange-red juice, which oozes quickly from any cut in its petiole or flower stalk, or from the buried thick horizontal stem from which these parts burst through the soil all neatly rolled up together. One leaf and one flower arise from each plant, the lobed leaf to open just below the level at which the eight to twelve white petals spread briefly around a short cluster composed of exactly twice as many stamens and a single central pistil.

Bright yellow juice comes from the celandine *(Chelidonium magnus),* a weak-stemmed member of the poppy family in Europe. Introduced into the northeastern part of America, it shows the same habit of opening yellow flowers in early spring when the swallows arrive and continuing until autumn when they depart for the winter. From this habit, Europeans call the plant swallowwort. Wherever it grows, its four bright yellow petals around a projecting pistil and less conspicuous stamens attract children who are gathering wildflowers. Unless warned, they are likely to paint their arms and bare legs with its pungent yellow juice, which contains substances poisonous to the skin of some people and alkaloids that can be fatal if swallowed.

In members of the fumitory family (Fumariaceae), the sap is watery and colorless, the leaves so deeply lobed that they appear dissected, and the flowers somewhat flattened and heart-shaped. Pendant blossoms of this type are familiar in the graceful bleeding heart *(Dicentra spectabilis)* of China and Japan, which is raised in gardens all over the world. Children delight in taking apart the pink flowers and identifying in each one the two big "rabbits" (the large pink petals, which end in spurs like rabbit ears), two shining "slippers" (the narrow white petals whose "blood-stained" tips fit together, "heel" to heel at the tip of the flower), two "earrings" (the clusters of three stamens each, whose arching filaments are separate but whose anthers cohere in a group), and the slim green "wine bottle" (the pistil, whose "cork" is the stigma, covered with pollen brought by insects). The same pattern appears in Dutchman's breeches *(D. cucullaria)* and squirrel corn *(D. canadensis),* which open their nodding white flowers in rich woodlands from the Carolinas into Canada and west to Nebraska. On the buried horizontal stems of squirrel corn are yellow tuberous knobs from which the plant gets its name.

Four petals is the rule also in the mustard family (Cruciferae), and they are always arranged symmetrically like the arms of a cross. As far back as the 1st century A.D., this group of plants was recognized to be a natural one by Hindu herb-gatherers, who called them "swastika-plants." All crucifers have a pungent, watery juice, simple leaves, and flowers with four sepals that fall off, six stamens (of which two are short), and two carpels joined together in a pistil that ripens to become a two-chambered pod.

In the early 17th century, when the use of lenses and compound microscopes to study living things began, a mustard seed was a common unit of measurement. Mustard seeds do fit into a narrow range of sizes, and are intermediate in dimensions between an average pea and an average-sized pepper seed. One pea equals in diameter about ten mustard seeds in a row, or a hundred pepper seeds lined up in single file. Mustard seeds of these dimensions could be those of black mustard *(Brassica nigra),* which are harvested to be ground up as the preferred condiment of Europe beyond the British Isles and as the major constituent of the blend that is sold in America. Most Englishmen prefer a hotter sauce on their roast beef and ham, and make it from vinegar, brown sugar, and the ground seeds of the white mustard *(B. alba),* which has less of the volatile oils that provide flavor, fragrance and "bite," but a different essential glucoside (sinalbin, which is "hot," instead of sinigrin). For American consumption, the blend of the two mustards is toned down by an admixture

Kerguelen cabbage (Pringlea antiscorbutica) *is a member of the mustard family native only on Kerguelen (or Desolation) Island in the Indian Ocean. (E. Aubert de La Rue)*

of starch. Except that it contains other seasonings, it is not too different from the home remedy that our grandparents prepared. A "mustard plaster" reddened the skin and supposedly drew away whatever ailed us.

Both black and white mustard have yellow flowers, each as much as three-quarter inch across, in a loose cluster at the ends of top and side branches from a coarse leafy stem rising six to ten feet above the ground. Now cultivated and escaped into waste land in most temperate regions, these mustards originated in Eurasia, where their "tops" have been used since ancient times for a green vegetable. Farmers and gardeners learn with annoyance how many years the small seeds of mustards survive burial in the soil, ready to grow as weeds as soon as a cultivator brings them to the surface again.

Yellow flowers develop also on any turnip *(B. napus)* or rutabaga *(B. napobrassica),* if these garden vegetables are given a second year in which to send up a tall stem and utilize the foods they have stored in a fleshy root during their first season of growth. A surprising number of the forty species in the genus *Brassica* have proved attractive and valuable to mankind. Chinese cabbage is *B. pekinensis,* while *B. oleracea* has many varieties that are known and

isolated as subspecies: ordinary cabbage *(B. o. capitata),* cauliflower *(B. o. botrytis),* broccoli *(B. o. italica),* kale *(B. o. acephala),* kohlrabi *(B. o. gongolodes),* and Brussels sprouts *(B. o. gemmifera).* All of these are mild, however, by comparison with their near relatives. In stimulating the salivary glands or the digestive movements of the stomach, only ground mustard seeds can compare with grated fragments from the fresh root of the horseradish *(Armoraia rusticana).* True radishes *(Raphanus sativus)* are more like diminutive turnips, and vary greatly in the degree to which they induce a burning sensation in the mouth. Some of this same "hot" flavor comes from foliage of the watercress *(Nasturtium officinale),* another of the contributions from Europe to the tastes of the world.

The mustard family is a large one, with about 2500 species, chiefly native to the North Temperate Zone, particularly around the Mediterranean Sea. Almost all of them are rich in sulfur compounds. Many produce an abundance of vitamin C and are fine sources of calcium—a double coincidence in initial letters that makes it easy to remember the nutritional values among members of the Cruciferae.

Possibly southern Russia gave the world the woad plant (or asp-of-Jerusalem, *Isatis tinctoria),* one of thirty members of this genus in southern Europe and central Asia. It came into cultivation long ago because its leaves can be processed to yield a blue dyestuff. Now woad has escaped to become a roadside weed in most civilized temperate lands. The plant itself is a slender herb two to five feet tall, bearing two different styles of foliage. At ground level it produces oblong leaves with a toothed edge, on distinct petioles. On the upright stem the leaves are smaller, smooth-edged, and clasp the stem with no petioles. Any of the leaves, but not the yellow flowers, contain indigotin—a substance identical with that in the indigo plant. If the picked leaves are crushed and dried, they can be stored easily until a convenient time for wetting and fermenting them—a malodorous process requiring several weeks. So strong is the sulfurous stench from fermenting woad that Queen Elizabeth I of England decreed a stiff sentence on any processor of woad caught producing this foul odor within five miles of her royal estates. Later (1577) she promulgated penalties still more severe

The brilliant golden cups of California poppy (Eschscholtzia californica) *brighten the semi-arid Western lands in springtime. (Josef Muench)*

on anyone importing indigo, a competing dyestuff which the Dutch were bringing from India. In Nuremberg, Germany, dyers were forced by local laws to take an oath every year that they would not use indigo. Yet the merits of the imported, smuggled dye won out and woad growers were forced out of business.

Few of the crucifers are more widespread than the little shepherd's-purse (or pickpocket, *Capsella bursa-pastoris*), which takes its name from the little heart-shaped capsules that mature throughout most of the growing season on lowly plants wherever sunlight reaches neglected soil. Naturalized all over the world from Europe, it competes with showier relatives that have a respected place in flower beds and rock gardens. They include the old-fashioned sweet alyssum *(Alyssum maritimum)* from Europe, and the various kinds of rock cress *(Arabis)* from Eurasia and North America. *Alyssum* comes from Greek that might be translated "anti-rabies," from an old belief that it could be used as an effective medicine to cure hydrophobia.

CHAPTER 10

The Meat-Eaters

CUES: *If the dicot plant is highly adapted for capturing small animals as food, as a plant with leaves shaped like pitchers that hold water, or as a sun-dew with leaves covered by projections bearing drops of sticky secretion, or as a flytrap with leaves forming a spring trap that closes rapidly, it is one of the members of the Order Sarraceniales.*

It is no news when an animal eats a plant and digests it. But when a plant catches animals and uses them as food, it is something strange—a story out of science fiction. Yet the pitcher plants and their allies depend upon the insects they catch for the nutrients that are least available to them from the bog water and other places where they live. Most plants get these nutrients, which contain nitrogen, by absorbing nitrates dissolved in soil water. But the acid water of a peat bog is full of tannins, and might poison a plant that absorbed it. The poorly drained soils of wet hillsides are often almost as toxic. And in the rain forests of the tropics, where insect-eating plants grow among mosses, ferns, orchids and other vegetation perched on the outstretched limbs of huge trees, there is no real soil at all. What little dust and decaying matter remains there is washed free of everything soluble by the repeated heavy rains. The carnivorous plants bypass this limitation in their environment by getting their nitrogenous nutrients from captured animals. Their habit lets them live where most kinds of vegetation cannot compete.

Plants whose leaves are modified into pitcher-like containers that hold water have evolved in both the New World and the Old. The first samples from America to reach European botanists were collected early in the 18th century near Quebec City by the official physician to the French Court, Dr. Michel Sarrasin de l'Étang. To honor him for this gift, the pitcher plants of eastern North America were named *Sarracenia,* and their family the Sarraceniaceae. In all of the nine or ten different kinds, the strange leaves develop in a radial pattern like the spokes of a wheel. From the center of the whorl a slender stalk rises, bearing a single, large, nodding blossom.

The fresh new leaves resemble slim vanes, flattened from side to side. Only as they attain their full length do they open up a central cavity which can hold water. In pitcher plants of the southeastern United States, the end of the leaf curves over the opening and prevents the pitcher from being overfilled by heavy rains. In *S. purpurea*—the official flower of Newfoundland, which inhabits peat bogs all across Canada and as far south in the east as Maryland, the end of the leaf is more like a funnel, perhaps matching the smaller rainfall.

Left above: Common European poppies (Papaver dubium) *and golden buttercups* (Ranunculus *species) are colorful weeds in many a farmer's field. Usually they fade and fall before the grain is ripe. (Ginette Laborde) Far left: Arctic poppies* (Papaver alboroseum) *attract pollinating insects in the brief summer just south of the Brooks Range in Alaska. Each flower lasts for one long day. (Steve McCutcheon) Left: From China came the bleeding heart* (Dicentra spectabilis), *plants of gardens all over the world. Bees know how to separate the parts and reach the nectar and pollen deep inside. (Lorus and Margery Milne)*

Usually a mature leaf is about half full of water, and either stands up erectly (in the hooded species) or lies mouth up on the moss, rather like a curved "horn of plenty." And despite the bodies of dead insects that have accumulated in the bottom of the pitcher, the water is usually clearer and more palatable than any in the peat bog below. People who have become desperately thirsty while crossing a peat bog have drunk the water from pitcher plants, and found that it did them no harm. For this reason, the leaves are often called "huntsman's-cups."

Above the water line, the inner surface of each pitcher is as shining smooth as though waxed and polished. Around the rim, actual flakes of wax may wait, ready to crumble if an insect walks on them, and to let it drop into the water. Neither insect nor sticky-toed tree frog can get a grip on the smooth pitcher walls and crawl out. It drowns, and the plant digests it, almost certainly with the aid of decay bacteria. The important feature, making a pitcher plant a true meat-eater, is that the green walls of the pitcher absorb the products of digestion.

On *S. purpurea,* the flaring end of each leaf is generally marked with dark red in a pattern that suggests the blood-filled veins in a rabbit's ear. Little glands there are believed to produce a substance that helps attract flies. But any fly that alights or ant that attempts to crawl across the outstretched end on the leaf is guided toward the region of perilous footing by stiff curved bristles, all pointing at the pitcher mouth. Even if the fly takes to its wings, it is likely to blunder into the opening and drown.

Some mosquitoes and other insects, however, make use of the pitcher water as a place to raise their young. The pitcher-plant mosquito, which lives nowhere else and does not bite, enters and leaves like a miniature helicopter without touching the walls. Some of the fly maggots that devour the

Left above: In the acid wet pinelands of southeastern United States, the carnivorous leaves of trumpets (or huntsman's-horn, Sarracenia flava) *have caps that shut out excessive rain. (Jack Dermid) Left: The hooded top of leaves on the pitcher plant* (Chrysamphora darlingtonia) *prevents rain from diluting the secretions that prepare insects for absorption. (Wilhelm Schacht) Right: Poised precariously, an ant is about to topple into the water-holding leaf of a pitcher plant* (Cephalotus follicularis) *which grows in marshes of Western Australia. The upper leaves of the plant are flat and carry on photosynthesis. (Michael Morcombe)*

remains of dead insects in the bottom of the pitcher cut a small hole through the pitcher wall at the water line and escape to transform outside into the fly that will lay its eggs on the pitcher rim and repeat the process. Certain spiders specialize in weaving webs across the mouth of pitcher-plant leaves, and in eating the insects that the pitcher would otherwise collect.

In the rain forests of the Old World, particularly in Borneo but also in the area from China to Australia, a different type of pitcher plant is known as monkeycups *(Nepenthes,* of family Nepenthaceae). In some of the sixty-six species, the pitcher is so tiny that a large pea would block its opening. Others hold more than a pint of water. All are borne by strange leaves of which the part nearest the stem is actual blade, the next part a slender tendril with which the vine climbs, and tip the pitcher or monkey-cup. These pitchers remain sealed until after the cavity inside them has formed. Clear water, secreted into the cavity by the plant, is uncontaminated and perfectly safe to drink, until the cap portion of the leaf rises up away from the rim, providing a way for insects to enter and get caught. In *Nepenthes,* as in the American pitcher plants, even the shell and the white of a hard-boiled egg is digested if this unusual contribution is made to the plant's varied diet.

If a pitcher-plant leaf is thought of as a pitfall for unwary insects, the members of the sundew family

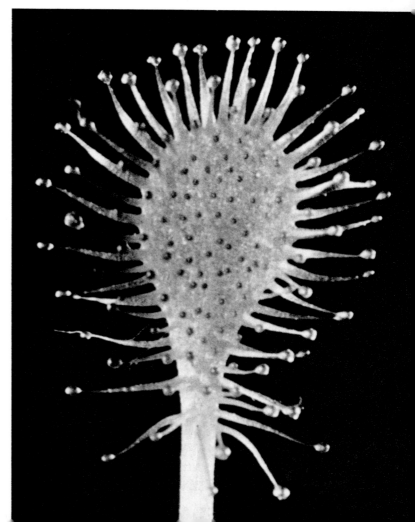

Far left above: Monkeycups (Nepenthes ampullaria) *of Borneo assume different shapes on the same plant. The overhanging leaf-shaped hood keeps heavy rain from filling the pitcher, in which insects drown and are digested. (G. G. Clark) Far left: Sunlight striking the pitcher of a monkeycup* (Nepenthes) *in the tropics of the Old World shines through translucent areas and brightens the interior. Most of these plants climb with tendrils that extend their flat leaves and end in insect-catching pitchers. Left: Like other sundews* (Drosera *species), this one in the vicinity of Darlington, Western Australia, attracts large insects as pollinators of its flowers while capturing small insects with the hairs on its reddish leaves. Right above: Resembling a beer stein with its hinged top, the liquid-holding leaf of monkeycups* (Nepenthes) *waits for insects to fall in and drown. (All by E. S. Ross) Right: The circumpolar round-leaved sundew* (Drosera rotundifolia) *secretes adhesive at the tip of projections that curl around a trapped insect and hold it as food. (Lorus and Margery Milne)*

(Droseraceae) can be regarded as providing the equivalent of spring traps and birdlime. Most spectacular of them is the Venus's flytrap *(Dionaea muscipula)* of coastal fields in the Carolinas. In this area, a policeman told us where to find this plant on a golf course. For most of the year, while it is not in flower, the rosettes of green leaves are inconspicuous among the grass. Each leaf has a long petiole with a narrow wing along either side, narrowing in to the midrib just before reaching the two halves of the terminal blade. Around the edge, the blade bears bristly hairs that suggest the sharp teeth along the rim of a steel trap. Three or four minute stiff bristles stick up from the center of the shiny flat portion of each half-blade. If these are touched—one several times or two just once—they act as triggers. In a second or less, the halves of the leaf fold together along the midrib, until their marginal projections interlock. If the insect gets away, or the alarm is false, the leaf opens again in half an hour or so. But if a fly or an ant is caught by the trap, the leaf blades slowly press against it until there is no space left. Only after the body has been digested, and the indigestible residues have dried, does the leaf open again and let the wind clear it of debris.

In *Aldrovanda vesiculosa,* which has no commoner name although it grows in shallow ponds all across Eurasia into the East Indies and Australia, the trap has a similar form but closes on insects and small crustaceans under water. Like the Venus's flytrap, it sends up a slender stalk with small white flowers, which are pollinated by flying insects too tiny to trip the triggers.

Most of the sundew family are sundews *(Drosera),* which secrete a dew-clear droplet of a nondrying adhesive from the tip of each bristle-like tentacle along the edge of every leaf. The round-leaved sundew *(D. rotundifolia)* may have leaf blades only one-quarter inch across, in a rosette smaller than a silver dollar. It produces one or two flower stalks, which extend to a height of perhaps ten inches, unfolding one new flower at a time, and this always higher on the stalk than the blossom that has just closed. The round-leaved sundew is found in bogs and on wet hillsides in the sun from Greenland to California, and Alaska to Florida. In many of its haunts it is accompanied by other members of the same genus, all of them able to curl the sticky tentacles over any insect that gets caught, and to digest the contents of its body. Australia has more varieties of sundews than any other continent, and

only Antarctica is without these amazing plants.

Among the meat-eaters, only the Venus's flytrap gives the slightest indication of being aggressive. Sometimes, when the sun is hot and the mechanism of closure particularly swift, it is tempting to think of the plant as snapping at each fly that settles for a moment on the trigger hairs. Purposeful movements of this kind are so rare in the plant kingdom that writers of science fiction have used it as a pattern on which to create exciting stories of man-eating plants, "somewhere" in the "mysterious tropics."

CHAPTER 11

The Roses and Their Varied Kin

CUES: *If the dicot plant has its sepals, petals, and stamens all rising together, either from five little scale-like elevations around the edge of the receptacle or as a cuplike ring that surrounds the pistil, the plant is almost sure to belong to the Order Rosales. It may then be a succulent hen-and-chickens, or a gooseberry bush, a witch hazel, a sycamore tree, a bluebonnet, a kidney bean, an apple tree, or a rosebush.*

Almost a tenth of the known kinds of flowering plants have a place in this huge, tremendously varied order. A small proportion—although still a large number of kinds—are known for their handsome flowers, or their edible fruits, or the wood they produce as trees. A few provide man with all three benefits in sequence.

THE SUCCULENT ONES (Family Crassulaceae)

So many people now fancy the cultivation of rock gardens that members of this family are widely familiar. All of them have fleshy leaves with such a heavy waterproof cuticle that they resist wilting and store water from one rain to the next. The leaves are evergreen, although usually a dull grayish green, and the short petiole (or the blade) joins the stem with no expansions that could be called stipules.

A century ago it was meaningful to refer to these plants as members of the orpine family, because the Eurasian orpine *(Sedum telephium)* was then cultivated all over the temperate world as the source of a home remedy for skin wounds. Now more kinds of *Sedum* are familiar as stonecrops—low-growing rock plants that transform into a carpet of golden flowers each year when they synchronously open on very short stalks a multitude of half-inch stars, each with five pointed petals.

Usually a rock garden has also a few clusters of hen-and-chickens (a *Sempervivum* of some species). Resembling succulent, flattened cabbages, these tight rosettes send out short horizontal stems at the tip of which a miniature facsimile of the parent plan develops. Houseleek (or thunderwort, *S. tectorum),* native to Mediterranean Europe as far as the Caucasus, used to be planted extensively on thatched roofs in the belief that it magically warded off lightning.

Tropical Africa has supplied the rock gardens and indoor gardens of succulent fanciers with several species of *Bryophyllum* known as lifeplants. In the notches around the margin of the succulent leaves, adventitious buds develop into tiny plantlets complete with leaves and roots. A leaf broken by wind or a passing animal reproduces in this way as it lies on the moist soil. In Latin America, senoritas often entertain themselves by pinning a leaf of the flopper *(B. daigremontianum)* to a curtain in the bedroom and naming the growing plantlets for prospective suitors. Tradition holds that the senorita should then accept the suitor indicated by whichever plantlet remains longest on the leaf.

The same method of reproduction is found in some of the species of *Kalanchoë* from the tropics of the Old World. In the cigarette plant *(K. verticillata),* which is named for the cylindrical shape of its two-inch leaves, the plantlets develop only at the tip and in an irregular cluster.

Some of the cultivated species of the large genus *Crassula* attain the form of small trees as much as ten feet tall. Heavy branching stems and thick rubbery leaves are particularly noticeable in the jade-plant *(C. argentea,* often called *C. arborescens),* which may produce flat clusters of small flowers in winter. Like others of its family, this plant has symmetrical blossoms in which a small scale-like projection

appears around the rim of the receptacle to correspond with each carpel in the ovary; on the projection a sepal, a petal, and either one or two stamens develop. In *Sedum* and *Crassula,* the four or five carpels are matched by eight or ten stamens. In *Sempervivum,* the pattern is repeated from six to thirty times, with twice this many stamens. From each flower that is pollinated, a small pouchlike follicle develops. It splits along one side to release its many seeds.

All of the Crassulaceae are so well adapted to arid environments that they tolerate long droughts caused by neglect in gardens or indoors, so long as they get an abundance of light and are kept reasonably warm. A few will tolerate frosts, and it is these that become favorites of alpine gardeners in cooler parts of the Temperate Zone.

THE SAXIFRAGES (Family Saxifragaceae)

The name saxifrage (a "breaker of stones") perpetuates an old wives' tale from the Middle Ages which claimed that an extract from the common Eurasian saxifrage *(Saxifraga cernua)* could cure kidney stones. Proof of this could be seen by anyone accepting the Doctrine of Signatures, in the supposedly divine clues given by pale pebble-sized bulblets found where each leaf of the saxifrage joins the stem. Not all members of *Saxifraga* produce these bulblets, from which new plants can grow. But some others in the family show a similar habit.

The herbs and shrubs of the saxifrage family differ from members of the orpine family in dropping their leaves for the winter, in never being succulent, and in having fewer carpels than petals or sepals. They resemble orpines and differ from other members of the Order Rosales in having plain petioles (or none), with no bladelike stipules where the leaf joins the stem.

Most valuable of the saxifrages are the members of the genus *Ribes,* which includes currants and gooseberries—fruit-bearing shrubs of Eurasia whose cultivation goes back at least to 1600 A.D. Currants are non-spiny bushes that produce their flowers and fruits in pendant clusters. Gooseberries are spiny, and bear their reproductive parts singly or in twos and threes. Both produce plump berries containing several seeds, tipped by the shriveled remains of the calyx tips.

Great Britain still grows more black currants *(Ribes nigrum)* than any other country, and about a tenth as many red currants *(R. sativum, R. rubrum,* and *R. petraeum),* chiefly for preparation of the dried fruit or the manufacture of jellies. These are species native to southern Europe and western Asia. Like the so-called "English" gooseberry *(R. grossularia),* which came originally from North Africa as well as most of Europe, these fruits may also be eaten raw. None of these habits became as well established in America, despite the early introduction of the plants themselves by European colonists. In states where white pine is an important timber tree, laws have now been passed prohibiting the possession of live plants of any species of *Ribes,* since they are hosts to the destructive blister rust that attacks this valuable pine.

The saxifrage family includes also the garden shrubs known as mock orange (or syringa, *Philadelphus coronarius,* from south and central Europe) and the hydrangea *(Hydrangea paniculata,* of China and Japan). Idaho has chosen the related wild syringa *(P. lewisii)* as its most representative flower.

THE WITCH-HAZELS (Family Hamamelidaceae)

The most bewitching feature of the six different kinds of *Hamamelis* may well be the odd ways in which people become acquainted with these low shrubby trees, or with products from them. American boy scouts are shown how to make an emergency toothbrush from a witch-hazel branch. Army recruits have been introduced to the shrub in the understory of forests in the eastern United States as being the best from which to remove branches to use as camouflage, because the dull green leaves wilt slowly and do not drop off for weeks. Rarely does an instructor point out that witch-hazels grow naturally only in forested parts of North America and in easternmost Asia, where the weather is similar. In neither area has much need for green camouflage been found.

Extract of witch-hazel leaves and twigs comes mainly from Connecticut, for use in aftershave lotions and other astringent solutions to which it gives a distinctive perfume. A similar odor, which many people find reminiscent of lemon extract, pervades the woodlands in late autumn when witch-hazels come into bloom. Usually they are the last to do so each year. While other deciduous trees drop their leaves for the winter, the witch-hazels unfold narrow ribbonlike yellow petals, four to a flower. After eleven months, the witch-hazel seeds mature in egg-shaped capsules close to the branches. In drying each capsule contracts and pressure builds

up inside. When the capsule splits open at its end, the single seed in a slimy covering is shot out like a rifle bullet—sometimes for forty feet.

Branches from American witch-hazel trees are sometimes chosen as a substitute for the forked branches of the European hazel tree *(Corylus)* in perpetuating a superstition brought from the Old World. The magic sticks are "divining rods" in the hands of people who call themselves dowsers and claim to be able to find the best place to dig a well to reach water.

Allied to witch-hazel are the sweetgum trees *(Liquidambar)* of Asia and America, from Costa Rican mountains to low woodlands as far north as Illinois and Connecticut. In autumn the star-shaped leaves, as much as nine inches wide, turn a glorious red. Sweetgum seeds, which bear wings and fall from the tree in autumn, are enjoyed by quail, forest rodents, and other animals of the forest. Sweetgum sap can be concentrated to make a resin called "storax," which is a fair substitute for gum benzoin —a material increasingly difficult to secure since it comes from Indonesia.

THE MOTTLED SYCAMORES (Family Platanaceae)

Tallest and heaviest of North America's deciduous trees is the sycamore *(Platanus occidentalis),* which may attain a height of 170 feet and a diameter of eleven feet at shoulder height. Like its relative, the slightly smaller plane tree *(P. orientalis)* of Europe and as far east as the Himalayas, and like six more kinds of *Platanus* in Eurasia, the sycamore can be recognized from a distance by its mottled bark. As the trunk and major branches enlarge, their covering flakes off in large pieces. The brown scaly plates fall to the ground, exposing pale layers of the inner bark in a piebald pattern. On all of these tall trees the leaves are large, their margins lobed in a palmate outline, their veins radiating out from the end of the petiole. At the angle between the leaf and the stem, the petiole is expanded into stipules which clasp the stem and conceal the bud from which a branch might extend during the next growing season.

Although the flowers of a sycamore are produced

Beach plum (Prunus maritima) *helps hold the sand dunes in place along northern parts of the American Atlantic coast. The fruits ripen in autumn, and can be made into jelly. (Vinton Richards)*

in clusters, like little balls each hung from the branch by a short length of string, each cluster is composed of either staminate or carpellate flowers with minute sepals and petals. The pistils that receive pollen each mature into a one-seeded fruit, which is a slender prism radiating out from the receptacle at the center of the cluster. All winter the ripe seeds may stay on the tree, before the balls break up and the individual fruits fall to the ground. Wind blows them about, and rivulets of water from heavy rains may strand them on suitable soil.

Sycamore wood is too weak for most structural uses, but it is so intricately cross-grained as to be almost impossible to split. This gives it a value for making into the cutting blocks upon which butchers divide meat, and provides also an attractive pattern when the wood is prepared as a thin veneer backed by some stronger material. A good many big sycamores, according to the annual rings in their wood, live to be six hundred years old. This gives them centuries in which to produce seeds, and makes up for the smallness of the number that find moist open soil without too much organic matter, in which the seeds will germinate.

THE GREAT ROSE FAMILY (Rosaceae)

With about 3200 species distributed over much of the earth, but most abundantly in the North Temperate Zone, the rose family shows great versatility in the ways by which one general style of flower can give rise to many different types of fruits. In all the sepals are partly joined to form a cup. In a *Spiraea,* after the petals fall, the several separate pistils can each mature into a slender follicle with a single seed and release it by splitting down one side. In a cherry or a plum *(Prunus),* the calyx falls off when the petals and stamens do, and the single pistil with a solitary seed becomes a fleshy fruit around an armored "pit." In a rose *(Rosa),* the calyx

Left above: Stanley prune plums (Prunus domestica) *were developed after this tree from Asia was cultivated in many remote lands. (Grant Heilman) Far left: Beach pea* (Lathyrus japonicus) *is a variable plant on sandy and gravelly shores of the North Pole. It grows also along the coast of Chile. (Matt Cormons) Left: Each of the numerous pistils in a bramble flower becomes a fleshy, delicious part of the ripe fruit. This is the prickly bramble* (Rubus fruticosus) *of northern Europe. (Ingmar Holmasen)*

cup itself enlarges and turns bright red, closing around the many individual carpels which mature as the hard little "pips" within the fleshy "hip." In a raspberry or blackberry *(Rubus),* the calyx remains green, attached to the elongated receptacle upon which multiple pistils develop into miniature fleshy fruits, each with a single small armored seed. In a strawberry *(Fragaria),* the calyx is the "hull" we remove before eating the colorful, fragrant, enlarged receptacle in whose surface the tiny indigestible nutlets are embedded, each the product from a separate pistil in the flower. In an apple *(Malus)* or a quince *(Cydonia),* a mountain ash *(Sorbus)* or a hawthorn *(Crataegus),* the calyx and all except the innermost layer of the ovary wall become fleshy in forming the familiar fruit, which botanists call a "pome."

Some eighty kinds of *Spiraea* grow as shrubs in the Northern Hemisphere, where they bear such names as steeple-bush, queen-of-the-meadow, hardhack, and meadow-sweet. They flower in all shades of pink to white. The popular cultivated form known as bridal wreath *(S. prunifolia)* bears small white flowers in convex clusters. The Asiatic spiraea *(S. japonica)* appears in gardens all over the world, raised for its tall spires of pink flowers. Usually a spiraea in bloom is a busy place, attended by bees, flies, beetles and butterflies by day, and by moths at night, every one of them rewarded with nectar or pollen.

Edible fruits with a single stony pit are the best-known products from the 150 members of the genus *Prunus.* Although they become small trees predominantly in temperate parts of the Northern Hemisphere, only those from the Old World have been developed into important horticultural varieties. From southern Europe came the sweet cherry *(P. avium),* from Asia Minor the sour, or pie cherry *(P. cerasus),* and perhaps the European plum *(P. domestica).* Central Asia provided the apricot *(P. armeniaca),* and the damson plum *(P. insititia),* as well as the almond *(P. amygdalus),* of which only the seeds are used, since the flesh is leathery. China gave us the peach *(P. persica)* and the flowering almond *(P. triloba).* All of these have been cultivated over a period of nearly two thousand years. More recently, new horticultural varieties of Oriental plums *(P. salicina*—native to China) have been introduced around the world from trees domesticated in Japan. By crossing several of these species with members of the same genus from America, it has been possible to breed fruit trees with greater hardiness to winter weather.

The low flat crowns of Acacia *trees are character-istic features of the savannas in East Africa and southward as far as South Africa. (James R. Simon)*

Best known of the American species is wild black cherry *(P. serotina)* from the eastern states and Canada, which produces hard, fine-grained wood. Chokecherry may be the native kind *(P. virginiana)* or the introduced Eurasian one *(P. padus),* both bearing small fruits that pucker the mouth but have great appeal for birds.

In the Western World, California is virtually alone in raising almonds. Special attention has been given to sweet almonds, as the source of nutmeats. Additional supplies are imported from Iran, Sicily and southern Italy, Spain, Portugal, and Morocco. In all of these countries, bitter almonds are raised too. They differ from sweet almonds in containing the same glucoside that makes peach seeds bitter and poisonous. It is amygdalin, which releases hydrocyanic acid upon digestion. By suitable treatment, however, the amygdalin in bitter-almond oil can be broken down and freed of its poison to yield benzaldehyde, which gives its characteristic flavor to almond extract.

By quite different processes, European plums are dried to yield prunes. And the blue fruits of the blackthorn, or sloe tree *(P. spinosa),* of the Mediterranean coasts provide an acid pulp from which the liqueur known as sloe gin is made.

From some of the highest slopes of the Ruwenzori Mountains along the border between Uganda and the Congo, and from similar elevations on mountains of Tanganyika, Kenya, and Ethiopia, has come an ornamental tree *(Hagenia abyssinica)* which forms forests in these inaccessible areas. Ethiopian people have cultivated it from time immemorial, not for its handsome pinnately compound leaves but for the pistillate flowers which comprise part of each scarlet cluster. From these flowers a drug can be prepared as an effective vermifuge for those who suffer from tapeworms. Known in Ethiopia as kuso or cusso, the remedy was discovered and publicized by a French physician in Constantinople, whose name has been taken for the drug in medical circles:

brayera, from Brayer. Curiously, the seeds that develop within small fruits surrounded by the persistent perianth soon die if not given a chance to germinate. Horticulturalists regularly tuck the whole, ripening flower into the earth as soon as the eight to ten stamens have dropped. Without this care, the tree appears unable to seed itself in parts of the world remote from its lofty African mountains.

Through a different process of great antiquity, rose petals can be made to yield rose oil and the famous rich perfume known as attar of roses. About two hundred and fifty pounds of rose petals are needed to make each ounce of attar of roses. Only in Bulgaria is it done on a large scale, and then under state auspices to take advantage of the damask rose *(Rosa damascena)* which grows so luxuriantly in the moist valleys that drain into the Danube and the Maritsa rivers. Less valuable oils from other roses go into rosewater and lesser perfumes from the gardens and factories of the Riviera.

For their fragrance and their symmetrical beauty, roses *(Rosa)* have been cherished since the dawn of history. In her "Ode to the Rose," the Greek poetess Sappho called them "the queen of flowers." Their elegant perfection led to their use as symbols of love and romance, as heraldic emblems made famous in England's War of the Roses, and as colorful tokens to strew before distinguished visitors. In countries as different as India and Mexico, despite unlikeness of cultural heritage and religious beliefs, rose petals are floated on garden pools and whole flowers buoyed up by water in transparent rose bowls, all to lend charm for special occasions.

With so many horticultural varieties in cultivation, it is no longer possible to be sure where all the wild ancestors of today's cultivated roses came from. Most were oriental, such as the tea roses *(R. fragrans* and *R. odorata)* of China, the memorial rose *(R. wichuriana)* and the multiflora rose *(M. multiflora)* of China and Japan, the sweetbriar *(R. eglanteria)* of western Asia, the cinnamon rose *(R. cinnamomea)* and the Scotch rose *(R. spinosissima)* from all across Eurasia into the British Isles. Dozens of different kinds of wild roses add beauty to the undisturbed landscape in the United States and Canada, providing valuable cover for game. Grouse, quail, wild turkeys, deer, bear, and many other animals of the fields and forest edges enjoy their ripe hips.

For many people, wild roses and wild raspberries are all briars and brambles, whose arching woody canes are studded with sharp thorns. To a rabbit, such as the hero of Thornton Burgess's stories for children, it makes no difference so long as the briar patch is fox-proof. But according to European usage, a briar is a rose *(Rosa)* and a bramble a raspberry *(Rubus)*. Both types of plant may have pinnately compound leaves. Those of a raspberry have two tiny green projections (stipules) where the petiole joins the stem, whereas those of a rose have large stipules that are united with the petiole like narrow wings along its sides and end in projecting tips. Often the winglike parts of the rose stipules bear a green fringe whose soft points are as conspicuous as the stipule tips, whereas a raspberry petiole bears nothing more elaborate than coarse hairs.

Raspberries constitute a vast genus, with perhaps a thousand species. Pliny mentions them as wild fruits. Their culture probably began in the 17th century, when some were found to bear particularly large and delectable berries or to be thornless. In Europe and Great Britain, only the red raspberry *(R. idaeus)* grows wild and has become domesticated. It is a circumpolar bramble of open fields and forest borders in cool climates. In its almost globular fruits, in the ease with which they drop off when ripe, and in the leaves, which are mostly pinnately compound, it closely resembles the blackcap raspberry *(R. occidentalis)* of eastern North America, whose fruits are purple-black when ripe and "red when they're green."

Often the blackcap is called a thimbleberry. Generally this word is reserved for the red-ripe fruit of a different bramble *(R. parviflorus),* which colonizes cleared land from Ontario to Alaska and down the mountain slopes from California into Mexico. This thimbleberry produces smaller flowers but a far more luscious fruit than the purple-flowered raspberry *(R. odoratus)* of eastern North America, whose blossoms may be two inches in diameter and whose leaves may be a foot across. Both *parviflorus* and *odoratus* have simple, lobed leaves and lack spines on the woody canes. Their seeds tend to be so large as to feel gritty if the fruit is chewed.

Blackberries are something else again, and usually the two *(R. canadensis* and *R. alleghentiensis)* found commonly in North America from Quebec to Tennessee, and as far west as Missouri. Despite the wide use of the name "sow-teat" for *R. alleghentiensis,* they are much sought-after by berry pickers, who often call them dewberries. They differ from raspberries in tending to dry on the bush if not removed by berry eaters.

Robinson strawberries are among the favored varieties that have been commercially developed to match growing conditions from northern New Jersey to eastern Canada. (Grant Heilman)

The names of our familiar fruits have a motley origin. Raspberry comes from the Old French, in which *vin raspé* was the kind of wine that could be made from their fruit. Loganberries, which are a hybrid between the western dewberry *(R. ursinus)* of California and the widespread red raspberry *(R. idaeus),* commemorate Judge J. H. Logan who discovered the first plants in 1881. A strawberry remained unknown, despite the presence of a few runnerless, small-fruited species in Eurasia, until the colonists to New England sampled the fragrant kinds that the Indians watched over in the fields *(Fragaria virginiana)* and in rocky woods *(F. vesca).* Already the red men knew how much better the plants survived the frosts of fall and spring, pro ducing runners, flowering and fruiting in greater profusion, if covered by at least two inches of straw or hay through the cold months. The first name of the colony at Portsmouth, New Hampshire, was Strawberry Bank, and it is tempting to think of the Indians as willing to drive out the settlers to regain the slopes where strawberries grew so luxuriantly.

Long before the Spaniards came to the New World, the Indians of Chile were cultivating a western

species *(F. chiloensis),* which ranged originally from Patagonia to Peru, and California to Alaska, as well as in the mountains of Hawaii. They had achieved red fruits with a yellow pulp, "as large as a walnut." Five plants from Chile were taken to England in 1714, and there crossed with *F. virginiana* from New England. The hybrid gave the world its commercial strawberries and one of its most popular flavors. The hybrids produce more large fruit, as well as firmer (more transportable) berries, but never quite match the sweet delicacy of the wild New England ancestor, of which Izaak Walton remarked, "Doubtless God could have made a better berry but doubtless God never did."

Although this regard for the lowly strawberry is widely shared, it is the apple *(Malus pumila)* that is the most broadly cultivated and best known of all fruits from the temperate zone that are eaten raw. This neither confirms nor denies the idea that was reached by Christians in the Middle Ages, identifying

Since new varieties of red currants (Ribes *hybrids) combine delicious fruits with immunity to pine blister rust, it is possible to raise them for jams and jellies. (Otto Croy)*

the apple as the fruit from the "tree in the middle" of the Garden of Eden, and the larynx bulging from a man's lean throat as "Adam's apple"—the fruit that stuck part way down! Apple trees apparently came originally from Asia Minor and perhaps southern Europe. They have been cultivated for more than two thousand years. In the 3rd century B.C., Cato listed seven different varieties of apple known to him. Caesar's armies introduced apple trees to Britain. By the time America was discovered, the number of horticultural types had reached the hundreds. The favorites were carried to the New World, and propagated by the famous Johnny Appleseed (Jonathan Chapman, 1775?–1847) and others, all the way to the Pacific coast. Washington state now produces the most apples, and North America accounts for about a fifth of the world production, amounting to nearly sixteen million tons (or 700 million bushels), counting apples destined for cider. Slightly more than half of the total comes from Central Europe, the Ukraine and the northern Caucasus. The remainder are important crops in Australia, New Zealand, Argentina, Chile, Japan, and Korea. In all of these areas the rather special living requirements of apples are met: at least one hundred days of frost-free growing season, with plenty of sunshine in late summer and early autumn to develop fruit color; at least 1200 hours per year of weather cooler than 45° Fahrenheit, but no prolonged exposure to 30° or more below zero.

An apple leaf has a fine-toothed edge, whereas that of a pear *(Pyrus communis,* originally from Eurasia) is wavy, and that of a quince *(Cydonia oblonga,* native to Central Asia), is smoothly curved. The golden-yellow fruit of a quince is unlike any pear or apple in that it is inedible raw. When cooked, it turns pinkish and, like apple, contains so much pectin that it forms firm, delicious jelly.

The same style of fruit on a diminutive scale is produced in great clusters on the mountain ash *(Sorbus americana)* of eastern North America, and the rowan tree *(S. aucuparia)* of Europe and northern Asia. *Aucuparia* means attractive to birds, which describes well the bite-sized "berries" whose indigestible seeds pass through and drop to start new trees as pioneers in any clearing.

THE GENEROUS LEGUMES
(Family Leguminosae)

Almost the only plants in the world that cooperate with the bacteria in the nodules on their roots and

Native to northern South America and Trinidad, the rain tree (Samanea saman) *has been introduced throughout the tropics for its shade, pink flowers, and valuable wood. (Lorus and Margery Milne)*

with insects that pollinate their attractive flowers are the members of this, the second-largest family in the vegetable kingdom. Most of them make notable contributions to the welfare of other plants near by, in the form of compounds containing nitrogen, formed by the nitrogen-fixing bacteria in the nodules. All of the legumes have a simple pistil with a single cavity, ripening to a characteristic pod with two symmetrical halves, such as is familiar in a pea pod or a peanut. With about thirteen thousand different species living in every kind of soil and, as aquatics, in every climate, the legumes are exceeded in variety only by members of the Family Compositae and in value to man only by the grass family.

In one section of the family, which is represented mostly by shrubs and trees in the tropics and subtropics, the flowers are small but grouped into dense heads which suggest balls of chenille. The stamens extend far beyond the short petals, and are walked over by all the myriad insects that come for nectar and pollen. The leaf blades are divided not just once but twice—into subleaflets (twice pinnately compound). Few members of this section are native to the United States, most notably the mesquite

Giants among the succulents of the orpine family are Aeonium canariense *from warm, arid slopes in the Canary Islands. Each rosette of thick leaves may be three feet across. (Lorus and Margery Milne)*

(Prosopis glandulosa), the screwbean *(P. pubescens)* and the cat's-claw, or tear-blanket *(Acacia greggii)* all in the arid Southwest. All three become small trees with hard wood and roots that reach far down to water, the mesquite to as much as fifty feet in depth on a tree less than twenty feet high. All provide good cover for desert animals, as well as food for insects, birds, mammals, and Indians. Cattle graze on the foliage, despite the spines which are modified stipules and project in pairs where each leaf is attached.

Nearly three-quarters of the world's six hundred kinds of *Acacia* live in the deserts and semiarid parts of Australia, where they are known as wattles from the use of their branches with mud ("wattle and daub") to build temporary sheepfolds, cattle barriers, and small houses. Golden wattle *(A. pycnantha)* is the national tree and flower of Australia, and mulga *(A. aneura)* the dominant shrub in the extensive arid scrubland known simply as the Mulga. In some of the Australian acacias, the leaflets are dropped almost as soon as they expand, and the green petioles expand a little to become narrow leaflike blades in

which photosynthesis continues while water is conserved in the face of chronic drought.

Tropical and subtropical Africa and India harbor most of the remaining kinds of acacia. They are the characteristic flat-topped thorn trees and thornscrub of the high plains where giraffes, other antelopes, zebras, rhinoceroses, and other spectacular animals have reached such astonishing abundance. African camel's-thorn *(A. giraffae),* becomes a small tree, whereas the sickle-lobe acacia *(A. drepanolobium)* reaches only shoulder-high, its branches studded with small spherical galls inhabited by tiny biting ants. These galls are a great favorite with baboons, which casually bite off each gall, munch it to get at the ants, and spit out the vegetable fragments.

The best grade of gum arabic, which is known also as gum acacia and is used in adhesives for postage stamps, envelopes and "stickers," comes from *A. senegal,* a small tree of both east and west tropical Africa. A poorer quality is obtained from *A. arabica,* which is almost the only tree left in many overpopulated parts of India. Another Indian acacia, known as the cutch *(A. catechu)* has long been the source of both tannins and a dye with which to give cloth an olive-drab or sandy color. Since the middle of the 19th century, this hue has been standard for military garb in many countries and known by its Urdu name of khaki.

Horticulturalists, who offer flower-laden branches of acacias in the middle of northern winter, often call them mimosas. Few members of *Mimosa* reach tree size. The majority of the 350 kinds are shrubs or vines or herbs. In Panama and other parts of tropical America we have played with the sensitive plant *(M. pudica)* in roadsides, where its pompons of pink flowers are more noticeable than the finely divided leaves. At the slightest touch, the leaflets quickly fold together. A greater shock causes each petiole to droop suddenly, as though wilted and

Right above: This member of the pea family, Calliandra surinamensis, *attracts pollinators to showy stamens rather than to colored petals. (Betty Allen) Right: Like the witch-hazels of eastern North America, this one from eastern Asia* (Hamamelis japonica) *produces delicately scented flowers in autumn. Far right: Acclaimed the most handsome of all Australian annual plants, the Sturt desert pea* (Clianthus formosus) *honors the name of a famous explorer. It grows in arid areas in all states on the continent. (Both by Conzett and Huber)*

ready to fall off. If undisturbed for ten minutes, the plant raises its leaves again and spreads its leaflets. It closes them also at night and in cold weather. Naturalists are always fascinated because the sensitive plant can be anesthetized with ether or chloroform, and then is unresponsive to touch.

The folding of leaflets in late afternoon and unfolding again before dawn is a common feature of leguminous plants. It is particularly spectacular in the rain tree *(Samanea saman)* of the American tropics. A handsome specimen tree of this kind is often shown to visitors on Queen's Park Savannah in the middle of Port-of-Spain on the island of Trinidad. Its low horizontal limbs extend out in all directions for a radius of about fifty feet. At midday no glint of sun penetrates its dense shade. Yet grass grows right up to the heavy trunk. On a cloudy day, as at night, the tree closes its leaflets and rain falls between them to the grassy turf below.

Almost the only large leguminous tree in the United States and Canada is the honey locust *(Gleditsia triacanthos)*, which grows to a height of 140 feet, and has its branches and sometimes its trunk armed with long sharp spines having prominent side spurs. Although it is native to the area from Quebec to Georgia, Texas, Kansas and Michigan, it has been planted in many other regions and grows well. Its flowers are small, growing in dense clusters suggesting pendant catkins from the branches that bore leaves the previous year. The five little petals are almost alike, and yet one is always at the top and slightly more conspicuous, giving the flower a bilateral symmetry. From the pistillate flower clusters, long brown pods mature and twist as they dry, dropping out their seeds.

Left above: From New England across America to Alaska and into eastern Asia, the briar rose (Rosa acicularis) has prickles along its canes and flower stalks that protect its solitary blossoms. (Steve McCutcheon) Far left: Khaki-brown enlargements on the thorny stems of the low-growing ant tree (Acacia drepanolobium) are hollow, and occupied by biting ants. Baboons in Tanzania and adjacent parts of East Africa often eat them, savoring the ants but spitting out the thorns. (Othmar Stemmler) Left: The golden-chain tree (Laburnum anagyroides) of southern Europe is widely admired for its pendant clusters of yellow flowers. Its seeds are highly poisonous, but its wood was once a favorite for fine cabinetwork in Scotland. (Hermann Eisenbeiss)

Hybrid lupines (Lupinus) *in many shades of purple, blue, pink, and white are raised for ornament in England and the eastern United States in light sandy soil. (J. Allan Cash)*

Bilateral symmetry is characteristic of the flowers in a whole section of the Family Leguminosae. It is found again in the blossoms on the small trees of redbud *(Cercis canadensis)* in eastern North America, and Judas-tree *(C. siliquastrum)* of Mediterranean countries, upon which Judas Iscariot is said to have hanged himself. This symmetry is a feature of the 450 kinds of senna *(Cassia)* in Australia, New Zealand, South Africa, and North America. Leaves of two species of *Cassia* are still imported as the base for a strong laxative which was introduced early in the Christian era by Arabian physicians. They knew this use for shrubs growing from Timbuktu in modern Mali, through the African Sudan all the way to the Punjab of India.

Larger flowers with the same symmetry and with attractive markings make the orchid-tree *(Bauhinia purpurea)* a favorite ornamental in warm parts of the world, such as southern Florida. It is native to India and Southeast Asia. Like the other two hundred kinds in this large genus, it has leaves shaped like the print of a deer's hoof—with a broad notch

At the 13,000-foot level on volcanic Mt. Pichincha, in the Andes northwest of Quito, Ecuador, a native lupine (Lupinus alopecuroides) produces handsome flowers. (E. Aubert de la Rue)

where a pointed tip might be expected. Since the leaf appears twinned, Linnaeus named the genus in honor of the brothers Gaspard and Jean Bauhin, whose work and writings in the early 17th century helped so much to make botany a respected science.

Most spectacular of the related tropical trees is the flamboyant (or royal poinciana, Delonix regia) of Madagascar, now planted widely in the tropics to provide shade and decoration when its clusters of orange-flame flowers open on all the high branches. A smaller version is seen in the prickly shrub known as peacock flower, or Barbados-pride (Caesalpinia pulcherrima), from the New World tropics. It is much more showy than the tree-sized sapanwood (C. sappan of India), lengths of whose trunk were in great demand during the Middle Ages as the source of a fiery red dye known as brazil (from the same word as the verb to braise, referring to glowing coals). When a related tree (C. brasiliensis) was discovered in the tropical forests of South America,

it gave its name to the entire country of Brazil. These were times when a new dye from any source had tremendous importance in trade. A black one, which found an immediate market for blackening hats in European markets, was obtained in Guatemala, British Honduras, and Yucatan, from another tree with symmetrical, five-petalled flowers: the logwood (Haematoxylon campechianum). The dye (hematoxylin) is still used in scientific laboratories.

No matter what living conditions they tolerate or what geographical addresses they occupy, trees that produce flowers with bilateral symmetry and leguminous pods are recognized as near kin. They include the palo verde (Cercidium floridum) of Mexico and the American Southwest, which lacks leaves altogether for most of the year, presenting only green trunk and branches to the dry air and sun. In the high dry country of Central Africa, the mopani-trees (Copaifera mopani) become the dominant vegetation and give character to the "mopani highlands," where thornscrub (acacias) are the chief lower vegetation. When struck by dry winds, these trees sometimes exude drops of resin; their name signifies copal-bearing. But a near-relative, the Zanzibar copal (Trachylobium verrucosum) provides the hardest resin of all, softer only than fossil amber. A few of these trees produce edible pods, as does the tamarind (Tamarindus indica of tropical Africa) and the carob (Ceratonia siliqua of the Mediterranean countries). The starchy pods of the carob are sometimes sold as St. Johns's-bread or locust pods, and may have been the food mentioned in the Bible as the "meat" of John the Baptist—"locusts and honey." The seeds from carob pods are suspected of being the original carats used in weighing precious jewels.

In the familiar flowers of the sweet pea (Lathyrus odoratus) is the general pattern that is repeated with minor variations in all of the most advanced members of the Family Leguminosae. Often this division of the Family is said to have "papilionaceous" flowers, from a fancied similarity in shape to the wings of a butterfly. The flower parts do show a bilateral symmetry, but any further comparison with the insect helps little. The top petal is the largest one (the "standard"), and flares upward or even curls back upon itself at each side, displaying its inner surface. The next two (the "wings") fit together like the shells of a clam, concealing between them the remaining two petals (which are narrow and joined along one edge to form the "keel"), as well as the ten stamens, and the central, elongated pistil. Most of the related flowers are like the pea in having the topmost stamen free from the others for its whole length, fitting into a narrow slot in an otherwise complete cylinder formed by fusion of the filaments of the other nine stamens. Plants with papilionaceous flowers have simple leaves, or singly compound ones that are usually pinnate.

The sweet pea itself came originally from Italy. Its fragrance and delicate pastel colors in a large flower excel most of the other hundred kinds in the genus, which is represented all over the North Temperate Zone, and in the mountains of both tropical Africa and South America. It bears relatively few flowers along each side stalk, unlike a lupine *(Lupinus)*, which raises an open, tall, conical cluster of many flowers at the top of each upright stem. Although the cultivated blue lupine *(L. hirsutus)* is native to southern Europe, most of the hundred different kinds are American plants. They include the beloved bluebonnet *(L. subcarnosus)* and others that transform dry, sandy fields into a sea of blue or purple flowers. Lupines are unusual legumes in having palmately, rather than pinnately compound leaves. Their name, which literally means "wolf flowers," came from the mistaken notion that their roots devour the soil, rather than improving it as they—and most other legumes—do.

Rosary pea *(Abrus precatorius),* a climbing vine native to Europe but now naturalized in much of the world's tropics and subtropics, is also known as Indian-licorice and crab's-eye. Its flat spiny-edged pods open as they dry to display brilliant red seeds, each with a black end. In India, they once were used as a standard of weight. In Florida and many warm countries they have been pierced and strung on necklaces as decorative beads. This is dangerous practice, for the seeds contain abrin—one of the most violent poisons known. A single seed, thoroughly chewed and swallowed, is enough to kill an adult person. Unbroken, the seed retains its toxic principle within its enamel-hard, glossy seed coat, and may pass through an animal's intestine without effect.

The sprawling, climbing plants of vetch *(Vicia, especially V. sativa* of Europe and *V. villosa* of Eurasia) have long been encouraged as pasture crops that could be grazed, or cut for hay, or plowed under to enrich the soil. The closely related broad bean *(V. faba),* along with the garden pea *(Pisum sativum)* and the lentil *(Lens culinaris)*—all from temperate Eurasia and the north coast of the Mediterranean—were the only major foods from legumes that people in the Old World enjoyed prior to the discovery of useful plants in America. For the most part, the broad beans, peas and lentils were dried and ground up to be made into soup or a porridge called pulse. So familiar were these seeds that "pea-sized" and "bean-sized" became common expressions, and the name *lens* for the flattened, circular seed of the lentil was transferred intact to the optical devices of polished glass whose shape was approximately the same.

Pulse was still a popular porridge when the Family Leguminosae received scientific recognition; it became known as the "pulse family." Later, because many people knew peas but not pulse, it was popularly renamed "the pea family," or its members referred to simply as legumes.

The New World contributed important members of the large genus *Phaseolus,* including the tropical lima bean *(P. limensis),* the Mexican scarlet-runner bean *(P. multiflora,* which has bright red flowers and red-and-black seeds), and the kidney bean *(P. vulgaris),* which the Incas were cultivating in South America when the Spaniards arrived. The kidney bean has been developed into horticultural varieties such as climbing "pole" beans, short-vined navy beans, white and yellow field beans, yellow-eyed marrow beans, and "pea" beans. Immature pods, in which the seeds have not yet ripened, are snap beans or string beans. Tropical Asia provided the cowpea, or black-eyed pea *(Vigna sinensis),* which is enjoyed by both people and domestic animals in the West Indies and the Southern States. Actually the cowpea is a type of bean, since in germinating it raises its seed-leaves (cotyledons) out of the ground, whereas garden peas do not. Soybeans *(Glycine soja),* which are used by people as food in Manchuria and Japan, have been adopted in other parts of the world as fodder for cattle, or as a "green manure" to be plowed under, enriching the soil.

Alfalfa *(Medicago sativa),* which has become one of the world's leading crops for hay, and the various kinds of clover are among the most valuable that are raised to feed cattle wherever the economy, the weather and the soil permit. More than three hundred different kinds of clover have been found in temperate and subtropical lands, but only about eight are regularly cultivated. Of these, red clover *(Trifolium pratense),* alsike *(T. hybridum),* white clover *(T. repens),* crimson clover *(T. incarnatum),* and sweet clover *(Melilotus officinalis)* are well known favorites whose tiny papilionaceous flowers attract bees. Their nectar makes some of the most delicious honey known.

In the Southern States, where the originally poor, sandy soils were depleted further by repeated crops of cotton, tobacco and corn, improvements are now being sought by planting legumes. The Japanese clover, or hoopkoop plant *(Lespedeza striata* and *L. japonica),* and the kudzu-vine *(Pueraria lobata)* hold the soil against erosion, enrich it with nitrogen-containing nutrients, and at the same time yield a limited amount of forage for cattle. Peanuts, which are known also as groundnuts and goobers *(Arachis hypogaea)* contribute only a little less to soil fertility, and produce a valuable crop from which commerce gains edible nuts, a salad oil, the basis for soaps, lubricants, and plastics, and a solid residue called cake which is one of the best stock foods. Peanuts originated in Brazil, were introduced into Portuguese African colonies, then to the rest of Africa, and returned to the New World in the hands of African slaves—principally to Virginia. The yellow flowers develop above ground in short spikes of one to three blossoms. Growth of the flower stalk thrusts the ripening ovaries into the loose soil, where pigs and people readily harvest them.

Leguminous plants with papilionaceous flowers have provided man with useful products for many centuries. Some of the wrappings around mummies in tombs at Thebes in Egypt, dating from about 3000 B.C., are dyed with indigo, which is a dark blue powder obtained by fermenting and oxidizing the juice from the leaves of the indigo plant *(Indigofera tinctoria),* which is native to the East Indies. Until the beginning of the 20th century, the cultivation of this shrubby plant and preparation of the dye (the "king of the dyestuffs") was a major industry in India. Introduction of cheap synthetic indigo from Germany at about this time ruined the market for the natural product, and brought about disastrous unemployment among Indians. The East Indies, particularly Borneo, provided the world also with the natural insecticide known as rotenone, from derris root *(Derris elliptica).* Roots of sweet-root *(Glycyrrhiza glabra)* from the north coast of the Mediterranean yield licorice. The plant itself produces blue flowers, and lemon-yellow roots many of which reach a diameter of about a quarter of an inch. If these are dried and chewed, they release a mild flavor, long known to soothe sore throats—partly by encouraging production of saliva. When the extract from these roots is concentrated commercially, the product is a black paste or semi-vitreous material ("stick licorice") which can be used to flavor cough lozenges, to conceal the disagreeable taste of some medicines, or to give a distinctive astringent sweetness to confectioneries.

The same style of papilionaceous flowers gives the golden color to shrubby gorse, or furze *(Ulex europaeus)* and Scotch broom *(Cytisus scoparius),* found native on uplands and dry hillsides over much of Europe and Great Britain. In pendant clusters of purple blossoms, the pattern is repeated on wisteria vines *(Wisteria,* mostly *W. sinensis* of China and *W. floribunda* of Japan). It is found again on large trees, such as the yellowwood *(Cladrastis lutea)* of the Southeastern States, grown now also in New England. Yellowwood bark is gray and almost as smooth as that of a beech. The tree's leaves suggest those of an ash, but arise singly (alternately) on the branches rather than in opposite pairs. The black locust *(Robinia pseudoacacia)* produces pendant clusters of similar flowers. Because it grows in height as rapidly as four feet a year and also sends up a multitude of new suckers from its horizontal roots, black locust makes a good anchor for shifting soil. The tree may become eighty feet tall, its slender twigs armed with pairs of sharp stiff thorns. During pioneer days, this tree of rocky high ground from Ontario to Georgia was much sought after as a source of wooden nails and pins which stayed in place because they neither swelled nor shrank with changes in humidity. Consequently the tree became the most widely distributed of North American hardwoods, both east of the Rocky Mountains and in the Great Basin states. A similar resistance to change in physical dimensions by absorption and release of water, and the ability to take a high polish, has given economic value to the rosewood *(Dalbergia nigra)* of Brazil and the blackwood *(D. melanoxylon)* of tropical Africa. They are the favorite materials for xylophone bars, and would be used more in pianos and other musical instruments if the supply were not so limited.

Right above: In North America, the mountain ash (Sorbus americana) *closely resembles the rowan trees of Europe and Asia. On both, the bright orange fruits ripen in heavy clusters late in summer. (Grant Heilman) Right: Despite its delicious fruit, the European red currant* (Ribes sativum) *is often outlawed near forests of white pine because it is the alternate host of the blister-rust fungus of pine. Far right: South Africa is home to almost three hundred different kinds of* Crassula *which store moisture in their succulent leaves. After a rainy period, they produce brilliant clusters of flowers in the sun. (Both by Lorus and Margery Milne)*

CHAPTER 12

The Bright Geraniums and Their Relatives

CUES: *If the dicot plant has the carpels in each flower united to form a single ovary that arises separately from the receptacle, the plant may well be a member of the Order Geraniales. Its stamens should be in two whorls or be united for a short distance by their filaments to form a tube. It may be a flax plant, a wood sorrel, a geranium, a creosote bush, an orange tree, a mahogany, or one of the spectacular euphorbias.*

All of these varied plants are grouped together because of a much less obvious feature in each flower—the way in which the ovules are attached within each carpel. On this evidence, more than a dozen families and nearly fifteen thousand species are believed to be related. Some are weeds, some trees, a few the source of fibers or drugs, and many are appreciated for their flowers or their foliage.

THE FLAX FAMILY (Linaceae)

The making of linen thread and textiles from the fibers of the flax plant is one of man's oldest techni-

Far left above: The crown-of-thorns (Euphorbia splendens) *of Madagascar has been introduced widely in warm countries as a prickly shrub for hedges in the hottest sun, and as a curious house plant. (Lorus and Margery Milne) Left above: The West Australian wax flower* (Eriostemon spicatus) *is among the loveliest of the flowering shrubs of the rue family (Rutaceae) in this genus, native only in Australia and Tasmania. (Eric Lindgren) Far left: The Barbadoscherry* (Malpighia glabra) *is a shrubby tree of the West Indies, now planted widely because its attractive fruits can be made into delicious jam or jelly. Left: The garden nasturtium* (Tropaeolum majus) *originated in warm, humid parts of Latin America. It is now cultivated world-wide for its gay flowers. (Both by Lorus and Margery Milne)*

cal achievements. Flax *(Linum usitatissimum),* native to Eurasia and the shores of the Mediterranean, may well have been cultivated as a crop five thousand years ago, for the mummified bodies found in the most ancient tombs of Egypt are wrapped in a linen cloth of fairly good quality. By the 18th century A.D., the use of flax fibers to make cloth for shirts, undergarments, tablecloths, bed sheets, face towels, and handkerchiefs became so general that the word "linens" now refers to any of these. Use of real linen decreased after the invention of the cotton gin in 1792 because cottons were cheaper. Today the cultivation of flax for fabrics is primarily a European custom, with the U.S.S.R. producing about three-fourths of the million tons a year that are grown in the Old World. Ireland and northern countries from Poland to France raise most of the remainder.

Flax is a slender, upright plant with few branches and narrow, almost grasslike leaves. At the tip of each branch it produces a delicate flower about three-quarters of an inch across, its violet-blue petals spreading from a cup-shaped throat. For fibers, the crop is harvested when about half of the seeds are ripe in their globular capsules, and the leaves have dropped from the lower two-thirds of the stem. Gathered in the field, the stems are tied in upright shocks to dry, then combed or beaten or threshed to free them of seeds, before letting decay bacteria separate the valuable fibers from the woody parts of the stems. In the U.S.S.R., the decay process is slow because the threshed stems are merely spread on the stubble until dew has supplied the water in which the bacteria work. Elsewhere a higher grade of fiber is obtained by soaking the stems in vats or ponds, hastening the "retting" process and making it more uniform. Either method yields flax fibers with a characteristic straw-yellow ("flaxen") color. Textiles made from long fibers are stronger wet than dry, and conduct heat away from the body more rapidly than do cottons or the newer synthetic materials. Short fibers are called "tow," and find use in the manufacture of Bible paper, cigarette papers, and the most time-resistant writing papers. So highly regarded are linen papers that cheaper types made from other fibers are often impressed with a "linen finish."

The seeds from flax capsules are "linseed," obtained most efficiently by raising varieties of flax other than those best for fibers. From a bushel of seed (fifty-six pounds), about 2½ gallons of valuable oil can be expressed, leaving behind a mucilaginous cake that is acceptable to cattle as food. Linseed oil,

115

particularly after being boiled, reacts readily with oxygen from the atmosphere to form a tough film that is waterproof. For this reason, it is added routinely to paints and varnishes, to printing inks, and putty. Coats of it on cloth are "oil cloth," while linseed oil mixed with cork dust or wood powder can be hardened on a cloth backing to make linoleum. Few of the roadside weeds in the world have such a distinguished history or such diverse uses. Yet flax grows in this humble site in most temperate areas and many parts of the tropics.

THE WOOD SORRELS (Family Oxalidaceae)

When St. Patrick's Day—the 17th of March—comes around each year, Irishmen all over the world seek a little sprig of shamrock to wear in honor of their ancestry. To make them happy and to get their money too, shamrocks by the thousand are shipped from Ireland to England, the Continent, and America. Almost all of these plants are the white wood sorrel (*Oxalis acetosella*), which is native to the North Temperate Zone on both sides of the Atlantic Ocean. It is a delicate plant of cool, moist, shady woodlands, bearing cloverlike leaves on long slender petioles and frail white flowers, which are often marked with pink or violet streaks.

No one knows for sure whether an *Oxalis* or one of the clovers is the true shamrock. According to Irish legend, St. Patrick chose the plant because its three leaflets symbolized for him the trinity of the Christian church. With the shamrock he is said to have driven the snakes of Ireland into the sea. But the familiar leaf might just as well have been on white clover (*Trifolium repens*) or suckling clover (*T. dubium*) or even black medic (*Medicago lupulina*), all of which can now be found either as weeds or escaped from cultivation in many parts of the world. *Oxalis* resembles the clovers in folding its leaflets as night approaches and spreading them again toward dawn. It will close them too if jostled roughly, but the reaction is much slower than that of the sensitive plant.

Children often discover that the bright yellow flowers of lady's-sorrel (*O. corniculata*) are fragrant, and that the juicy green stems and leaves have a pleasant sour flavor. This semicosmopolitan weed, which originated in Eurasia, turns up in most flower gardens. It too has the shamrock shape of leaf. The flavor is characteristic of most members of *Oxalis*, and is derived from oxalic acid. The Greek word *oxalis* signifies acid or sour.

In the high Andes of Peru and Colombia, the oca plant (*O. tuberosa*) is cultivated for its tuberous roots, which the mountain Indians harvest, mellow in the sun to get rid of the calcium oxalate, and then consume raw or boiled or dried and powdered to give body to soup. Only the potato, which is native to the same areas, outranks the oca as a source of starchy food for these people.

THE BRIGHT GERANIUMS
(Family Geraniaceae)

About 600 of the 850 species in this family are known as geraniums, although they are about equally divided between the genera *Geranium* and *Pelargonium*. In all members of the family, the ovary is deeply lobed, and five conspicuous glands alternate with the five petals where they are attached to the disk-shaped receptacle. In *Geranium* the flowers are radially symmetrical, but those of *Pelargonium* show bilateral symmetry. After the petals drop, the ripening ovary elongates, still bearing its slender cluster of five styles like a single point at the tip. In this fruit and the cuplike green calyx that closes around its base, Europeans have seen a resemblance to the diminutive heads of birds rising from the plant. The calyx represents the head, the ovary and styles the beak. *Geranium* is cranesbill, and another common genus (*Erodium*) storksbill. Many species have spicy, fragrant foliage that is lobed or actually divided into leaflets in a palmate pattern.

Wild geranium (*G. maculatum*) is a favorite wild-flower of late spring in the eastern part of North America, north of Florida. Herb Robert (*G. Robertianum*) is a smaller, almost cosmopolitan edition of the wild geranium, whose magenta flowers decorate rocky woodlands, shady ravines and even gravelly shores in Eurasia, North America, and North Africa. By following in the footsteps of Carl von Linné, the great Swedish botanist, to the spectacular gravel barrens of "Neptune's fields" on the Baltic island of Öland, we found herb Robert sprawling alone among the coarsest limestone pebbles thrown by storms high on the northwest shore.

The well-known "geraniums" that grow in tin cans on windowsills or in hanging baskets and window-boxes, brightening the buildings of Switzerland and big-city slums alike, are horticultural varieties bred from several species of *Pelargonium* that are native to the Cape of Good Hope in South Africa. All members of this genus differ from those of *Geranium* in having the upper two petals unlike the others—larger, smaller, or with different markings —and the sepal behind these two prolonged into a hollow spur that is joined for its whole length to the flower stalk. *Geranium* and *Pelargonium* can be distinguished merely by cutting through the flower stalk immediately behind the flower, for in *Geranium* there is no hollow spur from the one sepal whereas in *Pelargonium* the cavity of it shows in the cut flower stalk.

THE PUNGENT NASTURTIUMS
(Family Tropaeolaceae)

Until the Spaniards explored Latin America, no one in the Old World knew of the existence of nasturtiums. All of the eighty species are natives of America, from Chile to Mexico, and belong to the sole genus, *Tropaeolum*. The bright orange or yellow flowers and pungent circular leaves of the garden nasturtium *(T. majus)* and the canary-bird vine *(T. peregrinum)* have become familiar in gardens all over the world. They grow into luxurious carpets under the sea mists of Britain, with a continuous display of flowers almost hiding the leaves. Everywhere people discover the pleasing "hot," peppery flavor of nasturtium juice, by chewing the leaves or their stalks. Some gather the flower buds or the seeds to put in salads and pickles, providing a spicy tang slightly reminiscent of fresh water cress. Somehow this similarity led the Scottish botanist Robert Brown into giving the name *Nasturtium* to water cress. *Nasturtium* comes from the Latin for "nose-twisting," in reference to the pungent odor, and applies far better to the familiar nasturtiums than to water cress. These names have scarcely penetrated the high Andes, where the Indians continue as they have since Inca times in cultivating the sprawling vine they call anu *(T. tuberosum)* for the evil-smelling tubers on its roots. The odor, which is disagreeable but not nose-twisting, vanishes when the tubers (called *cubios*) are boiled to make their starch more digestible. At the time of the Spanish conquest, cubios competed with oca and potatoes as human food in the area from which all three originated.

THE COCA FAMILY (Erythroxylaceae)

When the Spanish conquistadores reached the South American regions that are now Bolivia and Peru, they found the native Indians chewing dried leaves with powdered lime—particularly in the middle of

Yellow flowers and red fruits adorn the vertical ribs on this cactus-like Euphorbia canariensis, *near Lake Bine-el-Quidane, Morocco, which makes dense stands on arid lands in northwest Africa. (Weldon King)*

the day while out cultivating their precipitous fields, or while walking for long, hard miles to market and back. The leaves were from the coca plant *(Erythroxylum coca),* which took on worldwide commercial importance after 1884 when a Viennese chemist discovered that cocaine—an alkaloid extractable from the leaves—could be used for local anesthesia. Cocaine readily penetrates mucous membranes, such as the gums, and blocks the sense of pain even as far into the tissues as the nerves serving a tooth upon which dental work is being done. Wild plants in western South America proved insufficient to supply the immediate demand for cocaine, and plantations of the coca shrub were set out in the East Indies, particularly in Java. Within twenty years, however, the chemical structure of cocaine $(C_{17}H_{21}O_4N)$ was worked out and a substitute for it found in synthetic procaine ("Novocaine"), which had the advantage of being non-habitforming. Pure white crystalline cocaine, known as "snow" to narcotics addicts, is now removed from coca leaves to produce a "de-alkaloidized" form, much of which goes into "cola" flavorings.

In the Andes, distances are still measured by the Indians in "cocadas," rather than in kilometers or miles. A cocada is the distance an Indian can trudge with a load while chewing one cud of coca leaves. With their juices in his stomach, he is almost immune to hunger, thirst, and the weight of the burden on his back. His preference is for symmetrical oval leaves that have been hand-picked from the six-foot plant at the stage when they break upon being bent. The green leaves are spread on coarse woolen cloths in layers, cured and dried at the same time in special sheds or in mist-filtered sunlight. The best ones are dry enough to keep indefinitely if protected from moisture. They show no curling, and are dark green above, gray-green below. Their odor is similar to that of tea leaves, but in the mouth they produce a feeling of warmth combined with a pleasant pungency. The flowers of the coca plant are small, borne in clusters on short stalks. Each blossom is regular, with five green sepals, five ivory-colored petals, ten stamens with heart-shaped anthers, and a pistil in which three or four carpels are joined together. The seeds ripen in small red berries, also in clusters among the thin green leaves.

LIGNUM VITAE AND ITS KIN
(Family Zygophyllaceae)

The national flower of Jamaica is the handsome blue one that appears on the lignum vitae tree *(Guaiacum officinale)* which, like its close relative *G. sanctum* in the West Indies and south Florida, produces some of the hardest and heaviest of commercial woods. Most of this greenish-brown wood will sink in water, having a specific gravity ranging between 0.95 and 1.25. Fragrant resins in the wood add to its inherent strength and tenacity a self-lubricating quality that make the wood especially valuable for bearings to operate under water. Dried, the wood is cut into dry bearings, pulley blocks, rollers, cogs, mallets, bowling balls, and furniture. Tear-shaped drops of gum guaiacum can be collected from the bark of the tree, and these have found use in the treatment of arthritic diseases, including gout. Solutions of the gum are oxidized readily by a number of agents, including blood, and change color abruptly. For this reason, they have found use in distinguishing blood stains from some other chemical compounds with a similar appearance.

The sapwood of lignum vitae contains a high concentration of saponins, as well as resin, volatile oil, and several organic acids. A decoction of the wood removes most of the saponins, which are moderately effective in treatment of syphilis. This therapeutic use was learned from West Indians on the island of Hispaniola in 1514 by the Spanish explorer Fernandez de Oviedo. He spread the news in Europe, where an epidemic of syphilis (known then as "morbus gallicus" or "malum francicum") had been raging ever since 1493. For a while a pound of lignum vitae sold for seven gold crowns, among the most expensive of remedies. Use of the decoction for this purpose continued until 1909, when Paul Ehrlich introduced arsphenamine ("Salvarsan" or "606") as a much more effective drug.

A close relative of lignum vitae grows on the dry savannas of Africa. It is the bito tree *(Balanites aegyptiaca)*, a scrubby thornwood whose irregular branches can be cut for fuel or to build lion-proof fences around herds of domestic livestock. The bark of the bito yields a fish poison, while its fruits (which resemble acorn barnacles so closely as to have led to the generic name, meaning barnacle-like) contain seeds with a medicinal oil known as zachun, much prized by the Arabs.

Often the Zygophyllaceae is called the "caltrop family," because so many people in Europe are familiar with caltrops—either the plant *(Tribulus terrestris)* or the four-pointed products of the blacksmith's art that once were used to halt charges of cavalry. No matter which way an iron caltrop fell, it stood on three of its sharp points and raised the fourth directly upward—ready to stab into the foot of any horse or man who stepped on it. Today the caltrop plant is still known by its old name in its native lands—Eurasia, from Tibet to the Mediterranean shores. But in other countries to which it has spread as a weed, it is more often known as puncture weed, and poses a real threat to bicycle tires or worn tires on automobiles. The spines that are so formidable are like metal caltrops, too, to bare feet. They develop on the cluster of ripening carpels from the ovary of each pale yellow flower.

The leaves of the sprawling caltrop plant, like those of the bito tree and the lignum vitae, are pinnately compound, with well-developed stipules where the petiole joins the stem. In some other genera of the family, the leaflets seem reduced to just two at the end of the petiole. This is true of the bean capers (species of *Zygophyllum*) and of the creosote-bush *(Larrea tridentata)* which is so important in the southwestern United States because it binds together the drifting sand. *Zygophyllum* consists of succulents on deserts and steppes of the Old World. In Asia Minor, the Arabs pickle the buds of *Z. fabago* and use them to give flavor in sauces and stews. They grind up the large aromatic seeds of *Z. coccineum* to take the place of black pepper. All of these plants are highly adapted to life under conditions of extreme aridity, and seem to rely upon a strong odor from their leathery leaves to repel hungry animals. Creosote bush has been found to survive when the water content of its stems and foliage has decreased to one unit for every two of dry weight. Most other plants die as soon as their water content falls to twice to twelve times this much.

THE CITRUS FAMILY (Rutaceae)

Eight of the ten species in the genus *Citrus* produce some of the world's most important fruits—the citrus fruits, which are so fine a source of vitamin C. They include the sweet orange *(C. sinensis)* of Indo-China and China, the sour orange (or Seville orange or bigarade, *C. aurantiacum)* and lemon *(C. limon)* of Southeast Asia, the Mandarin orange (or tangerine, *C. reticulata)* of Southeast Asia and the Philippines, the lime *(C. aurantifolia)* of the East Indies, the citron *(C. medica)* of India, Indonesia and China, the grapefruit *(C. paradisi)* and the tree that may have been its ancestor—the pummelo (or shaddock, *C. grandis)* of the East Indies and Southeast Asia. The first known grapefruit tree appeared in the West Indies, and may have sprung from an unrecognized hybrid seed dropped by other members of the genus *Citrus* already under cultivation there. Only the tangelo is a known hybrid (of *C. paradisi* × *C. reticulata)* that has reached commercial importance; it was developed in 1897 by W. T. Swingle, working in the Plant Introduction Laboratory of the U. S. Department of Agriculture in southern Florida. Most of the *Citrus* species have been diversified by horticultural methods into a vast variety of horticultural strains, none of which breed true. They are propagated just as named varieties of all other kinds of plants are, to minimize the chance of losing their distinctive features.

A hazard in lime fruits goes unmentioned in most books, but will always remain in our minds. We learned about it in the first fortnight of our initiation to the tropics, on the island of Barro Colorado in the middle of Gatun Lake, Panama Canal Zone. Unaccustomed to such continuous humidity and heat, with no electric refrigerator full of cool drinks—or even ice cubes to put in the warm drinking water, we quickly noted that a block of ice was brought in twice a week and that the little lime trees growing on the cleared hillside above the landing were stripped of their ripe fruit by the men who brought the ice. Before the next boatload of supplies was due, we gathered a few dozen limes ourselves, and gaily squeezed them into a tall pitcher of water when we heard the new ice cake go into the primitive refrigerator. We chipped ice and delighted in our beverage—the first really cold thing in ten days of steady heat. By the next

day the ice was gone, and we were left again to the hot sun or the shade of the rain forest all around. Then came the scare, with no realization that we had brought it on ourselves. Our skin turned dark brown in great patches, first one hand, then both, then up our arms in broad streaks to the elbows. We took the next boat to the mainland and hurried to the Dermatology Department of the Gorgas Memorial Hospital. What horrible disease had we contracted? The specialist just laughed at us. Diagnosis: photodermatitis from lime juice and then tropical sunlight. He couldn't do a thing to help, except to ease our minds. It would vanish as rapidly as the dead cells on the surface of the skin rubbed off at their normal rate. He told us of a girl who had rushed to the hospital earlier in the week from a remote part of Panama, sure that she had leprosy or something worse. Upon questioning she admitted having washed her hair and then rinsed it in lime juice, which was the *limon* the Spanish people had given her when she asked for lemon. She had taken a brief sunbath, wearing only her bathing suit. And now her face, neck, arms, midriff, and even patches on her legs had turned a chocolate brown! Everywhere that lime juice had run or splashed and then the sun had reached showed the same photodermatitis we had encountered.

No comparable side effects await the many millions of people in the East who make daily use of leaves from the Asiatic shrub *Murraya koenigii.* Dried, ground up, and mixed with a little turmeric powder, the leaves provide the favorite flavoring for rice dishes known as curries. When the British took over the governing of the subcontinent of India, they became familiar with the shrub, which belongs to a small genus of woody plants native to tropical Asia and Australia. They called the shrub itself the curry bush, and its leaves curry leaves. Local users, however, continued to refer to the plant by names showing no uniformity from district to district, dialect by dialect, so that it has never had just one common name to match the British term or the scientific genus and species.

Few of the other 1300 species in the citrus family have found importance for so many people. Many of them are trees whose hard wood is used for inlay work on fancy furniture. East Indian satinwood *(Chloroxylon swietenia)* from Indonesia is greenish, whereas West Indian satinwood *(Zanthoxylum flavum)* is yellow and a close relative of prickly ash (or toothache tree, *Z. americanum)* of eastern North America. From *Cusparia febrifuga* in the rain forests

of northern South America comes cusparia bark, known also as Angostura bark (from the old Spanish name for the Venezuelan city of Ciudad Bolivar, on the narrows of the Orinoco River, which was a supply center for many years). Extracts of cusparia bark contain bitter alkaloids that reduce the fever of malaria, or give a distinctive flavor ("Angostura bitters") to beverages. The alkaloid pilocarpine, used medicinally to promote salivation and urination, comes from *Pilocarpus perinatifolius,* a characteristic tree of the rain forests in southern Brazil. But the most spectacular member of the citrus family may well be the "gas plant" *(Dictamnus albus)* of western Asia and adjacent arid areas in southern Europe. On hot calm evenings so much volatile, inflammable oil evaporates from the leaves of this shrub that the fumes can be ignited. It may well be the bush Moses met in Exodus 3, and is often called "Moses' burning bush" or candle-plant.

THE QUASSIA FAMILY (Simaroubaceae)

Just as pinworm is the commonest roundworm parasite of children in civilized countries, so too the vermifuge known as quassia is the most efficient cure. Most people in Europe, North America, and centers of culture elsewhere have encountered this extract, at least at the age when they were most subject to pinworm. The medicine is obtained from the bark of tropical American trees, and its name honors Graman Quassi of Surinam, a Negro who made known about 1730 the effectiveness of the medication he knew locally. Linnaeus named the tree *Quassia amara*. Later plant explorers found it growing wild from Panama through the Guianas into northern Brazil. After 1809, however, quassia extract came more and more from a related West Indian tree *(Picrasma excelsa),* which grows to a height of sixty feet on Jamaica and St. Vincent. Known there as bitterwood or bitterash, it is cut into logs several feet long and as much as a foot in diameter, for shipment to Europe and America. For many years it was customary to turn out wooden

Left above: Water snowflakes (or floating hearts, Nymphoides *species) are members of the gentian family, although they grow in ponds like waterlilies. (E. Javorsky) Left: Wood sorrels* (Oxalis *species) of several kinds produce leaves divided like those of clover, but with a pleasant sour flavor. (John Shannon: National Audubon)*

cups from Jamaican quassia wood and sell them in pharmacies; they were filled with water or some tonic, and let stand for a few minutes until the bitter flavor of the wood was imparted. Chips of the wood are now extracted to yield the active principle (quassin). To a limited extent, quassia extract has been used also as a substitute for hops in the making of beer.

The more widespread member of the quassia family is the tree-of-heaven *(Ailanthus altissima,* now famous in the United States as "the tree that grows in Brooklyn") from Asia and Australia. Its names refer to the high altitudes at which it grows in its native lands. Today it thrives in cities around the world as an ornamental, because it grows quickly and survives despite poor soil, smoke and smog, dogs, and children with an urge to climb. Its compound leaves are twelve to twenty-five inches long, each with eleven to twenty-five leaflets, resembling those of staghorn sumac, but with no sawtoothing along the edges and no fuzz of hairs on the petioles and younger branches. As in all members of the family, the staminate flowers are on some trees, the pistillate ones on others. Since the former are evil-smelling, it is usual to find only pistillate *Ailanthus* planted. Their individual flowers are an inconspicuous green or greenish yellow and, if pollinated, produce an abundance of winged seeds as much as two inches in length, hanging in large terminal clusters on the branches.

THE INCENSE-TREE FAMILY (Burseraceae)

These too are shrubs and small trees bearing either staminate or pistillate flowers. About six hundred different species are known in tropical and subtropical areas of Africa, Asia and America. All of them have deciduous leaves and so many resin ducts in the bark that any bruise leads to formation of tear-shaped drops of aromatic gums, balsams and resins. In the Near East and Egypt, people have long known the value of these resins in salves and medicines (including vermifuges), and enjoyed their fragrance in perfumes and various kinds of incense. It was with a shipment of these materials that a caravan of Ishmaelites came riding on their camels to the place where Joseph's jealous brothers were plotting ways to get rid of him (Genesis 37). They were traveling from Gilead (now Jordan) to Egypt with "spicery and balm and myrrh." Balm of Gilead comes from a small tree *(Commiphora opobalsamum)* of Arabia, and is still used in many Moham-

The seeds of Ricinus communis, *of tropical Africa, mature in capsules and can then be freed of their valuable product, castor oil. The seed coats are poisonous. (John Gerard: National Audubon)*

medan households in preparing a fragrant unguent to rub on the skin (balm of Mecca). True myrrh is obtained from another shrubby tree *(C. abyssinica),* and today comes in small quantities from Somaliland. Under another name (stacte, from the Greek *staktos* meaning oozing in drops), myrrh is included in the official recipe for incense to be used in Hebrew tabernacles (Exodus 30): "Take unto thee sweet spices, stacte, and onycha[1], and galbanum[1]; these sweet spices with pure frankincense; of each shall there be a like weight: And thou shalt make of it a perfume, a confection after the art of the apothecary, tempered together, pure and holy." Frankincense can be collected from any of several members of the genus *Boswellia,* especially *B. carteri.* It was used by the ancient Egyptians in medicine, fumigation, and embalming of the dead. Always a rare and treasured substance, it was suitable (along with myrrh) as a gift for the Magi to bring the Christ child.

The shrubs and trees from which these gums exude are fairly common, even characteristic of the

[1] Onycha was a powder made from the horny operculum of a sea snail, such as a *Strombus;* galbanum was a yellowish-brown resin from certain shrubs *(Ferula)* related to carrots.

121

The citron (Citrus medica) *of the Far East has been cultivated in warm climates, particularly in Italy. Its rind is thick, fragrant and flavorful, and is often candied. (U.S.D.A.)*

savannas in East Africa and western Asia. The only reason known for the prolonged rarity of all of the resins extracted from them in commerce is the uniform lack of interest shown by people in these areas for giving any care to native plants that did not provide food. Only occasionally did anyone take the trouble to search out *Commiphora* or *Boswellia* trees, to cut or bruise the bark, and then return in a few months to gather the drops of hardened resin. Perhaps, on the return trip, the trees were too often gone—cut by someone else for fuel. No orchards of them apparently were ever planted.

In the Far East, by contrast, valuable resins have been harvested regularly from other members of the incense-tree family, particularly the black dammar tree *(Canarium strictum)* of western India and the Java almond *(C. luzonicum,* whose edible fruits are the source of roasted pili nuts) of the East Indies and Philippines. These resins are referred to as Malabar elemi and Manila elemi, respectively, the word elemi indicating a gum useful in medicine and in making varnishes. With inexpensive labor, com-

parable results might be obtained with the gommier tree *(Bursera gummifera)* of Central America and Mexico from which Mexican elemi has been gathered sporadically under the local names of cachibou and chibou.

THE MAHOGANY FAMILY *(Meliaceae)*

When the Spanish conquerors asked the Arawak Indians the name of the West Indian tree from which such fine-grained, easily polished hard wood came, the answer supposedly sounded like mahogany. This tree of Hispaniola, Cuba, Jamaica, southern Florida and the Bahamas quickly became the source of the foremost cabinet wood in the world, under the name *Swietenia mahagoni,* which had a similar sound and honored the 18th-century Dutch botanist Gerhard L. B. van Swieten. Later, preference was shown for the mahogany wood from *S. macrophylla* ("Honduran mahogany") which grows from Mexico to Venezuela and the upper Amazon valleys as far south as Peru. When freshly cut, the wood is often pinkish, but it dries to a deep red-brown or a brownish yellow that can be stained slightly to develop the popular color.

African mahogany is usually from a related tree *(Khaya senegalensis),* but other "mahoganies" are substitutes from quite different sources.[1] True mahogany trees have pinnately compound leaves, of which the paired, pointed leaflets are shiny and distinctly asymmetric. Like other members of their family they lack resin, and bear clusters of small greenish-yellow flowers whose stamens are united into one or two groups by their filaments.

Almost as well known over the world as mahogany is "cigar-box cedar" or Spanish cedar, from the West Indian tree *Cedrela odorata.* Although its aromatic wood is pleasant to human noses, and blends well with the tobacco odor of cigars, it seems to repel a great many insects—including those that are ready to tunnel in tobacco products and ruin their market value.

Still another member of this family has been introduced so widely into warm temperate regions that it is familiar to many people: the chinaberry tree *(Melia azedarach),* which came originally from southern Asia and northern Australia. Known also as pride of India, beadtree, and azedarach (an aboriginal

[1] In America today, the term "Philippine mahogany" is applied indiscriminately to wood from many different trees; commonest of these substitutes is *Toona calantas,* known also as Philippine cedar and used for cigar boxes as well as interior finishes; others are trees belonging to the families Leguminosae and Dipterocarpaceae.

122

name), it has escaped from cultivation and is now naturalized in Europe and America. If left to grow, it attains a height of thirty-five feet, producing clusters of pale blue flowers in spring, followed by fragrant yellow globular fruits with an astringent bitter pulp over a stony central pit.

THE KALEIDOSCOPIC SPURGES
(Family Euphorbiaceae)

Few families of plants show among their members so much variety as this one, whose 7300 different species comprise almost half of the whole Order Geraniales. Some of the spurge family float on water, others are clinging vines, or low herbs, or cactuslike succulents in African deserts, or tall trees of the tropical rain forest. Many, but not all, have a milky latex in which float distinctive corpuscles of almost as many forms as there are species possessing them. Some have leaves reduced to inconspicuous scales, while others (including the Para rubber tree) have broad palmately compound leaves. Most lack petals altogether, whereas a few (such as the tung nut tree and candlenut) possess large showy petals. All, however, show a complete separation of staminate from pistillate flowers. The staminates may be reduced to a single stamen with anther and filament atop a short stalk, in a cluster close to the pistillate flowers. Or they may be in separate clusters on the same plant, or on different plants. As in a kaleidoscope, every combination of features seems to have been tried and perfected among members of Euphorbiaceae. The name spurge is from the purgative use once accorded a resin derived from *Euphorbia resinifera* of North Africa, and *Euphorbia* honors Euphorbus, who was physician to King Juba of Numidia (now part of Algeria).

Of the vast genus *Euphorbia,* with about 1600 species of latex-bearing plants in warm temperate and tropical regions, the most widely known member is almost certainly the poinsettia *(E. pulcherrima)* of Mexico and Central America. It was introduced to the world via the United States in 1828 by Joel R. Poinsett of Charleston, South Carolina, who was then United States Minister to Mexico. On close inspection, the flowers of a poinsettia reveal their truly strange nature. The bright red (or greenish-white) "petals" are actually just leaves in the vicinity of the flower clusters, serving to attract insects as pollinators. These substitutes for petals draw attention to a number of flower clusters, each of which may be mistaken for a single flower. Less than a half inch across, each cluster is on a separate short stem and almost enclosed by green or yellow bracts that properly are called an involucre. They protect a single short pedicel bearing a rudimentary three-lobed calyx and a pistil, and four or five more pedicels each with a single short stamen. The pistil has a three-lobed ovary and three styles, each cleft at the tip. All of these parts are small, scarcely more conspicuous than the large nectar-producing glands which reward pollinators.

This strange style of flower cluster, with minor modifications, is found in all members of *Euphorbia.* They include a number of plants that have drawn attention to themselves: the roadside weed known as painted-leaf (or fire-on-the-mountain, *E. heterophylla)* from Virginia to Florida and Arizona to South Dakota, for the splash of orange-red across the petiole end of leaves near its clusters of flowers; the crown-of-thorns *(E. splendens)* of Madagascar, which extends from the tips of its spiny, woody branches a succession of slender stems bearing two or four scarlet "flowers," each a diminutive cluster; the tree *Euphorbias,* such as *E. abyssinica,* whose spine-fringed branching columns possess the same accordionlike ability to expand with stored water and to shrivel as it is used up or lost as is seen in organ-pipe cactus clumps on similar arid highlands —the cactus in America, the tree *Euphorbias* in East Africa; and the poison tree *(E. virosa)* of South Africa, whose simple broad leaves and easily bruised bark exude a latex that causes painful blisters to form on human skin and whose fruits are a deadly poison.

In the West Indies, children and visitors must be taught to avoid touching the manchineel tree *(Hippomane mancinella),* which provides pleasant shade beside many a sea beach. The fruits which fall beneath the tree resemble green apples but are extremely toxic. Even the water that drips from the foliage after a rain or a heavy dew carries with it enough poison from latex in the leaves and stems to blister the skin of people on whom it falls.

The seeds of the castor-oil plant *(Ricinus communis)* are similarly dangerous, containing a substance (ricin) that is among the most toxic compounds known. It is absorbed readily through the intestinal wall; by injection, it can cause death in doses as small as 0.000,000,01 per cent of an animal's weight. Fortunately it is insoluble in oil, and absent from castor oil, which used to be extracted for its purgative power and is now employed widely in industry as a lubricant. Castor-oil plants have been introduced from tropical Africa into most parts of the world where the frost-free growing season is long enough for the prickly red fruits to mature. The plants themselves grow rapidly to a height of fifteen to twenty feet, with handsome palmately lobed green leaves one to three feet across. The generic name is intended to show the similarity in form of the purple-streaked seeds to a fully gorged European tick *(Ixodes ricinus).* The plant itself is known also as palma christi.

A different poison (hydrocyanic acid) is abundant in the outer "skin" of potatolike tubers on the roots of cassava (or manioc or yuca, *Manihot esculenta).* Yet primitive people have found methods for preparing the tubers that effectively get rid of the poison. They may not know why each step in the traditional method is taken, but they are well aware of the disastrous consequences from any variation in ritual. In consequence, wherever cassava grows in tropical lands, it is second only to sweet potatoes as a root crop. The plant is native to tropical South and Central America, but it is now cultivated extensively in tropical West Africa and from Malaya throughout the East Indies. Its slender woody stems, growing up to nine feet high, bear large long-stalked leaves whose blade is deeply divided into three to seven long narrow lobes. The rosette of fleshy tapering roots includes tubers as much as three feet long and nine inches in diameter. These are dug up, peeled to get rid of most of the poison, shredded and soaked in water to extract still more of the acid, and then wrung out almost dry before being cooked in fresh water. The starch forms small lumps that are known as tapioca. They can be eaten immediately, or dried for export. The starch can also be ground to make a flour used in making cassava bread and cakes, often met in tropical America as "Brazilian arrowroot." All of these methods have come down from antiquity in the heritage of the people who first settled in well-watered parts of Central America. Only in the last century has science caught up, and given a satisfying reason for the procedures that have been handed down for so many human generations.

A tree-sized species of *Manihot (M. glaziovii)* of Brazil yields a latex that can be processed into Ceara rubber. The most valuable rubber, however, comes from the latex of various species of *Hevea,* especially *H. brasiliensis* and *H. benthamiana,* both native to the Amazon Valley. They are tall trees found in the rain forest, usually remote from one another and attaining a height of one hundred feet, a trunk diameter at shoulder height of nearly four feet. The high price of raw rubber from these scattered trees led in the 19th century to the introduction of *Hevea brasiliensis* to Ceylon, then Malaya and the East Indies, to be grown in plantations wherever the temperature ranged from 70° to 90° F and the rainfall amounted to about one hundred inches distributed rather uniformly throughout the year. Wild rubber trees now contribute a minor fraction of the world supply. Plantation trees are often tailor-made to match environmental conditions, perhaps with a root system of one *Hevea* chosen in relation to soil type, a trunk portion ("panel") of a different species with a particularly high yield of fine latex, and a leafy top of still another kind—one showing resistance to fungus diseases and insects. In all, however, a spiral cut through the bark is made daily with a special tool, stimulating an outflow of milky latex which runs down into a collecting cup. The latex contains thirty to forty per cent of small solid globules, which can be caused to unite (coagulate) and float as a soft, doughy mass. On drying, the white coagulum becomes firm, elastic crude rubber. Commercially valuable species and genetic strains of *Hevea* not only yield latex generously but also a crude rubber containing more than ninety per cent of the principal goal substance—caoutchouc. During the 16th to 18th centuries, this material found use chiefly in rubbing out marks made with lead pencils. Now it gives elastic and insulating qualities to a great variety of rubber products. A similar, if not identical substance can be obtained in smaller amounts from many other kinds of plants, including the unrelated, old-fashioned "indiarubber tree" (a fig, *Ficus elastica).*

The foliage of *Hevea* is graceful, each leaf with a long slender petiole and three radiating leaflets. The foliage of *Croton,* of which six hundred species inhabit the tropics and subtropics in both the Old World and the New, is showy although the individual leaves are simple; they are often colorful, or spotted and banded in reds, yellows and browns, or made velvety by a dense covering of star-shaped hairs and overlapping silvery scales. Many crotons are grown for their decorative interest. *C. cascarilla* of the Bahamas and southern Florida yields a thin bark, which has been used for making incense, tonics, and laxatives. Croton oil, formerly used in medicine as one of the strongest purgatives known, comes from seeds of *C. tiglium,* a shrub of tropical Asia. Native people in warm countries sometimes chew a seed or two from a croton, and swallow the juice to get quick laxative action. Perhaps they build up an immunity to the poison, for two soldiers who tried this home remedy recently in Hawaii died of the experiment despite anything physicians could do to help.

CHAPTER 13

From the Boxwoods to the Treacherous Akee

CUES: *If the dicot plant has flowers with three to five sepals and its petals (if any) separate, and if its stamens are opposite the sepals (alternating with whatever petals are present), and if the two to ten carpels of the pistil are united to form a superior ovary, it is likely to belong to Order Sapindales. It may be a boxwood (without petals), a cashew or a sumac (with all petals alike and regularly arranged), a buckeye or a touch-me-not (with petals of unlike sizes and shapes).*

More than 3500 different kinds of plants from all over the world meet the requirements for membership in this Order. They differ from members of Order Geraniales in the way their ovules are supported inside the ovary. Among them are the mango, called the "queen of tropical fruits"; the poison ivies, poison oaks, and tropical poisonwoods of the New World; the glorious maples; and the strange litchi nuts that seem to embody all of the mystery of the Orient.

THE BOXWOODS (Family Buxaceae)

In the writings of Virgil, Ovid, and Pliny the Elder —all about the beginning of the Christian Era— there is frequent mention of boxwood being used in making musical instruments and various decorative objects turned on the crude wood lathes of the day.

More recently, the same wood has been used for inlaying, for small wooden boxes such as jewel chests, for rulers and mathematical instruments, small carvings, and the special blocks into which wood engravings are cut. The dense, uniform wood of a delicate yellow color is taken mostly from two of the twenty different kinds of boxwood: Turkey boxwood *(Buxus balearica),* which attains a height of eighty feet on the mainland of Asia Minor, the islands of the eastern Mediterranean, and around the shores of the Black Sea; and English box *(B. sempervirens),* which seems to have grown naturally all the way from Scotland across the southern part of Europe, through Iran to the slopes of the western Himalayas. Both trees grow very slowly. English box attains a height of only about sixteen feet; its deep green, glossy leaves are about a third as large as those of Turkey boxwood. In all boxwoods the foliage is leathery, evergreen, and hence attractive for decorative plantings and hedges. English box and a hardier species *(B. microphylla)* from Korea lend charm to many a formal garden and big estate in Asia, Europe, and colonial grounds in the southeastern United States.

"Ground cover" in many gardens depends upon a low-growing relative of true boxwoods: the evergreen *Pachysandra,* whose name draws attention to the thick white filaments on each of the four stamens in staminate flowers. If sprigged into soil where the slope of the land or trees overhead give some protection from the sun, either the Asiatic *P. terminalis* or the North American *P. procumbens* soon makes a carpet that needs no mowing. The American species is native to rich woods with a limy soil, from western Florida and Louisiana north to Kentucky. Yet it thrives when introduced into northern New England, and has been adopted along with its Oriental cousin for estates in Europe and South Africa.

THE SUMAC FAMILY (Anacardiaceae)

From other members of Order Sapindales, these woody vines, shrubs and trees are distinguished by the presence of resin ducts, containing a milky sap, in all parts of the plant except the pollen grains. In this sap, many of them produce a strange poison called urushiol, which is nonvolatile and remarkably stable. Its effects are best known from the commonest offenders: the lacquer tree of China and Japan *(Rhus vernicifera),* poison ivy (especially *R. radicans*—known formerly as *R. toxicodendron)* and poison oaks *(R. diversilobum* in the Far West, and *R. toxicodendron*—formerly *R. quercifolia*—in the East) and poison sumac *(R. vernix)* of North America, and poisonwood trees (various species of *Metopium)* in the West Indies.

Lacquer trees have been milked of their latex in China since prehistoric times; lacquerware was already subject to official regulations during the Chou dynasty (1122–249 B.C.). The highest attainments of the art in lacquerware correspond to the Ming dynasty (1368–1644 A.D.), which is also the period when samples of this Oriental work first reached Europe in quantity. Deliberate cultivation of lacquer trees seems to have spread to Japan by the 6th century A.D., but there Chinese lacquerware was imitated and never equalled. The Japanese lacquer itself, however, was of so much better quality than the Chinese that the raw material came to be known as Japanese lacquer. To get it, the poisonous sap is released from the trees by making incisions through the bark of the trunk, and also by stripping the bark from branches an inch or more in diameter. Still smaller branches are cut off, soaked in water, and their sap collected. These practices kill the tree above ground, and yield as a byproduct a nonpoisonous wood useful in carpentry. New trees rise in a cluster of five or six from the roots, providing another harvest in six to ten years.

The sap, which is viscous, turns black by oxidation upon being left exposed to air. It is applied with a brush before it hardens. Strangely, this process requires high humidity, giving rise to the paradox that lacquer dries best in damp surroundings—such as a cave. When hard, the coating of lacquer can be smoothed with a stone tool and then rubbed to a high luster. Workers in the industry become immune to the toxic ingredients of the lacquer, and the poisonous character vanishes as soon as the material is hard and dry.

Color of the fruits is a good clue to which members of the genus *Rhus* are poisonous and which not. The lacquer tree and its toxic relatives all bear white or tan fruits, whereas the nonpoisonous sumacs have red fruits or fruits clad in brownish red hair. Some people in America save themselves from poison ivy by following the little rhyme:

Leaves in three,
Quickly flee!
Berries white,
Poisonous sight.

This is helpful for poison oaks too, which have three

leaflets at the end of each petiole. But three leaflets are characteristic also of the harmless fragrant sumac (or lemon sumac, or polecat bush, *R. aromatica),* a shrub of dry rocky areas and open woods from Quebec to Texas and Kansas to northern Florida. And poison sumac (or poison elder, or poison dogwood), which is just as dangerous despite its pinnately compound leaves, awaits those who rely on the rhyme in swamps from Florida to east Texas and southeastern Minnesota to Maine. Poison ivy itself (known also as cow-itch, since its poison can be picked up second-hand from cattle or animals that have brushed against the foliage and stems) is native to the whole area from Florida to Arizona and Manitoba to the Maritime Provinces in Canada. Western poison oak is found from Baja California to southern British Columbia, whereas the eastern one lives in pinelands and dry sandy barrens from Florida to Oklahoma and north to New Jersey.

Captain John Smith described in 1624 the effects of contact between human skin and the poison from these American species of the genus: it "causeth rednesse, itching, and lastly blisters, the which howsoever after a while passe away of themselves without further harme." Folk remedies offer little or no help, for the poison is insoluble in water (whether soapy or not), alcohol, and other household solvents. It was identified in 1956 by C. R. Dawson as a mixture of four closely-related compounds, all diphenols. Apparently it combines instantly with proteins in the skin, or in cells lining the digestive tract if pieces of the plant are eaten. For the first exposure in a lifetime, a person seems regularly to escape unharmed; no one is born with a sensitivity to the poison. But whatever the nature of the inborn immunity, it suffices to neutralize a limited amount of the substance formed in body cells that have absorbed the poison. About three people in every four respond to subsequent contact with the plant

Right above: Elephantwood (Pachycormus discolor) *is a small tree with thick trunk found in Baja California, Mexico. (E. S. Ross) Right: Staghorn sumac* (Rhus typhina) *colonizes cleared land in northeastern North America. Its hairy clusters of fruits attract birds, which carry the seeds. Far right: The cashew nut ripens in a hard seed coat, projecting beyond the end of a pear-shaped fruit known as a cashew apple. Cashew trees* (Anacardium occidentale) *are native to the West Indies and tropical Central America. (Both by Lorus and Margery Milne)*

(or smoke particles from burning parts of it) by inflammation, followed by blisters that exude a harmless serum but easily become infected, and by other symptoms in varying degrees of severity. Once the inborn reserve of immunity has been overwhelmed, the redness, blistering, and itching begin. No cure is known, although the symptoms can be made less painful and precautions can be taken against infection when the blisters burst. Months or years are needed to recover the original degree of natural immunity after any episode of poisoning. Some people acquire an immunity to occasional contact, and a few develop complete immunity by the time they are over sixty.

All of the harmless sumacs live in eastern North America, southern Europe and Asia. Sicilian sumac (*R. coriaria*) long has been a source of tannins for making leather. In America the Indians used to gather the ripe clusters of red-haired fruits from staghorn sumac (*R. typhina*) and smooth sumac (*R. glabra*) and dry them in the sun. Later the fruits could be rinsed with water, to extract a pleasing sour drink.

The fruit clusters of sumacs take on their conspicuous dark red color long before the foliage shows autumn hues. Seen from a distance, the sumacs then seem to us to be holding "ruby, upturned thumbs." Later, their characteristic pinnately compound leaves turn many shades of orange and rich red. They brighten the pastures and other open areas which these straggling shrubby trees so quickly colonize. During migration many birds make a meal of sumac fruits, and later drop the undigested seeds where conditions may be suitable for germination. The poisonous species of *Rhus* are distributed in the same way.

Poisonwoods produce fleshy fruits of larger size, to an inch in length. Of the three kinds found in the West Indies, Yucatan, British Honduras, and Gua-

Left above: The sugar maple (Acer saccharum) *of the eastern United States yields a sugary sap from which maple sirup and a hard wood for furniture are made.* (Gottscho-Schleisner, Inc.) *Far left: The American smoke tree* (Cotinus obovatus) *is known also as chittamwood in its native south-central United States. Its minute flowers on finely branching stalks resemble smoke. Left: A ring-necked snake glides among the opened fruits of the clambering bittersweet* (Celastrus scandens) *of the eastern United States.* (Both by Lorus and Margery Milne)

temala, only one (*Metopium toxiferum*) has reached southern Florida. It may be that fruits with ripe seeds rode hurricanes across the narrow strait from Cuba, and germinated in the limy soil of the Everglades. This particular shrub or small tree, which has pinnately compound leaves, occurs in Jamaica, Hispaniola, and Puerto Rico, as well as Cuba. Its toxic juice produces the same symptoms as develop from contact with poison ivy, and the poison may be identical.

A similar poison is found in the stalk that holds each fruit of the edible mango (*Mangifera indica*). Since the sap may spread from the stalk when the mango is picked, it is wise to remove the skin from the fruit before eating it. Wiping the fruit with a cloth that is to be used again is bad practice, since poisons of this kind do not evaporate or lose their potency for years. Otherwise, mango trees and mangoes are an unblemished delight. Among people in the tropics, mangoes take the place of apples as the most favored available.

Probably the edible mango trees came originally from Burma, Assam, and perhaps Malaya. Each grows to a height of forty to fifty feet, and its evergreen foliage casts a dense shade that is greatly appreciated in sunny lands. According to Oriental folklore, a whole grove of mango trees was presented to Gautama Buddha to shade him while he contemplated. The luscious fruit, too, was appreciated in India. Historic records show that between 1556 and 1605 A.D., at a time when large orchards of fruit trees were virtually unknown anywhere, the reigning emperor (Akbar, the Mogul) in Delhi had a plantation of a hundred thousand mango trees set out near Darbhanga. The Portuguese colonists met the fruit in western India, but not until early in the 18th century did anyone realize that the single large seed in each mango quickly loses its ability to germinate. Then sprouted seedlings were taken to tropical America and to Africa. In 1889 the U. S. Department of Agriculture introduced some desirable kinds into southern Florida, but an intolerance for occasional hard frosts has blocked any major production of mangoes in the continental United States. In Hawaii, the Philippines and throughout the tropics, however, improved horticultural practices have increased the yield and improved the quality—particularly by getting rid of the fibrous strands that mar the texture (but not the flavor) of earlier varieties. Mangoes can be picked just before they are ripe, and withstand being shipped if given about the same care that bananas receive.

A forest of cashew trees (Anacardium occidentale) *on the flat highlands of west-central Venezuela contains palms and many climbing vines. (Karl Weidmann)*

A far stranger fruit, again with a poison associated with it, is the product of the cashew tree *(Anacardium occidentale)* of eastern Brazil and northwestward into the southern West Indies. On sandy dry ground, the cashew is scarcely more than a shrub, but on fertile soil with adequate water, it grows to be an evergreen tree forty feet high. Unlike most members of the family, it bears simple elliptical leaves. As the single, kidney-shaped seed develops in the ovary of the small, inconspicuous flowers, the nearest part of the flower stalk enlarges to form a delicious cashew "pear," which may be eaten raw or cooked with sugar or fermented into cajú wine—a drink that is highly esteemed in Brazil. Projecting slightly from the blunt end of the pendant "pear" is the ripening ovary, containing the seed. The ovary wall and the seed coat together form a shell with a hard outer and inner layer and an oily poison between. In commercial practice, the fruits are picked by hand and the seed in its hard covering

separated from the soft "pear." Machines then break through the hard wall, salvage the oily material, remove the pieces of "shell," and send the washed seeds on to a roasting oven where they are freed of the astringent principle that would still discourage eating them raw. The "shell liquid" has found use in electrical insulation for use in aircraft, where it must withstand frequent large changes in temperature and never crack when extremely cold. Unfortunately, its poisonous qualities do not fully disappear, and repair men who must handle the insulated cables while maintaining the equipment have developed symptoms similar to those from poison ivy.

No poison seems to be associated with the small trees of the genus *Pistacia,* most of which are well adapted to life on poor soil with a cold winter or a long summer drought. All nine species have pinnately compound leaves, which often take on attractive colors before they drop off. Chinese artists often show the bright autumnal foliage of *P. chinensis.* The first turpentine used by oil painters came from the terebinth tree *(P. terebinthus)* of eastern Europe into western Asia; because supplies of it came chiefly from trees tapped on the Mediterranean island of Chios, it was (and still is) known as Chian turpentine. Pistacias, mixed with scrub oaks, compose the thorn forests of Asia Minor, such as the one through which Absolom rode wildly and was caught by the hair (II Samuel, 18). But one Mediterranean species *(P. vera)* outranks all others in fame, since it is the source of the world's pistachio nuts, each solid, green-pigmented, in its red, tissue-thin seed coat. These nuts are now cultivated throughout southern Europe, Asia Minor, and to a lesser extent in the southern United States. Turkey produces the largest crop, and processes them by removing the soft outer flesh of the fruit to expose the thin-walled "pit," which is in two parts hinged together like a clam shell around the seed. Cured in brine or dried (often with the "shell" dyed to make it more attractive), the nuts are shipped all over the world for use in confections or as delicious snacks.

In exploring the plant world for useful materials, the leather tanning industry has found its best source of tannins in an equivalent of sumac from the Southern Hemisphere. The red quebracho *(Schinopsis lorentzii)* of Argentina and Paraguay excels all other plants known in yielding an extract rich in catechol tannins. In recent years these scrubby trees, which were once cut for poor firewood or just to open up the land, have provided both South American countries with some of their most valued exports.

THE HOLLY FAMILY (Aquifoliaceae)

Although most of the 280 different species of holly *(Ilex)* are native to Central and South America and Asia, representatives are found in Africa and Australia, and Europe has a single species *(I. aquifolium)*. The European one seems to have been adopted into pagan rituals at an early date, having a place in Roman saturnalia and in the ceremonies with which Teutonic tribes made sylvan spirits welcome indoors when winter came. With the spread of Christianity, the traditional uses of holly were altered slightly to fit into Christmas festivities.

To be satisfactory, an *Ilex* should grow slowly to tree size, thirty to forty feet high, with a thick trunk containing wood so hard and stainable that it can serve as a substitute for ebony in handles of teapots and other ware in which hot things are served. The leaves should be evergreen, leathery, their surface glossy. The flowers may be inconspicuous so long

as the fruits are small hard red berries that stay on the tree in late December. All of these requirements are met best by the European holly, which has the additional advantage that birdlime can be prepared from its bark. Birdlime is a viscid adhesive made to be spread on the horizontal branches of trees, where it will entrap any small birds alighting on it. In European countries where small birds are sought to add a little meat to the soup, birdlime from holly is still in use.

In some English districts, holly with saw-toothed or prickly edges to the leaves is called "he-holly," and preferred to that with smooth-edged leaves ("she-holly"). If she-holly is used to decorate the house, visitors may even tease the family by claiming this to show that the wife is the master—not the husband.

When Europeans colonized eastern North America, they found another species *(I. opaca)* so similar to the European species that it too was sought for

Known variously as poison sumac, poison elder and poison dogwood, Rhus vernix *grows as a coarse shrub or small tree in swamps of eastern North America. (Hugh Spencer)*

Poison ivy (Rhus radicans), *noted for the rash it can cause, climbs freely or stands upright, with shiny leaves or ivory-white berries in clusters. (Hal H. Harrison: National Audubon)*

Early in the year, sugar maples (Acer saccharum) *display two types of flowers. The staminate ones (shown) are clustered on long stalks. (J. C. Allen and Son)*

Yuletide decorations. Indians of North America had a different use for the leaves of yaupon *(I. vomitoria),* which grows in sandy woods and clearings of the southeastern United States. They prepared from the foliage a strong decoction which served as an emetic when taken before, during, or after feasts, allowing the feasters to eat more than otherwise would have been physically possible. The decoction contained so much caffeine that the stomach reacted violently, but not before some stimulation had been gained. This same foliage has been used ever since colonial times by coastal people for the preparation of a mild, pleasant substitute for tea, known as yaupon or yaupon tea.

More refined methods are used in southern Brazil and Paraguay with the leaves of maté *(I. paraguariensis* and other species), which are gathered by local Indians from woodlands known as *yerbales.* Merchants pay the government for the Indians' services, and process the leaves to a powder or to dry fragments rather similar to tea leaves. The product retains its flavor despite continued exposure to damp

air. South Americans add it to a calabash or a cup in which a little sugar has been dissolved in freshly boiled water, to brew their favorite hot drink. They know it as Paraguay tea, or yerba maté, or tea of the Missions, or Jesuits' tea, commemorating the first cultivation of the holly as a crop by priests in the Jesuit Missions.

Only a few members of the genus *Ilex* follow the full tradition of hollies. Some produce black fruit instead of red ones, as does inkberry *(I. glabra),* which attained a height of twenty-five feet in some parts of its wide range—from Nova Scotia to Florida and westward to the prairies in patches of low sandy or peaty soil. Other hollies are deciduous, but their bright red fruits remain in place through the winter on otherwise bare stems. This is characteristic of winterberry (or black alder, *I. verticillata),* which brightens swampy places with its red fruits from Newfoundland to Georgia, and as far west as Minnesota. Over much of this same area, the damp woods and swampy thickets contain another red-berried, deciduous member of the family: the mountain-holly (or catberry, *Nemopanthus mucronata),* which differs from true holly in details, such as that its stamens are not attached to the base of the corolla or its calyx is retained on the ripe fruit, whereas in *Ilex* the converses are true. These differences seem more significant when they are seen to apply to all hollies in the tropics as well as both temperate zones.

BITTERSWEET AND ITS RELATIVES (Family Celastraceae)

With about five hundred different kinds native to all continents, this family includes many of the strong vines known as lianas, which link lofty tree tops and soil in tropical rain forests. Arabs in the Near East collect the leaves from the kat bush *(Catha edulis),* either to steep them in making a favorite substitute for tea, or to chew them for the stimulating alkaloids they contain. In Ethiopia and East Africa, where the kat bush also grows, some of the tribesmen seem to have learned the chewing habit from Arab neighbors. Elsewhere in the world, two genera *(Euonymus* and *Celastrus)* of small trees, shrubs and climbing vines attract attention chiefly because of their handsome foliage and strange, decorative fruits. As the fruits ripen, the thin wall of the ovary splits open and curls back, revealing four or five brilliant red or orange parts inside. Each of these is an aril, produced by fleshy enlargement of the tiny stalk that connects a seed to its support. Birds see the bright arils and eat them, swallowing the indigestible seeds at the same time, later dropping the unharmed seeds far from the parent plant.

The evergreen climbing *Euonymus* that so many people train on trellises against their homes is an Asiatic species *(E. fortunei)*. The European and Asiatic spindle-tree *(E. europaeus),* which begins as a shrub and may grow to become a tree twenty-five feet high, was formerly the source of wooden spindles for textile machinery; it has been introduced and escaped from cultivation in eastern North America, where it often grows near a native species *(E. atropurpuratus)* known as the wahoo or the burning-bush. The spindle-tree bears yellow-green flowers, pink fruit, and orange arils, whereas the burning-bush has purple flowers, purple fruit, and scarlet arils. Both earn the name "burning-bush" from the purplish red color to which their leaves turn in autumn. Both species seem to escape from gardens more readily than does the winged spindle-tree *(E. alatus)* of East Asia, which is something of a horticultural curiosity because its branches bear lengthwise vanes of corky material.

Bittersweet *(Celastrus)* is a shrubby twining plant in Australia, South and East Asia, and eastern North America. Its tough stems spiral through the branches of trees and, during the second season of growth, produce inconspicuous greenish flowers in small clusters wherever a leaf dropped at the end of the first year. The American climbing bittersweet *(C. scandens)* is often known as waxwork, because its freshly opened fruits with their bright crimson arils contrast with the orange ovary wall and appear manmade decorations rather than living plants.

THE GLORIOUS MAPLES (Family Aceraceae)

Before the Ice Ages, members of this family grew far into the Arctic and also well into the tropics. Now all but two of the 150 species are maples *(Acer),* represented in the Southern Hemisphere only in the mountains of Java and Sumatra; elsewhere they are woody plants of eastern Asia (particularly Japan), Europe, and North America. Sugar maple *(A. saccharum)* and its close relative, the black maple *(A. nigrum),* provided sugar to American Indians long before the arrival of Europeans and sugar cane. These magnificent shade trees grow as much as 116 feet high, and are native to the area from Louisiana and the highlands of Georgia to Newfoundland and southern Manitoba. Every springtime

they raise from their roots to their topmost branches a sap some of which descends again bearing sugar (sucrose). When most of the water has been removed from thirty to fifty gallons of the descending sap, the product is a single gallon of maple sirup that meets modern standards. Or the same quantity will yield about ten pounds of crystalline sugar with a similarly distinctive flavor.

Indians got rid of the water in sugar maple sap by freezing the sap and throwing away the sugar-free ice that formed. Or they boiled the sap in birch-bark buckets by dropping hot stones into it. Not until metal pots were introduced by the colonists could anyone boil the sap over a fire to make sirup. But the primitive equipment and methods the Indians used have been replaced. Sap is collected from whole orchards of great trees, each orchard referred to as a sugar "bush." Metal spiles are driven into half-inch holes drilled through the outer bark into the living bast tissue (phloem). The descending sap emerges through the spiles, runs by gravity through plastic hoses to a central collecting tank, and is generally hauled from there to the evaporators. Often a mild vacuum is maintained over the heated sap by pumps, in order to lower its boiling point while energy from the hot fire below drives off the extra water. Visitors from other parts of the world find maple sugaring, even in its most mechanized form, an exciting feature of this part of America.

Smaller quantities of a similar sap, sirup, and sugar can be obtained from a number of different maples, and also from some birches, ash, and hickory. In all, the highest yield and best flavor are obtained when the spiles are driven into the sunny side of the tree, and when the tapping is done during early spring when frosty nights alternate with daytime thawing, before the buds open. Neither the roots nor the unfolding leaves are essential to the production of sweet sap, however. Recently, scientists at the University of Vermont demonstrated that a branchless length of maple trunk, cut off top and bottom and stood in a container of water, will release useful amounts of satisfactory sap if it is subjected to an alternating twelve-hour schedule of temperatures above and below the freezing point. The newer technological improvements and fuller knowledge have not yet brought down the cost of maple sirup and sugar to the low price that remained so stable in colonial times. Then the sugar often served as a medium of exchange. This practice survived at least until January 1932 in remote parts of the Gaspé peninsula of Quebec.

The paired, winged fruits (samaras) of sugar maple (Acer saccharum) *diverge from one another, almost in opposite directions. (E. Javorsky)*

The leathery, prickly capsules of horse chestnut (Aesculus hippocastanum) *split when the seeds are ripe. (John Markham)*

People who learn to look for the U-shaped bays between the lobes of a maple's palmately-veined leaf as a guide in distinguishing a sugar maple from other members of the genus in which the lobes are separated by V-shaped indentations, should also break a petiole to see whether the sap that oozes forth is clear (as it is in sugar maple) or is milky—the mark of Norway maple, *A. platanoides,* a fine shade tree of Europe and Asia Minor, now introduced widely around the world. The leaf of Norway maple is similar in shape to that of sugar maple, but its bark is much smoother, its samaras are more divergent and drop off earlier, and its wood lacks the structural strength that makes sugar maple (and black maple) a "hard maple," second only to oak in its suitability for construction of furniture. "Soft maples," such as Norway maple, are faster-growing trees and often possess more conspicuous flowers. All of them, with the exception of ash-leaved maple (or box-elder, or Manitoba maple, *A. negundo)* of eastern North America, have palmately lobed and palmately veined leaves; the exception bears pinnately compound leaves with three to seven leaflets. In each leaflet of the ash-leaved maple, the veins extend to the tips of the teeth, whereas in the leaflets of ash, the lateral veins curve around and do not reach the tooth points.

America's west coast, from Baja California to British Columbia, has one native maple, the bigleaf (or broadleaf, or Oregon) maple, *A. macrophyllum,* a fine timber tree that is well named since its leaves may be twelve inches broad. Britain, too, has only one indigenous maple: the small hedge maple *(A. campestris)* of northern Eurasia. In Europe, maple timber comes chiefly from the handsome sycamore maple *(A. pseudoplatanus)* of central Eurasia, and the attractive Norway maple whose range extends into Asia Minor. One variety of the Norway maple is widely planted as an ornamental because its leaves in spring open with a reddish-bronze color that fades only slowly into green during the summer.

Few trees of the North Temperate Zone contribute so much to the magnificence of autumn coloration as the many kinds of maples. When their green disappears, the leaves remain for a week or more on the trees, brilliant in shades of yellow, orange, scarlet and ruby red. Daily the colors change on each tree, and from year to year the differences in the amount of sun and rain alter the final hue attained before the foliage drops from the tree. Usually the tall sugar maples provide their own special glory above the lower trees and shrubs, while in the swamps and along the wet edges of streams the red maple *(A. rubrum)* takes an especially fiery hue. So linked to the presence of maples are these displays that to see them at their best, a person must go to the northern United States and southern Canada, or to Korea and Japan.

In the Orient, specifically eastern China, live the two species of *Dipteronia* which alone now represent this once widespread second genus of the maple family. Their distinctive feature is that the wing extends all around the margin of each samara, rather than being limited to one side as in *Acer.* Yet, when the fruits drop one by one from their twinned positions on the tree, an asymmetry in the wing makes them spin in the breeze and drift sidewise from the parent tree, just as the samaras of maple do.

THE HORSE CHESTNUTS
(Family Hippocastanaceae)

Best known of the two dozen kinds of shrubs and trees in this little family is the widely-planted horse chestnut *(Aesculus hippocastanum)* which is native to the Caucasus and Balkans. From Constantinople it was introduced into Europe early in the 16th century in the belief that a medicine useful in treating sick horses could be made from its large seeds. No reason for this idea is evident today, since all members of the genus have been found to contain in their mature seeds, sprouts and young growth a glucoside (aesculin) that is toxic to stock animals if, by mistake, they swallow some. The presence of this poison explains the traditional way in which North American Indians prepared a bread meal from the seeds by leaching the dried, pulverized material for several days with frequent changes of water before using it. It may also be the basis for the claim that honeybees are poisoned by taking the nectar of the California buckeye *(A. californica),* and that people have become ill after eating the honey produced by the sick bees from the nectar of this shrubby tree.

In all horse chestnuts and buckeyes, the flowers are borne in clusters like showy candelabras pointing toward the sky. Each cluster has a distinctive style of growth: its main axis continues to develop while its side branches unfold a strictly limited number of blossoms. Each pollinated pistil matures into a spherical capsule whose leathery pieces split open. First they reveal, then release two or three (or just one, by abortion) large, glossy, brownish-red seeds. The attachment scar on each seed is so large and pale in color that the seed has a resemblance to the eye of a buck deer, hence the name buckeye.

Most of the species of *Aesculus* are native to Asia, from north of the Himalayas to Japan. North America has one in northern California and Oregon, and five more in the Central States west of the Appalachians and south of Lake Ontario. Ohio has named *A. glabra* as the "Ohio buckeye"—the state tree. All are large shrubs or trees of moderate size, different in that they possess opposite leaves that are large and palmately compound. The wood of these trees is light and strong, useful in making artificial limbs and also boxes of many kinds—including funeral caskets.

THE SOAPBERRY FAMILY *(Sapindaceae)*

This family of about 1100 species, most of which are tropical trees or shrubs, takes its name from the commercial soapberry tree *(Sapindus saponaria).* It is an evergreen with pinnately compound leaves, native to the whole area from Mexico to Argentina. Like the related soapberry of North America from Mexico into Louisiana and Arizona *(S. drummondii),* its ripe fruits are globular, yellow, about half an inch in diameter, and well supplied with a bitter saponin that produces a soapy lather in water. Only in underdeveloped regions today is this material valued for its use in home laundry work. Many people react to the saponin, which can cause a severe skin irritation. Perhaps these are the same individuals who develop a distressing inflammation of the stomach and intestinal lining if they drink home-made beer to which a few soapberries have been added to increase the depth of the foam on each glassful.

In Brazil the name guaraná is given both to the foaming beverage that is made from the fruits of a related tree *(Paullinia cupana),* and to the tree itself. In addition to sugars and saponins, this extract concentrates the alkaloid caffeine from an original 4.5 per cent to more than fifteen per cent, making the drink the most stimulating—and among the most bitter—of all with a caffeine content. The guaraná tree grows wild in many parts of South America, but is extensively cultivated only in Brazil.

Quite different poisons, still identified only as "hypoglycemic principles" *A* and *B,* have been recognized as the cause of "Jamaica poisoning" of children and adults who eat the fruit of a shrubby tree *(Blighia sapida)* from tropical West Africa. Known widely as the akee (or akee akee), this tree is named to honor the British admiral William Bligh, commander of H. M. S. *Bounty*—of mutiny fame. He introduced the akee along with the breadfruit to Jamaica in 1778, to provide inexpensive food for Negro slaves. African explorers had already found the akee to be a favorite with Negro people in the area from which the slaves came, and the breadfruit seemed a potential year-round source of a starchy vegetable—one popular in the South Pacific islands. The Jamaicans have adopted the akee as their national fruit. The stiff branches of the tree itself grow only to a height of about twenty-five feet. Clusters of small irregular flowers are followed by handsome orange or red fruits, each about three inches long. As the fruits ripen, the ovary walls split apart slightly at the end opposite the stem. Through the gaps, three large black globular seeds can be seen. Each is still supported by an ivory-colored fleshy aril, which is the only edible part of the fruit. It can be removed and cooked in various ways, all of which bring out a pleasant texture and nutty flavor—features that one would not expect from a dish with the name of "vegetable brain." We have eaten and enjoyed it only in Jamaica, while in the care of a Negro cook who liked akee herself and who attended to the purchase of the fruit in the curbside market as well as the preparation of the food for our table. At just the right stage of ripeness, the hypoglycemic principles decrease to a minimum concentration. In unripe fruit one of the principles is present in dangerous amounts, and in overripe fruit the other one seems to take its place. The seeds and the ovary wall never lose their toxic qualities. Most of the many deaths diagnosed as "Jamaica poisoning" in the West Indies (and in West Africa, and in many Latin American areas where the akee has been introduced) are among adults who use unripe or over-ripe fruits as the source of ariles, and children who eat even small amounts of the attractive fruit, ovary wall and all. The poison causes degenerative changes in the liver, and drastically lowers the amount of blood sugar in circulation until the cells of the body literally starve to death. So great is this danger that most communities in the United States where akee would grow, such as southern Florida, outlaw the tree altogether.

A very different tree of the soapberry family was introduced into Jamaica in 1775 for the benefit of white planters: the litchi *(Litchi chinensis)* of China and the Philippines. Its bright green foliage forms a compact crown that keeps its shape and appearance all year through. If grown where winters are just cold enough, or summers just dry enough, to discourage vegetative growth, litchi trees produce flowers and then fruits. These are the favorite of Cantonese, and have been so since ancient times, esteemed far more highly than either the orange or the peach. Under its brittle outer covering, a litchi fruit offers a white, translucent flesh surrounding the single large seed. Much of the flavor, which suggests that of a Muscat grape, remains if the fruit is dried completely. The product is the mysterious litchi "nut" of the Orient, which is now produced and exported from litchi orchards planted in many parts of India, in South Africa, in Hawaii, and in southern Florida.

THE TICKLISH TOUCH-ME-NOTS
(Family Balsaminaceae)

A fruit in the form of a fleshy capsule, that splits open explosively and hurls its seeds far from the plant, is so characteristic of this little family that variations in arrangement of leaves, placement of flowers, and some of the details of the irregular flowers themselves seem of lesser significance. All of the 450 different kinds are herbs with watery stems, most abundant in the tropics of Asia and Africa but represented on other continents and in cool temperate climates too. Most of the species belong to the genus *Impatiens,* which includes the touch-me-not *(I. nolitangere)* of Europe and Asia as far as Japan, the decorative garden balsam *(I. balsamina)* of Asia, and the jewelweeds *(I. capensis* and *I. pallida)* that brighten wet or springy places in North America from Georgia to Newfoundland and Saskatchewan to Missouri. Jewelweed gets its name from the abundant clear droplets of dew or exuded sap that, in the early morning, hang from the edges of its leaves—particularly the tips of the coarse sawteeth.

As bees shoulder their way into the partly closed flowers on any *Impatiens,* they seem to be entering a fragile imitation of the snapdragon. Although the upper and outer petals are joined on each side, the part upon which the insect alights and into which it creeps to reach nectar in a long backward-pointing spur is actually a sepal. Plantsmen puzzle over all the attention insects give these blossoms for, in most kinds, there are two kinds of flowers: larger ones that offer pollen and sweet bait but produce no seeds; and smaller ones that pollinate themselves early in the bud stage, push off their floral parts unopened, and grow larger as the explosive capsules in which the seeds are ripening. This paradox awaits attention in gardens the world over.

CHAPTER 14

The Grapevine and Its Attractive Allies

CUES: *If the dicot flower has its stalk end in a cup-shaped receptacle into which the superior ovary is sunk, while the rim of the cup supports a single whorl of stamens, each stamen opposite one of the four or five petals (or alternate with the sepals, if petals are lacking), the plant is almost sure to be a member of the Order Rhamnales. It may be a jujube, a buckthorn, a western lilac, a grapevine, or a Boston ivy.*

This is a little order of only about 1150 different kinds of plants, but they include several that have contributed outstandingly to man's traditions, and some others that add grace to modern living.

THE BUCKTHORNS (Family Rhamnaceae)

In Central Asia, southern Europe, and North Africa, people have long relied upon laxatives from buckthorns *(Rhamnus)* as remedies. The small plumlike fruits of the purging buckthorn *(R. cathartica)* yield a larger amount of the effective ingredient (anthraquinone) than can be obtained in "frangula bark" from the alder-buckthorn *(R. frangula).* But both of these shrubby trees were regarded as indispensable by the colonists on their way to the New World. They introduced the Eurasian buckthorns, which now have spread as far north as Nova Scotia, Quebec, and Minnesota, and from Virginia westward to Missouri.

The colonists might have saved themselves their trouble, for the Old World has no monopoly on buckthorns or on knowledge of how they may be used. North American Indians relied for laxatives upon related shrubs and trees; soon these too were gathered into the medicine cabinets of the white pioneers. Woodlands and forest edges in the North and East afforded the fruits of the alder-leaved buckthorn *(R. alnifolia).* Among the dense chaparral of the West was *R. purshiana,* from which bark is still harvested commercially in Oregon and Washington state, still under the Spanish equivalent of the Indian name for it—"sacred bark"—cascara sagrada.

The cascara buckthorn (and another, *R. california,* common in California) may be met as "coffee-berry," commemorating the quiet desperation of the early settlers over the absence of amenities from the Old World. These two buckthorns contain less of the laxative substance in their fruits than is usual among other members of the genus, and a weak beverage made from the fruit pulp faintly resembles coffee in flavor. It must have tantalized western pioneers for whom the nearest real coffee was thousands of miles away.

During the American Revolution, another member of this family *(Ceanothus americanus)* became famous as "New Jersey tea," because a substitute for that beverage could be made from its leaves. A western counterpart *(C. thyrsiflorus)* provides an evergreen cover on canyon sides from central California to Oregon, either as dense chaparral or in the form of trees as much as twenty-five feet high. Its three-inch clusters of small blue (or white) flowers earned the plant the name of California lilac, or blue myrtle, or simply "blue blossom." Especially abundant in the redwood belt, it has been adopted widely as an ornamental for temperate gardens around the world.

In China, the most important relative of the buckthorns is the jujube tree *(Zizyphus jujuba),* which has been cultivated there extensively for at least four thousand years for its dark brown fruits, each with a single large pointed "stone" enclosing a seed. Cooked in sirup, the fruits are called "Chinese dates." Or the fruit juice is used to flavor and give a firm gelatinous character to small lozenge-shaped candies known as jujubes. Although the fruits themselves are among the most popular in China, jujube trees have been planted elsewhere more as dooryard decorations and curiosities. A related bush native to southern Europe *(Z. lotus)* has larger, starchier fruits whose pulp has been used for making bread and also a wine—foods tentatively identified as those mentioned in Greek legends. The "lotus-eaters" were believed to subsist on this special fare and to be doomed by it to a trancelike state, forgetful of families and friends, and dreamily contented to do nothing.

THE GRAPE FAMILY (Vitaceae)

Distributed widely from the tropics into temperate regions, the six hundred species in this family are almost all climbing shrubs with clinging tendrils of an unusual origin: each slender tendril arises from a terminal bud and, at its base, the stem usually shows a distinct bend because it grew from a lateral bud. Generally there is a leaf close to the bend at the tendril, the leaf palmately veined or palmately compound. The clusters of fruits that succeed the small inconspicuous flowers ordinarily are opposite leaves more remote from tendrils. Each fleshy berry contains from one to four seeds that have a hard coating often described as bony.

The area around the Caspian Sea probably gave early man the first taste of the grape *(Vitis vinifera)* he domesticated in Asia Minor and Europe, then introduced wherever it would grow as he colonized new lands. Noah is recorded as planting a vineyard after the flood (Genesis 9, 20). Hieroglyphics from the 4th dynasty in Egypt (about 2400 B.C.) show details of grape culture and wine production. At the beginning of the Christian era, Pliny the Elder described ninety-one varieties of this one kind of grape. Today, more than eight thousand varieties have been named, but less than two dozen are regarded highly: just one, the Concord, for most of the sweet juice sold in America, a few each for wine-making and for canning, and the rest for sale as table grapes.

Until the 17th century, people in Eurasia and Africa relied almost completely upon the one European grape in its many horticultural varieties. A number of different types were eaten raw in season. Three (Muscat of Alexandria, Black Corinth, and Thompson Seedless) could be partially dried without losing their texture or flavor, or becoming sticky; they retained these qualities in storage as raisins. Still other varieties served as the base for the table (dry) wines with high acidity and low sugar content and the dessert (sweet) wines with low acidity and more sugar than the fermenting yeasts could use.

Without waiting to discover the nearly two dozen different species of *Vitis* in America, the colonists to the New World brought the European grapevines with them and planted out new vineyards. But aphids (phylloxeras) attacked the roots, and fungus diseases of several kinds all but destroyed the foliage, the flowers and the fruits. Aghast, the pioneers compared this disaster with the obvious immunity of American grapevines to all of these pests. By grafting a European grape onto the root of any of the immune species, damage by phylloxeras could be eliminated. Hybrids too showed varying degrees of immunity. Soon, however, the colonists developed a taste for some new horticultural strains of the American *Vitis labrusca,* which they had named the fox grape from an original dislike for its aromatic, thick skin. This one species became the ancestor of Concord, Chautauqua, Champion, Moore's Early, and other popular varieties, and by hybridization with European grape, of scores more. On each, the fox grape ancestor confers some toughness in the skin and makes the new fruit a "slip skin," from which the pulp can easily be squeezed free.

When the new American grapes were taken to Europe, phylloxeras and the fungus diseases to which European grapes were prone went along. Beginning in 1863, an epidemic of disastrous proportions swept across Europe. Within two decades the introduced insects and fungi ruined the grape industry there and forced a conversion to new methods. Fox grapevines were planted to get roots upon which European grapevines could be grafted, safe from the phylloxeras. Bordeaux mixture, consisting of water colored with copper sulfate ("blue vitriol") and made milky with lime, proved effective in controlling the fungus diseases and in repelling some insect pests that attack grape foliage. This earliest of all pesticides was invented for quite a different purpose: to hide the color of ripening grapes sprayed with the mixture, and thereby reduce losses to thieves who entered the vineyards.

The cultivation of grapes by wine-makers began so long ago that the origin of the custom is lost to history. Uniformly, however, the juice (called must) is pressed from the grapes and allowed to ferment through the action of the wine yeast *Saccharomyces ellipsoideus.* If the must is separated promptly from the grape skins, the product will be a white wine. If left for a short time in contact with the skins, it will be pink and called a rosé wine. If left still longer with the skins of black-fruited grapes, it will be a red wine with a much stronger flavor. Ordinarily, red wines are served at room temperature, whereas white wines are chilled before use.

Until the later years of the 17th century, when glass bottles and cork stoppers were invented, the full maturing of wine remained an unknown art. The Greeks, for example, fermented the must in crockery jars called amphorae, buried to the neck in earth. Contamination was avoided as well as possible by floating a film of olive oil over the surface of the fermenting liquid, and stuffing the neck of the amphora with rags before sealing it with clay to keep out air. As soon as bottles and corks became available, the technique of second fermentation became possible, producing sparkling wines such as champagnes. This discovery of the 17th century is attributed to the Benedictine monk Dom Pierre Pérignon. Champagnes, like non-sparkling or natural wines (called "still wines"), have an alcohol content between ten and fifteen per cent by volume, which is the concentration reached before the yeast is killed by alcohol poisoning.

Fortification of wines, increasing their alcohol content to as much as twenty-two per cent by addition of brandy to natural wines, began about 1750 in Madeira and spread rapidly. The infusion of white wines with quinine and various herbs to produce various types of vermouths is a later development which centered in France and Italy. Blending of wines, to match the traditions that have accumulated and the judgment of highly skilled wine-tasters, is perhaps the most delicate of the steps with which manufacturers of wines ensure the quality of their products.

The flavor of a wine is chiefly derived from its odor, savored as volatile components waft into the nasal passages from the throat. To a lesser degree it reflects the taste, which is sweet if sugar is still present, sour if bacterial action has been allowed to turn some of the alcohol into acetic acid—ruining the wine, and "dry" if neither sweet nor sour. Dry white wines are usually ready for use one or two years after fermentation has ceased and the product has been bottled. The flavor usually fades after about seven years. Sweet white wines take about three years to develop a satisfactory flavor, and reach their peak around ten years after bottling; they may last thirty years before the distinctive characteristics degenerate, leaving the wine with a watery quality. Red wines commonly are best between eight and twenty-five years after vintage, and often last with full bouquet for fifty years or more. It is customary to let red wines warm up to room temperature rather slowly, and to withdraw the cork an hour or more before use, to allow the odorous components to volatilize fully and be ready to please the nose of the imbiber.

Today, nearly a twentieth of the land in France is given over completely to cultivation of grapes, mostly to be made into wine, of which France is the leading producer in the world. Italy and Spain vie for second place, followed by Algeria, Argentina, South Africa, and the United States. California, which is the principal grape area in North America, provides only about three per cent of the world's wine, but sells about forty per cent of the world's raisins, and twenty per cent of the supply of table grapes.

Each wine-making district, each grower and wine-maker, and each year of production has its own distinctive characteristics, requiring a connoisseur to be informed in minute detail rather than to rely upon general classes in wines. From the Bordeaux region of France come light-bodied, strong-flavored Médoc red wines, which the British call claret, and natural semi-sweet Sauterne golden (white) wines, as well as a large number of others. From the Burgundy district come deep red wines that are described as "velvety," and very dry white wines such as Chablis. Most widely known of the Italian red wines is Chianti, from Tuscany, sold in straw-covered flasks. German white wines are famous and usually dry. Formerly they were called Rhenish wines or hock, but now Rhine wine is the more general term, with special esteem given to the pale golden (or slightly greenish) Moselle wine, which has a relatively low alcohol content. Hungary produces the moderately strong, topaz-colored Tokay wines, which may be either sweet or dry.

Of the fortified wines, the Madeiras from the Portuguese island of Madeira, the unblended "vintage" port and blended ports from the Oporto region of Portugal, the sherries from the province of Jerez de la Frontera in Spain, the heavy sweet Malaga wine from the Malaga area of southern Spain, and the Marsala wines from Sicily are best known. Madeiras may be red (called *tintas*) or white *(verdelhos),* Malmsey being a rich sweet one prepared from special malvasia grapes. Most port wine is red, and takes as much as forty years to mature. Sherry is an anglicization of Jerez, and gains its flavor from the action of a mildewlike growth encouraged by brief exposure to air after fermentation. Sherries range from pale dry blends, such as Amontillado, to the sweet, darker Cream types. Marsala wine is sweet with a burnt taste, and usually dark in color.

Champagne is fermented in casks from the harvest time until the first winter, when it is transferred to strong bottles after expert blending. A second fermentation within the bottle adds carbonation, making it sparkle. Gradually the bottles are turned cork down and left in this position until the wine is mature and marketable. Sediments settle onto the cork, which is then released, letting the explosive action clear the wine completely. Varying amounts of syrup melted in old champagne are added before the bottles are recorked, producing a range of sweet to dry in the bubbly, sparkling wine.

Part of European culture, now transplanted so widely around the globe, is the serving of traditionally correct wines before or at the beginning of a meal, as well as with each course, and after dessert. Fortified wines are chosen for the apéritifs as appetizers, such as dry Madeiras, amber-colored dry sherries, or vermouths—either dry or sweet. Sweet Madeiras, sweet sherries, dark red ports, and Marsala wines customarily follow the meal, as dessert wines. Natural wines go with main courses, as "table wines." Dry whites, such as Chablis, or rosé wines are preferred with hors d'œuvres, shellfish, fish, pork, veal, and salads. Rosé is traditional with ham, light reds (such as Médoc) with turkey and roasts, deep reds (such as those of Burgundy) with game and strong-flavored meats, and sweet white wines (such as Sauternes) with desserts.

The genus *Vitis*, which has added so much to wining and dining throughout the world, has only about sixty species. It is small in comparison with *Cissus*, with more than 250 kinds of tropical woody vines, some of which are found in temperate regions. Possum-grape *(C. incisus)* is a stout vine native to the Gulf states and up the Mississippi Valley as far as Missouri; its fruits are regarded as inedible, except to birds and small mammals. Trailing begonia *(C. discolor)* from Java is often introduced as an ornamental vine. In the Indomalayan rain forests, several species of *Cissus* with foliage in the tree tops and roots in the wet soil serve as hosts for the parasitic *Rafflesia,* which is the largest single flower in the world and one of the strangest.

A somewhat similar group of woody creepers in temperate Asia and North America are known as "virgin vines" *(Parthenocissus)* for no obvious reason. Each of their tendrils branches repeatedly and the tips all are expanded into adhesive pads that permit the plant to cling firmly to smooth vertical surfaces. One native to China and Japan *(P. tricuspidata),* with trilobed and palmately veined leaves on long petioles, has become a favorite wall vine known in America as Boston ivy. Another, *(P. quinquefolia),* with mostly five leaflets in each palmately compound leaf, is a wild climber from Mexico to Florida and north to Maine and Minnesota, where it is called Virginia creeper—except in the Canadian province of Quebec, where "virgin vine" reappears as *vigne-vierge.* Both the introduced and the native *Parthenocissus* display brilliant colors in autumn before the foliage drops, the Boston ivy usually an intense orange and the Virginia creeper a deep blood red.

CHAPTER 15

The Hibiscuses and Their Kin

CUES: *If a dicot plant has the four or five sepals of each flower distinct, never united more than at the base, and they open in the bud like valves, and if*

the stamens are numerous but united by their filaments into groups or into a tube around the compound, superior pistil, the plant is likely to belong to the Order Malvales. It may be a linden tree, a cotton plant, a cacao or a cola tree, or an African baobab.

Not all of the three thousand species in this order show every one of the distinctive features. A few have no more than five stamens. A few others have only a single carpel and hence a simple pistil. Most are natives of the tropics and of subtropical lands. Some produce flowers of outstanding beauty, and many furnish fibers important all over the world.

THE BASSWOODS (Family Tiliaceae)

Some of the most graceful among the deciduous trees of Asia, Europe, and North America are known variously as basswoods, lindens, and limes *(Tilia),* without much real distinction. In summer their heart-shaped leaves, toothed coarsely all around, cast a pleasant shade that is famous along Berlin's great avenue Unter den Linden, and lining the walkways to Trinity College at Cambridge University. Lime and linden are Anglo-Saxon names for these trees, quite unrelated to the French word from which lime is applied to a member of the citrus family.

All members of *Tilia* attract great numbers of bees at flowering season, perfuming the air and affording the insects a rich nectar. Honeybees make from it a pale, delicious honey with a distinctive flavor. The half-inch flowers themselves are cream-colored, and hang in loose clusters from a slender stalk. For part of its length the stalk appears to be the heavy midrib of a narrow, tongue-shaped bract, which remains in place after the ovary in each flower matures to become a dry woody fruit of globular form, enclosing one or two seeds.

The wood of each kind of *Tilia* is soft, firm, white,

Right above: Woody capsules, maturing after the flowers have fallen on the tropical Sterculia *trees of Portuguese West Africa, crack open to release their seeds. (E. S. Ross) Right: Spines protect the soft bark of the pink silk-cotton tree* (Chorisia speciosa) *of Brazil. A cotton-like fiber is harvested from the fruit pods of this kind of tree. Far right: In the West Indies, several members of the genus* Hibiscus *grow to tree size and are known as mahoes. The large brilliant flowers last only one day. (Both by Lorus and Margery Milne)*

and so uniformly fine in grain that it can be carved easily or cut into thin blades, such as those of venetian blinds or the frames for a honeycomb in a beehive. Long ago, it was customary to strip from the inner bark of these trees a soft fibrous tissue to serve as a bandage for wounds. Today, a fiber useful in the making of cordage, cloth and paper can be removed from the inner layer of the bark (the bast); hence the name basswood (bastwood).

Only in the U.S.S.R. is the inner bark of basswoods harvested on a large scale for its fibers. Elsewhere, the wood of *Tilia* trees is used increasingly as a material to be shredded in making excelsior as a packing material. But no substitute has yet been found for the bast fibers from two herbaceous relatives raised in India and Pakistan. From these two *(Corchorus capsularis* and *C. olitorius)* comes the fiber known as jute or gunny—for "gunny sacks." Neither plant is now known in the wild, but both have been cultivated for so many centuries in Bengal that they are thought to have originated there. Unskilled laborers broadcast the small seeds on suitable ground. Semiskilled workers weed and thin the stand a few weeks later. Thereafter the plants grow close together, almost without branches, to a height of from six to fifteen feet, as stems the thickness of a man's finger, with a loose crown of pale green leaves and small yellow flowers at the top. Each leaf is shaped like an arrowhead, with fine teeth along the sides and two coarse ones near the petiole projecting into long, bristlelike points.

In both Pakistan and India the foliage of jute is used as a potherb. When the flowers begin to fade, however, the stems are cut and subjected to bacterial decay in pools and streams until the long bast fibers can be stripped free, washed, wrung out, and hung to dry. The raw jute fibers, prepared and handled by cheap labor, leave by ship from the port of Calcutta,

Left above: Each of the strange buds of the shaving-brush tree (Pseudobombax ellipticum) *of Central America rolls back its protective coverings to expose a giant tuft of long stamens. (Lorus and Margery Milne) Far left: Flowers on short stalks from the trunk of the tropical American cacao tree* (Theobroma cacao) *produce huge pods, each containing many cocoa "beans." (Karl Weidmann) Left: The original marshmallow, a natural mucilaginous paste, was obtained from the perennial root of this tall herb* (Althaea officinalis), *which grows wild in wet soils of Europe and Asia. (Wilhelm Schacht)*

China jute, a fiber used in rugmaking, comes from cultivated plants of velvetleaf (Abutilon theophrasti), *a member of the mallow family native to southern Europe and Asia. (E. Javorsky)*

most of them destined for Dundee, Scotland, where they are spun into yarn. The higher quality goes into the manufacture of burlap for bags, the poorer for coarse sacking and for the covers of cotton bales. More than half of the people in Dundee engage in some aspect of the jute industry, marketing a product that is less expensive than any comparable fiber on the world market.

THE MALLOWS *(Family Malvaceae)*

The pointed flower buds on any member of the mallow family seem to open suddenly—just in an hour or two. Actually, for days before, the sepals of the expanding bud gape a little, exposing the swirl of colorful petals still tightly closed inside. After perhaps a week of visible preparation, the blossom opens widely, exposing a cylindrical tube studded with stamens around the long slender pistil whose stigma projects beyond the open end of the tube. Within hours the colors of the petals may change radically, and the whole corolla may drop to the ground by nightfall. It slides off the pistil along with the stamen tube to which the petals are individually attached.

Of the 1500 species in the family, about two hundred belong to the largest genus *(Hibiscus)*. Some of

them are tropical trees, others woody shrubs, and a few herbaceous annuals. More varied than the roses of the world, they invariably delight us wherever we find them—in hot countries or cool ones. Jamaicans have chosen the blue mahoe *(H. elatus),* a tree hibiscus, as their national flower. The most widely introduced species is the shrubby rose-of-China *(H rosa-sinensis),* whose one thousand horticultural varieties challenge the American Hibiscus Society members to name and classify them. All are big flowers with an out-thrust slender stamen tube and pistil tip, almost guaranteed to startle a person who comes around a bush and face-to-face with five flaring petals—white, or pink, or red, or yellow, or orange, or even violet pink, often with a deep ruby throat where hummingbirds reach for nectar. At the end of the day, when the petals close and fall to the ground, almost all of them darken and soften. They can be used to clean and shine black shoes, hence the unflattering name of shoeflower or shoeblack plant given to rose-of-China.

The unlobed leaves of these horticultural hibiscus varieties distinguish them from the gloriously red *H. coccineus* which opens scarlet blossoms six inches across in swamps and lowlands of its native Georgia, Florida and Alabama. The leaves of *H. coccineus* are deeply notched into five palmate lobes.

Countries of the eastern Mediterranean have given the world the rose-of-Sharon *(H. syriacus),* whose flowers are usually pink but sometimes purple and often more than three inches in diameter. It is a hardier plant than the rose-of-China or the hibiscus of the southeastern swamps, and often escapes from cultivation to become established in roadsides and thickets in northern Europe and in America as far as lower Ontario. Seldom, however, does it invade the borders of marshes and swamps—saline, brackish, or fresh-water. There America has native perennial herbs with handsome flowers as much as six inches in diameter, growing (as does *H. moscheutos,* a mallow-rose) to a height of ten to twelve feet.

In tropical West Africa, around Istanbul in Turkey, in India, and in the southeastern United States, people take a gastronomic interest in an annual hibiscus *(H. esculentus)* which has a branching hairy stem and heart-shaped, lobed leaves. Known as gumbo, or bendi-kai, or okra, it is raised for its partly-ripened

As the fruit of cotton (Gossypium *species) ripens, the capsule bursts in an explosion that displays the white fibers attached to the seeds. (Otto Croy)*

fruits. These can be cooked like asparagus, or pickled, or cut up to be put in soups and broths, to which they add a pleasant flavor and a "body" enjoyed by many people. The "body" is derived from mucilaginous materials and a pectin. The seeds can also be cured and dried as a substitute for coffee beans, or to be drilled and used as shining black beads. The leaves are used in many areas for poultices.

A similar mucilaginous material and pectin are accompanied by as much as eight per cent sugar in the dried bark collected from the heavy roots of the European marshmallow (Althaea officinalis), a plant that reaches a height of four feet with heart-shaped or oval leaves (often three-lobed) and a series of pink flowers about 1½ inches across. These ingredients, when extracted and concentrated by boiling in water, can be used to make a distinctive confection. Today, in the United States, marshmallow confections imitate those made from the plant; their ingredients are karo (corn) sirup, corn starch, gelatin, and cane sugar.

Far more widespread in the temperate zone and in highlands of the tropics is another Althaea: the hollyhock (A. rosea). It was a trophy brought to Europe by the returning Crusaders, and to America by the Pilgrim Fathers. Rising unbranched as high as nine feet, its stems produce a spirelike cluster of flowers. The lowest blossoms open first, then progressively the ones higher up. Few garden plants occupy as little area for their height or contribute as much vertically to the summer's display of flowers.

Several members of the mallow family produce bast fibers that locally can take the place of jute. In South America, the Caesar weed (Urena lobata) of Brazil yields the fiber known as aramina, used for making coffee sacks. In Asia and southern Europe, the velvetleaf (Abutilon theophrasti) is cultivated as the source of China "jute" for rugmaking; elsewhere the plant is widespread, and unappreciated, as a weed. Its flowers are small (to ¾ inch across), but of the same pattern as that in a hollyhock.

The most important fiber in the entire world today comes from still another mallow: the cotton plant (Gossypium, especially G. hirsutum). It is an annual, growing as high as eight feet, with many branches and lobed, heart-shaped leaves. Opposite some of the leaves it opens cream-colored flowers as much as 2½ inches across, which turn red and close on the second day. After the petals and stamens drop, the ovary enlarges, filled with seeds and the hairs that grow from their surface. The long ones are lint fibers, which begin to grow the day the flower opens; shorter are fuzz fibers ("linters"), which develop only

after the lint fibers reach almost full length—five to twelve days later. By then each of the seed hairs is increasing daily in the thickness of its cell wall. But as the seed ripens, the hairs die and dry. They collapse into spiral twisted filaments of almost pure cellulose, unlike any other natural fiber known. The twisting adds cohesiveness to any bundle of fibers, gives elasticity, and does not diminish the inherent strength, pliability and durability of the material. The white fibers become so bulky inside the ovary that it splits widely, exposing a white mass as the "cotton boll."

The use of cotton lint fibers to make thread and then cotton fabric has been traced as far back as 3000 B.C. in the Indus Valley. Thousands of years before any European met this material, patient women were laboriously pulling the fine white hairs from seeds of various native members of Gossypium under local cultivation in the Far East, India, Egypt, Central and South America. Until the 15th century, only a few European herbals hinted at the existence of such a plant; they mentioned and gave imaginative illustrations for a mythical "Vegetable Lamb, or Zoophyte" from which came a white "plant wool." These may have been inspired by explorers who brought back travel-worn cotton bolls.

Today about a third of the world's annual production of cotton lint fibers comes from the southern United States, where almost the only species raised is upland cotton (G. hirsutum). Its lint ("staple") ranges from 13/16 to 1¼ inch in length, which is intermediate in this dimension and in thickness as compared with "short-staple" Asiatic cottons and "long-staple" American types. The chief Asiatic species are G. arboreum and G. herbaceum, whose coarse lint fibers average 3/8 to 3/4 inch in length. Fine fibers from 17/16 to 2½ inches are obtained from various horticultural strains of G. barbadense, known as Sea Island cotton, American-Egyptian, or Peruvian Tanguis. Second as a producer of cotton fibers is the U.S.S.R. Other countries produce much less, but some (such as Egypt) show spectacular yields per acre and a cotton of very high quality.

Among the agricultural products of modern times, cotton seeds rank high. The short fuzz (linters), too short to be made into thread, provide a cellulose so pure that it can easily be converted into rayon, photographic film base, sheets and tubes of transparent wrapping materials, and explosives. The seeds themselves are pressed to obtain cottonseed oil, used in cooking and in the manufacture of margarine. The residue (hulls and cake) provide roughage in the

diet of domestic animals and a high-protein supplement that greatly increases the quality of meat on cattle, sheep, pigs, and poultry. These values from cottonseed after the cotton fibers are removed now almost equal in Europe and North America the benefits man finds from the lint fibers themselves. What a long way technology has come since 1498, when Vasco da Gama rounded the African continent to Calicut on the Madras coast of India and found the people wearing calicoes made of cotton! He brought samples back to Lisbon, and described the spinning methods now familiar from the hands of Mohandas Gandhi. Centuries before Vasco da Gama, the Arab traders had introduced cotton all around the Indian Ocean coasts, and taught Africans and Indians alike how to use the hairy seeds.

THE CHOCOLATE TREE AND ITS CLOSEST KIN
(Family Sterculiaceae)

Among members of the plant world, the chocolate tree *(Theobroma cacao)* may well come closest to paralleling the fairy-tale monster who turned into a prince. There is nothing about the tree itself that suggests the outstanding combination of food and flavor familiar all over the world today as chocolate. Growing untended in its native Central America or northern South America, its thick trunk rises to a height of as much as forty feet. Spreading branches with a downy surface support leathery leaves which droop from their own weight, the tip of each oval blade pointing toward the ground. From the trunk itself, small rounded "cushions" protrude, and on these the insignificant pink flowers appear. Dung flies are attracted by a malodorous fragrance, and attend to pollination. Then the fruit begins to swell toward its mature size and shape, resembling a reddish-orange to dark purple football ten to fourteen inches long and as much as five inches in diameter. During a year, any good chocolate tree will bear from sixty to seventy of these fruits, and every month a few of them will be hanging grotesquely from its trunk or large branches.

Left above: The hollyhock (Althaea rosea), *native to Crete and the Balkans, opens its flowers in succession up the spirelike cluster. Left: The handsome blossoms of shrubby hibiscus* (Hibiscus rosa-sinensis) *have become a symbol of the tropics. After they drop they can be used to polish shoes, whence the name shoeflower. (Both by Lorus and Margery Milne)*

Long before Europeans reached tropical America, the Aztecs domesticated the chocolate tree. They regarded its fruits as more valuable than gold, because chocolate could be drunk or eaten. Just as in Latin America today, the men of the Aztec tribes used a heavy knife to slash and split the woody husks of ripe chocolate fruits, exposing the mucilaginous pink pulp and from twenty-five to fifty large purplish seeds within. Their women plucked out the seeds and freed them of pulp. Next came a ritual whose origin is lost in antiquity, but whose role has come to be appreciated. The seeds are piled together and covered with the sweet pulp, either in a mound in some well-drained corner of a building or in a wooden container. In the tropic heat, fermentation begins almost immediately. The mound becomes distinctly warmer than its surroundings, and a trickle of smelly liquor drains away. Within a few days, everything that will ferment has liquefied, and the women can take up the "cured beans" (the seeds) for final cleaning and polishing. Several bitter substances in the seed coats have been altered by the curing, and the process is completed by drying the seeds further in the sun. They are now known as "cocoa beans," and ready for storage or shipment or use. In pre-Columbian days, they were a medium of exchange throughout the Aztec and Inca empires, and called in the widespread Nahuatlan language *chocólatl*.

Christopher Columbus took back cocoa beans to Spain in 1502, after his fourth voyage to the New World. There the strange bitter beverage made from ground roasted seeds, hot water, and vanilla from America was improved by the addition of sugar. About 1700 the English changed the recipe again, stirring hot milk into the delicious drink. More than a century later, a Dutchman patented a new machine for pressing the ground roasted seeds, yielding cocoa powder and a valuable by-product, cocoa butter, as a natural fat that does not turn rancid when exposed to air. If cocoa butter and sugar are added to ground roasted cocoa beans, the product is sweet eating chocolate. Today it is hard to realize that this favorite among the world's confections did not become available until about 1850, and that Swiss milk chocolate had its beginning in 1876. Chocolate trees are now cultivated in large orchards, and pruned to a size that keeps their fruits within easy reach for pickers. About nine-tenths of the world supply comes from Ghana, Nigeria, and the Dominican Republic, the rest (mostly of higher quality) from Latin America, the West Indies, Ceylon, and Java. Little of it is used in native areas, but demand for chocolate candy and flavorings in Europe and America keeps the production of cocoa beans important wherever the trees will grow well.

Far less elaborate preparation is required for use of the seeds from kola nut trees *(Cola nitida* and *C. acuminata),* relatives of the chocolate tree found native in tropical West Africa. There in the forests, the Negro people hunt out the modest-sized trees, recognizing them by their simple glossy leaves, their small clusters of red flowers among the foliage, or the star-shaped bunches of egg-shaped fruits in each of which are eight reddish seeds. These can be chewed fresh as a stimulant or to suppress any feeling of fatigue or hunger. They contain about two per cent of caffeine, as well as alkaloids and flavorful oils that may contribute to the satisfaction obtained. The same substances are enjoyed in cola drinks, made by boiling the pulverized dry seeds in water. Cola beverages are now known all over the world, many of them prepared with added extracts from coca leaves that have been freed of cocaine. Kola nuts, however, still come chiefly from wild trees in tropical Africa and cultivated orchards of them in the West Indies.

Similar materials are probably present in the seeds of the Panamá tree *(Sterculia apetala)* of Central America, Panamá, and northern South America. European explorers met them first in a village on the Pacific side of the isthmus of Panamá. The villagers were chewing Panamá seeds, from the Panamá tree, in the community of Panamá. All questions seemed to be answered with the same word. From this experience came the use of Panamá for the name of the Republic, and the adoption of the Panamá tree as the national emblem. It gives shade in a land where the sun's rays are intense. Only when its petalless flowers open do people shun it, for then the tree is like others in its family in attracting pollinating flies with an odor so characteristic that the Latin word *stercus* (dung) went into the name of both the genus and the family.

THE PARADOXICAL BOMBAXES
(Family Bombacaceae)

These strange trees of the tropics stand leafless for months at a time, their heavy boles spreading to bare branches. Many of them have gigantic trunks. Some, such as *Bombacopsis* in the rain forests of Latin America, remain upright in the soft muddy ground only because great buttresses extend to all sides as strong vertical vanes. Others, including many tropical American members of *Chorisia,* bear corky cones or stout spines at close intervals on their tall cylindrical trunks. Characteristically, these trees prune themselves as they grow until, at maturity, the lowest branch is far above the ground.

Heaviest of the bombaxes is the grotesque baobab *(Adansonia digitata)* of dry savannas in East Africa. From a graceful sapling, its trunk enlarges rapidly to a diameter of as much as thirty feet. In proportion to the twisted branches at the top, this seems so outlandish that we could scarcely believe our eyes when first we encountered these living trees. According to a local African legend, the baobab was planted by the Creator initially in the rain forests of the Congo basin. But the tree complained that the dampness made its trunk swell. The Creator moved it to the high slopes of the Ruwenzori range—the Mountains of the Moon—where the view on clear days is magnificent. Still the baobab grumbled about the humidity. Angered by the tree's wailing, the Creator seized the swollen trunk and thrust it into the soil of Africa's arid highland country. Inadvertently, he put the tree in upside down, with its roots in the air. And that, say the Africans, is why the baobab has its present appearance, as though suffering from elephantiasis.

The monstrous trunk is actually a reservoir of water, protected by a fibrous outer bark which native people sometimes use as a raw material for making rope and cloth. They also tap on old baobabs to discover those in which the center has dried out to a room-sized cavity. If a small doorway is cut through the thick wall, the tree affords shelter for a whole family. Such an inhabitable baobab near the coast of Mozambique, mentioned in the diary of the English missionary David Livingstone, was discovered recently to bear his carved initials on its inner wall, intact after nearly a century. The tree has been declared a national monument and given protection. It is too near permanent rivers to be endangered by thirsty elephants, as are baobabs farther inland. During times of prolonged drought, the big animals use their tusks to attack baobabs systematically. Tearing through the bark, they reach the moisture within and leave the baobab a dying wreck.

The six-inch pendant white flowers of baobabs are seldom seen among the foliage. But when the leaves drop at the beginning of the dry season, the large gourdlike woody fruits are conspicuous on high branches against the sky. Fuzzy on the outside, each fruit holds many small seeds embedded in a mucilaginous pulp with a pleasant, mildly acid flavor. Everywhere that members of the genus *Adansonia* grow—about ten kinds, in continental Africa, the island of

Much of the year the branches of Chorisia ventricosa *are bare but the bottle-like trunk stores water upon which the tree survives. Brazilians call it a* barrigudo *("big belly"). (E. Aubert de La Rue)*

Madagascar, and northern Australia—they are known also as cream-of-tartar trees from this cool-tasting pulp. In Africa where there are monkeys, baobab fruit is often called "monkey bread."

People of Malaya, Thailand, the Philippines and East Indies show surprising fondness for the custard-like pulp in fruits of the durian *(Durio zibethinus),* a tree with oblong tapering leaves and small greenish-yellow flowers. Under cultivation it attains a height of seventy to eighty feet, its main branches spreading like those of an elm. Its spherical fruit, six to eight inches in diameter, is encased by a five-part woody husk which bears so many sharp-pointed conical projections that no space remains between them. If split along the seams, where the spines arch toward one another, the fruit opens to reveal five chambers, each weighing about a pound and filled with a cream-colored pulp in which one or more large seeds are embedded. So offensive is the odor that Western people seldom sample the pulp of ripe durians, although they may enjoy the seeds roasted in the native style.

The silk-cotton tree (Ceiba pentandra), *a native of tropical America, yields kapok, most valuable of all stuffing materials, from the silky hairs on its seeds. (Rolf Blomberg)*

The African baobab (Adansonia digitata) *reaches as much as thirty feet in diameter. In extreme drought, elephants sometimes destroy them for their juicy tissues. (Southern Rhodesia Information)*

Several other members of the bombax family bear large fruits that split open to expose hundreds of seeds, each with a tuft of silky hairs ready to catch the breeze and carry it away. Because the hairs repel water for many hours and are hollow like those of cotton and milkweed seeds, they have found use in stuffing pillows and mattresses and in buoyant life preservers. Most valuable is kapok, the seed hairs from the silk-cotton tree *(Ceiba pentandra)* of tropical America. The palmately compound leaves of a silk-cotton tree cast interesting shadows in the bright sunlight as they spread from heavy branches in the tree's broad crown. The small, off-white flowers are seldom noticed. Great plantations of silk-cotton trees have been established in Africa and Asia, where mature trees each produce annually about one thousand fruits. This number will yield around ten pounds of useful fiber and a harvest of seeds valuable in making soap, margarine, and stock feed. Similar fibers and useful seeds come from trees native to the East, such as the red cotton-tree *(Salmalia malabarica)* of rain forests from Indo-Malaya to northern Austra-

lia. Its foliage, thick trunk and spreading buttresses are similar to those of silk-cotton trees, but its heavy branches come out horizontally in handsome whorls. In January, while the red cotton-tree is regularly leafless, its long flower buds open into a spectacular display of bright crimson petals and many purple-tipped stamens. Hundreds of birds and insects come for nectar and pollen. In Burma, people gather the fallen calyxes from freshly opened blossoms and make them into a curry vegetable. Even the thick, strap-shaped petals and the stamens are relished by native animals, such as deer, when they drop from flowers whose fruits are beginning to swell.

Still more spectacular displays of stamens mark the shaving-brush tree *(Pseudobombax ellipticum)* which flowers at the same time of year in its tropical American homelands. Pinkish brown buds as much as eight to ten inches long may be compared to sticks of shaving soap. When they open abruptly, the five tongue-shaped petals curling back, a mass of long red stamens is revealed in a cluster that resembles a shaving brush. At their center is a slender pistil, extending well beyond the stamen tips, ready to capture pollen from any visiting bird or bee.

The lightest of all commercial woods is also a product from the bombax family. It is balsa, from the tree of that name (or West Indian corkwood, *Ochroma lagopus),* which grows rapidly in the rain forests of tropical America. The cell walls of the wood are remarkably thin, which seems to limit growth to small-tree size except where sturdier vegetation blocks the wind. Both the palmately compound leaves and the white flowers, which attain a diameter of about six inches, are lightweight. When well seasoned, balsa wood floats in water with only about an eighth of its bulk immersed. It can be shaped easily with a file or sandpaper, and is used extensively for model-making, for interior construction in aircraft, for thermal insulation, for minimizing vibrations from machinery, and for floats of many kinds.

Balsa is also the name for a raft made of balsa wood. By diligent hunting, Thor Heyerdahl and his party of Norwegian scientists found nine giant balsa trees almost three feet in diameter at the base. One

was more than eighty feet tall, well protected in the forest. But with help from Peruvian laborers, the scientists cut all nine and got the logs into the water along the coast, where rope lashings could hold the balsa lengths together as the floating structure of the raft *Kon-Tiki.* The longest log, forty-five feet from end to end, went into the middle of the array, with progressively shorter ones on each side of it. On this structure the exploring scientists proved the feasability of drifting from Peru to Tahiti in the Polynesian islands of the South Pacific Ocean.

CHAPTER 16

Tea, and Plants Somewhat Like It

CUES: *If the dicot plant has its sepals overlapping in the flower bud and its compound ovary containing just a single chamber, its ovules (and seeds) all attached around inside the outer wall, it will usually have ten or more stamens and simple leaves, and belong to the Order Parietales. It may be a* Camellia, *a tropical mangosteen, a salt cedar, a violet, a passionflower, or a begonia.*

The attachment of ovules and seeds inside the ovary is the inconspicuous feature upon which botanists have relied in grouping together nearly 6600

The giant granadilla (Passiflora quadrangularis), *a vine native to tropical South America, produces edible juicy fruits as much as ten inches long. (Othmar Danesch)*

Right above: Tea trees (Camellia sinensis) *are kept low and shrubby on plantations, but grow to modest height if untended, particularly in their native areas from India to Japan. Photographed in Ceylon. (ZFA) Right: Known as the "lost camellia tree"* (Gordonia alatamaha), *this attractive flowering tree appears to have become extinct in the wild since 1790, when living branches collected in Georgia were successfully propagated in Bartram's botanic garden in Philadelphia, Pennsylvania. (E. Javorsky) Far right: Violets* (Viola *species) of many kinds are favorite flowers of springtime in the North Temperate Zone. They are native also to cool moist woodlands on slopes of the Andes, on mountains in tropical Africa, and in South Africa. (J. C. Allen & Son)*

species belonging to more than three hundred genera. Only a few bear leaves that are lobed or divided. In most, the foliage consists of simple leaves with smooth, untoothed edges, rounding in a curve from the base to the tip.

THE TEA FAMILY (Theaceae)

Buddhist priests are credited with phenomenal success in spreading the cultivation of tea and its use as a beverage in the Far East as a means of combatting intemperance there. Tea itself (*Camellia sinensis*— formerly known as *Thea sinensis*) grows wild in the monsoon forests of eastern India, western China, and Indonesia. It thrives best in cooler air, and as an evergreen shrub attains a height of as much as thirty feet in the tropics. It cannot tolerate frost, however, and hence is limited to an elevation of no more than six thousand feet near the Equator and to lower altitudes in adjacent parts of temperate zones. On tea plantations, the shrubs are set out in rows three to six feet apart and never allowed to develop more than three to five feet high. When about three years old the shrub comes into production, reaching its peak at age ten, and ending its useful life when twenty-five to fifty years old. All through its productive life, the tea plant annually opens one or more sets of fragrant white blossoms suggesting those of a single rose. Each has several whorls of stamens and a compound pistil which matures as a dry capsule and opens to free three big seeds.

In the tropics, new growth begins on tea plants several times a year. As each "flush" of fresh leaves opens, pickers go systematically along the rows, collecting into bags or baskets the buds and young foliage that is to be processed locally. To make one pound of manufactured tea requires about 3200 branch tips, each usually a bud and two leaves. After

Giant fruits, each botanically a berry, mature on the trunk of the papaya (Carica papaya). *Cultivated widely in frost-free areas, it is native to tropical America. (Grant Heilman)*

plucking, the tea tips are wilted for eighteen to twenty-four hours, and then rolled up tightly by hand or machine to break the leaf cells and expose their contents to the air. This treatment is cut short for "green teas," which go into a steam bath to stop fermentation while some color from their chlorophyll remains. Oolong teas are allowed to ferment for half an hour or more before being steamed. Black teas develop their color and flavor by being subjected to as much as $4\frac{1}{2}$ hours of fermentation in baskets, or on cement floors, or on glass shelves, under damp cloths. The steamed buds and leaves may receive another short period of rolling before entering the drying ovens. After being dried, tea leaves of each type are cut, sifted, and sorted into distinctive grades. Of the black teas, the best quality of buds and small foliage become "orange pekoe." Next larger and coarser is "pekoe," then Souchong (coarsest leaves), and finally "pekoe dust." A pound of any kind of tea represents the year's output of about four bushes in their prime, or more bushes at lesser or greater ages.

Almost eighty per cent of the tea in world markets comes from India and Ceylon. About nine-tenths of it goes to countries in the British tradition, where annual consumption ranges from around nine pounds

Far left: The large, edible, melon-like fruits of the papaya (Carica papaya) *are sometimes assailed by the blue tanagers in tropical Latin America where these sturdy plants are native. (Karl Weidmann) Left above: "Johnny-Jump-Ups" are Eurasian pansies* (Viola tricolor) *that have escaped from cultivation. In Europe they are often called ladies'-delight and heart's-ease. (Lorus and Margery Milne) Left: On the mountains of equatorial Africa, several species of the genus* Hypericum *attain tree size, with large golden flowers often tinged with red. Photographed high in the Ruwenzori range. (E. S. Ross)*

153

per person in Britain itself to three in Canada and two in South Africa, as compared to two-thirds of a pound in the United States. Internal production and consumption of tea in China and the U.S.S.R. are estimated to total less than a third of the amount visible in world commerce. This represents a major change since the 1940's, India displacing China as the largest tea-producing country.

The earliest authenticated reference to the beverage use of tea is in a Chinese dictionary of A.D. 350. Cultivation of the shrub and the drinking of tea spread to Japan about A.D. 593, and to Java in 1684. The sale of tea by the cup or the pot commenced in coffee houses of Venice (1559), Lisbon (1600), Amsterdam (1610), Moscow (1618), Paris (1648), and cities of Britain and America about 1650. In his famous diary, Samuel Pepys of London recorded drinking his first cup of tea in 1660. The unpopular British tax on tea, begun in 1773, precipitated the Boston "Tea Party" and spurred on the American Revolution. Ever since, Americans have drunk about twenty-five times as much coffee as tea. In Britain, coffee continued to outrank tea until a century later, when the price of coffee skyrocketed due to ruination of coffee plantations in India and Ceylon by a rust fungus. On the same land, tea plantations were promptly set out and, because it was cheaper, tea replaced coffee in British habits.

An average cup of British tea contains about two grains of tannins, one grain of caffeine, and various other soluble substances that provide the flavor. Britishers tend to increase the food value of their beverage by adding sugar to sweeten it, and follow a procedure recorded first among the Chinese in 1655 by mixing in milk or cream, whose proteins combine with the tannins and eliminate the natural astringency. The caffeine is absorbed slowly, and provides pleasing stimulation after about fifteen minutes, whereas the heat from the hot beverage, the water, and the sugar are all distributed by the blood in a much shorter time. An average cup of American coffee, by contrast, contains eighteen to thirty-six grains of caffeine, with less tannins than in a cup of tea.

Tea is but one of the eighty-odd species in the Oriental genus *Camellia*. Best known among the others are *C. japonica* and *C. sasanqua,* the latter sweet scented, of which many horticultural varieties are cultivated for their handsome flowers. These come in shades from white to red, contrasting with dark evergreen foliage.

In many of the world's botanic gardens and around homes where the climate is no more severe than along the Atlantic coast of America as far north as Long Island, a "lost camellia tree" is treasured as a curiosity—a living fossil among plants. The American botanist John Bartram discovered it in 1765 along the banks of the Alatamaha River in Georgia. From seeds and cuttings he propagated it in his Philadelphia garden under the name *Franklinia alatamaha,* honoring Benjamin Franklin. Attempts to find more wild trees of this kind met with no success. Apparently Bartram gathered his material from one of the last few specimens of a tree that was on the verge of extinction. If he had not happened along and taken a fancy to the Franklinia, no one today would know that this American camellia-like tree ever lived or was lost. In modern cultivation it attains a height of fifteen to twenty feet, and produces attractive flowers as much as three inches in diameter. The petals are of unequal lengths, and cup loosely around a golden cluster of stamens. Each flower lasts for several days and then is followed by another opening from a nearby bud, keeping the tree in bloom from midsummer until frost. The tree sheds its leaves before winter.

The "lost camellia" or Franklinia is now known as *Gordonia alatamaha,* or mountain-bay, to show its actual kinship to the evergreen loblolly-bay *(G. lasianthus)* of swamps from South Carolina to southern Florida, and to thirty more kinds of *Gordonia* native to the Orient from India to China, where they bear glossy green leaves and large waxy white flowers. In most of them the many stamens are united for a short distance by the base of the filaments, but in a series of separate whorls around the single central pistil.

THE MANGOSTEEN FAMILY *(Guttiferaceae)*

Among the nearly 825 kinds of plants grouped in this family because they show similarities in floral details there is more variety than can be anticipated. Beauty leaf *(Calophyllum inophyllum),* from the shores of the Indian Ocean and the western Pacific, is planted for its magnificent glossy evergreen foliage; its six-inch leaves, with blunt or notched tips, are unharmed by salt spray, and its clustered fragrant white inch-wide flowers make it the favorite among tropical seashore trees. Mangosteen *(Garcinia mangostana),* a handsome small tree that rarely grows taller than thirty-five feet in its native East Indies, gains its fine reputation from its delicious fruits; inside the purple rind that maintains firmly the spherical or pearlike shape are several segments of snow-white flesh which are juicy, faintly acid, and so delicate that shipment of the fruit to distant markets is impractical. Ceylon ironwood (Mesua ferrea) is a sacred tree among Buddhists of India and Malaya, and has been planted outside most Buddhist temples in the area or to grace avenues in the East Indies as far as Java; not only do its waxy leaves shimmer with reflected light underneath, but its fragrant flowers are collected to stuff in pillows for bridal beds; traditionally, one of the five arrows of the Indian cupid god Kamediva is made of Ceylon ironwood, or at least tipped with it; the dried flowers, each like a four-petalled rose, are sold in Indian bazaars. In the rain forests of the New World tropics, many of the two hundred kinds of Clusia begin life as seedlings among orchids and bromeliads on high limbs of giant trees; gradually they extend roots down the trunk of the supporting tree and envelop it, becoming "strangler trees" comparable to the strangler figs.

The most widely known members of the mangosteen family are neither tropical nor trees, but perennial herbs and small shrubs of the genus Hypericum. One that makes an attractive ground cover, low-growing and profuse-blooming with three-inch golden flowers like five-pointed stars, is H. calycinum of southeastern Europe and Asia Minor; it is among several different plants to which the name "rose of Sharon" is applied, and grows naturally on the famous Plain of Sharon between Israel's port of Jaffa and Mount Carmel. Several related species, with yellow petals and brown or reddish sepals on pendant flowers, attain tree size on the mountains of equatorial Africa and Ethiopia. On lofty, misty slopes they grow as much as fifty feet tall in forest groves, hung with beardlike lichens. At lower elevations, different species form a shrubby understory below other kinds of trees.

Far less appreciated is St. John's-wort (H. perforatum), a tough weed from Europe that has become naturalized in pasturelands and neglected areas of Asia, America and Australia. Usually domestic livestock avoid eating its branching stems, its small eliptical leaves which seem perforated by translucent dots, and its golden, half-inch flowers. Since edible plants are eaten all around this weed, it has few competitors and proliferates rapidly by extending its roots and dispersing its lustrous black seeds. In overgrazed lands, however, the animals add St. John's-wort to their diet. So long as less than three per cent of the vegetation they eat during any twenty-four hours is from this weed, they may escape harm. But greater amounts provide them with too much of the fluorescent pigment (hypericin) found in the pellucid dots seen in the leaves.

Hypericum-poisoning becomes evident in a day or two in animals exposed to the sun or to cold water, to both of which the pigment makes them hypersensitive. The skin of a black-coated animal is rarely affected, but the corneas of its eyes may become bloodshot after a day in the sun, as a prelude to permanent blindness. Animals with paler coats develop an intense itching that may lead them to rub raw the areas of skin exposed to the light. Sheep that have been sheared are similarly susceptible, although the symptoms are quite unlike those of sunburn. Often the poisoned animals refuse to eat, and starve to death. Or they may plunge blindly into cold streams, and die from the cold water. In California and other western states between 1930 and 1951, and in many areas of Australia, Hypericum-poisoning was regarded by ranchers as their greatest single cause of financial loss. Some of the difficulty vanished wherever the number of stock animals was reduced until the edible plants could grow and compete with the St. John's-wort. By 1951, Australians discovered a more selective means for eradicating the poisonous weed: release of certain glossy blue beetles from South America, whose larvae attacked the roots and stems of the plant and whose adults fed avidly on the floral parts and seeds. Introduction of the beetles was successful too in the western United States. Often the ranchers found that elimination of St. John's-wort left their animals without anything to eat on overstocked ranges; only a reduction in the number to be nourished on the plants that would grow could provide each animal with enough for proper development.

THE DIPTEROCARPS (Family Dipterocarpaceae)

The Greek words from which the family name is derived mean "two winged fruits," and this distinctive feature makes it easy to recognize these tall trees native to the tropical area from India to New Guinea and the Philippines. Their trunks grow straight, with few branches, yielding fine hardwood such as that from sal (Shorea robusta)—a forest tree officially protected in India. Among their evergreen leathery leaves, little clusters of regular flowers appear. Each one to be pollinated develops into a one-seeded nut enclosed by the five sepals of the calyx. Usually just two of the sepals extend like wings, catching the wind and carrying the seed within the nut far to one

In Baja California and the western Sonora in Mexico, bizarre boojum trees (Idria columnaris) grow as much as thirty feet high, branchless and leafless except after rains. (Joe Stacey)

side of the parent tree. Many of the dipterocarps yield valuable resinous gums, known as dammar. White dammar (or Indian copal) comes from *Vateria indica,* of India and the Seychelle Islands. More fragrant is the gum called Gurjun balsam, from various kinds of *Dipterocarpus* in the monsoon forests of southern Asia. Most aromatic of all is the resin of *Drybalanops aromatica* of Malaya and Borneo, which is in great demand throughout the East Indies as "Sumatra camphor" or "Borneo camphor" for use in incense and embalming of the dead.

THE TAMARISKS (Family Tamaricaceae)

Among the few shrubs that can grow on alkali flats and in salty soil along sandy coasts are the tamarisks. Their small, hair-tufted seeds germinate quickly in wet weather, sending down long roots that reach water at levels below those available to most plants. Their gray-green leaves are narrow and pressed against the branching stems, retaining moisture well. Even their flowers are minute. But they do serve well as windbreaks, and a few (such as French tamarisk, *Tamarix gallica,* of Eurasia) are grown as ornamentals. In arid areas from Egypt to Afghanistan, the Bedouin people seek out the shrubby *T. mannifera,* upon which scale insects feed. These sapsuckers

exude a honeylike substance rich in sugars—one of several known as "manna," but probably not the one mentioned in the Bible (Exodus 16).

THE CANDLEWOODS (Family Fouquieraceae)

For most of the year in the Arizona-Sonoran desert of North America, clumps of unbranched eight- to ten-foot wands cast slim shadows in the hot sun. They are coachwhips *(Fouquiera splendens),* each stem armed with a multiplicity of short thorny projections that justify another name: "cat's claw." Under the magic touch of rain, the plant sends out new leaves with bright green blades. At the proper season, it may also open a terminal cluster of brilliant orange flowers, whose sepals and stamens are all separate but whose petals and carpels are each united into a group. Desert dwellers call the plant "banner cactus" from these waving spikes of bloom. Or they remember that the dry woody stems, collected between rains, can be burned from one end as "candlewood." Ocotillo is still another name for this distinctive shrub of the American southwest. As soon as the moisture from the rain is used up, the plant drops its leafblades. The midribs and petioles harden into thorny points, which protect the plant from any animal with tender lips.

The only other genus in the family is *Idria,* with a single species *(I. columnaris)* known as the "boojum tree" in the unique deserts of Baja California. The trunk is shaped like an inverted carrot ten to thirty feet high, bearing a few slender leafless branches only at the very top. After a rainy period, these extend a new crop of tender leaves to the sun and some clusters of white flowers to attract pollen-carrying insects. With the return of drought, the plant seems to go dormant again. Actually its green trunk is still providing useful energy from sunlight,

Right above: In Pacallpa, Peru, passionflowers (Passiflora) grow on clambering vines, as do more than 350 species in this genus, most of which are native to South America. (E. S. Ross) Right: From Arabia and East Africa comes the shrubby fried-egg plant (Oncoba spinosa), which gets its name from the large flowers, each about four inches across. (Lorus and Margery Milne) Far right: At high altitude near Tixán Chimborazo, Ecuador, these wild perennial members of the genus Begonia are near one of their centers of distribution. Others occur in Hawaii and New Guinea. (E. S. Ross)

and making use of the water stored there. As the water diminishes, the boojum tree becomes more slender and often bends over in a bizarre arch.

THE DYE WE EAT (Family Bixaceae)

Long ago the South American Indians discovered how to extract from the seed coats in showy orange fruits of a local tree a brilliant dye with which to decorate their bodies or add color to woven cloth. They claim the orange color to be effective in repelling insects that bite or sting. Today the fruits and seed coats from this tree *(Bixa orellana)* are collected on a far larger scale for export as a "harmless vegetable dye." For many years after the discovery of this American dyestuff, the dairy industry provided almost the only market for it. Dairymen added the dye as "butter color" (or by its South American name of annatto) whenever the color faded from butter or cheese made from the milk of cattle to which green fodder had become unavailable. No complaint arose when the permanent yellow component of the dye was employed to color varnish. But in many parts of the world, the dairymen continue to resist addition of annatto dye to margarine, to make the low-priced spread resemble butter-colored butter.

THE VIOLETS (Family Violaceae)

A pansy flower more than two inches broad is actually a cultivated violet *(Viola tricolor)* of a species that was adopted long ago on its native Eurasian soil and developed into a delightful ornamental. Pansies come in so many different colors today, often marked in ways that suggest a little face, that they are favorites on every continent inhabited by man. But whenever they cast their seeds out of the flower border into the lawn, the new plants that come up produce smaller flowers in different patterns; generally they are then known as Johnny-Jump-Ups. We can't bear to run the lawnmower over them, and regularly leave little clumps in tufts of grass until they stop blooming in late spring.

The genus *Viola* is one of the largest in the plant kingdom, with more than four hundred species recognized. Many of them produce hybrids by cross-

The ocotillo (Fouquiera splendens), *known also as cat's-claw and coachwhip, is as distinctive as cacti in the deserts of the American Southwest. It produces a new set of small green leaves after every rain. (Bill Ratcliffe)*

breeding. Although the hybrids reproduce less freely, they do add to the variety of violets to be discovered. Most species inhabit the wetter slopes of the Andes, which appears to be the ancestral home of the whole family. Violets have spread widely, however, until Europe has seventy-five species and America more than sixty. All are low herbs with simple leaves, whose flowers show a special development of the lowest petal into a backward-pointing spur. A large, horn-shaped nectar gland reaches into the hollow of the spur and releases there the sweet liquid for which insects visit the flower. If pansies are to be picked for indoor enjoyment, the freshly-opened ones should be gathered early in the morning—before the insects arrive. The colorful petals remain on much longer if the three united carpels of the pistil have not been pollinated. After pollen arrives, the five petals and five stamens fall, and the pistil begins to swell into an explosive capsule.

During the warmer months of summer, most violets produce an inconspicuous set of flowers without petals. In some, these flowers are hidden underground. They never open, but instead fertilize themselves in the bud and are amazingly productive of viable seeds. Whether these cleistogamous flowers or the familiar showy ones are produced depends chiefly upon the length of night. As soon as autumn approaches and the nights lengthen out to a number of hours comparable to those of early spring, violets (and pansies) begin producing conspicuous blossoms again and attracting the bumblebees that are their chief pollinators.

In the tropical rain forests of South America and Africa, members of the violet family reach tree size. The achocon tree *(Leonia glyptocarpa)* of northern South America produces a trunk two feet in diameter and sixty to seventy feet tall. In season, the lower part of the trunk is hidden by large pendant clusters of cream-colored flowers. They are followed by a peach-sized fruit whose soft, sweet flesh is much sought after by many Peruvians.

THE PASSION FLOWERS (Family Passifloraceae)

When a visitor to the tropics is served a tall glass of passion-fruit juice (a "refresco"), or is given a large delicious passion fruit to eat, the folklore of aphrodisiacs comes to mind. But the truth is that the name of the passion flower *(Passiflora)* arises from a supposed religious symbolism: the three styles, each ending in a button-shaped enlargement, for the Holy Trinity; the "corona" of threadlike projections from the central stalk that supports the five stamens and single ovary, for the crown of thorns; the five petals and five sepals (which are similar and form a single ring below the corona) for the ten apostles—leaving out Peter and Judas. All of the six hundred species in the family show this special form of flower—unlike any other in the plant world. The four hundred members of *Passiflora* are chiefly South American, mostly woody climbers with tendrils from the axil of leaves along the stem. Widely cultivated as a horticultural curiosity is the passion vine *P. incarnata,* which is native to the southern United States from Florida to Virginia, Missouri to Oklahoma; its pink and white flowers are followed by edible yellow fruits two inches long. The fleshy arils that support the seeds inside taste much like those of the tropical purple granadilla *(P. edulis)* and the giant granadilla *(P. quadrangularis),* the latter with fruits as much as ten inches long. Australians and people in the Far East raise these tropical species for fruit and juice, to a degree unmatched elsewhere.

THE PAPAYAS *(Family Caricaceae)*

The "melon-that-grows-on-a-tree" is known by many names even in its native Mexico and Central America: papaya, pawpaw, *melon zapote.* Cubans call it *fruta bomba,* and Puerto Ricans *lechosa.* It grows on a tree-like herb *(Carica papaya)* now cultivated throughout the tropical world and into the warmer parts of the temperate zone. From a seed, the plant may attain a height of twenty feet in five years, its woody trunk unbranched but crowned by large deeply lobed leaves on long petioles. The stamens are borne in separate staminate flowers in a pendant cluster as much as three feet long. Pistillate flowers are larger, with five fleshy petals, but usually develop singly where the leaf petioles join the stem. The large ovary, topped by five fan-shaped stigmas, develops into a somewhat cylindrical fruit that may be twenty inches long and weigh twenty-five pounds. Its thin skin and deep yellow or salmon-colored flesh surrounds a large cavity the walls of which bear many black, pea-sized seeds. The texture of the fruit suggests that of a canteloupe. When ripe it cuts easily with a spoon and to our taste is most enjoyable when drizzled with the juice of a lime or lemon.

The unripe fruit, the leaves and other parts of the papaya plant contain a milky juice which is rich in an enzyme (papain) that is like pepsin in tenderizing meat. Tropical people often wrap a tough chicken in papaya leaves the day before it is to be cooked and eaten, and let the enzyme soften the meat. Or the unripe fruits can be cut into superficially, causing juice to exude and dry where it can be collected and used as a meat tenderizer—or for making home remedies to aid indigestion.

THE BEGONIAS *(Family Begoniaceae)*

Almost all of the succulent plants in this family are members of the huge genus *Begonia,* with about eight hundred species in tropical wetlands—principally South America, Hawaii, and New Guinea. Some are native to South Africa, and others to the slopes of the Himalayas. All species produce two types of flowers. The pistillate type have from two to five petal-like parts but no distinction between petals and sepals, and two to three united carpels in an inferior ovary which bears conspicuous angles or even winglike extensions. The staminate flowers have numerous stamens, and showy parts consisting of two petals and two larger petal-like sepals. Most species grow easily from cuttings, or even from pieces of leaf that are kept half-covered by damp soil. So many horticultural varieties have been developed that people interested in these plants have formed begonia societies in Britain, America, and other parts of the world.

The commonest "house begonia" is *B. semperflorens,* a native to Brazil, usually with rose-pink flowers in clusters and oval leaves as much as four inches long. From Assam has come the rex begonia *(B. rex),* with a prostrate stem or buried rhizome and leaves handsomely variegated, often a foot in length. Most of the so-called tuberous begonias are horticultural hybrids, derived from ancestors whose regular annual period of dormancy matched unfavorable living conditions of cold and drought. Despite all the variations that have been perpetuated by the begonia fanciers, all members of the genus continue to produce lopsided leaves.

CHAPTER 17

The Prickly, Spiny Cactuses

CUES: *If the dicot plant has stems modified for water storage, taking the place of the leaves in photosynthesis, and if its flowers have a large number of showy parts (sepals and petals usually grading into one another) and the stamens arise from the base of the petal-like parts, the plant is almost sure to be a member of the Order Opuntiales. Ordinarily it will be a spiny cactus, with barbed bristles rising from a pit or a raised spot. The ovary will be inferior because the other flower parts arise part way up the ovary walls.*

About 1700 kinds of cactuses constitute the single family *(Cactaceae)* in this order. Probably all of them were restricted to the New World before man began redistributing the plants he found in America. Today only one cactus, *Rhipsalis cassytha* of continental Africa, Madagascar, Mauritius, and Ceylon, cannot be shown definitely to have come from the Western Hemisphere. All of the other sixty members of *Rhipsalis* are native to South America, chiefly Argentina and Brazil.

Truly exceptional are the various species of *Pereskia,* for these plants of Latin America and the West Indies bear broad flat leaves as well as the characteristic cactus spines. Barbados-gooseberry *(P. aculeata)* is a climber, sometimes called lemon vine. Its lemon-yellow fruits, reaching three-quarters of an inch in diameter, are delicious; its showy white flowers are pleasantly fragrant; but many people object to the odor of its leaves even when it is grown outdoors as a hedge plant or as a covering for buildings in the tropics. In South America, several kinds of *Pereskia* attain a height of twenty-five feet or more as real trees. Venezuelans often set out the guamacho *(P. guamacho)* as living fence posts, since they grow quickly from cuttings and later produce delightful yellow flowers and then succulent edible berries.

The best-known symbol of American deserts in the United States is the giant saguaro cactus *(Cereus giganteus,* sometimes called *Carnegiea gigantea).* It is native only to the Arizona-Sonoran desert, where its vertical columns rise as high as seventy feet, reaching a diameter of as much as two feet, often as unbranched fingers pointing to the cloudless sky. Tall saguaros, however, usually support as many as a dozen armlike branches, which curve to rise parallel to the main stem or twist grotesquely. In spring, showy snow-white flowers appear at the tip of the central column and the ends of the arms. By night they are visited by hawkmoths and fruit-eating bats, and by day by desert doves, hummingbirds, native bees and introduced honeybees.

From infrequent storms the giant cactus collects water through a radiating system of roots near the

Cactus flowers appear occasionally on a peyote button (Lophophora williamsii), *a cactus of northern Mexico and Texas that yields a hallucinogen. (Claire Meyer Proctor)*

surface of the ground, extending as much as fifty feet in every direction. The moisture passes into a vertical series of interconnected wood rods spaced equally around the sturdy stem. Between these supports the outer surface is conspicuously pleated. After a rain the pleats tend to disappear because the plant expands like an accordion, holding a ton or more of moisture in the pulpy tissue between the vertical rods. During the normally rainless remainder of the year, the water is used up or lost to the dry air, and the pleats become deeper. Rosettes of strong curved spines stud the ridges between the pleats, and ward off all the larger animals except the ladder-backed woodpeckers, which cut nest cavities out of the wet central pulp. Against the dry air in the woodpecker's hole, the gummy sap of the saguaro hardens, shutting out infectious microbes and sealing in the precious water. Even after the plant has lived its full two hundred years, died and disintegrated, the hard rind around the woodpecker nest remains. Prospectors find the nests intact on the desert floor and call them "desert shoes." By then the local Indians have usually salvaged the strong dry woody support rods of the saguaro, to make frames for homes—a practice they have followed for unknown centuries.

Each red juicy fruit of the saguaro contains about two thousand seeds. Desert animals and Indians collect the fruits as food. The pulp can be boiled down to a thick sirup, and sealed for storage in earthenware jars. The seeds may be dried separately, and mashed to a paste, which is cooked like corn meal mush. Even after livestock were introduced into saguaro country, a fair number of seeds escaped desert animals and Indians; some of them germinated in the shadow of desert shrubs, where cattle did not trample the delicate plant. Ten years later, the seedling might be four inches tall. By age twenty, it would be armed with strong spines. A decade more, and a height of three feet would be normal. After that, a saguaro continues to grow about four inches a year. But stock raising in the Arizona-Sonoran desert may still have doomed the saguaros to early extinction. Cattle eliminated many of the native plants which supplied alternative foods to animals that eat saguaro seeds. Cattlemen decimated the predatory animals, allowing such an increase in the number of seed-eating rodents that almost no saguaro seed today escapes. Although a large area of saguaro "forest" has been set aside near Tucson, Arizona, for the preservation of this remarkable kind of cactus, almost no young plants can be found in it. The saguaros distribute their seeds each year. There are no cattle to trample seedlings in the protected area. But there are no saguaro seedlings to trample unless they are raised in a rodent-proof enclosure and transplanted later one at a time.

Far less disturbed by western man and his livestock is the organ-pipe cactus (Cereus marginatus, often placed in the genus Lemaireocereus or Pachycereus) which is native to several provinces of Mexico and to a small area in southernmost Arizona. Its erect stems, each with five or six spiny-studded ridges, are usually unbranched, even when they rise to a height of twenty-five feet. The small flowers, which are funnel-shaped, are followed by globular fruits slightly more than an inch in diameter, full of black shining seeds. In Mexico and Central America, people plant this cactus in single rows, side by side, to form an impenetrable hedge between dwellings or separating a house and the road. Known as organos, they do suggest the large pipes of an organ. Several closely-related species, which develop a central trunk and many branches all rising to about the same height, simulate on the arid highlands of Latin America the tree euphorbias of similar country in Africa. Latin Americans often use them as storage structures for hay, each cactus supporting a fair-sized haystack above the reach of domestic animals.

Cereus has become a popular name for various night-blooming cactuses that can be raised indoors in pots of modest size. For perhaps eleven months of the year, these plants display only flat blades or stems of triangular cross section. Then suddenly buds like miniature artichokes appear, swell rapidly, and some evening open to a glorious white blossom ten to twelve inches in diameter. After releasing fragrance all night, the flower closes finally at dawn. To live with such a cactus is to share in the world of Cinderella. Its beauty can be fitted more closely to human schedules if the flowers are picked as soon as they open widely, to be put in the refrigerator until morning. Then they will stay open part of the following day when removed from the cold.

Probably the most famous hedge of night-blooming cereus was planted prior to 1840 by Mrs. Hiram Bingham, grandmother of a Connecticut senator, along the stone wall that encloses Punahoe School in Honolulu. This climbing cactus (Hylocereus undatus), attains four or five peaks of flowering between June and November. As many as ten thousand blossoms open to the mile in a single night, and the illusion of wonderland is fostered by a Honolulu ordinance forbidding anyone from picking a flower from the hedge before 10 P.M., when every visitor will have had a chance to marvel at the display. After witnessing this glorious wall of bloom, half a mile on a side, we stepped back through the Looking Glass into reality, convinced that imaginative names (such as "Queen of the Night" or reina de la noche) for the cactus are complete understatements.

Some of the smaller cacti with bright green, fleshy, flattened stems and no spines to trouble careless fingers, thrive indoors and blossom anywhere at the time of year characteristic of their native lands. The short days and long nights of December bring Zygocactus truncatus of Brazil into bloom as "Christmas cactus," whereas the longer days and shorter nights of spring affect Schlumbergera gaertneri from the same part of South America, earning it the name of "Easter cactus." The one produces brilliant scarlet flowers at the tip of each flat arching branch, the other coral-red blooms in the same places.

Cacti with conspicuously jointed stems were among the spiny plants of the New World that amazed conquistadores and colonists alike. They encountered

Waxy white flowers crown the giant saguaro cacti (Cereus giganteus) *each spring in the Arizona-Sonora desert between the United States and Mexico. (Josef Muench)*

the prickly-pear *(Opuntia humifusa)* on dry sands and rocky ground all the way from southern Massachusetts through southernmost Ontario to Minnesota, south to Oklahoma and the Gulf States, and across to the uplands of Georgia. Very similar cacti inhabit the Canadian provinces from the prairies to the Pacific coast, and southward in the mountains to arid lands of southwestern states and Latin America; subtropical Florida has other members of *Opuntia*. One of these flat-stemmed, jointed cacti was introduced into Australia with the idea that it would furnish food for cattle in arid areas if only the spines and barbed bristles were burned off regularly. The *Opuntia* spread disastrously, and was not brought under control until suitable insects were freed to riddle its stems with their burrows. A different species *(O. ficus-indica)* is the bushy or treelike "Indian fig" of which spineless varieties are now cultivated in most warm parts of the world, both for stock food and for the edible pulp in their scarlet fruits, which can be peeled easily.

The famous "jumping chollas" (pronounced choy-yas) of the American Southwest are members of *Opuntia* too. Their segmented stems are cylindrical, with lengthwise rows of rounded eminences and spectacular spines. Their reputation for leaping at passing animals arises from the ease with which the terminal segments (the "chollas"—Spanish for "heads") break off and the sharpness of the hooked spines which extend and catch so readily on any animal that brushes against the plant. Usually the weight of the detached segment drives some of the stiff spines through the animal's skin, pricking it as suddenly and painfully as a wasp sting, starting the animal into a short run before the source of annoyance is identified and scratched free by skilful use of a hoofed foot. The cholla segment may take root where it drops, starting a new plant some distance from the parent one.

Similar in many ways to the flat-stemmed members of *Opuntia* is the cochineal cactus *(Nopalea*

Left: Prickly pear cactus (Opuntia engelmanni), *with its flattened stems and rosettes of spines, some long, many short, is well adapted to life in the hot sun of the arid American Southwest. (Josef Muench) Right above: The green segments of stem on many kinds of* Opuntia *cactus are well protected by long spines. (Conzett and Huber) Right: Under the tough epidermis, the opuntia cactus stores water. (Beringer and Pampaluchi)*

cochinellifera) which the Spaniards found in 1518 being cultivated by the Mexicans. Transplanted to Spain, the plant was spread to the Canary Islands, northern Algeria, India and elsewhere, always as the host for minute scale insects which suck juice wherever they are placed on the fleshy, flattened, spineless stems. Brushed off into bags and then killed either by dry heat in a stove or by hot water, the cochineal insects yield a brilliant scarlet dye whose active ingredient is carminic acid. Until it was replaced in many uses by cheaper aniline dyes, carmine ("cochineal dye") was among the most valuable pigments in international commerce. England imported from the Canary Islands alone in 1868 more than six million pounds of dry cochineal, paying for it the equivalent of four million dollars. Now carmine dye finds use chiefly in lipstick and rouge for women who are allergic to the synthetic pigments, but who show no sensitivity to this harmless product from cactus insects.

The Supreme Court of California ruled in 1963 on a different use for an American cactus. It reversed the judgments of two lower courts, holding that "to forbid the use of peyote is to remove the heart of peyotism" and so to infringe upon a religious freedom. Peyote *(Lophophora williamsii)* is a small cactus native to arid lands from central Mexico through southern Texas. Exposed to the air is a hemispheric rubbery portion marked off by six to thirteen grooves into a pattern of large rounded tubercles. This green part of the plant may reach three inches in diameter, atop a coarse carrot-like taproot about four inches long. Indians of the Rio Grande Valley and Mexico have collected peyote since pre-Columbian times, calling it by its Aztec name of peyotl, or xicori, or huatari, or "mescal buttons," or "sacred mushrooms." Inscriptions on ancient monuments show that the manner of use has not changed to the present day. For peyote ceremonies, the Indians assemble at nightfall in doors and sit in a circle facing one another while first chewing the spineless top of the cactus to soften it and then swallowing

Left above: Flowers adorn the giant saguaro cactus (Cereus giganteus) *of the Arizona-Sonora desert. The shorter cactus is jumping cholla* (Opuntia fulgida). *(Bill Stackhouse) Left: Night-blooming cereus* (Hylocereus undatus) *has been introduced from Latin America into Hawaii. Nightly, for months, it opens gold and white fragrant flowers. (Hawaii Visitors Bureau)*

small pieces. Digestion quickly releases several alkaloids, which appear not to be habit-forming but to induce hallucinations. The peyote cultists sit quietly and contemplate the remarkable visions released by the drugs, partly conscious of their surroundings yet feeling an exhilarating unity with supernatural powers. The introduction of Christianity strengthened rather than weakened the peyote religion, since the Indians saw no conflict between the two and could embrace both—at least privately. Between 1870 and 1890, peyotism spread over most of the Plains tribes and northward into Canada. Today it is the main native religion of more than fifty American Indian tribes, including many of the best-known ones. Over much of this area, the peyote cactus is valued too as a panacea to be nibbled or to be used in making a medicinal tea.

CHAPTER 18

The Pomegranates and Some Similar Plants

CUES: *If the stems of the dicot plant are neither succulent nor spiny, and if its flower parts arise from the sides of the compound ovary (making the ovary inferior), with several seeds developing in each chamber of the ovary, it is likely to be a member of the Order Myrtales. It may be a pomegranate tree, a Brazilnut, a mangrove, a tall eucalypt, a fireweed, or a graceful fuchsia.*

Almost ten thousand different kinds of plants are grouped together in this Order. They are regarded as allied most closely to the cactuses on the one hand and to the Order embracing the great carrot family on the other. A few, including the members

Left above: Accordion-pleated cacti expand to accommodate rain water without losing protection from herbivorous animals afforded by interlocking spines. (Alan B. Stebbins: Black Star) Left: Western red-tailed hawks nest on a giant saguaro. (K. H. Maslowski: National Audubon)

The pomegranate (Punica granatum), *known for its delicious fruits, is a small tree native to southern Europe and Asia to the Himalayas. (Walter Dawn: National Audubon)*

of the loosestrife family *(Lythraceae),* have a superior ovary but so many features in common with plants having an inferior ovary that botanists can overlook this irregularity—like a forgivable quirk in an old friend who has many redeeming qualities.

THE LOOSESTRIFE FAMILY (Lythraceae)

Although the ovary in flowers of this family is completely free from the other flower parts, it lies deep in a snugly fitting cup called an androperianth tube. The tube is formed by fusion for a short distance of the bases of the sepals, the bases of the petals (if any), and the bases of the filaments on the stamens.

Loosestrifes *(Lythrum)* are slender herbs of damp ground, bearing purple or white flowers in a tall spike. Most handsome is the European one *(L. salicaria)* which the French call *bouquet violet.* Introduced into America, it has spread among the native loosestrifes over the whole area from Newfoundland to Minnesota, south to Missouri and Virginia. Each summer it grows as much as four feet tall in wet meadows, ditches and similar places, its stem topped by a spire of purple flowers each with six long petals. This particular loosestrife produces three different types of flowers on each plant: one with very short stamens and a long pistil; one with very long stamens and a short pistil; and one with both of these reproductive parts of medium length. This peculiarity is believed to aid the plant in ensuring cross-pollination and avoiding inbreeding. Yellow loosestrifes are quite different plants.

Henna is both the name of a small shrub *(Lawsonia inermis)* and of the orange dye made from it. The shrub may have been native in the same areas where it is now cultivated: Iran, East Africa, India, the East Indies, and northern Australia. Its smooth, lance-shaped leaves are collected, dried, powdered, and sold in native markets to be made with hot water into a paste to color toenails, fingernails, the soles of the feet and palms of the hands, men's beards, and ladies' hair to the hue of ironrust. Its use is widespread today among Mohammedans and probably dates back to prehistoric times since mummies exhumed from Egypt's oldest tombs have nails painted with this dye. Henna may also have been the plant referred to as camphire in the Bible *(Song of Solomon* i, 14; iv, 13). The white hair of aging people was often concealed in early times by dying it with henna one night and indigo the next; the combination left the hair a jet black.

India and adjacent areas in the Old World tropics have contributed another member of the loosestrife family as an oriental shrub *(Lagerstroemia indica)* grown in mild climates on all continents and known as crape myrtle. In the southeastern United States it is often set out to beautify parkways and the entrance roads to fine estates. "Lilac of the South" is a common name for it, suggested by its open terminal clusters of lavender blossoms and its paired simple leaves. Some varieties have white flowers, others pink, or purple, or watermelon-red. It grows easily from cuttings or seeds, and its flower buds open quickly indoors on branches thrust into a vase full of water.

Right above: Fireweeds (Epilobium angustifolium) *spring up in burned woodlands and clearings in Europe, Asia and North America. (Steve McCutcheon) Right: The evening-primrose* (Oenothera *species) opens its four-petalled flowers in late afternoon, and closes them in early morning. (Bill Ratcliffe) Far right:* Pileanthus filifolius *ranks high among the attractive native myrtles in Western Australia. Atop slender erect stems two to three feet high, buds enclosed by two lemon-yellow bracts open late in the year to display colorful petals that endure the heat of summer. (Eric Lindgren)*

THE POMEGRANATES (Family Punicaceae)

The early Romans knew the pomegranate as the "apple of Carthage" *(malum punicum)*, although the tree upon which this delightful fruit grows apparently was native to the region from the Balkans to the Himalayas and had reached Carthage along the trade routes through the Mediterranean. The Latin adjective punic, referring to things Carthaginian, provided the scientific name of the pomegranate *(Punica granatum)* and of the one other member of this little genus and family, found only on the island of Socotra in the Indian Ocean near Aden.

No one knows how far back in history the edible pomegranate was first set out in orderly orchards. During their years of slavery in Egypt, the Israelites enjoyed this fruit abundantly. Later, as they followed Moses through the wild deserts on their way back to Israel, it was the pomegranates and figs of Egypt that they longed for as they complained of their hard life in freedom *(Numbers* 20, 5). Still later, Solomon had his own pomegranate orchards. As today, the trees attain a height of fifteen to twenty feet, with bright green simple leaves and a profusion of brilliant orange-red flowers among the foliage from early May through most of the summer. The fruit develops to the size of an orange, with a thin dry skin of yellowish or reddish hue, covering two series of fleshy segments one above another. Each segment of reddish flesh is part of the seed coat, but separates readily from the single angular seed and yields a slightly acid sweet flavor that is greatly appreciated in warm, semiarid parts of the world. Grenadine, a sweet sirup, is prepared from the fruit.

Far left above: Purple loosestrife (Lythrum salicaria) *adds handsome color to wet meadows and lake shores in Europe, where it is often known as bouquet violet or salicaire. (Ingmar Holmasen) Left above: Only the low-growing deergrass or meadow-beauty* (Rhexia) *of eastern North America represents the family Melastomataceae outside of the tropics. (Matt Cormons) Far left: Central and South America have given the rest of the world many different members of the genus* Fuchsia, *all with beautiful flowers, many with a characteristic purplish-red color. (Lorus and Margery Milne) Left: The conspicuous stamens of* Eucalyptus kruseana, *a forest tree of Western Australia, draw attention to the flowers and to the greenish-gray, rounded foliage that is characteristic of new growth. (Stan and Kay Breeden)*

Conspicuous stamens draw attention to the flower clusters on the bottlebrush tree (Callistemon) *of Australia. The hard, dry fruits are held tightly against the stem. (E. Javorsky)*

SOME STRANGE TREES OF THE TROPICS (Family Lecythidaceae)

In both the tropics of the Old World and of the New, some of the tallest timber trees bear little clusters of simple leaves at the very ends of their branches, and produce a woody capsule several inches in diameter. So hard and heavy are these capsules that men who work in the rain forests below the trees, either cutting timber or gathering the fruits, commonly wear padding on their heads or industrial safety helmets to prevent serious injury when the bomblike capsules drop to the ground.

Best known of these trees is the Brazilnut *(Bertholletia excelsa),* sole source of the nuts sold all over the world for people to nibble. Brazilnut trees attain a height of 160 feet and a diameter of four feet along the banks of the Amazon and Rio Negro. Native people harvest the six-inch fruits during the first six months of each year, between work on other tasks, and open them with an ax to free the twelve to twenty-four large three-sided seeds which fit inside the husk like a segment of an orange. Millions of pounds of Brazilnuts are shipped annually from Para, Brazil, as an export second only to rubber in value, surpassing coffee in most years. In Pará itself, the smooth bark of the tree is used in calking ships, while fine hardwood cut from it is shipped as *castanha do Pará*

Western Australia produces valuable hardwood in its forests of karri (Eucalyptus diversicolor), *a giant gum tree. (Fritz Ros)*

(Para chestnut). Oil pressed from the seeds has found special uses among watchmakers and artists.

Northeastern South America and adjacent islands of the West Indies are home to a related tree that startles many people when they first encounter it, as we did, in a sunny clearing amid the steamy rain forest. From the main trunk extend hundreds of short crooked branches, supporting either rust-colored eight-inch spherical fruits or large red flowers at the very tips. From its inedible fruits the tree is called the cannonball *(Couroupita guianensis),* which seems most appropriate. In their exposed positions the flowers can be reached easily at night by nectar-sipping bats which attend to pollination. Presumably the shape of the blossom is one that sends back a characteristic echo to bats on the wing, guiding them in to a landing on a special perch where they can rest while probing for nectar and unwittingly transferring pollen.

In the same parts of the world, about fifty different kinds of tall trees are known as monkeypots *(Lecythis).* From their woody capsules a small circular door breaks away, allowing the wind to shake out the ripe seeds. Reputedly, the doorway is large

enough to admit the outstretched hand but not the clenched fist of a monkey, such as the capuchins that inhabit these forests. Local people claim to be able to capture monkeys by half-filling the empty monkeypot capsules with coarse sugar; the monkeys discover the bonanza, and will let themselves be caught rather than let go of a final handful of sweets. The same story is told of monkeys that find a fallen fruit of the Brazilnut tree, if rodents have gnawed through the woody wall and left an opening of critical size through which the monkey's empty hand will pass but not a fistful of nuts. For this reason, the name "monkeypot" is also sometimes given to Brazilnut trees.

THE MARCHING MANGROVES
(Family Rhizophoraceae)

Although the red mangrove *(Rhizophora mangle)* of America and West Africa and the corresponding one *(R. natalensis)* along African coasts of the Indian Ocean are typical of the seventy species in this family, they also represent a way of life followed by other plants in different families—the mangrove way of life. The trunk of a mangrove sends out horizontal aerial roots that branch and enter the water, sending up new leafy trunks. Arching branches on the tree itself send down pendant roots that add to the tangle, giving additional support and nourishment. Gradually the mangrove marches out over the muddy bottom, forming a dense thicket among which racoons and crabs scurry. Oysters and barnacles attach themselves to the roots where the tide covers them every day. Despite waves and storms, the mangroves capture and hold all sorts of debris and sediments, building up the land until other kinds of trees take root and shade them out.

The red mangroves are named for the color of their wood, which is remarkably dense (sinking instead of floating in water) and resistant to attack from shipworms and other borers. From it an extract called cutch is prepared, as a valuable tanning agent for leather and a dyestuff for fabrics. The residue after extraction is a more porous wood from which a high grade of charcoal can be prepared. Red mangrove flowers are small and regular, leading to formation of leathery edible fruits with a strange habit. Within them the seeds germinate and become new green plants as much as a foot long, with a few leaves and a sturdy javelin-like tap root, although still attached to the parent plant. In *Rhizophora,* the fruit and seedling drop together like javelins and embed themselves in the soft bottom mud, there to remain erect and grow. If insecurely held, they may float loose at high tide, to be carried far and deposited on some mudflat where the seedling can get a roothold. The similar and related mangroves of the genus *Bruguiera,* which are native to East Africa, tropical Asia, Polynesia, and northern Australia, but well distributed by introduction elsewhere, such as the Hawaiian Islands, drop only the germinated seedlings, while the fruits themselves remain attached to the parent tree.

Mangrove thickets commonly include members of other families showing similar features. White mangrove *(Laguncularia racemosa)* and button mangrove *(Conocarpus erecta),* both found commonly in tropical Africa and America, are members of the Family Combretaceae, which bear distinctive wings at the angles of the fruits. Black mangrove *(Avicennia nitida,* a member of Family Verbenaceae) of the West Indies and southern Florida, like another with the same popular name *(Aegiceras majus,* of Family Myrsinaceae) in northern Australia, send out long horizontal roots below the mud and from these extend upward into air a multitude of cylindrical breathing structures about the diameter of a lead pencil.

THE SPICY MYRTLES *(Family Myrtaceae)*

Australia and tropical America are the two centers of distribution for about three thousand different kinds of shrubs and trees whose simple evergreen leaves are dotted with translucent glands containing fragrant volatile oils. Although the leaves usually appear in opposite pairs, they show considerable variation in shape—often on the same plant—particularly between foliage on new adventitious stems and on older branches of the same tree.

Only one of the one hundred species of myrtle *(Myrtus communis)* is native to Europe, but it is the shrub whose young twigs were taken to make the fragrant wreaths of classical times, with which to crown a victor in war or the Olympic games. Like the wild members of this genus in tropical America, the true myrtle from Mediterranean countries has a major vein encircling each leaf just inside the margin, as well as a central midrib. This distinctive feature is missing among other kinds of plants to which the name "myrtle" is given, such as crape myrtle *(Lagerstroemia indica)* and creeping myrtle *(Vinca minor).*

Largest of the genera in the family is *Eugenia,*

Snow gum, a cold-tolerant *Eucalyptus of the mountains of Australia, is often deformed by storms.* (Australian News and Information Bureau)

with over a thousand species—a vast assortment of shrubs and trees in tropical and subtropical regions. It yields the most important of all spices, the clove, from a tree *(E. caryophyllata)* still growing wild in the understory of the lofty rain forests on East Indian islands. Centuries before the beginning of the Christian era, Chinese records mention cloves as fragrant objects that envoys from far-off Java held in their mouths to perfume their breath during audiences with the emperor. At the beginning of written history in the West, Arab merchants were already sailing the Indian Ocean to bring cloves from the East Indies. Venice grew wealthy, in fact, by dominating the Mediterranean and taxing the spice trade between the Arabs and Europeans, who paid high prices for cloves to use as flavorings and food preservatives. Only in the latter half of the 18th century did the French succeed in spreading clove culture out of the East Indies, where first the Portuguese and then the Dutch had sought to monopolize production, starting new plantations in Madagascar, Zanzibar and other islands off the east coast of Africa, whence now comes most of the world's supply.

Clove trees are raised from seed in the shadow of tall vegetation. At about five years of age they begin flowering twice a year, and clove growers pluck the unopened buds as soon as they show red. Dried on grass mats along the roadsides, the yellow and red buds turn dark brown, and shrivel until the four sepals project stiffly just below the tight cluster of

Red-flowering gum (Eucalyptus ficifolia) *provides a blaze of color from December to February in its native Western Australia, and in frost-free areas to which it has been introduced. (Australian News and Information Bureau)*

unopened petals. Coastal vessels bring thousands of huge bags full of dried cloves to the harbor on Zanzibar, supplementing production on the island itself. Thrilled, we watched black longshoremen in sweating relays carry the heavy bags to a distillation plant, where oil of cloves is prepared for use in medicine, in mouthwashes, as a mild anesthetic for dental work, as an ingredient of perfumes, and as a base material in the synthesis of artificial vanillin. The plantations themselves are far less conspicuous than the mosaic of mats with drying buds, for clove trees in the shady groves are rarely allowed to grow out of easy reach, to the fifty feet of which they are capable. Their foliage, however, adds measurably to the spicy tang in the tropic air.

A hint of clove flavor, as though it were compounded with cinnamon and nutmeg, was discovered in the dried flesh of fruits from the pimento tree *(Pimenta officinalis)* of Central America and the West Indies. The aromatic material, either in pieces or powder, became known as allspice after 1601 when it first was imported by Europeans. Today it is called for in most recipes for mincemeat and takes its place among the mixed spices used for making pickles. On Jamaica, from which most of the present supply is exported, local people use the fresh flesh of the allspice berries as the principal material from which to prepare a delicious liqueur in time for each Christ-

mas season, as a gift or special form of hospitality representing the big island. From a related tree *(P. racemosa)* they also collect the fragrant foliage for the manufacture of bay rum. Formerly the chopped wilted leaves were steeped in rum and water before distillation, hence the name. Now they go directly into water and the distillate, which is rich in phenols with a bactericidal action, is the "bay oil" that amounts to about one per cent in the alcoholic solutions marketed in barber shops and at drug counters as a skin conditioner.

Horticulturalists have succeeded in developing a popular fruit from the guava trees *(Psidium guajaba)* from the West Indies, by selecting strains with a minimum of pungent oils and grittiness in the pinkish flesh that surrounds the central cluster of small black seeds. Visitors to guava orchards can recognize the small trees by their square stems and opposite leaves, as well as from the white flowers with four petals, or the round to pear-shaped fruits. Particularly rich in vitamins A and C, the fruits can be eaten raw from the hand, or sliced in cream with sugar, or be prepared as a firm jelly or jam. In well-tended orchards, guava fruits reach three inches in diameter, and are soft enough when ripe to need picking by hand.

Hard dry fruits are produced by many other members of the myrtle family, particularly by the tall timber trees of Australia and adjacent tropical areas of the Old World. The fruits in the six-hundred-odd different kinds of *Eucalyptus* are preceded by flowers from which the sepals and petals drop as the buds open, exposing a tuft of stamens—often brilliant red, long, and golden tipped—to attract pollinating insects. Eucalyptus leaves, which yield a fragrant oil, are mostly narrow and pendant, casting virtually no shade on the ground below. They are actually Janus-like, having two upper surfaces and no lower one, with a tightly packed layer of palisade cells under

Right above: The small brilliant flowers of Kunzea recurva, *an Australian shrub with evergreen leaves, develop into aromatic fruits that are edible. (E. S. Ross) Right: The cannonball tree* (Couroupita guianensis) *of northern South America extends flowers on stems from the main trunk. The fruit are woody capsules resembling rusty cannonballs as much as eight inches in diameter. (E. Javorsky) Far right: White ironbark* (Eucalyptus leucoxylon) *is one of Australia's many fine timber trees in this genus. (Eric Lindgren)*

each epidermis—comparable to that found only near the upper surface of any ordinary leaf. Many of these trees shed their pale bark in long thin ribbons, which accumulate in tangled heaps at the foot of the trunk.

The "mountain ash" of Australia *(E. regnans)* becomes the tallest of all hardwood trees. Some have been measured to be 326 feet high, with a diameter of twenty-five feet at a man's shoulder height above the ground. This is more wood in a single trunk than is to be found in any other tree except the coastal redwoods of California. In Australia, New Guinea, and the Sunda Islands, an average of three trees out of every four proves to be a *Eucalyptus* of some kind. In the shadeless forests there, the proportion may be as high as ninety-five per cent. Often the only trees on flood plains that are inundated periodically are the river red gum *(E. rostrata)*. Other species survive in the dry interior plateau country, or tolerate repeated frosts on windswept mountain sides. A fast-growing kind (the Australian blue gum, *E. globulus*) has been introduced widely elsewhere in the world because it so quickly provides wood and a token forest. In places as distant as South Africa and California, this blue gum yields a second-quality wood that is resistant to termites but not to soil fungi; it stains easily but checks badly while being cured; it provides bees with abundant nectar but most people find the honey too aromatic for complete enjoyment. Often they are surprised to find that after a tall *Eucalyptus* has been cut down, new "suckers" spring up from the outspread roots and stump, bearing broad thick leaves in pairs with a bluish surface bloom on them, quite unlike the narrow thin foliage of the mature tree; florists often offer these adventitious stems for sale as decorative "blue spiral."

Close kin of *Eucalyptus* are the dozen different kinds of bottle-brush trees *(Callistemon)* from Australia, some of them tall trees and others mere shrubs. They bear their bright scarlet stamens in cylindrical spikes near the ends of the branches, actually in a spiral of blossoms from which the sepals and petals drop when the buds open. From March until May these exotic clusters appear, waving in the wind like torches in the sunlight. Later the stamens fall and the ovaries develop into hard close-set fruits like gray buttons sewn tightly to the stem; beyond them the branch continues to grow and open its new leaves of the year.

THE BRIGHT EVENING-PRIMROSES
(Family Onagraceae)

In temperate and northern parts of Eurasia and North America, some of the most vigorous weeds are native members of *Epilobium,* known from the shape of their leaves as willow-herbs, and from the speed with which they colonize burned-over areas as fireweeds. One of them is river-beauty *(E. latifolium),* which remains low and densely matted on river gravels and damp slopes. Another, great willow-herb *(E. angustifolium),* rises to a height of as much as eight feet on new clearings and roadsides, or where a woodland has gone up in flames. Both brighten the area with a spire of magenta flowers that continue to open all through the summer. From Scandinavia to northern Italy and Siberia, from Alaska to California, North Carolina to Newfoundland, and in Greenland too, these familiar flowers greet the traveler and make him feel at home. In the leaves, the side veins do not quite reach the edge, but curve forward to join the next side vein nearer the tip. Each of the flowers has four broad bilobed petals, four narrow sepals, eight stamens and a longer pistil which matures into a long slender capsule. When the capsule opens, an abundance of seeds with plumes of white hair waft away in the wind, ready to settle and germinate wherever the sun can reach the soil.

Four broad petals and eight stamens is the mark also of evening-primroses *(OEnothera),* the hundred different kinds of which are native to America from the Arctic to Patagonia. Characteristically these herbs open their flowers in the late afternoon and close them again permanently the following dawn. Usually they are a bright butter-yellow or white, sometimes turning pink or magenta before they close. By then the hawkmoths should have found them in the fading light of dusk or by scent during the blackness of the night. The seeds lack hairs to catch the wind, but some have a thin membrane as a crest and are so light in weight that a gust can carry them some distance from the parent plant. In the evening-primrose *(OE. biennis)* which has spread as a weed to Eurasia and to temperate parts of the Southern Hemisphere, the foliage of the first year is a low rosette, each leaf of which has a pinkish cast. In the

Eurasian angelica (Angelica archangelica), *a member of the carrot family* (Umbelliferae), *is gathered as a vegetable in the Faeroe Islands and Iceland. Elsewhere its roots and fruit yield angelica oil, a flavoring and perfume, and its tender shoots furnish a sweetmeat.* (Ingmar Holmasen)

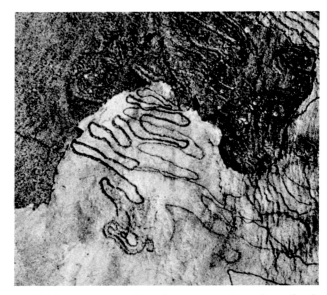

Cajeput oil, a universal remedy in the Orient, is extracted from the leaves of Melaleuca leucadendron, *a gum tree of Australia and adjacent islands.*

"Scribbly gum" is a Eucalyptus *tree in whose bark the larva of an insect eats a tunnel, going up and coming down in parallel twists. (Both by Lorus and Margery Milne)*

second summer, the plant raises up a taller stem with spreading leaves and branches near the tip, opening its low flowers first and then the higher ones, in a succession that may last from July to September. Another species *(OE. grandiflora),* with larger flowers, spread to Europe in the 19th century and became world-famous under another name *(OE. Lamarckiana)* as the plant whose inheritance Hugo de Vries studied, leading to his theory of evolution by sudden mutations.

Except for two species in New Zealand, the members of the genus *Fuchsia* are native to Latin America, where they grow to be small shrubs or trees with a trunk several inches in diameter. Named in honor of the 16th century herbalist Leonard Fuchs, who died long before any of the genus was discovered, the fuchsias have become popular all over the temperate world as greenhouse plants or as kinds that can be set out to decorate a summer garden. Only the botanists pronounce the name to show its derivation (as fooks'–ee-a); other people say few'-shah, with the approval of major dictionaries. The handsome flowers are pendant, with a brightly-colored four-part calyx in the form of a funnel with spread wings. Below it hang four petals and eight or ten long stamens that parallel the threadlike style and project in a loose cluster where hummingbirds can reach through them easily.

The fruit of a *Fuchsia* is an edible berry with many seeds. By hybridization and selection, horticulturalists have developed an almost limitless assortment of long-flowered and globe-flowered plants, some of them double instead of single, in an entrancing array of colors—pinks and purples predominating. The parent of most garden varieties is *F. magellanica* of Peru and Chile, which attains a height of twenty feet in its homeland but is rarely allowed to grow so tall in cultivation. *F. splendens* of Guatemala and Mexico rarely exceeds six feet in height, whereas *F. procumbens* of New Zealand is a creeper.

CHAPTER *19*

The Carrots and Their Kin

CUES: *If the dicot plant bears its flowers in clusters that are flat-topped or globular, each flower held by its own stalk at the same level as neighboring flowers, and if the four or five petals are separate but the four or five sepals join to form a tube that is fused to the ovary (making it inferior), the plant is almost sure to be a member of the Order Umbellales. The plant may be an English ivy, a poison hemlock, a parsnip, or a dogwood.*

Somewhat more than 3800 kinds of plants show the distinctive features of this Order. Many grow as tall trees or as clambering woody vines (lianas) in the rain forests of the tropics. Most, however, are herbs of the temperate zones, where man has found uses for a remarkable assortment—for flavoring and perfume, for food, decoration, and poison. A few, particularly in the Southern Hemisphere, provide wood with special virtues. Still others survive under the harsh weather of the high Andes, or on the Falkland Islands and Tierra del Fuego, growing into dense cushion-shaped masses between the bare rocks that shelter them from the wind. But all of them, when they come into flower, unfold clusters of the same general type, in which the first flower to open is the one at the center, followed by those to the sides.

THE GINSENG FAMILY *(Araliaceae)*

Among our earliest memories is one of being allowed to break off tiny pieces from a flat rectangular wafer of rice-paper and of happily dropping them onto the water in the goldfish bowl. One at a time the white fragments soaked up moisture, lost buoyancy, and sank—to be gobbled up by the fish. The explanation seemed appropriate: goldfish were glorified carp from the Orient and preferred flakes of rice to eat. Only much later did we discover that rice-paper is made from the soft pith of a small tree *(Tetrapanax papyrifera)* native to Formosa, unrelated to rice in any way. For centuries, Oriental people have removed the pith from branches in which it is as much as an inch in diameter. The material is rolled into smooth sheets, which may be a sixteenth of an inch thick for goldfish food or a few thousandths for artists' paper. It retains its ivory-white color indefinitely, and accepts water colors well. When dampened, the thinnest rice-papers remain astonishingly tough but can be pressed into close conformity with the surface of any stone or metal that has been carved in bas-relief. These papers are ideal for use in making "rubbings," producing copies almost as handsome as the hard original by marking on the paper with a lithographic crayon. While watching someone using rice-paper in this way on the floor of a cathedral in England or the side of a stone temple in Thailand,

we seldom think of the thicker grade of the same material we used as goldfish food. The error in naming rice-paper was made by Europeans in the 17th century, when this strange product of a culture built on rice was first imported from the mysterious East.

A near relative of the rice-paper tree is ginseng *(Panax),* from the thick roots of which extracts of high commercial value have been made since time immemorial. This value arises from a still-unexplained belief that is widely held among Chinese people that the extract has broad curative powers and also acts as an aphrodisiac. Neither view is supported by evidence acceptable to scientists in the West. But the generic name matches the Oriental belief, and can be translated "cure-all"—panacea. No crude agricultural product in international commerce carries as high a price as ginseng root in Hong Kong—thirty dollars per pound in 1965 for first quality, preferably forked into a vague resemblance to legs from a human torso. Asian ginseng (or sang, *P. schinseng)* is native to Manchuria and Korea, and cultivated in both Korea and Japan. Because demand for it far exceeds the supply, people in the New World collect and cultivate American ginseng *(P. quinquefolia),* which grows wild in cool, moist woods in Canada and the United States east of the Great Plains. Between 1895 and 1903 or 1904, a ginseng "boom" began and collapsed in America, in an attempt to raise larger amounts of the valuable root. Unfortunately, the plant requires rich soil, the right amount of shade, about seven years to mature from seed, and is susceptible to diseases. Even when given the best of skilled care, the cultivated roots rarely bring more than two-thirds the price paid for the best wild roots dug and prepared by regular collectors.

Both rice-paper trees and ginsengs have a compound leaf. The most widely known member of the family, by contrast, is one that has a simple, lobed leaf: English ivy *(Hedera helix).* It grows wild all across southern Europe, from the Canary Islands in the Atlantic to the foothills of the Himalayas. Its stems produce a multitude of adventitious roots, which remain blunt and serve to hold the climbing branches to supports no rougher than a brick building. Or they quickly become nutritive if buried in moist soil, allowing the ivy to reproduce from cuttings. It is cultivated in many parts of the world as an evergreen soil cover, or to hide a brick wall, or indoors as a plant that can be draped over window ledges and doorways. From handling the foliage or stems, some people develop an inflammation of the

The stiff, prickly flower head of Eryngium giganteum, *a member of the carrot family native to Asia Minor, resembles a wire sculpture. (Beringer and Pampaluchi)*

skin, but it rarely produces intense itching and blisters characteristic of poison ivy. Children have been poisoned by eating the globular black or yellow fruits, each usually with fewer than five seeds. This is the ivy that covers the buildings of so many long-established universities in Europe and North America, earning for them the name of "halls of ivy" or a membership in the "Ivy League."

On Karekelang Island, northeast of Celebes in the East Indies, the late Dr. David Fairchild discovered an amazing relative of English ivy, as a tall tree in full bloom by the sea. High above its large palmately lobed leaves he saw one enormous flower cluster the size of a bushel basket, suggesting to him a gigantic pincushion into whose purple-brown mass were stuck dozens of large yellow-headed pins. A cutting from this tree has grown tall in the Fairchild Tropical Garden near Miami, Florida, letting visitors see these same remarkable flower clusters at closer range. Named *Boerlagiodendron,* after J. G. Borlage who studied the plants of Java, it is native to several of the big islands in the Far East. In Borneo an Italian botanist discovered the unique way in which this tree is pollinated. The purple-brown parts of the flower cluster are seedless "false fruits," enjoyed by wood pigeons. As the birds alight on the sturdy cluster to get the "false fruits," they brush pollen from the yellow flowers onto their breast feathers or spread it on the waiting stigmas. After the "false fruits" have all been eaten or dried up, the real fruits develop. Perhaps different feathered aides distribute them, since all members of the Family Araliaceae produce fleshy fruits containing indigestible seeds.

THE CARROT FAMILY (Umbelliferae)

Petioles that ensheath the stem, paired styles that are conspicuously swollen at the base, and ovaries that ripen into dry fruits splitting into two, each half containing a single seed, are features common to nearly three thousand different members of this family. All are herbs with aromatic foliage. Most attract flies, which walk over the flat clusters of flowers and accomplish cross-pollination.

One of the most infamous members of the family is confusingly called poison "hemlock" *(Conium maculatum),* from Anglo-Saxon words meaning "meadow death." This coarse, branching weed with parsley-like leaves is found native in moist areas of Europe, Asia, and North Africa. It spread early into corresponding parts of the New World, and has even been cultivated in some places as a hedge plant under the name of "California fern." Sometimes it forms dense thickets as much as ten feet high. All parts of the plant are poisonous, containing a mixture of at least four alkaloids. More than two thousand years ago, extracts rich in these poisons became a legal means for putting to death convicted criminals in Athenian Greece. The philosopher Socrates was condemned to this punishment, and the detailed description of his death by his student Plato reads almost like a modern account by a pharmacologist. The poisons paralyze the muscles concerned with breathing, and death comes without convulsions, the mind remaining clear to the end. The same fate awaits modern people who make the mistake of eating the roots of the plant, believing them to be parsnips, or generously sprinkling their food with the seeds, supposing them to be caraway.

The Latin name of the poison "hemlock" has been applied to related plants in both the Old World and the New: the water-hemlocks *(Cicuta),* which are at least as deadly. The commonest in Great Britain and continental Europe is *C. virosa,* which grows rankly at the edges of rivers and other small bodies of water. Eastern North America, and as far southwest as Texas, produce spotted cowbane *(C. maculata—* known also as musquashroot and beaver-poison), which may well be the most violently poisonous plant of the whole North Temperate Zone. A single root, perhaps exposed by a plow, ordinarily will kill a cow that eats it. The succulent petioles of new leaves, which have often been mistaken for celery, have the same effect on people. Death may come within fifteen minutes or not until after eight hours, but usually follows great pain, convulsions, and delirium.

Edible parsnips *(Pastinaca sativa)* and carrots *(Daucus carota)* were well known in Greek and Roman times, and used along Mediterranean coasts as food for people and livestock. Wild forms of the parsnip, far more fibrous and pungent than cultivated types, still grow widely in roadsides and neglected areas of Europe and temperate Asia. Between the beginning of the Christian era and the 16th century, parsnip cultivation spread into northern Europe. In 1609 the colonists introduced the plant in the New World, where it soon became even more of a favorite than in its native lands. American Indians adopted it, perhaps delighted with a root crop that seemed to thrive on casual husbandry. Parsnips are unharmed by being left in the ground and frozen there. Cold, in fact, is needed to transform the starch in these roots into sugars that bring out the full flavor. In all other ways, parsnips are handled in the same manner as carrots.

Carrots appear to have come originally from Afghanistan. The Greeks ate them as medicine. Gradually the custom of cooking them for food spread in Europe—into Italy in the 1st century B.C., to France and Germany in the 13th century A.D., to England about 1600, and to the New World with the colonists. Until about 1920, however (when the importance of carotene—vitamin A—was discovered), carrots did not rival such old-time favorites as peas and potatoes in Western diets. Today, growers in California and Texas alone market more than half a million tons annually and regard four hundred bushels to the acre as normal production. This is twice the average yield for parsnips. The custom of eating carrots raw has become popular only in the present century. Carrots that grow wild produce flowers in their second year and are known then as Queen Anne's lace—a weed that is hard to eradicate.

Parsley *(Petroselinum crispum)* and celery *(Apium graveolens)* are both biennial herbs of the Mediterranean region. Banquets in classical Greece and Rome saw sprigs of dark-green parsley added as a tasty garnish on fish, meat, and vegetable dishes. The parsley omelette was created along the south coast of Europe. England gained the plant in 1548 from

The western water-hemlock (Cicuta bolanderi), *limited to sheltered valleys in west-central California, is among the most poisonous of plants. (M. Woodbridge Williams)*

Sardinia. A little later it was brought to the New World. Still the only part eaten was the frilly, much dissected leaf, which is now known to be extremely rich in vitamin C. It also contains some essential oils that can cause damage to liver, kidneys and stomach if eaten in excess. But until about 1800, no one paid much attention to parsley roots. Then a new variety was discovered in northern Europe and named the Hamburg, or turnip-rooted, parsley. When cooked, the fleshy root is a pleasant vegetable. Curiously, its use remains almost completely restricted to parts of the Old World.

Celery leaves have been used for centuries to add flavor to soups. Less than two hundred years ago, gardeners in France recognized a different type of celery which had upright, fleshy petioles. They learned to keep these leaf stalks pale and succulent by "hilling" the soil high around the growing plants. The petioles replaced the leaf blades in popular appeal, and were eaten raw, or stuffed with cheese, or cooked in various ways. Celery leaves actually contain too much oxalate to be eaten safely in large amounts. Still more recently, horticulturalists developed a turnip-rooted celery, and called it celeriac. Celeriac roots are usually cubed and cooked to give flavor to soups and stews.

Some members of the carrot family produce a

milky juice so copiously that early man learned to collect it and gain from it by drying a spicy resin in the form of translucent shining "tears." Perhaps the earliest of these to gain favor was galbanum, from a parsnip-like weed *(Ferula galbaniflua)* common in Iran. It is called for in the preparation of temple incense. Hippocrates mentioned it as a medicine, and Pliny compiled for it a long list of curative qualities; today it has little place in pharmaceutical preparations. A similar plant, *F. foetida,* is a coarse weed of Iran and Afghanistan that local people cook as a green vegetable. Its gum resin is asafetida, which is much in demand as a condiment in Iran and India, despite its strong onion-like odor and bitterly pungent taste. Perfume-makers of Europe and the United States import and purify asafetida as a spicy addition to the scents they blend. Sportsmen who enjoy riding to the hounds sometimes lead the dogs over hill and dale by laying down an imitation trail with a rag soaked in a solution of asafetida. To the dogs' noses, the odor appears almost indistinguishable from that left by a real fox.

Seeds of some members of the carrot family are popular because of their essential oils. Caraway *(Carum carvi)* outranks all the others in importance. Originally the plant came from a wide area of Eurasia. Now it is naturalized as a weed in the British Isles and in North America from Newfoundland to Colorado. Cultivation of caraway is centered in Morocco, in central and northern Europe, and southern England. Most of the paired hard seeds are added whole to bread, cakes, and cheeses. From the remainder a volatile aromatic oil is distilled for use as a flavoring in cookery, in manufacture of after-dinner liqueurs, and to provide stimulating and gas-reducing (carminative) effects in medicines.

This ability to reduce gas in the human digestive tract is found also in the seeds of anise *(Pimpinella anisum)* and dill *(Anethum graviolens)*. For years they have been used to confer this quality—and a pleasant flavor—in medicines, dentifrices, foods, and even some of the beverages that might cause production of gas. Anise is a perennial herb native to Egypt, but now cultivated extensively in Asia Minor, India, and parts of South America. If the dry seeds are chewed, a sweet taste is gained, faintly suggestive

Flowering dogwood (Cornus florida) *is famous for the white flowers with which it fills gardens and woods of eastern Mexico and the eastern United States in spring. (Grant Heilman)*

of licorice. The flavor is extracted completely in a volatile oil distilled from the seeds. It is sometimes combined with cheap ingredients to make artificial licorice candy. More often it is blended into expensive liqueurs, including the highly distinctive anisette.

Biblical scholars debate over the translation given in Matthew 23:23, as to whether the tithes paid by the Pharisees were in anise or dill. Dill itself is a weed in the grain fields of Egypt and southern Europe, and can be found both wild and cultivated in the Holy Land, in India, and North America. In recent years, an extract distilled from the plant and called "dill herb oil" has largely replaced the use of dill seeds or immature flower clusters or leaves for flavoring soups and pickles. Hungary and some of the western United States are the principal producers of commercial dill herb oil. The material has a reputation for aiding insomnia and stimulating lactation, but in medicine finds use primarily as a carminative and diuretic agent.

Neither good cooks who add a little of this and a pinch of that from their line of herbs in the spice rack, nor the manufacturers of quality whisky, gin, and other liquors ever give away their recipes. But most of them admit using regularly either the dried fruits of coriander *(Coriandrum sativum)* or an extract from the hard seeds. This member of the carrot family is mentioned in ancient writings of Egypt, the Near East, Greece, and Rome. Greeks knew the plant by the same name as the bedbug, showing how similar is the unpleasant odor given off by the ripening fruits. When dry, however, the fruits and seeds are delightfully fragrant. Often they are candied and sold under the name of sugarplums. The seeds themselves are added to many sweet dishes in India and some Mediterranean countries. So great is the demand there that large plantations of coriander are tended in Morocco, southern Europe, and India.

THE DOGWOODS (Family Cornaceae)

Those who have wondered what a dogwood had to do with dogs will be enlightened to learn that the tree should be called a "dagwood" from its ancient use as a source of material for making wooden daggers. The wood is hard as horn (Latin *cornu),* hence the generic name *Cornus* for almost half of the one hundred species in the family. Two of these are beautiful little herbs in the Far North: the Lapland cornel *(C. suecica),* which is circumpolar, and bunchberry *(C. canadensis),* which brightens the northwoods across America from Newfoundland to Alaska. One species

is a shrub in the highlands of Peru. The rest are shrubs and small trees in north temperate regions.

Lapland cornel and bunchberry are unusual among the dogwoods in having flowers that people notice. Each of them unfolds from the base of the compact floral cluster four shining snow-white leaflike bracts, which catch the eye like broad petals. The flowering dogwood *(C. florida)* of northeastern Mexico, eastern United States, and southernmost Ontario in Canada, repeats this pattern of floral display. Western flowering dogwood *(C. nuttallii)* in California and Oregon outdoes them all with six (or sometimes five or four) of these white bracts, and in blossoming twice a year—with scarlet ripe fleshy fruits on the tree at the same time as the new lot of flowers. A black spot, the remains of the single style, tips each fruit.

Other kinds of dogwood, whether of tree size or low shrubs, bear conspicuous fruits that are greatly enjoyed by birds and admired by people. Horticultural uses for these plants now outweigh the old values, such as cutting the wood of European dogwood *(C. sanguinea)* and Cornelian cherry *(C. mas—* native to much of Eurasia) into pointed skewers for pinning meat into manageable roasts or "joints."

Some plantsmen stretch the limits of Family Cornaceae and of Order Umbellales a little, to make a place in them for the pepperidge tree (or tupelo or

American ginseng (Panax quinquefolius), *found in eastern North America, has often been exported to China as a substitute for Manchurian ginseng, a prized medicine there. (U. S. Forest Service)*

sourgum, *Nyssa sylvatica)* and other members of this genus from northern swamps and southern mountains of Eurasia and North America. These tall trees, with a trunk diameter as great as five feet, produce a heavy wood that once found great demand for ox yolks, wheel hubs, wooden shoes, and wharf pilings. Two kinds of inconspicuous flowers appear in early spring: compact pendant clusters with stamens, and paired pistillate flowers at the tips of upright stalks. By early autumn, when the oval leaves turn a glorious brilliant red, the fruits are ripe, dark blue, about two-thirds of an inch long, with a stony covering for the central seed. Birds fly to them. Bears climb to get them. Deer stand on their hind legs to reach the fruits. And rabbits pick up those the other animals drop among the falling leaves. Like the dogwoods, the sourgums reward the animals that carry away the seeds, helping a few reach a good place in which to germinate.

CHAPTER 20

The Heaths

CUES: *If the plant has flowers with a regular or only slightly irregular corolla, and its anthers on the stamens open by a terminal pore or a chink, and if the ovary (with two to ten chambers inside) has a single style, it is likely to be a member of the Order Ericales. The plant may be a ghostly Indian pipe, a handsome rhododendron, a blueberry or cranberry, or a heather carpeting some misty moorland.*

Literature gives most of us a special admiration for the heaths. We know them as the shrubby, flowering carpets over the exposed hillsides of Scandinavia, the Scottish Highlands, the English moors, or have met them in corresponding areas from Labrador and Kamchatka to South Africa and Tierra del Fuego. We find them thriving in quaking bogs among the peat, or in the dim mysterious places of great temperate forests. They blaze with color on the steep slopes of the high Himalayas, provide the makings for blueberry pie, and add the red tartness of cranberry sauce to Thanksgiving or Christmas meals.

The heaths tend to be stiff-stemmed, leathery-leaved evergreens, whose simple leaves lack stipules. Those that reduce competition by tolerating the dark-stained water of a peat bog match the limited availability of fresh water there with a reduction in loss of moisture from foliage. Their leaves are even more leathery, often glossy above but hairy below, and curling along the edges in ways that deflect the wind from the pores through which gas exchanges take place. Even the plants that grow on the acid soil of temperate woodlands or on the thin soils of the moors have thick leaves.

The extraordinary versatility shown by members of the Order seems linked also to a virtual lack of absorptive root hairs. Instead, particularly in acid soils, the root tips are enmeshed by great masses of fungus strands which extend out among the soil particles. In some cases, the fungi obtain nourishment from decaying organic matter or living roots of trees, and share it with the flowering plant. No one is sure yet what the fungus gains from this strange partnership. But in soils where the fungus partner grows poorly, the heaths too fail to thrive.

Despite the many features shared by the 2400 different kinds of plants in this Order, botanists see the heaths and their kin straddling a distinction regarded elsewhere as important. Some members of the Order have flowers with petals joined to form a one-piece corolla, which is a feature regarded as an advance, one characteristic of all dicot plants covered in Chapters nineteen through twenty-five. But other members of Order Ericales have flowers with separate petals, as have all dicot plants in Chapters six through seventeen. Even within a single family, one genus may follow the separate-petal tradition, and all others the one-piece-corolla pattern. *Pterospora* is an example in Family Pyrolaceae. Or one genus may be exceptional in the opposite direction, as is *Befaria* with separate petals in Family Ericaceae. Family resemblances are simply stronger than this convenient subdivision of floral patterns, and the plantsmen accept the situation as they find it.

THE WINTERGREENS AND KIN
(Family Pyrolaceae)

Long before the plants of the New World were discovered and given common names, people in Great

On the rim of the canyon in Yosemite National Park, California, the red snow plants (Sarcodes sanguinea) *raise flower clusters in early spring. (Josef Muench)*

Britain and Europe chose "wintergreen" as suitable for some low-growing members of this Family. Included were species of both *Chimaphila* and *Pyrola,* whose generic names signify respectively "winter-loving" and "little pear" (from *Pyrus,* whose leaves have a similar shape). By the time plant explorers realized that *C. umbellata* and several species of *Pyrola* were circumpolar, new and interesting names had been adopted for these wintergreens of the New World. *Chimaphila* there took the Algonquian Indians' name of pipsissewa or prince's pine, and *Pyrola* became shinleaf—perhaps a corruption of shineleaf, referring to its glossy foliage. Americans referred to a quite different plant, in the Family Ericaceae, as "true" wintergreen, and distinguished the pyrolas as "false wintergreens" or English wintergreen. In the eastern states and provinces, the native *Chimaphila maculata* took the name of spotted wintergreen.

The pyrolas and chimaphilas are handsome little plants, actually diminutive woody shrubs not more than ten inches high. On the dimly-lit floor of the deciduous forest in early summer they display comparatively large flowers with waxy white petals widely flared. Those of *Chimaphila* are sometimes called waxflower, and have a short, inconspicuous green stigma from the central pistil. Among pyrolas the stigma is long, and often droops conspicuously like some kind of a green handle from the center of the blossom.

Some non-green members of the family, which appear even more waxy and artificial, tend to steal attention in America. These plants lack chlorophyll, and depend completely upon nourishment obtained by their root fungi from decaying vegetable matter or from the roots of living trees. Most spectacular of them is snow plant *(Sarcodes sanguinea),* which thrusts up a blood-red spike of fragile flowers through the thick humus below the big trees *(Sequoia gigantea)* in California, often through the remaining drifts of winter snow. Less gaudy relatives rise from the forest floor later in the season, elsewhere on the continent, as they do also in Eurasia.

Far left: Diapensia (Diapensia lapponica) is a cushion plant, growing in tussocks in arctic and alpine regions on all sides of the North Pole. (Ingmar Holmasen) Left: The cross-leaved heath or bog heather (Erica tetralix) is well known in northern Europe, its native area. In late summer it sends up deep pink flowers, which attract many insects. (John Markham)

Tallest of the non-green species is pinedrops *(Pterospora andromedea),* whose vertical, unbranched sturdy stem may be three feet tall. From its purple-brown sides extend numerous whitish flowers and many brown, scalelike leaves. It is found in rich coniferous woods from the mountains of Colombia, South America, north to British Columbia, and east to Prince Edward Island, Canada, and Vermont.

Pinesap *(Monotropa hypopitys)* grows in pine woods of Asia, Europe, the British Isles, and North America coast to coast, south into the mountains of Mexico. Its yellowish upright stalks attain a height of ten inches, bearing at the bent tip a small cluster of fragrant orange flowers of which the lowest blossom opens first. All but the flower at the tip of the stalk have three or four sepals and petals apiece, whereas the one at the end—the last to open—ordinarily has five sepals and five petals.

Far more ghostly is Indian pipe (or corpse-plant, *M. uniflora)* of America's mixed woodlands from Newfoundland to Alaska and southward into Mexico. In the deep shade, the solitary flowers of Indian pipe nod stiffly, usually in little clumps thrusting up to a height of eight to ten inches through the fallen leaves. Until pollinated, each stalk and flower is a waxy white or faintly tinged with flesh-pink. Then the whole of the exposed parts of the plant blacken. The sepals and petals drop and the ripening ovary turns upright. The Indian pipe becomes only an inconspicuous vertical twig, shriveled and stiff, supporting its dark capsule full of minute seeds. A similar plant, which may be the same species, greets climbers through the woodlands on the slopes of mountains in Japan and Nepal.

THE HEAD FAMILY (Ericaceae)

THE HEAT FAMILY (Ericaceae)

About half of the 1900 different kinds in this family inhabit frost-free areas of the tropics and subtropical lands. It is there that the twenty species of the Andes "rose" *(Befaria)* grow luxuriantly on the mountain slopes. The northernmost outlier of this genus *(B. racemosa)* is called fly-catcher or tar-flower in the pinelands of Florida and southern Georgia, because small insects become mired in the sticky secretion that coats the opening buds and spread calyxes. Fly-catcher blooms profusely all summer, each of the seven to ten separate white petals tipped with rosy pink.

The huge genus *Rhododendron* includes nearly half of the species in the heath family. Of the 850 different kinds, about seventy drop their leaves each

The waxy flowers of Indian pipes (Monotropa uni-flora) *rise out of woodland litter, their roots forming a ball around decomposing wood. (Esther Heacock)*

winter and are called azaleas. The rest are evergreen "rhododendrons," a majority of which form dense thickets in the wet monsoon forests on the eastern slopes of the Himalayas and into Yunnan and Szechuan provinces of China. Still more are native to higher ground in Malaysia, the Sunda Islands, New Guinea, and Australia. Horticulturalists have produced many handsome hybrids and named varieties of rhododendrons by crossing Himalayan species (such as *R. arboreum* and *R. campanulatum)* with *R. caucasicum* from the Caucasus Mountains, *R. ponticum* from Mediterranean Europe, and some of the showier kinds (especially the catawba rhododendron, *R. catawbiense,* and the rose-bay, *R. maxi-*

mum) of eastern North America. Many of these flowering shrubs will grow well in cooler parts of Mexico, Central America, South America, Africa, and Great Britain, although none of these lands has a *Rhododendron* of its own. Scandinavia, however, has low-growing *R. lapponicum,* which is found wild also in Greenland and northeastern North America.

Both rhododendrons and azaleas drop their corollas after pollination is accomplished. Rhododendrons generally have a more bell-shaped blossom, which may be red, orange, yellow, white, or in shades of purple almost to blue. Azaleas more frequently have flaring petals, with the flowers in loose clusters rather than compact heads, but often in such profusion that the shrub is virtually hidden under a mosaic of splendid color. Even small azaleas will produce this delightful display year after year, thriving indoors where they are protected from temperatures lower than thirty-five degrees Fahrenheit. As decorative house plants, they cannot be surpassed, partly because so many horticultural varieties have been developed for this express market. Some are from Korean and Japanese ancestral stock, others from well-known North American species including the flame azalea *(R. calendulaceum),* the pinkster *(R. nudiflorum),* and the rhodora *(R. canadensis),* which Ralph Waldo Emerson made famous in a poem. All members of *Rhododendron* produce dry capsules, which split open along the seam between each seed-filled chamber and the next.

The petals of a rhododendron or an azalea are rarely joined for more than half their length; the tips are free and generally pointed. The same flower form can be recognized on a diminutive scale in the trailing arbutus *(Epigaea repens)* of eastern North America, and in the similar *E. asiatica* of Japan. These are trailing woody vines, with thick leaves and tough roots. Their flowers are wonderfully fragrant, opening in very early spring and often known as Mayflowers, mountain pink, winter pink, gravel pink, or shadflowers. Queen bumblebees hunt them out for nectar and accomplish pollination. Thereafter the three-quarter-inch corollas turn brown and drop off, leaving the ovary to swell into a spherical capsule that splits widely into five parts, each with a fleshy interior enclosing the indigestible seeds.

In the several different kinds of *Kalmia* ranging from northern Canada to Cuba, the flower buds provide a fascinating display as they open. After swelling to full size, the corolla of flower after flower in a cluster spreads widely, forming a shallow crater-shaped cup around the margin of which are little notches indicating the boundaries between fused petals. Each petal has a little pit, in which the anther of the corresponding stamen remains concealed, its filaments arching toward the central pistil. At a touch, however, as when a bee alights in the floral cup, all of the anthers pop out. Usually they spring against the sides of the insect and coat it with pollen, which may rub off in the next flower or on the next plant. Mountain-laurel (K. latifolia) attains a height of twenty feet as a shrub forming dense thickets in craggy country of the eastern United States. It is sometimes harvested for Christmas decorations. The smaller sheep-laurel (K. angustifolia) grows in old pastures and on barren ground from Labrador to the mountains of Georgia. Domestic animals that are starved into eating the foliage of these plants commonly die from the poison they contain. Indians in Delaware formerly regarded drinking a tea made from the leaves of any Kalmia as a sure way to commit suicide.

The Indians over much of North America made a quite different decoction from the leathery leaves of checkerberry (Gaultheria procumbens), which remain evergreen in clusters atop short erect branches from a woody creeping stem. This extract lessens the pain of a headache or rheumatism, and reduces the discomfort of a fever. The plant is the aromatic one Americans named wintergreen. Its medicinal value comes from a high concentration of methyl salicylate, known all over the world today under its commercial name of aspirin. Its flavor is far from unique, and the "oil of checkerberry" or "oil of wintergreen" sold in drugstores is now more likely to be either an extract from birch, or to be synthetic—as is all of the aspirin on the market. This same flavor can be enjoyed in the woods by chewing the fresh leaves that the checkerberry plant adds each spring, or the brilliant scarlet fruits that ripen in autumn and increase in size under the winter's snow. The fleshy part of each fruit is actually the calyx, which grows up around the central small flat capsule containing the many seeds from the ripened ovary. Chipmunks carry wintergreen "berries" in their cheek pouches, to nibble away the fleshy calyx where danger can be watched for in all directions. Grouse, pheasant, deer, and bear swallow the fruits whole, and drop the indigestible seeds somewhere else.

The one hundred species of Gaultheria almost encircle the Pacific Ocean. They include low shrubs all the way down the Andes to Tierra del Fuego, in New Zealand and Australia, and in Southeast Asia, but not elsewhere in the Old World. Many of them resemble salal (or shallon, G. shallon) of the Pacific coast of North America in forming an evergreen dense mat on sandy soil near the sea where no trees give shade, but attaining a height of as much as six feet as a slender shrub in more protected places of high humidity, such as in the fog-filled shade of the coastal redwoods in California. Fresh leaves and new growth on salal have a pleasant sour taste, leading landscape gardeners to market the shrub as "lemon leaf." The plant grows wild far up the Pacific coast into British Columbia, and provides emergency browse for the elk of Olympic National Park in Washington state, and more routine food for Roosevelt elk farther south. The fruits mature in autumn, changing from green to purple, to indigo or black, and are then sought for intensively by deer, bear, birds, and squirrels.

Fruits appreciated by wildlife and by human beings too are produced abundantly by the forty different kinds of huckleberries (Gaylussacia) and the two hundred species known variously as bilberries, blueberries, and cranberries (Vaccinium). All of these shrubs and low woody plants bear small, bell-shaped blossoms which differ from those of most other members of the Family Ericaceae in having the corolla and calyx fused to the ovary for a short distance, making it inferior. The ovary ripens to a true berry, with unarmored seeds, in any Vaccinium, whereas each huckleberry fruit contains ten seeds protected by stony coats like those of a plum, although far smaller. The center of distribution for huckleberries is the mountains of western Brazil; outliers are found in cool parts of South America to the south and north, and in North America. Vaccinium, by contrast, is well represented in temperate Eurasia, in mountain areas of Madagascar, Indo-Malaysia, New Guinea, Polynesia, in the Andes, and in cooler parts of North America. Many are wiry little shrubs sheltering between boulders at high altitudes or in the Far North, or inhabiting cold peat bogs. Others, particularly the cultivated blueberries, become tall shrubs that shed their leaves each winter.

Great Britain has four native kinds of Vaccinium, all of them now known to have a circumpolar distribution. The whortleberry (V. myrtillus) and bog whinberry (V. uliginosum) are both bilberries, bearing their fruits singly rather than in clusters, as is familiar in the cultivated blueberry (V. corymbosum) of North America. Red fruits (or black ones, on some horticultural varieties) are characteristic of the red whortleberry (or cowberry, V. vitis-idaea) and the succulent sour cranberry (V. macrocarpon), which is grown extensively in artificial bogs for its festive fruit in northeastern North America. More than half of the immense annual crop in the United States is made into a canned sauce to go with fowl. The rest is sold raw or converted into a red juice. Gourmets discover that the tartness of a cranberry can be counteracted by adding sugar in abundance, but that a teaspoonful of salt may equal a cupful of extra sugar after a reasonable amount has been added to the fruit.

Properly the word heather is applied only to the ling (Calluna vulgaris), which differs from true heaths (Erica) in that the lobes of the bright purple calyx extend far beyond the petals and conceal them. This is the conspicuous covering of the Scottish Highlands, attaining a height of three feet in favorable areas and remaining less than three inches high where the weather is particularly severe. Its generic name reflects the use of the taller woody stems to form the working parts of brooms, with which to sweep or to put out fires. The same plant is gathered and dried for fuel in regions where almost nothing else combustible can be found. The long trailing stems may be made into baskets, or skilfully woven and then coated with peat mud and straw to form the walls of highland huts—the "shielings" of the independent Scottish Highlanders. It is a poor thatching material, but a durable mattress can be made of it. Heather was introduced early into New England, and has become naturalized in the New World in small areas from Newfoundland to New Jersey, westward to Michigan and the mountains of West Virginia.

True heaths (Erica) are most numerous in the western part of South Africa, and in Europe. Low ones are the characteristic shrubby vegetation of the moors, spreading over vast areas of thin poor soil in southwestern England but furnishing much of the food upon which grouse and partridge fatten. Even the wild ponies of Dartmoor seem to get some good from it, and bees collect honey from the open flowers. The purple or Scotch heath (E. cinerea), which often competes with heather for dominance on the moors, is often regarded as producing the most beautiful sprays of minute flowers. Individually, however, they are so tiny as to require a strong lens to appreciate them fully. The blossoms are scarcely larger on the largest member of the genus, the white heather (E. arborea) of southern France and the Mediterranean coast, where some individual plants attain a tree form and a height of sixty-five feet. From the French name bruyère for white heather has come the word brierwood, for the woody burls cut from the roots of this heath for making tobacco pipes.

CHAPTER 21

The Primroses

CUES: *If the flowers of the dicot plant bear their ovules on a central eminence within the single chamber of the ovary, and the four to eight stamens rise in a single ring from the base of the petals, which are joined at least part way to form a united corolla, the plant is almost sure to be a member of the Order Primulales. It may be a cowslip, an Alp's-violet, a moneywort, or a scarlet pimpernel.*

Three little families share the 2100 different kinds of plants grouped in this Order. One, the Myrsinaceae, consists of tropical and subtropical shrubs and trees, which produce a berry or a plumlike fruit. Since they do not tolerate frost, they are seldom familiar to people living in temperate zones. An exception is *Ardisia crenulata*, which is raised extensively in greenhouses and grown as a house plant since it bears from fall until spring a profusion of brilliant red berries making handsome decorations for Christmas. The leadwort family (Plumbaginaceae), with about three hundred species, differs in that the flowers of its members have five styles

Heaths. Right above: Many birds and wild mammals enjoy the ripe fruits of blueberries (Vaccinium species). (Grant Heilman)   Right: The lingberry of Europe (Vaccinium vitis-idaea), the "grape of Mt. Ida," is known also as mountain cranberry, rock cranberry, and cowberry. (Werner Schultz)

Overleaf, left: This (Dodecatheon hendersoni) is one of about thirty different wildflowers of western North America known as shooting-star or American cowslip. It is native to Pacific coastal states and blossoms in early spring. (Ray Atkeson)   Right above: Many representatives of the genus Primula tolerate the harsh conditions at high altitudes. Their foliage remains low, shielded in crevices from wind, making the flowers seem disproportionately large and showy. (Wilhelm Schacht)   Right: The thick leaves and upright flower stalks of this primrose (Primula parryi) show it to be a plant of moist ground where the growing season is many months long. (Ernst Peterson)

instead of a single one on the ovary, and in producing small nutlets as fruits, with a firm seed coat that may cling closely to the seed or balloon out from it and give buoyancy for distribution by water. The sea coasts of the world consequently are good places to find thrift (or sea-pink, *Armeria* species) and sea-lavender *(Limonium* species), particularly where the soil is limy and barren.

The most familiar members of the Order are the eight hundred different kinds of Family Primulaceae, almost all of them low-growing herbs with opposite or whorled simple leaves, flowers with a single style, and fruits in the form of a capsule that splits open to release its numerous seeds. By far the largest group is the genus *Primula* of the Northern Hemisphere, found in greatest variety in the Alps, the Caucasus, and the slopes of the Himalayas into western China. Other centers are the mountains of Ethiopia and Java. In all of the five hundred species, the flowers on each individual plant are of two types: "thrum-eyed" if the anthers of the stamens protrude beyond the tubular part of the corolla and the stigma is inconspicuous, and "pin-eyed" if the style and stigma protrude and the stamens are so short that they cannot be seen easily in the depth of the corolla tube. Charles Darwin showed experimentally that primulas produce seed most reliably when pollen from a thrum-eyed flower is carried to a pin-eyed one. He found that the texture of the stigma and the size of the pollen grains both differ in the two forms of flower.

The alpine *P. auricula* has been developed into many horticultural varieties, known as auriculas. For garden decoration they far surpass the "flowering primroses" that are more intolerant of heat, frost, drought and wind, such as the Chinese *P. obconica,* whose hairy leaves cause a skin rash on many sensitive people. The cool humid summers and mild winters of the British Isles seem to favor the growing habits of primulas, and have led to development there of a delightful range of different flower colors and leaf forms. The scale-like folds at the mouth of the blossoms in *P. veris* of Eurasia have earned for it the name cowslip; a similar plant from central and eastern Europe lacks these folds and is oxlip *(P. elatior);* both are usually bright yellow, with a dark "eye" in the throat.

Fringed gentian (Gentiana crinita) *is one of the rarest and most admired wild flowers in wet meadows in eastern North America. (Vinton Richards)*

The perennial habit of primulas depends upon a heavy underground stem (rhizome), whereas in the approximately twenty kinds of *Cyclamen,* the buried part containing food reserves is a swollen root (tuber) from which the leaves develop on long petioles. Cyclamens are plants of the Mediterranean region, the foothills of the Alps, and Asia Minor. The one known as Alp's-violet *(C. europaeum)* ranges from France to the Caucasus, producing nodding magenta flowers that are a smaller version of those on the cultivated *C. persicum.* In all, the five large petals join to form a short tube, beside which they curve back, often fluttering in the breeze and drawing attention to the flower. After pollination, the petals fall off, carrying the stamens with them, and the flower stalk coils in a spiral, pulling the ripe fruit close to the soil.

Tradition holds that Lysimachus, the king of Thrace in 300 B.C., once saved his life by waving a loosestrife plant in the face of the mad bull that was attacking him. This legend is perpetuated in the generic name *Lysimachia* for the 110 different kinds of loosestrifes found around the world. Probably the story refers to the Eurasian species *(L. vulgaris),* often called yellow loosestrife from the color of its star-shaped flowers, although most members of the genus have blossoms of this color. Yellow loosestrife grows along river banks, attaining a height of four feet. A creeping relative with succulent leaves and large open golden flowers is moneywort *(L. nummularia),* which has escaped from cultivation and become naturalized as far from its native Europe as Japan and North America.

On many continents, an inconspicuous European member of the primrose family has been introduced for sentimental reasons. It is known in Britain as shepherd's-clock or poor-man's weatherglass *(Anagallis arvensis).* Its quarter-inch red flowers became famous among readers of the Western World as scarlet pimpernels—the identifying boutonniere of a nameless daring hero in an exciting novel by the Hungarian-born English novelist Emmuska Orczy, telling of an "underground railroad" during the days of the French Revolution. Those who enjoyed the book can relive its thrilling moments merely by finding a scarlet pimpernel anywhere in the world. We lift this delight from our memories by looking into the neglected windowbox of a fisherman's shack on the forbidding Isles of Shoals off the New England coast, or a craggy corner of Vancouver Island looking out over the Pacific Ocean, or a sandy moor on the Swedish coast facing the Baltic Sea. The salmon-red (or white, or sky-blue) blossoms open widely in sunshine and close tightly upon the approach of any storm.

CHAPTER 22

The Sapodilla and Some Others

CUES: *If the dicot plant is a woody shrub or tree with alternate, simple, leathery leaves, and its stamens are borne on the bases of the united petals—either one stamen opposite each petal lobe or with two or three whorls·of stamens, some of which may be modified into showy, petal-like staminodes—the plant is likely to be a member of the Order Ebenales. It may be a persimmon, or produce such diverse substances as ebony, chicle gum, balata rubber, aromatic resins, or shea butter.*

The 1350 different species that show the features of this little Order are met most frequently in tropical and subtropical countries, where their foliage is more conspicuous than their flowers. Commonly the side veins in each leaf curve toward the tip before reaching the margin, and join the next side veins, which repeat the pattern.

THE SAPODILLA FAMILY (Sapotaceae)

In many markets of tropical America and India, rusty-brown fruits of spherical or egg-shape are piled high. They come from a small evergreen tree *(Achras zapota)* that is native to southern Mexico, Guatemala, and Honduras. In most Latin American areas it is known as chicozapote, but in regions to which it has been introduced, other names for it are used: in India, naseberry; in Florida, sapodilla. Each ripe fruit offers a translucent yellowish brown flesh that is soft and sweet like that of a pear, with a suggestion of a brown-sugar flavor. While still green, however, the fruit is unpleasantly astringent, and charged with

a milky latex like that found in the inner bark of the parent tree.

When freed of some of its water, the latex is called chicle. It is the raw material that started the commercial chewing gum industry. Particularly since World War II, manufacturers have found difficulty in buying chicle in the quantities and qualities they need, and have gradually replaced it with other gums and synthetic materials. Few plantations of the trees have ever been set out, and the native collectors (known as *chicleros)* who climb and tap the wild sapodillas in the forests vary greatly in their skill and reliability. Ideally, each tree should be tapped only once in each six to eight years. Even then, about fifteen per cent of them die from diseases that attack through the zigzag channels cut in the bark to start latex flowing. If handled well, a harvest of a ton of latex per two hundred trees can be expected in a season. With more casual methods and more frequent tapping, more trees die and the survivors become so few and scattered that the potential industry languishes.

On our first visit to Guatemala, the government generously flew us by military airplane into the northern province of Petén, where we could see the chicleros at work. In this thinly-populated part of the country, transportation is still difficult. Human porters and mules travel the trails through the forest, and light aircraft are used to take out the valuable products: chicle, mahogany, and dyewoods. From their temporary camps the chicleros go out each morning to the "walk" of trees they are tapping, armed with a machete, a length of rope and a bucket. With the rope they can climb to renew the cut surfaces in the bark. Each afternoon, while the day's latex is being heated over a wood fire to drive off the water, the men explore the forest again to locate other sapodilla trees that seem ready to produce when the supply of latex decreases along the current "walk" and a new trail is to be followed. The whole operation is handled casually in most areas, and changes unpredictably according to the yield, the location of surviving mature trees, and the mood of the men who do the hard work for so little return.

Chicle has always been treated as though it were crude rubber. This is no accident, because the first shipments to reach the United States were sold about 1890 as a possible substitute for caoutchouc. The latex for chicle is boiled down to about two-thirds of its original volume, and then molded for shipment into rough cubes each weighing about twenty-five pounds. This brownish material must be freed of impurities at the chewing-gum factory, before it is blended with other gums, powdered sugar, corn sirup, and flavorings, and prepared in bite-sized pieces ready for wrapping and sales. Almost the entire world demand for chicle still comes from the United States, where chewing gum displaced in the early 1900's the traditional chewing of spruce and cherry gums—a practice adopted by the pioneers in imitation of the American Indians.

Rubber manufacturers might get much better latex for their purposes from other trees of the sapodilla family. Some of these, such as the gutta-percha, used for covering golf balls and electrical wiring, are well known. This hard, nonbrittle material is the boiled latex from trees of the Indomalaysian genus *Palaquium*. Some of them have been introduced into Brazil, but plantations have been small. Wild trees, chiefly of *P. gutta* in the Malay Peninsula and *P. oblongifolia* on Sumatra, Java and adjacent islands of the East Indies, are still tapped to contribute toward the world supply. Since *Palaquium* latex is viscid and does not run readily from tapped trees, it is usual to fell the tree, strip off the bark, and extract the latex. All of these operations add to the cost and the scarcity of the gutta-percha. They also stimulate greater reliance upon similar latex of poorer quality, known as balata, obtained from related trees in the West Indies and northern South America. Perhaps a mispronunciation of balatawoods has led to the use of the name bulletwoods for these trees, many of which are of the genus *Mimusops*. Among the most productive, although still in the rain forests rather than plantations, are the bully trees *(M. globata* and *M. darienensis)* of Colombia and Panamá, and the West Indian dilly trees *(M. emarginata)*.

Starapple *(Chrysophyllum cainito)* and marmalade-plum (or sapote, *Calocarpum sapota* or *C. mammosum)* are among the delicious fruits from other members of the sapodilla family from the West Indies and Central America. Both are common dooryard trees in the Caribbean area, with evergreen leaves, and frequent crops of fruits. The foliage of starapple is easy to recognize because each leaf is covered below by a velvety coating of brownish hairs, contrasting sharply with the glossy green above. A starapple fruit is purplish, from two to four inches in diameter, shaped like an apple, with a thick and pleasantly sweet pulp marked at the center by a star of five chambers containing the small seeds. The marmalade-plum fruit, known in some areas as a mamey apple, has much larger seeds and thinner pulp, and affords a much more spicy flavor either fresh or when cooked and made into jamlike preserves.

The seeds alone are harvested from a tropical African member of the family *(Butyrospermum parkii),* and yield a white fat known as shea butter. It is used extensively in the western Sudan for food and melted for burning at night as an illuminant. Every year, however, the supply of this fat decreases because education and religious conversions reduce the number of people who hold the seed-producing trees in superstitious awe, and increase the population who wish to fell them and burn the wood for fuel.

THE EBONY FAMILY *(Ebenaceae)*

Among the kinds of wood that man has treasured for thousands of years, the intensely black heartwood from trees of certain species of *Diospyros* has held a place of special esteem. Known as ebony, it is hard, durable, heavy, and capable of taking a high polish. The Hebrew prophet Ezekiel in the 6th century B.C. listed this wood among the important merchandise brought to the city of Tyre. Herodotus commented that Persia received two hundred logs of ebony every third year as tribute from Ethiopia. It was carved into scepters, statues, and even drinking vessels, following the belief that poisons added to a drink would be neutralized by the black material. Today it still finds extensive use in cabinetry, for the black keys on pianos and organs, knife handles, and the heads of golf clubs.

India and Ceylon have long led the world in production of ebony, from *D. ebenum,* which attains a height of more than one hundred feet and a remarkable thickness of trunk. After a tree is felled, its jet-black bark is removed and then the considerable sapwood, which is almost pure white, to reach the valuable heartwood forming the center of the trunk. Similar material in much more slender pieces is obtained from an East Indian ebony *(D. melanoxylon),* which becomes sixty to eighty feet tall and three feet in diameter at the base. Niger ebony, so widely used by home craftsmen for carving in equatorial Africa, is a still smaller tree *(D. dendo)* native to forests from Liberia to Angola and eastward to the limits of the Congo basin.

In many of these areas, the local people know that bees make a distinctive and delightful honey from the nectar in flowers on ebony trees, and that these flowers are of two types: solitary pistillate ones in the axils of the large leaves, and clusters of staminate ones often toward the ends of the branches. American

Indians appear to have been quite familiar with this characteristic of *D. virginiana,* a small tree of the southeastern states from Texas to New Jersey. They competed, in fact, with raccoons, opossums, squirrels and birds for the small fruits that developed. Known as persimmons, these yellowish or orange-colored solitary berries retained an extreme astringency until ripe, and then proved very perishable as well as delightfully soft, sweet and edible. The early colonists learned to enjoy persimmons too, and found that the dark brown wood of the tree could be carved and polished to make heavy shuttles for looms. Modern luxury markets sometimes offer cultivated persimmons twice as large as the common one-inch wild fruits. Persimmon wood has the hardness and durability of ebony, and is often used for golf-club heads. The proportion of the heartwood, which is black or brownish black, is small in comparison with the pale sapwood.

THE STORAX FAMILY (Styracaceae)

Differing from members of the sapodilla and ebony families in producing plumlike fruits with a stony covering around the single seed and in having epidermal hairs that branch into fanciful patterns, the 125 species in the storax family belong mostly to the big genus *Styrax* and are common in tropical and subtropical lands. In place of latex their bark contains resins, for which a variety of uses have been found.

Benzoin is among the most valuable of these resins, from woody shrubs *(S. benzoin)* of Southeast Asia, including the islands of Sumatra, Java, and Borneo. It is fragrant enough to serve as an incense, effective as a kidney stimulant (diuretic), as a mild laxative, and as an ingredient to put into mouthwashes and toothpasts to stimulate flow of saliva and antagonize the growth of bacteria. Its derivatives, such as sodium benzoate, are often added to foods to retard spoilage on the grocer's shelves. Seemingly the amounts used have no harmful effects.

Storax is a hard fragrant resin collected from the bark of the snowdrop bush *(S. officinalis)* of Mediterranean coasts. Unfortunately the name was used also for a more valuable resin obtained from Asiatic and American sweet-gum trees *(Liquidambar,* of the witch-hazel family), and it is this misnamed substitute that is still in use for manufacture of medicinal salves, perfumes, perfumed powders and soaps, and for flavoring tobacco. Collection of the tear-shaped drops of fragrant resin from the snowdrop bush has virtually ceased.

CHAPTER 23

Plants Whose Petal Tips Uncurl

CUES: *If the dicot plant has regular flowers with sepals united into a cup, and petals (if any) similarly joined although their tips are conspicuously lobed and curled tightly in the bud, and if all stamens arise from the petals near their base, the plant is likely to be a member of Order Gentianales. It may be an olive tree, a privet bush, a floating heart, a milkweed, or even a kind of pitcher-plant.*

Among the 5100 species in this Order, the leaves are usually paired, the ovaries paired (distinct or joined), and the stamens fewer than the petal lobes. Wherever the stamens and petals are equal in number, the filaments arise from the lines of junction between the petals—not opposite the petals as is characteristic of Orders Primulales and Ebenales. The petal tips are so curled and twisted in the bud that the Gentianales has been called the "Contortae."

THE OLIVE FAMILY (Oleaceae)

Although the cultivated olive is named *Olea europaea,* the origin of this valuable kind of tree may never be known exactly. It may have come from the semi-arid coasts of Mediterranean Europe or from Asia Minor. Archaeologists have evidence of olive orchards existing on Crete in 3500 B.C., and believe that Semitic peoples have been raising olives for at least five thousand years. If we are to accept Noah's identification of the branch with leaves that the dove brought to him in the ark after the Flood, olive trees were among the first to recover after the deluge. They have tolerated the felling of the forests around the Mediterranean, the erosion of the land, a rainfall of only eight to ten inches after hot summers lasting six to eight months, and the presence of multitudes of people with their domesticated animals. Gradually over the centuries, the olive branch in the dove's beak became a traditional symbol of peace.

Olives need no insects for pollination, but depend upon the wind and produce no petals that might get in the way. To bear fruit, in fact, olive trees require winter temperatures near freezing, but none lower than 15° F. These conditions are met in Spain, Italy, Greece, Turkey, and Portugal, which today produce most of the olive oil and pickled olives used in the world. Suitable climates can be found too in lands as remote as Argentina, South Africa, Australia, and the state of California. Nowhere, however, are fresh olives sold to be eaten raw. Until processed at some length, the fruit contains a bitter glycoside that renders it inedible.

Table olives are picked before they get ripe. The Spanish procedure requires that they be harvested while still green or straw-colored, and then go directly into a lye bath. The dilute sodium hydroxide in the bath neutralizes the bitter glycoside, and both can be washed out together with several changes of water. The olives then go into large wooden barrels containing a six- to eight-per cent salt solution for a month to six months, during which their full flavor is developed by lactic-acid fermentation. The process is controlled by occasional additions of sugar, but exposure to air is avoided since this leads to a darkening of the fruit.

"Black olives," in the California style, are picked while straw-colored or cherry red and placed immediately in a brine for fermentation. After this is complete, the black color is developed by controlled exposure to air. Only then is the treatment with sodium hydroxide begun and the repeated washings that remove the bitter flavor. Final storage, as with Spanish-style olives, is in dilute brine.

For oil, the olives are allowed to ripen fully on the tree. By midwinter they are black, and contain from twenty to thirty per cent of oil. The best quality, for cooking uses, comes from the first pressing of the pulp; to be called "virgin oil" it must be removed quickly from any residues of fruit tissue which might putrefy, releasing fatty acids that would go rancid. The remaining pulp, known as "pomace," is extracted again, using hot water, to obtain a poorer grade of oil that is still called *lampante* from its former use as a fuel for oil lamps. Lampante is decolorized, deacidified, and deodorized to become "refined olive oil," to be blended with virgin oil for export. Ordinarily the product is aged for a short time in large tanks before being sold, because fresh olive oil of any quality has an unpleasant flavor. The pomace yields a third type of oil if extracted once more, this time with fat solvents. It is suitable chiefly for manufacture of laundry soaps. These can be called Castile soaps, since they are made with olive oil and sodium hydroxide. But the better the grade of oil and the higher the purity of sodium hydroxide used, the harder and more tasteless the soap becomes and the more it is free of both color and mottling.

Some olive trees have been known to attain an age of one thousand years, growing slowly all this time. Only the one species, however, among the thirty different kinds in the genus *Olea* produces edible fruits or useful oil. The other species are native to Mediterranean countries, South Africa, Indomalaysia, Polynesia, and New Zealand.

Near the French Riviera, where for centuries the depleted soil supported only olive orchards, goats and sheep, another member of the olive family is now tended carefully for its valuable oil. It is a jasmine *(Jasminum grandiflorum)* from the Himalayas, whose twenty-foot woody vines are trained along trellises like those used for raising grapes. Particularly around Grasse, in a great natural amphitheater open toward the sun and sea, these vines bloom almost continuously. Each evening they open white five-petalled flowers like stars. Each dawn, women and children carefully pluck the flowers before they wither in the sun, and hurry them into the perfume factories. About 3500 flowers in springtime, and twice this many in October or November, are needed to weigh a pound, from which less than a fiftieth of an ounce of the fragrant oil can be extracted. At Grasse, the favorite method is by enfleurage—spreading the fresh blossoms on trays containing a mixture of beef and pork fat mixed with gum benzoin. After a few hours, the flowers are brushed onto fresh trays coated with fat. Repeatedly, for as many as fifteen transfers, the blossoms are given a chance to share their volatile perfume with the films of fat. This continues for as much as three days, until the flowers shrivel. The fat is scraped from the trays, shaken up with a solvent (such as alcohol) in which the jasmine oil will dissolve but not the fat, and then separated again for reuse. Using no heat that might affect the jasmine oil, the alcohol is evaporated out of the solution, leaving the valuable extract to be bottled or blended with other perfumes.

In many parts of the world, English-speaking people give the name jasmine to almost any vine or shrub that bears fragrant star-shaped flowers. Often they are correct, for *Jasminum* includes about two hundred species and several have escaped from cultivation far from their native lands, which extend from Indomalaysia to northern Asia, Europe, North America, and South America. Winter jasmine *(J. nudiflorum)* from China is widely planted in temperate climates on both sides of the Equator for the pleasure its golden-yellow flowers provide on warm days in earliest spring—opening on stems from which all leaves have fallen and where no other buds will open for weeks or months to come. Star jasmine *(J. gracillimum),* like the horticultural variety known as *J. illicifolium* ("holly-leaved"), produces evergreen foliage and white flowers with seven or more slender points spreading starlike from the end of the short tubular portion of the joined petals.

Four petals is a more characteristic number for flowers in the olive family. It is familiar in golden-bells *(Forsythia),* whose one species from Albania and three from China and Japan are now planted for decoration in many lands, as shrubs with graceful arching branches on which yellow flowers open before the leaves expand in spring. Each little flower in a cluster on a lilac *(Syringa)* has the same form, and most afford the extra pleasure of a distinctive perfume; these shrubs include *S. emodi* from the Himalayas, Persian lilacs *(S. persica)* from Asia between Iran and northwestern China, and the "common lilac" *(S. vulgaris)* from southeastern Europe. Because lilacs reproduce readily by suckers from the roots, it has been fairly easy to develop a delightful range of colors and other features among cultivated varieties, with all shades from the wild purple to white, and red, and almost pure blue.

In his *Herball,* published in London in 1597, the English botanist John Gerard illustrated and described the introduced European lilac as "blue pipe privet." He distinguished it from "white pipe privet," which is the principal shrub *(Ligustrum vulgare)* used for hedges in Britain and on the European continent, in both of which it is native. The "California privet" *(L. ovalifolium),* which originated in Japan, thrives in Britain but offers few advantages there. In the northern United States and Canada, however, *L. ovalifolium* remains evergreen or remains leafless for fewer months than *L. vulgare* and is less subject to killing by sub-zero temperatures; for these reasons it is the preferred privet in colder America.

Aside from European privet, the only member of the olive family native to Britain is the ash *(Fraxinus excelsior),* which grows wild all across the continent and into the mountains of Asia Minor. Like other members of the genus, this ash has pinnately compound leaves and winged fruits (samaras). The four petals in each flower are small, distinguishing it easily from the flowering ash *(F. ornus)* of Mediterranean coasts and Asia, which has showy white petals, and from the twenty species in America, most of which lack petals altogether. Several of those in the United States and Canada grow tall—to 105 feet in green ash *(F. pennsylvanica)*—and are highly regarded for their solid shade and useful wood.

THE STRYCHNINE FAMILY *(Loganiaceae)*

Strychnine, which is world-famous as a powerful poison causing quick, convulsive death in people and most other animals, was isolated first in 1818 from the pale greenish yellow seeds of the St. Ignatius vine *(Strychnos ignatii)* of the Philippines. It is now recognized to be the chief alkaloid, usually associated with brucine, in the seeds of about 150 different species of this genus, which is well represented among the trees and woody vines of the world's tropics. The effects of this poison were well known to primitive people long before chemists identified the substance. It is the toxic ingredient in curare, an arrow poison prepared by the Indians in the South American valleys of Guianian rivers, of the Orinoco, the Amazon, and the Magdalena. They make it from *S. toxifera* and *S. castelnaei* by secret processes they were reluctant to reveal. Similar material is used in the same way in the East Indies from New Guinea westward. But strychnine for a druggist's shelves comes chiefly from India and Ceylon, as an extract of "vomit nuts"—the seeds of *S. nux-vomica.* From all sources, the material acts in a similar manner. It stimulates the nervous system excessively, leading to violent contraction of muscles, suppression of normal breathing movements and asphyxia. Presumably the poison keeps wild animals in tropical lands from repeatedly eating the seeds of *Strychnos* plants. Each seed is usually disc-shaped, and surrounded with three or four others by a bitter gelatinous white pulp within a thin-skinned fruit the size and shape of a small orange.

Members of the strychnine family produce perfect

Right above: Probably this old olive tree (Olea europaea) *bore fruit in 300* B.C., *when the temple behind it near Agrigento, Sicily, was a center for the Greek community. (Wilhelm Schacht) Right: Cup-of-gold* (Allamanda cathartica) *climbs vigorously and opens new flowers each morning in tropical America, often in a canopy atop forest trees. (E. Javorsky)*

flowers each with four or five apiece of sepals, petals, and stamens, and two styles from the two-carpel pistil. A few are cultivated for their attractive flowers and handsome leaves. Butterfly-bush *(Buddleia alternifolia)* with lilac-colored flowers in conspicuous spikes is a member of this big genus from northwest China, appreciated by butterflies in gardens all over the world. Yellow jessamine *(Gelsemium sempervirens),* which is sometimes called "jasmine," is native to the southeastern United States but grown widely as an evergreen vine whose fragrant clustered golden flowers are a bright contrasting pinkish orange behind the flaring petal lobes. Jessamine in its home sandhills and swamps often clambers up the tallest trees, such as pines, and gilds them in early spring with a rising tide of bloom as sun-catching flowers open higher week after week while the weather warms up.

THE GENTIANS (Family Gentianaceae)

About five hundred of the eight hundred different kinds of herbs in this family are true gentians *(Gentiana).* A majority of them produce distinctive tubular flowers of an intense ultramarine or blue color; only a few are yellow; some, particularly in the Andes, are pink or red. Those that grow, as most do, high on the world's mountains or at high latitudes in Scandinavia, Canada, Alaska, South America, and New Zealand, excite interest because of their harsh environment. Those that inhabit shady river banks and damp bottomlands, or pinelands or uplands nearer human habitations tempt so many people to pick them that they are in constant danger of being exterminated. Some gentians tolerate cultivation in gardens, particularly in the British Isles where the climate is cool and moist. A few, especially the handsome large *G. lutea* of the Apennines, Alps and Pyrenees, have been sought extensively for their roots, from which a home medicine is prepared—supposedly to improve digestion.

The water-snowflakes *(Nymphoides),* which are often mistaken for water-lilies, produce such similar

Left above: This milkweed (Asclepias *species) flowering northwest of Abercorn, Northern Rhodesia, exposes paired bags of pollen ready to be caught on the leg of an insect. (E. S. Ross) Left: Velvet-soft petals on the perfumed flowers of frangipani* (Plumeria rubra) *of tropical America contain a milky latex. (Lorus and Margery Milne)*

flowers that they are grouped in the gentian family. These water plants have floating leaves tethered by very long petioles from buried stems in the bottom mud of ponds and slow streams in Africa, Eurasia, and America. Some, such as floating-heart *(N. cordata*—native to North America from Newfoundland to Ontario, Louisiana to Florida), have been adopted by people with garden pools all over the temperate world. The petioles grow beyond the leaves into air during summer and support little clusters of white or yellow flowers, each from a quarter of an inch to more than an inch across.

THE DOGBANE FAMILY (Apocynaceae)

The 1300 members of the dogbane family include herbs, shrubs, woody climbing vines (lianas), and trees of moderate height. They resemble the gentians (Family Gentianaceae) in lacking stipules where each petiole joins the stem, and are like milkweeds (Asclepiadaceae) in having a milky latex, but differ from both in having a single stigma instead of two.

Some of these plants have become notorious because of the poisons extracted from them by primitive people. The Madagascan ordeal tree *(Tanghinia veninifera)* and the Hottentot's poison bush *(Acocanthera venenata)* both produce plumlike fruits whose poisonous seeds can be offered to test a suspected criminal. Supposedly an innocent person who swallows these seeds will disgorge them again too quickly to be harmed, whereas a guilty individual will digest them and die. A convicted criminal, found by other means, can be put to death in a few minutes if an arrow point smeared with an extract from the crushed bark of these plants is jabbed into the person's skin. On the game reserves of equatorial and southern Africa, poachers use poisoned arrows made lethal with the extract of *Acocanthera* bark. Enough of it can be bought on the black market for ten shillings to coat twenty arrows; used arrowheads can be dug out for reuse without additional coating. A minute amount suffices to kill an antelope, and only a little more to cause the rapid death of a hippopotamus or a full-grown elephant.

Several of the ornamental shrubs grown along city streets in warm countries are almost as poisonous. Pliny, the Roman encyclopedist who died in A.D. 79, mentioned the dangers in oleander (or rose-bay, *Nerium oleander)* from Mediterranean coasts—the full native range is from Portugal to Iraq—and North Africa. The yellow oleander (or be-still tree, *Thevetia peruviana)* of tropical America is a similar hazard.

In temperate regions of the Old World goldenbells (Forsythia species*) open yellow flowers in earliest spring—and sometimes in late autumn. (J. Allan Cash)*

Both are tall shrubs often as much as thirty feet high. greatly admired for their evergreen leaves and fragrant, roselike flowers. Those of *Nerium* are pink or white, those of *Thevetia* bright yellow or orange. In Hawaii, the two genera share the top position as causes of fatal or near-fatal poisoning in man (especially children) and domestic animals. A few leaves

or seeds constitute a deadly dose. People have died merely from eating meat that was roasted while skewered on oleander wood from peeled branches. Horses have succumbed from nibbling at foliage on a bush to which they were tethered very briefly. The poison is a glycoside with effects similar to those of digitalis.

Arrow poisons in which the effective agents are glycosides have long been prepared from the seeds of various species of *Strophanthus,* of which Africa and Asia have some forty-three different kinds. Recent attempts by biochemists and pharmacologists to learn the nature of the purified compounds have led to the recognition of several classed as strophanthins. They prove helpful in medical treatment of people with heart disease who could not be given digitalis orally because of digestive upsets. Strophanthins, particularly those from *S. sarmentosus,* can also be converted readily into cortisone, which is valuable in the treatment of arthritis. Some members of this genus, which reach tree size, produce spectacular flowers in which the stamens exceed twelve inches in length, protruding from long tubular corollas that are scarcely shorter.

Modern investigation of extracts from other members of the dogbane family confirm the good judgment shown by medicine men in India as far back as 1000 to 800 B.C. Through the intervening centuries, Hindus have continued to use derivatives from the roots of shrubby *Rauvolfia serpentina,* which is native to India, Ceylon, and Java. The Sanskrit name of the plant is *sarpagandha,* referring to its use in treatment of both snakebite and lunacy. Today a crystalline alkaloid (reserpine) is obtained from these roots and from those of *R. vomitoria* of Africa, following the discovery in 1952 that the substance had dramatic effects in lowering high blood pressure and in tranquilizing certain types of mental patients, most notably those with schizophrenia. The eighty species of the genus have representatives in the tropics of the New World as well as the Old. Some are trees. All produce flat clusters of small flowers and paired plumlike fruits.

Both the shape and size of the individual blossoms vary tremendously among members of the dogbane family. Some are extraordinarily handsome, and the plants that bear them are cultivated as ornamentals. Big yellow flowers form the chief attraction on cup-of-gold (*Allamanda cathartica*), a woody liana of tropical America. Far more beautiful, to our eyes, are the smaller perfumed blossoms of frangipani *(Plumeria,* especially *P. rubra)* from Central

America, which are now favorites in most warm parts of the world. In India, frangipanis are known as "temple trees" because they are used so often for decorative plantings around Hindu shrines. Frangipanis grew luxuriantly in the rocky soil of a remote island off Zanzibar, where we found giant tortoises eating the fallen corollas, apparently in an attempt to satisfy their thirst and get a little sugary nectar too. They refused freshly cut flowers, which contained more moisture but also the milky latex.

A few members of the family have other features to recommend them. From Natal and adjacent parts of South Africa has come the popular, spiny, evergreen shrub known as Natal-plum *(Carissa grandiflora)*. Its waxy-white blossoms, often two inches across, are followed by decorative scarlet fruits as much as two inches long. They are edible raw, or make a delicious jelly. Wherever we find them, they seem to defy the law of gravity—poised atop short stalks, instead of hanging from them.

Without evergreen periwinkle (or creeping myrtle, *Vinca*—particularly *V. minor* from southern Europe and Asia Minor), the ground would be bare beneath many shade trees in Britain, other parts of Europe, and much of America where this trailing perennial now grows. It serves as a soil anchor, and produces almost continuously in springtime either violet-blue or white flowers that contrast handsomely against its dark green foliage.

Dogbane *(Apocynum)*, for which the family is named, is native to the North Temperate Zone, where its small clusters of pinkish-white flowers on branching stems often attract brilliant leaf beetles of metallic green, glinting with coppery hues. Later in the season, long slender paired fruits hang from the same stems. The name of the plant commemorates an old idea that dogs run from it. Domesticated animals find its foliage distasteful. Those suffering from extreme hunger may eat it, but they usually die from a poisonous glycoside, a poisonous resin, and perhaps other toxic ingredients that can be extracted from the leaves and stems.

Most bizarre of the plants in this family is the

Right above: The giant carrion-flower (Stapelia nobilis) *of Kenya belongs to a genus resembling American cacti in succulence, but without spines. (Othmar Stemmler)   Right: The split pods of milkweed* (Asclepias *species) expose seeds to the wind, each with a parachute of fine hairs. (C. G. Maxwell: National Audubon)*

ghostman *(Pachypodium namaquanum)* of arid lands across South Africa and in Madagascar. Virtually leafless except at the top after a desert rainstorm has wet the ground, the plant rises as a tapering, slightly bent column as much as twelve feet tall and a foot in diameter at the base. This grotesque succulent resembles in many ways the boojum tree *(Idria columnaris)* of similar areas in the southwestern deserts of North America.

THE MILKWEED FAMILY *(Asclepiadaceae)*

Perhaps it would be better if these plants were called silkweeds, instead of milkweeds, since more of the 1700 different kinds produce a silky tuft on each seed than contain a milky latex in the roots, stems, and leaves. All have regular flowers, usually with a unique organization involving stamens and stigma. The pollen in the stamens adheres in masses called pollinia. Pairs of pollinia are linked by yokelike bars contributed by the stigma, and catch on the legs or bristles of pollinating insects—if these visitors are of the correct size. Sometimes a honeybee collecting nectar from a milkweed flower gets caught by several of the yokes at once and is unable to free itself. More often it carries away the paired pollinia and wipes them off in another milkweed flower, whose stigma is just the right shape to unload the insect and gather the pollen.

The fruits of plants in the milkweed family are podlike, opening along one side to expose both the seeds and their silky hairs. When a gust of wind blows past the open fruit in the correct direction, the hairs are pulled and lift out the seeds one after another, to float off, sometimes for miles. On each seed, all of the hairs join to form a minute ring that surrounds a peglike extension on the seed coat. If the seed dries and shrivels while being blown along, or the humidity rises and the ring around the peg expands, the seed is freed and drops to the ground. Milkweed silk has been tried as a substitute for

Left above: Old olive trees in Europe and Asia Minor often lose their center by decomposition. (E. Aubert de La Rue)   Left: The snow gentian (Gentiana corymbifera) *attains a height of eight inches in the mountains of New Zealand's South Island, and flowers so profusely from January to March that it often dies soon after setting seed. (New Zealand Information Service)*

kapok. But since the best silk is from species native to the United States, where hand labor is expensive and no one has yet devised a machine to harvest the silk and prepare it economically, no industrial uses have developed.

Milkweeds (*Asclepias*—dedicated to the Greek god of medicine, Aesculapius) include about ninety species, a dozen of which are South American and the rest divided almost equally between North America (temperate and tropical) and Africa (southern and eastern). At least fourteen kinds are known to serve as the host plant for the handsome and remarkably migratory monarch butterfly. Introduction of milkweeds has been followed by colonization by monarchs in many distant lands: Hawaii, about 1845, the Marquesas Islands in the South Pacific, about 1860, Australia in 1870, and New Zealand in 1874. Attempts to raise milkweeds in Britain are likely to have the same effect, for "visiting" monarchs have been recorded there many times since 1876. In North America, the annual migration of monarchs from the northern states and Canada to mid-California in the West and the Gulf States in the East is a regular autumn event. Females fly back again in early spring, depositing eggs soon after the milkweed plants have raised new stems to a height of a few inches from their perennial roots.

By comparison with milkweeds, other members of the family seem strange in form and way of life. Least bizarre may be the eighty different kinds of climbers in the genus *Hoya*, native to Asia and Australia; the wax-flower *(H. carnosa)* of southern China, which has paired fleshy leaves and clusters of flowers from which fragrance spreads and sweet nectar drips at night, is often raised indoors as an ornamental. The carrion-flowers of South Africa *(Stapelia)* resemble cacti because of their succulent stems and reduced leaves. Their flowers emit an odor suggesting carrion, which attracts flies as pollinators. In Australia and parts of Polynesia and Indomalaysia, the epiphytic plants of the rain forest include about fifty different species of *Dischidia* which climb with aerial roots. Most astonishing of them is the pitcher-plant *D. rafflesiana,* whose pitcher-shaped leaves catch rain water and hold it where it can be absorbed easily by adventitious roots that grow into each pitcher. Ants often ruin the pitchers, cutting drainage holes in the bottom and filling the cavity with plant fibers among which they raise their young. If the plant is disturbed, the ants rush out, biting and stinging, defending the *Dischidia* as well as their young.

CHAPTER 24

The Tube Flowers

CUES: *If the dicot plant has petals joined to form a tubular corolla that is free from the single compound ovary but supports the stamens, and the stamens arise from the lines of junction between petals and at least halfway toward their tips, it is almost sure to be a member of the Order Tubiflorales. It may be a morning-glory, a sagebush, a teak tree, a forget-me-not, a tomato vine, a bladderwort, or an African voilet.*

Among the nearly twenty thousand different kinds of plants assigned to this Order, botanists find structural features of flower, seed, and embryo they regard as meaningful, pointing to an ancestral line of great antiquity. During the millions of years since this line branched away from the other members of the dicot group, adaptations have accumulated in a host of directions, providing the wealth of differences we can find today. For no apparent reason, none of the species in this Order possesses stipules as leaf-like expansions of the petiole where it joins the stem.

THE MORNING-GLORY FAMILY
(Convolvulaceae)

Except in the tropics, where the members of this family include a few trees and woody vines, these plants are herbs with alternate leaves. In one genus the leaves are represented by mere scales. Most species twine around supports or trail along the ground. "Wild morning-glories" *(Convolvulus)* show this spiral habit of growth, and are properly called bindweeds because they twist so tightly around the vegetation upon which they climb. Field-bindweed *(C. arvensis)* originated in southern Europe, but now has become a cosmopolitan weed. Hedge-bindweed *(C. sepium)* has spread almost as widely from the Old World, where it seems to have been native all across Eurasia and to New Zealand. Both bindweeds open new flowers before dawn, the smaller ones of field-bindweed in white or pinkish shades, the larger funnel-shaped blossoms of hedge-bindweed usually rose-colored. By afternoon the flowers begin to wither. Soon they are replaced by small globular capsules with many seeds in two chambers.

Common morning-glory (Ipomoea purpurea), with flowers to three inches across, is a contribution to gardens and waysides in many lands from tropical America. Some flowers are purple, as the name suggests. Other plants produce blooms that are sky-blue, red, white, or variegated in these colors. In sweet potato (I. batatas, a native of South America), the blue or rose-colored flowers have darker, rather than paler throats, but the plants are ordinarily propagated from cuttings of the vines, or from pieces of the thick roots for which they are raised. So adapted to the tropics is the sweet potato that, unless the plant is given comparable warmth and light and moisture, it fails to set seed farther from the Equator than New Orleans, Casablanca or Shanghai (30 degrees latitude) and rarely flowers north of Gibraltar, Tokyo, or the state of Kentucky.

Sweet potatoes were a staple food among the Aztecs when America was discovered. They were carried to Europe from the West Indies in 1526, and raised as a crop by the settlers in Virginia in 1650. The thick roots are rich in starch, and become distinctly sweet when boiled or baked. Horticultural varieties with an orange "flesh" contain valuable carotene—pro-vitamin A—which the body absorbs and converts to the vitamin. These foods are prized highly in tropical America, in the warmer islands of the Pacific, and in English-speaking areas of the United States and Canada. In Japan, sweet potatoes are grown chiefly for manufacture of starch and alcohol.

A very different way of life is found among related plants of the genus Cuscuta. Known as dodders, they are rootless, leafless twiners that lack chlorophyll and subsist as parasites on other vegetation. The slender stems, which may be golden-yellow or white or red, resemble strands of wet catgut as they spread from one host plant to another. On each victim they twine and cling tightly with special branching organs called haustoria penetrating the host, absorbing from it both water and elaborated foodstuffs such as sugars and amino acids. In the tropics, where great masses of dodder often give a golden color to the tops of small trees, the plants are often called "love bush" and provide the basis for an amusing folk custom. To learn whether a loved one is being faithful, the suspicious partner frees a mass of dodder strands from its host plants and tosses the tangled stems on another bush; if, a week later, the dodder has not

taken hold in its new site, the suspicions are groundless—or so the superstition holds. In temperate lands, dodders often cause serious damage to crops. The European clover dodder (C. trifolii) attacks various legumes, and is a real pest in fields of beans, clover and even alfalfa. Where flax and hemp are raised, C. epilinum often destroys hundreds of plants. Injury of this type rarely develops in America. Everywhere that dodders grow, however, they produce clusters of small white flowers, followed by capsules that open to free the seeds. Many strict laws have been passed and enforced to prevent the international and interstate transport of dodder seeds, which otherwise travel as impurities and are sown by growers of clover, alfalfa, and other crops.

THE PHLOXES (Family Polemoniaceae)

Deep in the tubular throat of each flower in members of this little family is the most distinctive feature: a three-part ovary that matures into a three-valved capsule. All other members of the Order have two-part ovaries and fruits. From the end of the tubular portion of the corolla, the five petal lobes flare in a flat whorl that provides a good target for night-flying moths and diurnal hummingbirds. These pollinators reach easily into the deep throat for nectar, and transfer pollen from stamens that rarely show their tips.

So many of the 265 species in the family have been adopted into flower gardens all over the world that it is easy to overlook the New World origin of most of them. Phlox, with about a fifth of the different kinds, has one representative in eastern Siberia and the rest in North America. Some form a ground cover and are grown in massed areas that flame with color during the flowering season. Moss-pink (P. subulata) is a perennial favorite, wild on poor soil from New York and Michigan south to Florida and Kentucky. Texan pride (P. drummondi) attains a height of eighteen inches and flowers profusely, dying at the end of its single year but usually seeding itself and holding its place, even in waste ground beyond gardens from which it has escaped—far from its native east Texas. Tall wild phloxes of moist woodlands in eastern North America have contributed the common tall-growing border plants. The

Lungwort (Mertensia *species) is found in ravines on mountain slopes in Eurasia and North America, and on gravel beaches on arctic coasts. (Ernst Peterson)*

early-flowering ones are mostly horticultural varieties of *P. carolina* and *P. glaberrima*. Late-flowering usually are *P. maculata* and *P. paniculata*. So many people in the United States admire both the wild and cultivated phloxes that decorate their home regions that garden clubs have urged the adoption of the whole genus as a national flower.

More than twice as many species are included among the members of *Gilia*, which are mostly natives to western North America but have a few outliers in the tropics of the New World. Several grow wild in the National Parks of Wyoming, Montana, and California. Many have been adopted into gardens in all temperate lands. Attaining a height of about three feet are scarlet *Gilia* (*G. aggregata*—which may have white flowers) and bird's-eyes (*G. tricolor*), which has violet petals from a purple throat in a flower with a yellow tube. Standing-cypress (*G. rubra*) is seldom over five inches tall but starred with bright red flowers having a yellowish center.

THE BORAGE FAMILY (Boraginaceae)

Many of the poets who have celebrated the forget-me-not (*Myosotis*, especially *M. scorpioides* and *M. sylvatica* of Eurasia) avoid any mention of how the flower got its name. According to a romantic old German legend, these are the last words from a gallant gentleman who drowned in a boggy place beside a stream while trying to gather a bouquet for his lady. The generic name is Greek for "mouse ears," referring to the shape of the leaves. The flower buds are pink, but open and expand into saucer-shape, the bright blue corolla usually sky-blue with a yellow throat. In addition to the forget-me-nots of temperate regions in the Old World, there are wild ones in Australia, in many parts of North America, and one (*M. alpestris*) so common in Alaska as to have been chosen for the floral emblem there.

Heliotropes (*Heliotropium*) are also favorite flowers in old-fashioned gardens of the world, adding so much fragrance that the roughness of the plant and

Left above: Flame-violets (Episcia) *of about thirty kinds thrive in the moist shade of tropical America. Far left: Cape-primroses* (Streptocarpus) *are native to South Africa and Madagascar. (Both by E. Javorsky) Left: Clusters of large cup-shaped flowers make the African tuliptree* (Spathodea campanulata), *which grows twenty to seventy feet tall, one of the showiest in the tropics. (Tropical Films)*

the scraggly way it grows are easily overlooked. Most of the 250 different kinds are from tropical South America, particularly Ecuador and Peru, where they are shrubs, vines, or small trees. The cultivated one known as cherry-pie (*H. arborescens*) was introduced from Peru to the Paris botanic garden, and from there to England about 1757. Along with a second species (*H. corymbosum*), presumably from the same part of the New World, this heliotrope was developed into many horticultural varieties, all with the same delightful perfume. The English name "turnsole" for the plant is a corruption of the French *tournesol*, referring (as does the generic name) to the habit both the flowers and leaves show of turning to follow the sun each day.

By finding in each blossom five stamens and a pistil whose style rises from a depression between the two lobes (carpels) of the ovary, it is possible to recognize a member of this family even though it shows few other resemblances to a forget-me-not or a heliotrope. The geiger-tree (*Cordia sebastena*) of Florida, the West Indies, and southward has been planted widely in the New World tropics for its shade, its handsome orange-red flowers, and its edible plumlike fruits. At the other extreme we would think of a bristly, noxious weed: viper's bugloss (*Echium vulgare*) or blue devil. It has spread unwanted from Europe, and is difficult to eradicate, particularly where the soil is well supplied with lime. Individually its flowers are beautiful. The pink buds open one after another, exposing a showy blue corolla and long out-thrust stamens paralleling a three-parted style. Something of the plant's hardiness can be seen in the vigor of a stand of it on the Baltic island of Øland off the Swedish coast. As stiff as soldiers on parade and almost as closely side by side, the viper's bugloss plants rise twelve to fifteen inches high from a broad beach of coarse limestone pebbles, where every other plant is stunted, raising flower stalks no more than two inches above the barren, stony ground.

THE VERBENAS (Family Verbenaceae)

More times than we like to admit, we have reached out a thumb and forefinger to feel the stem of a member of the verbena family—just to remind ourselves that it was cylindrical and not square, as would be true almost certainly if the plant were a mint. The similarity among members of these two families is confusing so long as only the native species in temperate parts of Eurasia and North America are compared. In the tropics and subtropics, where many of the Family Verbenaceae are shrubs, woody vines or trees, the confusion vanishes. Except in these warm countries, all verbenas and kin have opposite leaves—as all mints do. In both families the flowers have a right side and a left (a bilateral, rather than a radial symmetry), and the four stamens attached to the corolla include two short ones and two long ones. Close inspection of the pistil reveals a consistent difference: in Family Verbenaceae the ovary tapers smoothly into the style, whereas in mints (Family Labiatae) it bears a definite indentation between the two carpels, and from this groove the style arises.

Today no medicinal value is known for Eurasian vervain *(Verbena officinalis),* which the Druids and other early people of Britain regarded as a sacred cure-all. Their reverence for the plant is reflected in the name *Verbena,* which is a Latin word the Romans used for any sacred herb or branch. Wild verbenas in America are often called vervains, including blue vervain *(V. hastata),* a tall, slender, rank-growing plant of swales and damp shorelines, whose upright flower spikes bear rings of small purple blooms from July until the end of August over much of the United States and Canada. Garden verbena *(V. hybrida),* which was introduced into North America from Brazil about 1840, produces attractive flat heads of flowers, each on its own floral stalk, either all pink or purple or blue or white, or mixed attractively in one head. A similarity in the form of flower cluster can be seen in the cultivated lantana *(Lantana camara)* from tropical America, which is often grown indoors as a house plant, but which has escaped in Hawaii to become a weed—forming almost impenetrable thickets. In lantana, the individual flower buds unfold to expose pink or yellow corollas, that usually change to orange or scarlet as they age. Since not all flowers in a cluster open at the same time, this too provides a mixture of colors in a single head.

Commercial oil of verbena is extracted from the leaves of *Lippia citriodora,* often called "lemon-scented verbena," and native to Central America. Other species of this genus are native to North America and to South Africa. They differ from *Verbena* in having only two seeds, not four, from each pistil.

Shrubby members of this family from the tropics include some of the most beautiful and odd-flowered to be found in gardens of warm lands. Pagoda-flower (or glory-bower, *Clerodendrum paniculatum)* from Java grows to a height of nearly six feet, spreading large heart-shaped leaves covered with soft hairs and producing huge clusters of brilliant scarlet

tubular flowers from spring through autumn. Bleeding-heart vine *(C. thomsoniae)* from West Africa needs high humidity and protection from cold; its glossy deep-green heart-shaped leaves are handsome, and its clusters of flowers demand attention because the calyx of each is white, heart-shaped and conspicuously persistent while the fragrant blood-red corollas and the stamens drop off a day or two after expanding. Chinese hat-plant *(Holmskioldia sanguinea)* from the Himalayas can stand on its own as a shrub or be trained as a vine; its flowers in cascading clusters are unusual in that the intensely red tubular corolla sticks out from the center of a flaring round calyx that is membranous and orange-colored. All of these flowers attract hummingbirds in the New World, but must depend on other pollinators in their native lands since no hummingbirds live outside America.

Very different animals come to mind in connection with the most valuable member of the Verbena Family: hard-working Indian elephants carrying and hauling logs of teak *(Tectona grandis).* Native to Indomalaysia, the teak tree has been used widely in India for more than two thousand years. It grows in forests remote from the coast, particularly in India, Burma, and Thailand. Teak plantations have been set out in Ceylon, Java and other islands of the East Indies, in Central and northern South America. Wild trees attain a height of more than one hundred feet, and a probable age of over two hundred years. Under cultivation, a teak tree becomes exploitable at about eighty years of age, when it may be sixty to eighty feet tall and two feet in diameter, not counting the buttresses that spread from the trunk at the base. Teak bark is grayish, and covers a white sapwood that is susceptible to attack by termites and fungus rots. The heartwood is relatively immune to both, and retains some of its pleasant aromatic fragrance while the seasoning process changes its color from golden yellow to brown, mottled with darker streaks. If protected from rain, teakwood is outstandingly durable. Timbers from one thousand to two thousand years old have been found in good condition among the ruins of old temples in southern and western India. The wood is remarkable also for its dimensional stability, changing little with fluctuations in temperature and humidity. This quality

South Africa and Madagascar have about fifty species of cape-primroses, all of them low-growing, shade-loving plants. (E. Javorsky)

makes it especially valuable for flooring, panelling, and fine furniture. It would be suitable too for boat hulls, as well as decking, if not for the destructive action on it of marine borers such as shipworms.

Teak branchlets are four-sided, with a large quadrangular pith. They support large leaves shaped somewhat like those on tobacco plants, as much as two feet long and a foot wide. The branches terminate in large upturned clusters of small white flowers. Many, however, seem sterile, and the plumlike fruits that develop contain few viable seeds.

THE SQUARE-STEMMED MINTS
(Family Labiatae)

Perfumes, flavorings, and handsome flowering plants with aromatic foliage—these sum up our usual reactions to members of this family. Almost all of them are herbs with epidermal glands secreting spicy oils the human nose finds pleasant. The 3200 different species include representatives on every continent, but more in the Mediterranean region than elsewhere. A majority have a two-lipped corolla, which is celebrated in the family name—the "lipped" flowers.

Lavender and rosemary have long held their popularity among old-fashioned perfumes. Both are low evergreen undershrubs of the European southlands, with narrow gray-green leaves and fragrant pale violet flowers. The odorous oil is contained in glands on the calyx as well as the corolla. To extract it, the blossoms are picked at their peak of expansion and subjected to distillation procedures that vary according to the preferences of the perfume-maker. Today, lavender (Lavandula, chiefly L. officinale) is raised and extracted in areas as remote as the environs of Grasse, France; Aberdeen, Scotland; Philadelphia, Pennsylvania; and Sacramento, California. The plants grow best on rocky soil exposed

Far left above: Chalice-vine (Solandra guttata) *from Mexico and the West Indies is sometimes called "cup-of-gold." Its flowers, as much as nine inches across, change color as they age. (Lorus and Margery Milne) Far left: Jimson weed or thorn-apple* (Datura stramonium) *spreads readily to bared ground. An ill-scented, dangerously poisonous weed, it originated in Asia but became cosmopolitan. (E. R. Degginger) Left: Lousewort* (Pedicularis sceptrum-carolinum) *appears in wet meadows from Japan to northwestern Europe. (Ingmar Holmasen)*

to the sky and, under cultivation, do not produce seed. "Lavender water" is an alcoholic solution of the oil, with other scents added. Rosemary (Rosmarinus officinalis) is one of the few members of the mint family to have only two stamens in each flower. As a perfume it has a long history in literature and folklore; most famous is Ophelia's "rosemary's for remembrance." Medical importance is no longer attributed to either of these fragrant extracts.

Good cooks in the Western World who rely upon their skill in blending flavors from the herb cabinet to add interest to food use a great many dried products from plants of the mint family. Sage, thyme, marjoram and the various varieties of mint (plain mint, peppermint, spearmint, and the like) are all contributions from European species. Garden sage (Salvia officinalis) has gray-green wrinkled leaves that give flavor to meat and poultry stuffing; a showy relative from Brazil is the scarlet sage (S. splendens) known to every gardener in Europe and America simply by its generic name. Garden thyme (Thymus vulgaris), like pot marjoram (Origanum vulgare) and sweet marjoram (Majorana hortensis), provides tiny leaves and clusters of small purple flowers with a spicy fragrance and pleasant taste. The subtle differences among them are lost when the plants are distilled to obtain the essential oil from which thymol is produced for medical purposes.

Shakespeare had Oberon, King of the Fairies in *A Midsummer Night's Dream*, tell Puck "I know a bank whereon the wild thyme blows ... There sleeps Titania sometime of the night, Lulled in these flowers with dances and delight"; the wild thyme is *Thymus serpyllum*. It provides a soft mat half an inch thick over soil and small rocks far north in the British Isles and Eurasia, and in North Africa too. Big bumblebees buzz from one tiny magenta flower to the next, apparently richly rewarded by sweet nectar. The plant is now naturalized in eastern North America, from Nova Scotia to Ohio and Indiana, southward as far as the mountains of North Carolina.

True mints (Mentha) include only about fifteen different kinds, most of which have now escaped from cultivation in so many parts of Asia and the New World that the European ones seem inextricably mingled among the few native species. Garden mint (or spearmint, M. spicata) is distinguished by its smooth leaves arising in pairs with no petioles, and its floppy, tapering spikes of flowers. Water mint (M. aquatica) has hairy leaves with petioles and an almost spherical form to each flower cluster. Peppermint (M. piperita) may be a cross between these two.

Sausage-shaped woody fruits hang from the branches of the sausage-tree (Kigelia *species) native to tropical Africa and Madagascar. (Paul E. Genereux)*

It has smooth leaves on petioles, and produces an oblong blunt spike of flowers; from its leaves a valuable volatile oil (menthol) is extracted for flavoring. The custom of using mint jelly or a sauce made of fragments from dried mint leaves in sweetened vinegar to flavor roast lamb at the table may be traced back to the mint of Scripture *(M. longifolia),* whose bitter spicy leaves were traditionally eaten with the paschal lamb.

In India and other areas where Hindu customs are followed, one of several kinds of plants known as basil has a place of special distinction. Sacred basil (or tulsi, *Ocimum basilicum)* is grown on a pedestal in the courtyard of orthodox homes; addition of small pieces of its leaves to foods consecrates them at the same time that flavor is introduced. In the West, a different basil *(Satureja vulgaris)* from Mediterranean Europe is used as a seasoning, particularly in turtle soup. A relative *(S. thymus)* may have been the fragrant "hyssop" of the Bible, called for in many ceremonies. Real hyssop *(Hyssopus officinalis)* does not grow in the Holy Land; formerly it was cultivated in Europe as a source of a leaf tea that could be sweetened with honey and used hopefully to treat external wounds and internal infections, particularly those of the nose, throat, and lungs. True hyssop ranges eastward to Central Asia, and has become naturalized across Canada and down both coasts of North America.

As with hyssop, reliance has dwindled in the medical value to be found in most members of the mint family. At the same time, the old phrase "as good as betony" (referring to the former high regard held for a drug from *Stachys officinalis*—Eurasian betony) has vanished from modern literature. Even horehound candies and flavoring in cough medicines has become old-fashioned; horehound *(Marrubium vulgare),* native to the Canary Islands and Eurasia, escaped and naturalized widely elsewhere, is still growing in waste lands, as a wooly-leaved, bitter-aromatic perennial with wrinkled foliage and whorls of small white flowers.

Because of their fragrance and the subtle differences in scent that a human nose can distinguish, members of the mint family have become favored plants to be raised in gardens for blind people. Those with good vision can delight even more in some of the handsomer cultivated varieties. Among these, the 120 different species and countless horticultural forms of *Coleus* would rank high. One *(C. blumei)* from the Old World tropics is often called "Jacob's coat," because of the variegated color patterns in its leaves. Clumps of the bergamots *(Monarda)* lend color and distinction to any temperate garden. All twenty species are from North America. They include three-foot Oswego tea (or bee balm, *M. didyma)* which bears terminal whorls of brilliant scarlet flowers, and "wild" bergamot *(M. fistulosa),* which attains a height of six feet, holding up a profusion of fragrant, lilac-colored or pink flowers in whorled heads.

Some members of the mint family appeal even to domesticated animals. House cats show a special fondness for nibbling at and rolling on catnip *(Nepeta cataria),* now naturalized in many lands but originally a plant of southern Europe. They ignore a related species *(N. grandiflora)* from the Caucasus, which has larger flowers and hairless leaves.

With so many members of Family Labiatae encouraged to grow in flower beds, it is not surprising that some have moved successfully into the grasses of the lawn beyond the border. The most persistent of these invaders are from Europe too, but now established over much of the world. One that remains low-growing, seldom more than an inch or two high, is creeping Charlie *(Glechoma hederacea),* known also as Gill-over-the-ground, crow-victuals, hedge-maids, cat's foot, robin-runaway, snakeroot, and tunhoof. Another, attaining a height of two feet in shady protected places, is heal-all *(Prunella vulgaris),* called also selfheal, hookheal, hookweed, blue-curds, brownwort, thimbleflower, carpenter-weed, and heart-of-the-earth. Such a multiplicity of common names attests to the number of times these plants have turned up in new human communities, usually from seeds that were introduced accidentally along with those of more desirable species.

THE NIGHTSHADE FAMILY *(Solanaceae)*

Poisonous drugs, life-giving foods, ancient superstitions, and cherished ornament are all values that have been found among the 2200 species in this family. No other family of dicot plants provides so many people with so much edible food and economic gain. Yet this importance to man could scarcely be predicted from the distinguished features of the family: a five-parted, regular corolla that may be tubular or funnel-shaped or flare so widely as to be called "wheel-shaped" (rotate); five stamens all alike, arising from the throat of the corolla; an ovary of two united carpels.

The toxic qualities present in nightshades and some other members of the family were recognized long ago, and some advantage taken of them. Deadly nightshade (or belladonna, *Atropa belladonna)* bears dull green leaves on a profusely branched bushy stem; its tubular purple flowers precede berries that become purple or black when ripe. Just three of these berries contain enough poison to kill a child. Yet the plant is cultivated in Switzerland, France, southern Germany, and some areas of the United States to obtain leaves and roots from which the drug atropine can be extracted for medical uses. Its chief use is to cause the pupil of the eye to open for easier examination by a specialist. This recalls the old dangerous practice of women in the southern and central parts of Europe, where deadly nightshade is native, of putting

in their own eyes before a party a drop or two of diluted juice squeezed from a belladonna fruit—to cause their pupils to enlarge and make their eyes seem more attractive; that vision is hopelessly blurred through a dilated pupil and that damage to the eyes from excessive amounts of the drug was possible did not immediately put an end to the custom. Lesser amounts of other poisons are present in most parts of woody nightshade (or bittersweet, *Solanum dulcamara)* and black nightshade *(S. nigrum).* Both originated in Europe, parts of North Africa, and temperate Asia, but came as weeds to the New World and are now widely distributed.

The genus *Solanum,* with fully 1700 species, is one of the largest in the plant kingdom. It has representatives on every continent, but more in America than anywhere else. They include *S. giganteum* of the Andes, one of the few trees in the family; it attains a height of fifty feet or more. More importantly, the Andean region provided the world with the white potato (or "Irish" potato, *S. tuberosum).* Sir Francis Drake found the Indians using it as a food when he visited southern Chile in 1577. They dug up the subterranean swollen lengths of stem, now called tubers, and either used these promptly boiled or baked, or air-dried them and baked the starchy material into a breadlike chuño that despite frost can be stored above ground better than the tubers themselves. Similar methods were followed by Indians in other parts of the far-flung Inca empire, using tubers from *S. andigenum* and still different species that abound in the Peru–Bolivia–Ecuador mountains.

No one is sure when the white potato reached Europe first. Apparently it was eaten aboard Spanish ships in the early 1580's. Thomas Heriot included a description of the plant and its tubers in his account of the *New Found Land of Virginia* published in London, 1588; he claimed to have carried living potatoes to England in 1586 when he and the other colonists at Roanoke Island, North Carolina, abandoned their frontier post and sailed back to Europe with Sir Francis Drake. Whether potatoes were growing in the colony is not clear. Sir Francis might have had them aboard, perhaps taken from some of the Spanish ships or shore installations he had recently destroyed. Sir Walter Raleigh may have introduced potatoes into Ireland about 1588. The first known illustration of the plant appeared in that year as a woodcut by Jacob Bergzabern in his *Neuw Kreuterbuch.* It was reproduced in John Gerard's *Herball,* published in 1597. From England, potatoes are known to have been taken to Bermuda, and thence to Virginia in 1621.

In European hands, the small potatoes of the Chilean Indians developed to far larger size. Better ways to store them were discovered. Soon the tubers became a prime food for Western people, for their hogs, and the source of starch, flour, sirup, and alcoholic beverages. In Ireland, the potato provided so much more nourishment than had ever been available before that the human population increased within less than 250 years from under two million to more than eight—not counting a million or so who emigrated to the New World before 1845. An acre of potatoes would support a family of five. Irishmen who settled in southern New Hampshire about 1719 started the first large-scale cultivation of this crop in North America. Much later, Maine and Idaho became great centers of potato raising. Today, more than ninety per cent of the world's potatoes are grown in Europe, particularly in the Netherlands, Germany, and Denmark. Demand for them in the British Isles still exceeds the massive production there, and potatoes are imported from as far away as northern Italy. Historians are no longer sure whether the Industrial Revolution or the introduction of *Solanum tuberosum* was the principal factor that allowed a sudden increase in Europe's population beginning about A.D. 1600. Certainly the potato crops increased nearly fivefold the number of people the soil of the continent could support.

Although many other species of tuber-potatoes are cultivated by the Indians in the Andean highlands, none of them would have been so fortunate a choice as the white to improve nutrition in Europe and the Anglo-American parts of America. These others are adapted to the shorter days and longer nights of low latitudes, whereas *S. tuberosum* matched the longer days during the growing season at forty to fifty degrees south latitude. It could match equally well the long summer days north of the Equator by a corresponding distance, at lower altitudes but in suitable climates.

At first the white potatoes in the Northern Hemisphere grew and produced with virtually no diseases or insect pests. Then a fungus began about 1830 to attack the whole plants in both the United States and Europe. Known as the "late blight" to distinguish it from another fungus, it still varies in severity of infestation according to the weather. Low temperatures and high humidity favor the fungus or reduce the resistance of the potato plant. These conditions may have combined in 1845 and 1846, when the late blight struck Irish potato crops with such intensity that this one food resource was wiped out. So completely dependent upon the potato had the Irish become that more than a million people died of malnutrition on the island, or of diseases made lethal by hunger. A million and a half abandoned their potato fields and homes, most of them moving to America to escape the famine. Although soon after 1860 a number of blight-resistant types of white potato were developed, the Irish who remained in Ireland had already adjusted to a new economic situation. Their customs were altered to a new pattern that led to stability in the population, at about two-thirds the number that previously had depended upon potato crops. For about a century these customs continued, until new sources of income were developed after World War II and once more a larger population could be supported.

The Old World has several species of *Solanum* with conspicuous fruits. The largest and most edible is the eggplant (*S. melongena*) from northeastern India, where it has been cultivated since antiquity. The egg-shaped berry, which may be as much as twelve inches long, is borne on a coarse bushy stem which is often armed with stiff spines. Eggplant is now grown for market in southern Europe, England, South Africa, the Orient, Australia, New Zealand, and wherever the climate is suitable in the United States. In Japan, eggplant is the fourth most popular "vegetable."

At Christmas time in many Western countries, Jerusalem cherry (*S. pseudocapsicum*) is offered for sale by florists. On this small evergreen shrub from Asia Minor, the half-inch white flowers are followed by bright yellow or orange fruits about the size of a cherry. Children should be cautioned not to eat these berries, for they contain several poisonous compounds.

Similar warnings are now needed in Hawaii for Sodom apple (or popolo, *S. sodomeum*), which was introduced there and became common. We first noticed the spiny bush in elephant country, from Kruger Park in northeastern South Africa to Tanzania, Kenya and Uganda. It is native to these areas and to Asia Minor, producing conspicuous purple flowers and then yellow fruits about the size and shape of a tomato. The elephants and other African animals avoid Sodom apple, letting the plant grow by default and spread in big game country. This is an African parallel to the manner in which heathers take over the barren landscape of high latitudes, wherever sheep are permitted to eat very nearly every other kind of vegetation.

Tomatoes *(Lycopersicon esculentum),* too, were believed to be poisonous by many people until about 1900, particularly in North America. The wild plants originated in the Andes, and were cultivated all through the Inca empire long before Columbus and the Spanish explorers reached the New World. Probably the first tomatoes seen in Europe came from Mexico and were yellow-fruited varieties. The earliest description (1554), in Italian, calls them *pomi d'oro* ("golden apples"). By 1600 in France they had become *pomme d'amour* ("love apples") from a supposed value as an aphrodisiac, but remained a horticultural curiosity. Red-fruited kinds were cultivated on this basis at the same time by gardeners in Italy, England, Spain, and other countries of Europe. Within fifty years, courageous people in many places tried eating tomatoes, and found them delicious as well as safe. Italian spaghetti became really tasty after the addition of tomato paste and tomato sauce. The fruit and the plant that bore it were reintroduced into North America about 1800 by Italians and other immigrants from Europe, who had no knowledge of small wild tomatoes that the American Indians were eating in pre-Columbian days and that had spread northward from tribe to tribe from the Andean area.

The Andean fruits are scarcely bigger than marbles. But in developing from them the luscious large firm tomatoes of commerce, some of the food values have been lost. The wild fruits contain, in particular, more vitamin C (as well as vitamin B and pro-vitamin A) than cultivated fruits weighing a hundred times as much. Small tomatoes on the market tend, in fact, to have the same total amount of vitamin C as large fruits of the same kind, or even more of it. Horticulturalists are now striving to improve the nutritional quality of modern tomatoes by crossing them with wild Andean strains, without losing the appealing color, texture, flavor, and other features we have come to expect.

From Central and South America have come some perennial woody plants whose fruits captured a place on European tables. These are the many varieties of New World peppers *(Capsicum frutescens).* Columbus and other early explorers encountered them and were delighted by the pungency of these fruits, which led to the misuse of the word pepper for them. The small "hot" varieties are used for making chili, cayenne pepper powder, and the tabasco sauces of the southern United States; they contain large amounts of an oleoresin, very small quantities of which stimulate the appetite and stom-

ach activity whereas larger doses irritate the lining membranes of the digestive tract. Mere traces of this material cause intense pain if they reach the surface of the eyes, and only slightly more of it will produce "burning" sensations on the skin of many people. Water does not wash away the oleoresin, but milk usually will.

The mild sweet peppers, often called "bell peppers," have the least of the oleoresin. When ripe and red they contain about ten times as much pro-vitamin A as when green, and a third more of vitamin C. In both of these they excel most other vegetables. Sweet peppers are eaten raw in salads, cooked in various ways, stuffed with meat, and known also in the cooked form as pimento (or pimiento) as a material to add flavor to pitted olives, to cheese, or be dried as a spice. A variety cultivated extensively in central Europe yields paprika.

Smaller fruits of a form that is superficially similar but entirely different in structure are produced by each of about fifty species of plants in the cosmopolitan genus *Physalis.* An Asiatic one *(P. alkekengi)* is raised all over the world as Chinese lantern-plant, to obtain its dried fruits for flower arrangements. In all members of *Physalis,* the calyx becomes inflated and membranous, concealing the berry within. The calyx of lantern-plant is bright red to orange, and retains this color for months. The calyx is discarded to reach the scarlet berry by people who raise ground-cherry (or husk tomato, *P. heterophylla,* from the eastern two-thirds of North America) or cape-gooseberry *(P. peruviana* of western South America); the berry, when ripe, tastes like a tomato.

Over the years, attitudes toward many members of the nightshade family have changed markedly. From the Dark Ages into Shakespeare's time, the mandrake *(Mandragora officinarum)* of Mediterranean Europe was regarded with superstitious awe and regarded as a potent aphrodisiac when properly prepared. Its short stem from a thick and commonly forked root seemed symbolic of the human body, its terminal tuft of oval leaves a parallel to the human head with disheveled hair. The plant was to be dug up only at the right time of the moon, usually by exposing its stem, tying a cord around it and to a dog, and forcing the animal to provide the traction. Supposedly the plant shrieked as it came from the ground. From the tone a wise herb gatherer could tell whether the trophy was a mandrake or a woman-drake, and use its magic extracts accordingly in medicine. These include alkaloids that were given to dull the pain of early surgery. "Give me to drink mandragora" remains as a line commemorating this role in Shakespeare's *Antony and Cleopatra*. In some parts of Africa it is still used as a source of narcotic substances. In the East, its extracts and powdered tissues serve in potions claimed to facilitate pregnancy in childless women. Elsewhere the mandrake has fallen into disrepute.

Among the largest flowers in the nightshade family are those of angel's trumpet (or borrachero, *Datura arborea*) from Chile and Peru. They are pearly white, eight to nine inches long, and hang from a tall shrub, emitting a musky odor into the night air. We met them first in North Carolina, then in Florida, next in Panamá and Jamaica, later in South Africa and Monaco. They are admired all over the world, although both the foliage and the fruits contain dangerous poisons.

Gypsies are supposed to have spread an even more poisonous relative from the Asiatic area between the Caspian Sea and India. Known as stramonium (or thorn-apple, *D. stramonium*), it has become a cosmopolitan weed, with pharmacologists urging its extermination wherever possible. The Gypsies prepared extracts from stramonium seeds to induce fantastic visions. Thieves made "knockout drops" from various parts of the plant to stupefy their victims. Reputedly, even the nectar is poisonous. In North America the plant is generally called Jimson weed, or more properly Jamestown weed, from an outbreak of fatal mania and convulsions that struck a company of British "red coats" sent in 1676 to quell an uprising in Jamestown, Virginia. Living on whatever they could find, the soldiers ate a meal of stramonium foliage cooked as a vegetable. All parts of the plant are poisonous, even the thorny egg-shaped fruits which contain sweet-tasting lethal seeds.

In the annals of science, Jimson weed attained a respected place when two observant geneticists on Long Island, New York, discovered consistent correlations between different forms of fruit and the chromosomes visible in the *Datura* cells under the microscope. One of the men, Dr. A. F. Blakeslee, summed up these important discoveries in 1934 under the title "New Jimson Weeds from Old Chromosomes."

Among the most violent poisons known is the alkaloid nicotine, as extracted from tobacco plants *(Nicotiana tabacum)*. A single drop of the purified compound is fatal if applied to human skin. In extremely weak solutions, it kills plant lice, caterpillars, and many other insects on contact. Yet the Indians of coastal North Carolina showed the earliest settlers there how to smoke the cured tobacco leaves. Tobacco, along with potato, was described as a strange plant of the New World in Thomas Hariot's 1788 book. Samples of the leaf and a pipe in which to smoke it were carried in 1786 to Sir Walter Raleigh in England at the time of Hariot's return. Today the United States, China and India raise among them more than two million tons of cured tobacco leaves, which is less than half the total of world production. The proportion used in making cigarettes, pipe tobacco, cigars, chewing tobacco, snuff, and insecticides continues to vary from year to year. Only modest changes followed the statistical proof in 1964 that tobacco smoking contributed importantly to the incidence of lung cancer, heart disease, and other causes of death whose frequency has risen at a pace comparable with that of tobacco sales.

An aboriginal Indian name for tobacco *(petun)* has been perpetuated in *Petunia* for about fifteen species of tropical American plants on the fringe of the nightshade family. Unlike other members of Family Solanaceae, the petunias show a disproportionate enlargement of the upper two petals and a reduction in the size of one stamen among the five, converting them from a radial symmetry to bilateral; the capsule that develops from the ripening ovary is two-valved, not four-valved. And although the lower leaves on each plant are alternate in arrangement, as is usual in this family, the upper ones tend to be paired (opposite). Despite these differences, the pleated petals in a petunia bud show that the plant belongs in the same group with the tobacco, the angel's trumpet, the potato, and the spooky mandrake. Cultivated kinds are mostly hybrids between Brazilian and Argentinian species. Some are weak-stemmed and lie on the ground or adjacent vegetation. Others stand erect. In all of them the foliage has a clammy nature, due to adhesive hairs, and the bright corolla is a flaring funnel, usually fragrant, attractive to both hummingbirds and hawkmoths. Since the seeds that form rarely breed true, propagation is mostly from cuttings.

THE SNAPDRAGON FAMILY (Scrophulariaceae)

Most of the 2600 species in this large family are herbs of temperate lands. The flowers are bilaterally symmetrical, often with the petals forming an upper and lower lip which remain pressed together except when an insect pushes between them to reach nectar and pollen within the inflated corolla. The Eurasian toadflax (or butter-and-eggs, *Linaria vulgaris*), now a widespread weed in both North and South America, and the cultivated snapdragons *(Antirrhinum,* chiefly *A. majus* from Mediterranean Europe) are familiar plants of this kind. They are sought out by bumble-bees and butterflies, the one strong enough to force entry into the flower, the other able to slip a slender sipping tube into the corners of the "mouth" between the lips where the pressure is insignificant.

Entry for insects and other pollinators is far easier into the open flowers of foxgloves *(Digitalis,* especially *D. purpurea).* The two dozen members of this genus range from the Canary Islands and western Europe to Central Asia, their tall spikes of hanging tubular flowers appreciated for their beauty, and their leaves harvested as the source of three important drugs for treatment of congestive heart failure. The extract, known generally as digitalis, contains at least three effective glycosides and a number of saponins which modify the action. In Ireland, foxgloves are called fairy thimbles. In southern Scotland the symbolism is more morbid: bloody fingers; and farther north, still more extreme: dead men's bells.

When the whole world is scoured for members of the snapdragon family, a few are found representing each of many ways of life. A few are degenerate parasites, with only scalelike leaves and no chlorophyll. South African species of *Hyobanche* and *Harveya* show this complete dependence upon nourishment taken from other plants. Some get only a little boost in nutrients from the roots of grasses and other neighbors, as partial parasites. These include the fifty species of paintbrush (or painted-cup, *Castilleja)* of the Americas, and the 350 kinds of lousewort *(Pedicularis)* in North America, the Andes, and Eurasia; in both genera, the leaves associated with the flowers are small and bractlike, in paintbrush so brightly colored in red and yellow as often to distract a person's eyes from the actual blossoms.

Among the vast majority of plants in the Family Scrophulariaceae, independence is well established. Bright sun, country air, occasional rain, and the dissolved materials in stony soils seem enough for many, such as the 260 different kinds of mulleins (or velvet-plants, *Verbascum)* of the Old World's temperate zone. "Common mullein" (or devil's tobacco, *V. thapsus)* is one from Europe that has become a widespread and not unattractive weed in fields all across northern Asia, North America, and into South America. Its sturdy stem rises above a great rosette of coarse, gray-green, wooly leaves, and holds a stiff spike of golden-yellow flowers sometimes to a height of eight feet.

A *new plant of gloxinia* (Sinningia speciosa), *native to Brazil, can be grown from a single healthy leaf. But after flowering, the plant must encounter drought before putting forth new leaves. (E. Javorsky)*

A mullein flower would never be confused with one from a snapdragon. Its petals, in fact, show only a slight modification away from radial symmetry into the bilateral pattern characteristic of the family. It has five stamens, all of them producing pollen, although the two lower ones are longer than the three upper ones; usually a member of Scrophulariaceae has only four (or two) stamens, or a fifth one is reduced to the form of a slender, petal-like part (staminode) without pollen. Similarly, the imperial tree *(Paulownia tomentosa)* of China and Japan, which is often planted in parks throughout the temperate zones, is an exception to the general rule that members of the snapdragon family are nonwoody herbs; *Paulownia* attains a height of forty feet or more, holding great clusters of purple bloom toward the sky. To place these plants in the correct family, botanists rely upon hidden details they can ignore most of the time. *Paulownia,* despite its woody trunk and branches, has seeds in which the small embryo is surrounded by a copious albumen—as is true throughout the Scrophulariaceae. If the embryo were larger, flat, and without albumen, the plant would be assigned to the next family—among the bignonias.

THE BIGNONIA FAMILY (Bignoniaceae)

In the rain forests of northern South America, the tall trees are laced together and tied to the ground by thousands of woody vines (lianas), many of which are members of the genus *Bignonia*. Few of them grow beyond the tropics. But about six hundred other species in the same family include vines, shrubs and trees, among them some of the most decorative on earth. No longer is it necessary to travel to their homelands to see them in profusion, for they have been planted in most countries where the climate is suitable. On the Natal coast of South Africa, a schoolboy can predict that when the *Jacaranda* trees along the avenues are purple with showy bloom, it will be time for final examinations. In Madeira, the same tree species flower magnificently in the months when winter cruise ships arrive. In the West Indies and Brazil, where the forty kinds of *Jacaranda* are native, the people are more likely to know that the name for the trees came from the Tupi Indian language and is pronounced as though it began with an H.

We first met the African tuliptree (or tulipan, *Spathodea campanulata*) in Honduras. Only much later did we see it on its native continent, as the *Flame Trees of Thika,* with lacey Thika Falls cascading in the near distance, just as Elspeth Huxley lovingly described it in her book of that title. Nor does it satisfy us in Latin America when local people tell us that the roadside tree under which are so many big fallen blossoms is a *roble* (oak). No oak has palmately compound leaves or flowers with two-lipped corollas such as drop to the ground below any of the 150 kinds of trumpet-tree *(Tabebuia)* native to the American tropics. Even knowing the genus does not always help. We recall in the rain forests of Panama finding on the bare red mud of wild-pig trails the freshly dropped corollas of at least a dozen species of this genus, without being able to tell from which tree they came. They drifted down from branches several stories higher than we could see in the green world about us. Some of the giant trunks on all sides must have been the ones we wanted to recognize. But which was which?

A few members of the bignonia family do thrive in temperate lands. Indian-bean *(Catalpa speciosa)* of North America attains a height of ninety feet and a trunk diameter of four feet from central New England to Iowa, and comparable size where introduced on the Oregon coast, or in Europe, or South Africa. It is just one of ten members of the genus to be found wild in East Asia, North America, and the West Indies. The flame vine *(Pyrostegia ignea)* from Brazil can glorify a sharecropper's shack in some back corner of Florida or south Texas or California only a little more lavishly than the trumpet-creepers of eastern North America *(Campsis radicans)* and China *(C. grandiflora)* do for buildings farther north.

Woody capsules containing a multitude of winged seeds are characteristic of the trees and vines in the bignonia family. Some of these fruits seem strange when first examined closely. The "beans" on a *Catalpa* tree are actually tubes, divided by a lengthwise thin partition. The calabash-tree *(Crescentia cujete)* of tropical America produces globular fruits as much as twelve inches in diameter, with a woody covering from which the central pulp and seeds can be dug out, leaving a calabash as a watertight container appreciated by primitive people in any hot country. Calabashes develop tight up against the bare trunk and major branches of the tree, remote from any foliage. In this position the flowers that precede them can be located easily and visited at night by nectar-sipping bats which somehow find the blossoms by the echoes of ultrasonic cries. Similar isolation of flowers from foliage that might confuse the echoes is characteristic of the sausage-trees *(Kigelia)* of tropical Africa and Madagascar; the bologna-shaped and -sized fruits that develop remain suspended on long slender stalks far below the leafy branches of the tree.

SOME OTHER CARNIVOROUS PLANTS (Family Lentibulariaceae)

The capture and digestion of small animals, which provide a source of nutrients containing nitrogenous compounds, is so unusual among flowering plants as to demand attention. The habit and its basis in structure and function has been developed in about 360 species that bear two-lipped corollas, constituting half a dozen genera in a family unrelated to those that include the pitcher plants, sundews, and flytraps.

The forty different kinds of butterwort *(Pinguicula)* grow on wet, ill-drained hillsides, often among sundews, in Eurasia, North America, and down the Andes to Tierra del Fuego. Each plant consists of about six oval, pointed leaves in a rosette close to the ground. The edges of each leaf curl upward slightly, and roll even more if an insect settles on the soft, fleshy blade. A slight pressure on the upper surface is enough to cause minute glands there to secrete a sticky, acidulous digestive liquid. Since there is an average of 160,000 of these glands to the square inch and their reaction is quick, an insect running across the leaf blade is likely to become mired. Soon it is overwhelmed and digestion proceeds.

To us it seems contradictory that an insect-trapping plant should depend upon other insects for pollination. Yet this is characteristic. A butterwort sends up a slender vertical stalk bearing a single flower with a purple tubular corolla. The related bladderworts (*Utricularia*), whose stems, narrow leaves and animal traps are all submerged in ponds, rely similarly upon insects to visit and pollinate the small clusters of flowers they elevated many inches above the water surface. Often bladderworts provide a profusion of bloom, attracting hundreds of insects at once. Seeing such a display and knowing that any seeds formed will contain nourishment drawn from the bodies of digested aquatic insects, we can never quite suppress a feeling of satisfaction from observing other animals actively preventing pollination. It may be a hovering flycatcher, above the white-flowering bladderworts in a little pond on the slopes of volcanic Lassen Peak in California, eating the insects attracted to the blossoms. It has also been a big alligator in the Florida Everglades swamp and a chicken turtle in the mysterious Okeefinokee swamp of southern Georgia, plowing through the floating mats of bladderworts and overturning them, pushing their golden flower clusters down where the traps wait and no insect will help set a seed.

The finely divided submerged leaves of bladderwort bear egg-shaped hollow chambers, each as much as an eighth of an inch in length, with a hinged trapdoor at one end. Fine bristles extend from the door into the adjacent water. If a small insect, or a water flea or a worm, agitates these bristles, the trapdoor opens inward quickly, creating a current of water that may carry the animal inside. Almost at once, the door closes and the bristles lose their sensitivity for a time. If a victim is caught, the trap remains closed until digestion is complete. Otherwise, the simple mechanism becomes again a hazard for any passing animal of the right dimensions. Since about 250 different kinds of bladderworts get their nitrogenous nourishment in this way, in tropical and temperate ponds on all continents and even in the Arctic, there can be no question as to the success of the adapted leaves.

In Brazil and tropical Africa, several species of a related genus (*Genlisea*) capture similar prey from the surrounding water by another means. Charles Darwin compared the mechanism to the eel traps he knew. A New Englander would be more likely to think of a lobster trap. Each *Genlisea* plant consists of a cluster of leaves arising from a short horizontal stem buried in the muddy bottom of a pond or swamp. Some of the leaves are spatula-like, and carry on important photosynthesis. The others consist of a petiole whose tip forms a bulbous hollow tube from the open end of which arise two spiraling green ribbon-like extensions held apart by a series of buttonlike projections. Minute animals swim or creep into the slits between the buttons, into the tube, and are prevented from escaping by numerous sharp stiff hairs. Some of the hairs divide the interior of the trap into a smaller antechamber and a larger "dining room" in which the presence of an animal stimulates the secretion of digestive agents. To a botanist it seems amazing only that such diverse ways in which to get nitrogenous foods from animal bodies should have arisen among plants whose flowers are as similar as those of butterwort, bladderwort, and *Genlisea*—which still lacks a common name.

THE PROLIFIC GESNERIAS
(Family Gesneriaceae)

Among the handsomest and most common herbs in the forests of tropical America, both on the mainland and in the West Indies, are the fifty species of *Gesneria*, a genus dedicated to Konrad von Gesner of Zurich. By his forty-ninth year, when he succumbed to a plague epidemic (1565), von Gesner had earned international respect as a botanist and patron of learning. His *Historiae Animalium* in five folio volumes (1551–1558, 1587) provided the best of the early encyclopedic accounts of animals and served as the starting point for modern zoology. His important botanical works were not published until two centuries after his death (1751–1771), but his detailed description of vegetation at different levels on Mount Pilatus, thirty miles south of his home, is perhaps the earliest work (1555) on mountaineering. For so distinguished a man, it seems proper that a family of outstanding ornamental plants should serve as a monument.

The 1200 members of the family are all tropical and subtropical. A few are favorites of people who enjoy house plants that can be propagated easily just by thrusting a severed leaf into moist soil. African-violets (*Saintpaulia ionantha* and *S. kewensis*) have become particularly popular in North American homes for their attractive foliage springing from a thick compact stem and for a profusion of bloom in all shades from white through pink to deep purple. They are native to humid lowlands in East Africa, and are easily "burned" by full sunlight. Similar habitats in Central America gave indoor gardeners the carpet-plants (or flame violets, *Episcia),* which produce extensive clambering stems and mosaic patterns of beautiful paired leaves, as well as bright red (or blue or white) tubular flowers. Gloxinia *(Sinningia speciosa)* from Brazil has coarser foliage and much larger, bell-shaped flowers; it regularly goes dormant for several months before starting a new cycle of activity.

"OPEN SESAME" (Family Pedaliaceae)

Ever since we learned as children the magic password in the *Arabian Nights* story of Ali Baba and the Forty Thieves, sesame has meant more to us than just the pale flat seeds stuck to the tops of bakery rolls and bread. This use for them, and their conspicuous combination with a sticky sirup to make a delicious wafer (pasteli), goes back into ancient times in the whole area of the Old World from Greece to India. The sesame plant itself *(Sesamum indicum)* probably originated in East Africa. Different horticultural varieties grow rapidly to heights from two to ten feet, usually erect and unbranched, bearing one to three flowers in the axil of each leaf as these arise in pairs up the slightly hairy stem. In China, India, and Mexico, where almost two million tons of sesame seeds are harvested each year, the stalks are cut by hand just before the capsules become ripe. When dried in the sun, the capsules shatter and the seeds can be separated by trampling, beating, or shaking. With the discovery of nonshattering capsules in 1943 and subsequent horticultural improvement, there is hope that new strains can be produced that yield as well and will be adaptable to machine harvesting.

By pressing newly dried sesame seeds, a valuable oil can be removed. It amounts to about half of the weight of the seed, and is second only to olive oil in resisting deterioration in hot countries. Africans call it benne, Indians teel or gingili, and buy it instead of olive oil for cooking and in salads. It can be made into margarine, shortenings, and soap. With pyrethrum in insecticides, it greatly increases the killing power and hence decreases the amount of expensive pyrethrum needed, lowering the cost of treatment for agricultural crops. The sesame cake from which the oil has been removed still contains a high proportion of protein, which is unusually rich in the important amino acid methionine; it can be used as a food supplement, contributing at the same time valuable amounts of calcium, phosphorus, and the vitamin niacin.

Today we can appreciate these advantages in a sesame seed, and read new significance into the quantities consumed in the Mediterranean countries, in the United States, and Japan. The goodness is there too in a bar of halva from Turkey or Israel, or the Arab world, whether we buy it in a bazaar or a delicatessen. This traditional candy of the Near East has the appearance of brown sugar without the sweetness. It is ground sesame seeds and perhaps some almonds too, along with a little sugar and some other flavorings. Few snacks offer as rich nourishment as those containing seeds from the sesame plant.

CHAPTER 25

The Coffee Plant and Its Close Kin

CUES: *If the dicot plant has opposite or whorled leaves, regular flowers with a four- or five-lobed calyx and corolla, its stamens arising separately from the inner surface of the petals, and its pistil with an inferior ovary, its membership in the Order Rubiales is almost certain. It may be a coffee tree, a gardenia, a honeysuckle, or a spiny teasel.*

Slightly more than 5800 different kinds of plants show the features of this Order. Many of them provide man with the means to make life pleasant.

THE COFFEE FAMILY (Rubiaceae)

Over about a third of the world, people are in good agreement that a cup of coffee represents the finest nonalcoholic beverage to be had. In British and former British areas, where tea-drinking now ranks higher, coffee-drinking was well established until about 1870, based upon coffee beans from plantations in Ceylon and other parts of the British Empire in the Old World. But when a fungus disease suddenly destroyed the coffee trees, forcing a quick conversion to tea-growing as an alternative to bankruptcy, tea-growing and tea-drinking became patriotic, then traditional. Only now is it becoming challenged again by coffee-drinking among British people who can afford to buy imported coffee, which is more expensive than imported tea. Probably more money is spent on coffee than on any other nonalcoholic drink.

The origin of the coffee habit remains elusive, despite the fact that its spread through the Western World began only about five centuries ago. Legend holds that the name of the plant *(Coffea)* and of the beverage made from its treated seeds comes from Kaffa, which is the old name for a mountainous region of southwestern Ethiopia now in the province of Jima. Arab traders carried the beans and then the plants into most of the Moslem world, making coffee-drinking an Arabian custom despite initial conflict with orthodox conservatives who claimed the beverage to be intoxicating and hence prohibited to Moslems by the Koran. Similar opposition developed from Christian theologians when the custom spread into one European country after another during the 16th and 17th centuries. Starting about 1652 in England and 1689 in eastern cities of North America, coffeehouses grew popular as meeting places, and then as centers of business influence (such as famous Lloyd's of London) or of political unrest.

Until about 1700, the coffee plantations in Arabia provided almost all of the beans in commerce. Shipped from the Red Sea port of Mocha in the area that is now the Republic of Yemen, they gave the world the name Mocha as a workable synonym for coffee. The orchards consisted of only one species of tree *(C. arabica),* an evergreen with paired glossy elliptical leaves and dense clusters of white, fragrant flowers. Clusters of green fruit ripen irregularly, each becoming in succession brownish, brownish red, and red. Pickers harvest the ripe berries ("cherries") by hand, going through the plantation every few days to pick whatever fruits show full color. Skilled pickers gather one hundred to one hundred and twenty-five pounds of "cherries" daily, yielding twenty-five to thirty pounds of raw seeds ("green beans") which become about twenty-one to twenty-five pounds of saleable coffee beans when roasted. This is equivalent to the average annual production of from twelve to twenty trees, and explains why

coffee plantations must be very large to yield at a commercially significant rate.

As demand for coffee grew, plantations were extended into new areas: Ceylon (1658), Java and other parts of the Dutch East Indies (about 1696), Hispaniola in the West Indies (1715), Brazil (1727), Cuba (1748), Costa Rica (1779), Colombia (about 1790), El Salvador (1840), and elsewhere in mountainous tropical lands where temperatures might average 65 to 75 degrees all year and the humidity be high. Additional species among the twenty-five in genus *Coffea* were tried, but only *C. robusta* from the Congo basin and *C. liberica* from West Africa have proved suitable. Neither seems capable of competing seriously with *C. arabica,* even though they yield generously and are somewhat less susceptible to disease.

Curiously, the taste in a cup of coffee seems to depend more upon the species of tree, the climatic condition under which it grows, and the roasting treatment of the dried beans than upon the procedures by which freshly picked "cherries" are converted into unroasted beans for shipment. In an unroasted bean, there is no coffee flavor at all. Mild, lowland coffee is produced in quantity by Brazilian plantations, and accounts for more than half of the beans in international commerce. The United States, which buys more than half of the coffee produced in the world, shows a clear preference for blends of Brazilian with flavor-rich mountain coffees, giving a taste approaching that characteristic of the old blend of Mocha and Java beans of Arabian coffee. Since coffee production usually exceeds demand and top prices go to the producers of mountain-raised grades of Arabian coffee, growers are reluctant to sacrifice quality for the sake of quantity.

The amount of water available on a plantation determines the procedure that will be followed when the "cherries" have been collected. Where water is scarce, the freshly picked fruit is merely rinsed before being spread on large cement platforms to dry in the sun and open air. This is the "natural" or "dry" process. When suitably desiccated, the fruits are run through a hulling machine that breaks off the dry skin, fragments the pulp, tears off the parchment-like coating around each bean, and also the "silver skin" which is the outer layer of the seed coat. In Africa and Asia, this older method is widely employed.

In Latin America, the water supply is usually more generous. The cherries from the plantation (finca) go into a machine that squeezes out the seeds in their parchment coverings and sends them on their way to fermentation tanks. The pulp and skins are hauled

Coffee trees (Coffea arabica) *often bear fragrant flowers, unripe and ripe fruit at the same time. Each ripe red "coffee cherry" contains two "coffee beans" as seeds. (Pan-American Coffee Bureau)*

The leaves and tubular flowers of honeysuckle (Lonicera *species) are in pairs, and as the ovaries of each pair of flowers ripen, they fuse to form one berry or join at least part way. (Otto Croy)*

away in carts for burial, which reduces the menace of flies, and later provides a suitable fertilizer to be spread under the trees—returning to the soil some of the good that would be lost otherwise. Fermentation for about twenty-four hours leaves the coatings of the coffee beans in fragments that can be washed away by repeated flushings back and forth in large troughlike washing canals. The washed beans are then spread on concrete platforms (beneficios) in the open air and sun. To expose every bean to the sun's heat, men work with rakes and shovels all day every day for about two or three weeks. Then, at last, the product can be bagged ready for shipment and sale.

Left to itself, a coffee tree would attain a height of forty feet or more. On a plantation it is ordinarily pruned severely at frequent intervals, keeping its branches within easy reach from low ladders. In areas that have been reclaimed from open rain forest, the pruning and weeding and picking and fertilizing of the coffee orchards requires a large number of hands and, for a good yield of high-quality fruit, both skill and a modicum of luck. Young trees must be given shade from the tropical sun, usually by tall trees of other kinds, such as *Erythrina*. These too have to be cut back to let the

sun through as the coffee grows and needs more light.

Among the many plantations we have visited in Central America, the West Indies, and Africa, none has impressed us more than Finca Mocha in the highlands of Guatemala, where its owner took time to talk to us at length of his failures and successes in adjusting practices to the climate and the soil, the fungus and insect pests, the people who worked for him, and the jungle that was always ready to obliterate his holdings. He told us too of his efforts at the beginning of World War II to raise a related tree: the cinchona *(Cinchona,* particularly *C. ledgeriana)* from the Andean highlands, as a source of bark from which quinine could be extracted.

Until the jigsaw pieces comprising the whole story fitted together, it made no sense to us that he had had such difficulty starting a cinchona grove, for the thirty-eight known species of *Cinchona* are native to seemingly comparable mountain country from Bolivia northward through Colombia, with outliers in Panamá and Costa Rica, chiefly at elevations of five thousand to eight thousand feet. The procedure for extracting the bitter antimalarial drug from the bark seems to have been the same ever since about

1630, when Spanish Jesuits learned the secret and began using the quinine from trees *(C. officinalis)* near Lima, Peru. The red bark covering the roots, trunk and branches of uprooted whole trees is beaten with a mallet to loosen it, then peeled by hand and machete. Quickly the bark is dried over fires or in ovens, for it deteriorates rapidly if moisture is left in it. Extraction of the antimalarial drug can then be done at a convenient center to which the dry bark is shipped.

Exploitation of wild cinchona trees in their native lands proved extremely inefficient. As demand for the "red bark" (or Jesuit's bark, or Peruvian bark) grew in Europe to combat the fevers of malaria there, enterprising men went to South America specifically to train the Indians of the Andes to become bark collectors *(cascarillos)* and driers. Soon the number of trees decreased markedly. The need to be selective in harvesting the remainder became clearer in 1820 when the French chemists Joseph Pelletier and J. B. Caventou isolated and identified quinine as the effective ingredient; the average run of bark yielded about seven per cent of the drug, while some samples ran as high as seventeen per cent.

The English botanist Richard Spruce set out to secure young plants and ripe seeds of *Cinchona,* toward establishment of plantations under efficient management elsewhere in the world. He journied up the Amazon, nearly died of malaria on a side trip into the Orinoco jungles, but finally reached Ambato, Ecuador, about seventy-five miles south of Quito and the Equator. Under commission from the British government to gather these living materials and ship them to India, he overcame local distrust among the Ecuadorians and visited the cloud forests where the trees grew. He sent six hundred seedlings and over one hundred thousand ripe seeds; few survived. A second British expedition under the command of Sir Clements Markham achieved barely more. The Dutch government tried to start *Cinchona* culture in Java, and sponsored an elaborate collecting trip by J. K. Hasskarl. Part of the failure in these expeditions lay in an inability to recognize varieties of tree with a high content of quinine. Part came through ignorance of soil requirements, need for shade, susceptibility to diseases, and proper horticultural practices in the countries where the plantations were attempted.

The Dutch in Java overcame most of these difficulties in time to profit mightily from a shipment of approximately a pound of *Cinchona* seed sent in 1865 by Charles Ledger of Puño, Peru, collected from a stand of high-yield trees along the Marmoré River in Bolivia. British efforts near Madras, India, with an equal amount of the same seed, failed disastrously. Gradually the superior bark from the Javan plantations took over the market, and yielded about ninety per cent of the quinine used in 1940. Simultaneously the demand for South American bark fell off, and the production there dropped from about four thousand tons annually in 1880 to less than one thousand by 1930. This was the world situation when the Japanese suddenly cut off the shipments from Java, interned the Dutch planters who knew how to propagate *C. ledgeriana,* and created a need for unprecedented tropical warfare where malaria was more dangerous than bullets.

Emergency measures aimed at revitalizing and extending the Latin American production of *Cinchona* bark reached our friend in Guatemala, among others. But by the time he learned by experiment that seeds of *C. ledgeriana* grow best in the rotting wood of fallen *Cinchona* trees, and how to combine by grafting techniques the root portion of hardy "succirubra" strains and the top portion of high-yielding "calisaya" types, and what program to follow in providing shade, pest control, and effective thinning of the stand, the market for *Cinchona* bark had vanished. Quinine therapy had been replaced almost completely by synthetic drugs: quinacrine dihydroxichloride (Atabrine), and then the whole sequence of improved substitutes, such as Chloroquine, Paludrin, and Plasmoquine. All could be produced far more cheaply and had no unavoidable side effects, such as the ringing sensation in the ears that continues under quinine therapy so long as the concentration of the drug in the blood is high enough to be deadly to active malaria parasites.

We saw some of the fine trees he had raised. They reminded us of graceful elms in their pattern of growth although all the branching was in opposite pairs. A few were in flower, like lilacs with loose clusters of pink blossoms. The fragrance, however, proved distinctive and memorable. He saw no future for these trees, nor for the great *Cinchona* plantations in Java over which the Dutch held such monopolistic control in the prewar world. Quinine itself was synthesized in 1944, but the demand for the drug had waned too far to justify commercial production.

The cinchonas and coffees represent two different parts of the Family Rubiaceae. In *Cinchona* and its near kin, the fruit is a capsule that opens when ripe to free many seeds from each chamber. Similar fruit on a diminutive scale develop over much of North

America on a lowly herb known as bluets *(Houstonia,* particularly *H. caerulea).* In shady meadow corners it sometimes achieves a height of seven inches in clumps worth transplanting to the flower border. More often we see it blossoming just above the grass in meadows, less than three inches from soil to upfacing blossoms, each about one-quarter of an inch across, pale blue with a bright yellow eye, its four petals spread like a little cross. People know this little wildflower affectionately as innocence, Quaker ladies, little washerwoman, and brighteyes, or eyebright.

The plants related more closely to coffee produce only one seed in each of the ovary's two chambers. Some, such as coffee, bear two-seeded berries. These fruits are bright orange and as much as 1½ inches long in the cultivated gardenias, such as the cape-jasmine *(Gardenia jasminoides)* of China. All of the sixty species of gardenia are evergreen shrubs with attractive dark-green glossy leaves. Wild ones in subtropical parts of the Old World bear five flaring petal lobes, backed by five green sepals joined together into either a tube or a spathelike piece with a slit down one side. Horticultural varieties usually produce double flowers with so many petal lobes that they resemble camellias. The waxy white blooms are much more fragrant, however, and usually last for many days before fading. Perhaps these features make a gardenia plant an ideal gift for a bride; no attention need be given it in return for its fragrance until the honeymoon is over. This helps us too when someone asks, "Could you tell me the name of the small bush with green leaves and white flowers that we got as a wedding present?" If the flowers were fragrant, the probability is high that it was a gardenia.

Two-lobed scarlet fruits as much as a third of an inch in diameter capture attention for trailing evergreen herbs known as partridge-berry (or two-eyed berry, or running-box, *Mitchella).* One species *(M. repens)* is common in the woods of America between Minnesota and Florida or Texas and Newfoundland. Another thrives in similar places on the islands of Japan. On both, the paired leaves are almost circular and often conspicuously white along the midrib but glossy dark-green otherwise. The paired fragrant flowers each produce the characteristic, edible berry, which remains in place all winter unless eaten by wild animals. The fruits are scarcely sweet enough for human tastes.

On most other members of the family, the paired carpels in the ovary become only slightly fleshy, then dry out and separate, each containing one seed. They become tiny burs on the weak, straggling plants of madder *(Rubia)* and bedstraw *(Galium).* The forty different members of the madder genus are all Eurasian, and differ from the bedstraws in having five rather than four lobes in the corolla. Both bear whorls of small leaves and commonly catch on a finger or even on clothing because of prickles arming their stems. Perhaps the little hooks help the madders and bedstraws hold their position atop other low vegetation over which they grow.

An Indian madder *(R. cordifolia)* native to the hillier parts of India, and to Northeast Asia and Java, has provided the raw material for a red dye called manjit since long before the beginning of written records in that part of the world. Similar methods of cultivation and preparation were applied later in Asia Minor, perhaps from India and possibly from Egypt. Cloth dyed with madder clothes mummies found in ancient Egyptian tombs. Libyan women used the pigment to color their cloaks in Herodotus' time. The pigment prepared in countries around the Mediterranean seems to have come from a different madder *(R. tinctoria),* which yields a brighter dye known as "turkey red." For centuries it was important in commerce between the Near East and western Europe, where its color had become a symbol of courage. But after about A.D. 1500, the intermittent supply coming by camel caravans across the deserts of Arabia was replaced by a new industry in Holland, where the Dutch became skilled at cultivating the plant and extracting its pigment. When properly fixed in fabrics by suitable mordants, each a metallic oxide in solution, the dye compounds ("lakes") are insoluble, resist bleaching by sunlight, and range in hue from red through pink, purple, orange, brown, and black according to the mordant used. The use of the dye is still important, but the industry in Holland collapsed about 1868 when chemists found a way to synthesize the essential ingredient (alizarin) for about a quarter of the cost.

Some of the bedstraws could be used too as sources of dyestuffs. A few are sweet-scented, and have been used as dry herbs to stuff into mattresses, making them fragrant. Others are known as cleavers, because they cling so readily to almost any surface; or as goosegrass, supposedly because geese will eat them; or as false baby's-breath, from a general resemblance of the clustered flowers to those of *Gypsophila.* As common weeds with almost cosmopolitan distribution, these lacy-flowered herbs tend to be noticed and their rough weak stems remembered.

The welfare of some animals in which man is

interested has recently been shown to be bound up in the success of some related shrubs and small trees of the genus *Coprosma*. Fossilized remains of these plants dating back to Eocene times fifty million years ago have been found on Kerguelen and other remote islands toward Antarctica. *Coprosma* still lives on many of these, as well as on New Zealand, Australia, and small islands all the way to Hawaii. The generic name signifies "smelling like dung," which is easiest to understand where the plants grow among the congested nests of sea birds. To this strange habitat, *Coprosma* seems particularly well fitted. And some of the native animals appear to have become dependent upon the abundance of these woody plants.

The need to protect *Coprosma* from feral goats has become most obvious on island sanctuaries near New Zealand where the unique lizard-like tuatara *(Sphenodon punctatus)* survives by spending the day in burrows. It is the last living representative of an ancient group of reptiles, the Rhynchocephalia, which were numerous contemporaries of the extinct dinosaurs. Although the tuatara can dig fairly well in loose soil, it commonly inhabits the nest burrows of albatrosslike birds known in Australia and New Zealand as "mutton birds" and elsewhere as shearwaters. Both the tuatara and the shearwaters depend upon finding loose soil of exactly the type produced by the birds' activities in mixing fallen leaves and twigs of *Coprosma* with eggshells, feathers, and dry guano. Seedlings of the plant thrive in the mixture, maintaining the habitat as it may have been for millions of years before man introduced domestic goats. Wherever the goats are allowed to feed on the *Coprosma*, the soil becomes hard, the birds tend to leave before nesting, and the tuatara soon disappears.

THE HONEYSUCKLE FAMILY (Caprifoliaceae)

To tell a plant of the honeysuckle family from one of the coffee family, it is necessary to look only where the leaves join the stem. Members of the coffee family either have the leaves in whorled groups without stipules, or in pairs with a stipule where each leaf arises. Members of the honeysuckle family either have leaves paired without stipules, or the two leaves of a pair so joined at the base that the stem seems to go right through the continuous blade.

About two-thirds of the species in this little family are honeysuckles *(Lonicera)*, of which there are a hundred and eighty different kinds. Honeybees and hawkmoths, even more than people, enjoy these erect or climbing shrubs of the Northern Hemisphere for their paired tubular flowers, in which the five joined petals are usually quite unequal in size, giving the corolla a strong bilateral symmetry.

Ordinarily, the children of each generation share with those of the next younger age the secret of getting honey from a honeysuckle. The corolla must be pinched free at the calyx end, and slid carefully over the pistil that remains attached. The expanded stigma at the end of the style serves as an efficient piston, pumping at a single stroke all of the nectar from inside the corolla into one big drop to be caught on the tongue. It is delightfully sweet, and a reward for dexterity, but gained only by wrecking the flower. The trick is easiest with large-flowered honeysuckles, such as the woodbine *(L. periclymenum*—Britain's only native honeysuckle) of Europe, which bears red fruit, and the Japanese honeysuckle *(L. japonica*— widely naturalized as a weed in many parts of the United States), an Asiatic species with black fruit. The nectar drops are smaller and the corollas hard to handle separately in the swamp fly-honeysuckle *(L. oblongifolia)*, which is native to wet woodlands over so much of the eastern United States and Canada, producing orange-yellow to deep red berries that the robins and cedar waxwings devour hungrily in early autumn.

A diminutive, trailing evergreen found in cool, mossy woods on all sides of the North Pole was the favorite plant of the immortal Swedish naturalist, Carl von Linné. His friend, the Dutch botanist Jan Gronovius, recognized that this little wild flower needed a genus of its own, and named the twinflower *Linnaea borealis* in honor of von Linné. Its creeping woody stems send up short vertical branches bearing pairs of small rounded leaves and, at the tip, pairs of fragrant, nodding bells. Each bell is pinkwhite, streaked outside with rose-purple, and hairy inside.

The honeysuckle family includes also some shrubs and small trees bearing flat clusters of tiny flowers, each with a spreading five-lobed corolla. About 120 different kinds are viburnums *(Viburnum)*, with simple leaves and small plumlike fruits each with a single pit. Another twenty species are elders *(Sambucus)*, with pinnately compound leaves and juicy fruits each with three small armored seeds. Both genera are well represented in Eurasia, North Africa, and North America, providing nectar for bees early in the summer and nourishment for birds by autumn. Wayfaring-tree *(V. lantana)*, which is native to Europe and North Africa, has escaped from cultivation in eastern Canada and New England, where it often reaches a height of fifteen feet along roadsides. Nannyberry (or sheepberry, *V. lentago),* which is widespread in North America east of the Rocky Mountains, grows along the edges of woodlands and offers large blue-black fruits with a sweet pulp. European elder *(S. nigra),* found wild from western Asia and North Africa to the Baltic Sea, and the common American elder *(S. canadensis),* which is native to the eastern United States and Canada, have provided the makings for many an elderberry pie and for countless bottles of delicious elderberry wine. These and other elders can still make little children happy, if their parents will take the trouble to cut a six-inch length of stem, push out the soft central pith, and make of the tube that remains a whistle or a flute—as has been done all over the world since time immemorial.

THE SPINY TEASELS (Family Dipsacaceae)

At the approaches to the village of Skaneateles, on one of the Finger Lakes in New York state, are large signboards proclaiming this to be the center of the teasel industry in America. Teasels *(Dipsacus)* still grow there as they do in many areas in eastern North America where they were raised toward the end of the 19th century. All teasels are native to southern Europe, north Africa, Ethiopia, and across the Caucasus to India. Each is a coarse plant that attains a height of five feet or more by the end of the summer, when small blue or purple flowers begin to open halfway up its several elongated oval or conical heads. The progression of flowers continues simultaneously toward the tip and the base of the head. Stiff bristles extend out between the individual flowers, and the whole head is guarded by about eight stout spiny projections like tentacles which arise just below the head and curve out around it.

Woolen manufacturers used to cut off the spiny projections from ripening heads of teasel, split the heads lengthwise and mount them on belts or rollers to work over the surface of cloth. The stiff bristles raised the nap on the fabric, making it thicker and warmer for clothing or blankets. The process, known as fulling the cloth, gave the name fuller's teasel to a variety of *D. sylvestris* called *D. s. fullonum,* in which the bristles are particularly stiff and long-wearing. A relative *(D. laciniatus),* with deeply cut margins to the paired leaves and each pair joined broadly at the base, forming a cup, is often cultivated in flower gardens for its strange heads.

The teasel family is represented in the Old World by about 150 other kinds of plants in equatorial and southern Africa, and temperate Eurasia. All of them produce dense heads of flowers with leaflike bracts instead of tentacle-like projections from the stalk at the base of the head. This type of floral arrangement would earn every member of the family a place in the huge assemblage of composites (Family Compositae) if not for the fact that the four stamens that arise from the inner surface of the tubular corollas are all separate from one another. In composites, such as daisies and coneflowers, the stamens are joined to form a tube.

CHAPTER 26

The Capacious Gourds

CUES: *If the dicot plant has alternate leaves with palmate venation, and solitary flowers in which the tubular corolla and lobes of the calyx arise from a ridge encircling the sides of the ovary, it is likely to be a member of the Order Cucurbitales. It may be a watermelon vine, or bear pumpkins, cucumbers, or vegetable sponges.*

All of the 850 different kinds of plants in this Order are included in the one family Cucurbitaceae. Most of them are creeping or climbing plants with tendrils developing opposite their leaves. Generally the staminate flowers are distinct from the pistillate, and have the stamens united by their elongated anthers or by their filaments. The ovary, seen as an elongated enlargement between the flower stalk and the calyx lobes, grows to become a fleshy fruit with large flat seeds embedded in a soft juicy pulp or in a central cavity derived from three united carpels.

Right above: The evergreen leaves and colorful fruits of Coprosma repens *appear on a low-growing member of this large genus of the coffee family in New Zealand. (G. G. Clark) Right: In* Mussaenda *species, which are herbs and small shrubs of the coffee family found in the Old World tropics, one sepal of the calyx is enlarged as a showy part of the flower. (E. S. Ross)*

Early man almost certainly discovered the thirst-quenching nature of the flesh in melons produced by plants of the several kinds native to Africa and Eurasia. These fruits of the Old World often remain full of juice after the vines on which they grew die and shrivel in the sun. Only a step more leads to primitive agriculture: tucking into the soil a seed here and there, upon the good chance that edible fruit will be waiting on the next visit to the area. Such casual cultivation seems to hide the site of origin for muskmelons *(Cucumis melo)* and watermelons *(Citrullus vulgaris),* which are unknown now in the wild except where they have obviously escaped. Muskmelons were mentioned in Egyptian records from 2400 B.C. They were enjoyed in ancient Greece and Rome, and spread to China in the first century A.D. A small, highly perishable variety in which the fruit has a hard rind with heavy netlike markings was discovered and developed first at Cantaluppi in Italy, and is known widely as a cantaloupe; its fruits are peculiar in developing a circular crack around the junction between fruit and stalk when the sugar content reaches its peak and harvesting should be done; slight pressure will then break off the stem cleanly. Larger types of muskmelon include the smooth skinned honeydew, the netted skinned Persian melon, and the yellow casaba melon; all of these are harvested by cutting the fruit stalk, which does not separate from the fruit until it is quite ripe. These larger melons, which can be stored satisfactorily for weeks, are sometimes called "winter melons." As they mature slowly in storage, they become softer but not noticeably sweeter.

Watermelons probably came first from tropical Africa, but found their way into the diet of ancient Egypt, then into Oriental and European areas. A single prostrate vine may produce anywhere from two fruits each weighing over fifty pounds to as many as fifteen smaller ones. To match the appetites of small families and to overcome the difficulty in knowing when a watermelon is ripe, horticulturalists recently have been striving to develop types with quick-ripening smaller fruits, and color in the skin that will change slowly as an indicator of the state of readiness to eat. For eating raw, the juicy red- and pink-fleshed melons are preferred. But for making into watermelon-rind pickles, the firmer yellow

Ripening on the arid central plains of Australia, these small gourds (Citrullus *species) are close relatives of the edible watermelon of tropical Africa. (E. S. Ross)*

or white-pulped strains offer certain advantages.

About half of the cucumbers *(Cucumis sativus)* raised today are made into pickles. The rest are eaten raw, in salads. Both customs have come down to modern times from the Prechristian era. The plants that bear the firm fruits probably came from Asia south of the Himalayas, where several related species of little consequence clamber among the low vegetation. The genus is represented also in the New World, a West Indian vine *(C. anguria)* providing the small prickly cucumbers known as gherkins, which are now raised in many temperate and subtropical parts of the world.

Often the tsamma melon *(Citrullus lanatus)* of South West Africa and Bechuanaland is the only source of water for the Bushmen living in the great Kalahari Desert. These and other primitive peoples of Africa have relied for centuries on whatever fruits of this type they could find, savoring the wet and faintly sweet pulp, the edible seeds, and then saving the hard rind as a convenient, temporary container. Hottentot tribes in the Namib area of South West Africa regard the dried fruit pulp of the naras melon *(Acanthosicyos horrida)* as a staple food at almost any time of year. The seeds of this plant contain a considerable quantity of fat, adding further to the nutrient value. The plant itself is unlike most members of the family in being a woody shrub that survives under the most murderously arid conditions, producing a root as much as forty feet long. Each seedling expends its fat supply in rapid growth following one of the rare rains, and thereafter is usually able to reach water during many months when neighboring plants must be dormant because of the extreme drought. The small melons, which attain four inches in diameter, are well protected by spine-studded branches.

Nearer the Equator, many African tribes suffer no handicap from their ignorance of pottery and metalworking because they have available a hard-shelled melon from a native vine *(Lagenaria siceraria).* When these fruits (known as gourds) are completely dry, they serve admirably as buoyant floats on fish nets. Or they can be cut into forms suitable for containers, scoops, ladles, other utensils, or even the resonators below the tone bars of marimba instruments. When cleaned out through a small hole, they can be plugged again to hold a few pebbles and make fine rattles for ceremonial dances. One crooked-neck gourd that we cherish, because it was given to us in the Transvaal of South Africa, is covered completely by colorful, artistic Ndebele beadwork.

The frost-resistant fruit of winter squash (Cucurbita maxima) *may weigh as much as one hundred pounds, most of it edible rind. (Grant Heist: National Audubon)*

Only a botanist who examined one of these African gourds carefully, or who saw the leaves of the vine on which it grew, would know it from a similar fruit from a vine of the New World. American Indians found comparable uses for the gourds on this vine *(Cucurbita pepo ovifera),* which is an extremely variable one and a close kin to the field pumpkin *(C. pepo pepo)* and the summer squash *(C. pepo condensa).* One of our favorite American friends keeps us supplied with crooked-neck gourds of *C. p. ovifera,* each with a one-inch doorway cut in the side, a short twig glued below this as a landing perch, and a strong copper wire through the stem end as a support. It is then a fine nest box for a wren, and we delight in seeing it used once or twice a summer right outside the study window.

The field pumpkin is too soft to keep well, but it adds a New World touch to the old Halloween legend when hollowed out, carved to imitate a face, and made glow bright orange in the dark from a lighted candle placed inside. Summer squashes are soft too, and come in so many different shapes, some plain colored and others in distinctive patterns, that

horticulturalists have worked out the hereditary basis for the differences.

Similar inherited features distinguish the winter squashes, which have tough rinds and good storage characteristics, into Hubbard, Boston Marrow, Turks Turban, and other types, all of which are *Cucurbita maxima.* The inner flesh of the thick fruit wall is more starchy and nourishing than the juicy counterpart in summer squashes, and more flavorful than that of the true pumpkin. Thus it is that most of the "pumpkin" used for pumpkin pies is actually winter squash.

The versatility of the gourd family is far from exhausted in the fruits found commonly in temperate markets. Among the most delicious "vegetables" on Latin American tables is the cooked chayote (or chocho, *Sechium edule),* a pear-shaped, one-seeded melon whose greenish, soft-spined fruit well deserves a far wider acceptance. But few people would attempt a second time to eat a loofah fruit *(Luffa cylindrica),* for the elongated melons on this twining vine in the American tropics are firmly supported by a tough network of vascular strands between the outermost skin and the pulp containing the seeds at the center. By enlisting the aid of decomposition bacteria in the process of retting, all of the soft parts of a loofah can be liquefied and washed away. The product is a cylindrical object as much as fifteen inches long and four in diameter, closed at one end, composed of an interlocking meshwork of inert fibers. Some people claim a loofah to be the best filter for fuel oil going into naval vessels. Others use these objects, known as vegetable sponges, for air filters, brushes, packing materials, or curios with which to confound the folks back home.

CHAPTER 27

The Daisies and Their Relatives

cues: *If the dicot plant has its petals joined to form a bell-shaped or a tubular corolla that arises from the ovary, it is likely to be a member of the Order*

Campanulales. It may be a bluebell of Scotland, a cardinal-flower of eastern North America, a giant groundsel on one of Africa's highest mountains, an aster, a hawkweed, or a dandelion.

Because this Order includes the largest family of flowering plants (the Compositae) with 20,000 species, it is also the most widespread, found in all parts of the world under all terrestrial conditions. Within the Order, however, this one family is unique in bearing flowers in compact heads which are protectively covered in the bud by whorls of leaflike bracts, forming an involucre; the individual flowers may be sterile, or staminate, or bisexual, or pistillate, but each fertile one produces only a single dry seed-like fruit (an achene). Among the members of the other families in the Order, the flowers arise singly or in clusters, but never in heads with an involucre; these flowers each produce a capsule or a berry. In all families, the stamens are usually united to form a tube surrounding the style and stigma; all composites show this feature, and differ thereby from the teasels.

THE BLUEBELL FAMILY (Campanulaceae)

In the Northern Hemisphere, there is no real need to travel to Scotland to meet a Scottish bluebell (or harebell, *Campanula rotundifolia*), for this very slender-stemmed, narrow-leaved little plant with its nodding purple bells is native to the Eurasian and North American area. Extremely hardy in rocky and sandy places, it blooms from June until September, even high on mountain slopes and into the Arctic. Only the leaves close to the soil and to the roots may be broadly oval, matching the name of the species ("round leaved").

The shape of the flower and even the blue color, which usually has a strong purple cast, are remarkably uniform among members of this family. Generally they are called "bellflowers," which matches well the Latin *campanula,* a little bell. The genus *Campanula* includes among its 250 species the Canterbury bell *(C. medium)* of southern Europe, now so widely cultivated in temperate gardens, and rampion *(C. rapunculus)* of Europe, where it is often gathered and cooked as a green vegetable.

In the Southern Hemisphere, the family is well represented by nearly one hundred different kinds of tuftybells *(Wahlenbergia)*. These plants are particularly numerous in South Africa, but add color

also to the limited flora on the remote islands of St. Helena and Juan Fernandez.

THE LOBELIA FAMILY (Lobeliaceae)

Most of the seven hundred different kinds in the lobelia family are tropical plants, distinguished from the 650 members of the Family Campanulaceae by their bilaterally symmetrical, tubular flowers, rather than radially symmetrical, bell-shaped blooms. As among the bluebells, the predominant color of the flowers in lobelias is blue, varying to purple, violet, and white. The few exceptions, whose showy blossoms come in shades of red, have been adopted and hybridized as garden plants. Prized among these are the cardinal-flower *(Lobelia cardinalis)* of eastern North America, the scarlet *L. splendens* and *L. fulgens* of Mexico and Texas, and *L. tupa* of Chile, all of which are normally pollinated by hummingbirds rather than by the hawkmoths that visit blue-blossomed lobelias. From South Africa comes the dwarf blue lobelia *(L. erinus)* which has become one of the commonest of edging plants in Europe and North America. Taller denizens of temperate gardens now include the blue cardinal-flower *(L. siphilitica)* of eastern North America, whose name reflects a supposed curative quality—now disproved. In greenhouses and where frost is no problem, gardeners commonly raise the handsome *L. tenuior* from Australia and *L. georgiana* from the American Southeast. None of these lobelias, however, prepares an explorer for meeting one of the giants of the genus in the tropics of the Old World. Ceylon has *L. leschenaultiana,* which attains a height of ten feet. And equatorial Africa offers little colonies of the tree lobelia *(L. keniensis)* on the misty slopes of Mt. Kenya, Mt. Kilimanjaro, and the Ruwenzori Range at the headwaters of the White Nile. We found a few outlying plants of the tree lobelia near the twisting road down the outer rim of the Ngorongoro Crater in Tanzania, raising flower spikes six to eight feet tall atop leafy stems that rose ten to fifteen feet high among the lush vegetation.

Probably the lobelias in gardens should be treated with respect, for several of them are known to contain a dangerous assortment of poisonous alkaloids with a chemical structure not greatly different from that of nicotine. Indian tobacco *(L. inflata),* which is a shrubby annual with inconspicuous blue flowers, got its name when the colonists in New England observed the Indians drying and smoking the leaves of the plant. Attempts to use various concoctions as medicine led to quick realization that lobelias—especially this one—are deadly if their foliage, fruits, or extracts from them are taken internally.

THE COMPOSITE FAMILY (Compositae)

About a tenth of all the kinds of flowering plants in the world have a place in this family. They display to insects as pollinators a large number of small flowers arranged somewhat like the pile in a rug. Well below the surface over which the insects walk, thrusting their mouthparts into one floret after another, is the support—like the backing on the rug. Usually, as in a sunflower or a daisy, this backing is the expanded circular end of a single flower stalk, as a receptacle encircled by the green bracts of the involucre. Less often it is a compound structure, as in the famous edelweiss (Leontopodium alpinum) of the European Alps, in which several flower heads (each with many florets) are supported by branching stalks at a common level, allowing the bees and flies to walk easily from one group of florets to the next. The ultimate in this arrangement is found in the globe thistles (Echinops), which are grown in many temperate gardens and attract bumblebees especially; each spherical cluster consists of nearly a hundred separate flower heads, each with a single floret and its own involucre, held by its radiating private stalk from the end of an upright stem.

Some botanists prefer to split the huge Family Compositae into two unequal parts, each with family rank. Others prefer to think of a larger subfamily Tubuliflorae (not Family Asteraceae) to include all those composites that possess tubular florets and lack a milky juice (latex), and a smaller subfamily Liguliflorae (not Family Cichoriaceae) for composites with only florets having a strap-shaped corolla and with a milky juice. Many of the members of Tubuliflorae have their tubular florets occupying the large center of the flower head while around its rim is a ring of florets bearing strap-shaped corollas as extra pennants that catch the attention of insects. However, the straplike corollas in Liguliflorae are basically five-lobed, whereas those of the Tubuliflorae are three-lobed—formed in development by the fusion of only three petals.

THE TUBULIFLOROUS COMPOSITES

Only a few genera are composed of plants in which all florets in every flower head have the tubular form of corolla. Among these few are the 450 species

of Eupatorium, known variously as Joe-Pye-weeds, bonesets, and snakeroots. Most of the 450 are native to tropical America, where they attract butterflies just as reliably as do those species found in Mexico, the southwestern and eastern United States and eastern Canada, and the few outliers in the Old World—such as hemp-agrimony (E. cannabinum) in Britain and Europe. Joe-Pye-weeds (chiefly E. maculatum and E. purpureum) are among the most conspicuous flowers in wet meadows and along the damp edges of woodlands from Newfoundland to Minnesota and southward. They are coarse perennials as much as four feet high, with leaves in pairs or whorled, and pale purple to creamy white flowers in heads that are held at almost a single level, signaling attractively to insects. Until home remedies were largely ousted in America by modern medicine after World War I, housewives used to hunt out boneset (E. perfoliatum) in thickets and beside swamps to dry its paired leaves as the basis for a bitter tonic hated by small boys, and a powerful emetic that cured many an upset stomach in short order.

The closely related white snakeroot (E. rugosum) should probably be exterminated wherever it is found —over the whole area from eastern Canada south to Georgia, across through Louisiana to east Texas, and north to Saskatchewan. It has poisoned more people in North America since the days of the American Revolution than any other native plant. Yet its action is indirect, and was not understood until the early 1930's. Over much of its range, the plant forms dense stands on freshly cleared land and along the edges of the forest. There, in early autumn or late summer when other foods become harder to find because of

Right above: After accumulating reserves of nourishment during at least twenty years, the giant silversword (Argyroxiphium macrocephalum) *produces daisy-like flowers ten feet high on the Hawaiian island of Maui. (Lorus and Margery Milne) Far right above: Golden marguerite or yellow camomile* (Anthemis tinctoria) *of Eurasia is enjoyed for its showy flowers and its fragrant leaves. Right: Called the "New York aster"* (Aster novi-belgii), *this is one of the most common and conspicuous of blue asters from Newfoundland to Florida, westward to the Mississippi Valley. (Both by E. Javorsky) Far right: Often called the "French marigold"* (Tagetes patula), *this spicy-fragrant plant is native to Latin America from the tropics to Argentina. It has been cultivated world-wide. (Lorus and Margery Milne)*

drought, domestic livestock may eat the foliage of white snakeroot. Curiously, cattle that are being milked are slow to develop symptoms of poisoning, for they are discharging the toxic ingredient (trematol) in their milk. Their calves die of the poison, and people develop "milksickness" from the milk or from butter produced from the cream. Cows that are not giving milk, sheep, and horses react to a diet containing small amounts of white snakeroot foliage by muscular quivering called "the trembles" and a reluctance to move known as "the slows." It may pass, or be followed by a coma ending in death. People who seem to recover from a touch of milksickness collapse and die after slight exercise. During the first half of the 19th century this fatal illness seemed to follow the settlers as they cleared the land of the central states. Sometimes half of the inhabitants of a village died of it within a few weeks, and the site was abandoned as though cursed. Abraham Lincoln's mother is suspected of succumbing to milksickness, although the cause of her death seemed mysterious at the time.

Today milksickness has ceased to be a problem for people whose milk and butter come from large dairies in which the milk from many farms is pooled—diluting any poison that a few cows might have eaten in a shady corner of the pasture. But the nature of the poison is still far from clear, since it seems to act only when linked to a resinous acid of unknown structure present in the white snakeroot plant.

Just as a naturalist in North America comes to associate hot summer days with the flowering of the various kinds of *Eupatorium,* so also an approach to the end of the year's growing season seems signaled when the goldenrods *(Solidago)* begin waving their bright yellow wands. Of the ninety different species, only one (the European *S. virgaurea)* grows in Britain. A few others are native to Eurasia and to South America. The majority are wildflowers of North America, leading members of garden clubs to agitate for selection of goldenrods as a national flower for the United States. Some people have objected, claiming that these plants cause "goldenrod fever," an allergy of the hayfever group that may come from the small amounts of goldenrod pollen carried by the autumn breezes, or from the large quantities of ragweed pollen blown about at the same

The bull thistle (Cirsium vulgare), *a prickly plant of meadows and fields in its native Europe, has become an aggressive weed in America. (Bill Ratcliffe)*

Cushion-like clumps of alpine plantain (Plantago rigida) *grow high in the Sierra Nevada del Ruiz of Colombia among reed grasses* (Calamagrostis *species) tolerant of cold. (H. G. Barclay)*

season. These views have not stopped Europeans from enjoying some of the taller goldenrods from the New World as introduced perennials for their gardens. When we first discovered these familiar "weeds" of American waysides and neglected fields in carefully-tended clumps among the roses and Canterbury bells in Britain and Scandinavia, we could hardly believe our eyes.

The individual flower heads of goldenrod scarcely call attention to themselves. Instead, they are grouped in many different ways to produce the familiar yellow display: sometimes in gracefully arching lines; at others in more compact masses. Each head includes a few florets with strap-shaped corollas, but these form no single encircling row around the florets with tubular corollas. A radiating pattern is the mark of other composites, in a wide variety of flower heads characteristic of asters, sunflowers, and daisies. The encircling "ray florets" surrounding the tubular "disc florets" call to mind the light rays from a star (Latin *aster)* or from the sun. The Anglo-Saxon word daisy, on the other hand, is a contraction of "day's eye," and refers to the common habit shown by these flowers of opening early in the day by spreading the ray florets, and closing again by folding them together over the disc florets as the daylight fades toward evening.

To the botanist, *Aster* is a generic name for some six hundred different kinds of plants, a few of which lack ray florets altogether. The six hundred are especially well represented in North America, but include wildflowers native to South America, Africa, and Eurasia. Only one *(A. tripolium)* is a natural denizen of the British Isles, where it grows commonly near the sea in salt marshes. Horticulturalists have produced new combinations, such as the "Michaelmas daisy," which is a handsome hybrid whose ancestors include the Italian aster *(A. amellus)*, the large pinkish-purple New England aster *(A. novae-angliae)* and the tall blue New York aster *(A. novi-belgii,* referring to the old name of New Belgium which preceded New Amsterdam for the New York area). In the American Southwest, true asters include the reedlike devilweed *(A. spinosus)* which grows to a height of nine feet, and the woody desert aster *(A. tortifolius)* with harsh, twisted leaves.

To a naturalist in New Zealand, Australia, or New Guinea, an aster is a woody shrub—a tree aster or daisy-bush *(Olearia),* of which more than 125 different kinds have been discovered. We found these plants blossoming profusely close to the Irish Sea where they have been introduced at Inverewe Gardens near Poolewe in the Scottish Highland country. Close by were fine beds of Chinese asters *(Callistephus chinensis),* an annual with large, soft, double flower heads in pastel shades of pink, or blue, or white, a horticultural favorite in the Orient for many centuries, in Europe for over two hundred years, and in America since about 1850. Our parents regularly started seedlings of this indoors, and set them out in the garden only after the last killing frost of spring seemed past. They surrounded each plantlet with a paper cuff to protect it from hungry cutworms until its stem grew too big and hard for these caterpillars to bite.

Human aid on a far grander scale seems called for today to save from extinction the five different kinds of silverswords *(Argyroxiphium)* still living on the volcanic mountains of Hawaii. Most spectacular of them is the Haleakala silversword *(A. macrocephalum)* which was so abundant around the rim and in the dead crater of Mt. Haleakala that these slopes at the 10,000-foot level on the island of Maui appeared silver gray and the cinder soil scarcely showed. The species name, which can be translated "big headed," refers to the habit of the silversword plant in growing steadily larger as a giant bud of almost spherical form. Year after year it enlarges, until its diameter is about two feet. Still all of its surfaces are covered with silvery gray glandular hairs, which ward off much of the intense sunlight at this elevation and also hold in moisture. Finally the plant produces a six-foot, swordlike upright stem, topped by a very conspicuous cluster of small flowers, each a yellowish disk surrounded by about two dozen purplish ray florets. Ordinarily, the plant dies while its seeds ripen.

Between 1900 and 1927, many visitors uprooted Haleakala silverswords and carried them off as ornaments. Others broke off the giant buds for the brief amusement of rolling the strange plants down the mountain slope like silver snowballs. Now the few survivors are threatened by introduced leafhopper insects that attack the slow-growing buds, and by moth caterpillars and fly maggots that eat out the florets before they open. The present custodians of Haleakala National Park hope to save the remaining plants by fencing off visitors and spraying the buds repeatedly with insecticides. Once a generous supply of seeds can be produced, they rely upon the silverswords germinating again in numbers in the cinder slopes where once they grew so abundantly.

Near inactive crests of the mountains known as Mauna Loa and Mauna Kea, close to the 13,000-foot level on the island of Hawaii, similar attempts are being made to preserve the remnants of the Hawaiian silversword *(A. sandwicense),* which visitors notice now only within fenced preserves in a few parts of Hawaii Volcanoes National Park. The three other species are smaller and more remote, mostly in undrained boggy areas on lofty Hawaiian plateaus where the almost constant mist and rain discourages all but the most persistent tourists. Conservationists hope to preserve these necessary habitats and their unique silverswords by keeping visitors away. Often this policy is misunderstood by officials who believe that the special features of the island should be seen by everyone, even if this will soon lead to the disappearance of the living resource.

The flower, rather than the plant on which it grows, ordinarily attracts the most attention in the sixty species of sunflowers *(Helianthus),* which are denizens of the New World. A few are native to Chile and Peru, the remainder to North America. Tallest of all are the coarse horticultural varieties of the Great Plains sunflower *(H. annuus),* which is now raised all over the temperate world, in India, and Egypt, for its nutritious seeds. A single plant may attain a height of fifteen feet, bearing at its top a flower head ten inches broad, with long golden petals radiating from a brown disc. The several thousand disc florets attract bees, then produce separate dry fruits with a black-striped whitish shell around the single seeds.

From sunflower seeds, a sweet yellow oil can be expressed and used in place of olive oil or almond oil as is done in many parts of Eurasia and North Africa. The residue from pressing is a nutritious oilcake now exported in quantity from the Soviet Union to Scandinavia and elsewhere as a food supplement for poultry and livestock. In America, bird watchers buy tons of dry sunflower seeds each winter to place in outdoor feeders attracting chickadees, finches and grosbeaks of several kinds, bluejays and hungry squirrels. By spring, the ground below the feeders outside our windows is inches deep in discarded shells of sunflower seeds. If we are not careful about storing the bags of seeds we buy, we find empty shells in all sorts of unlikely places where nocturnal mice have dropped them, or sunflower seedlings sprouting from flowerpots of earth in which the mice have buried their stolen treasures.

Samuel de Champlain is credited with carrying back with him to Europe an American plant *(H. tuberosus)* of which he saw the Indians on Cape Cod eating the enlarged roots. De Champlain tasted some of the strange vegetable, and found its flavor nearest to that of artichokes. His description was combined later with a mispronunciation of the Italian word *girasole* for the plant, to yield the commonest name today: Jerusalem artichoke. In France and northern Europe, where it is cultivated extensively as a stock feed, it is often called "Canadian potato." The plant grows as a coarse perennial, dying to the ground if winters are frosty, but producing each season a new cluster of branching upright stems which may attain a height of twelve feet by late autumn when the tips of the uppermost ones bear an abundance of sunflower-like heads each four inches across. It is native over the whole American area from Manitoba to Arkansas and eastward to the Atlantic Ocean. The tubers on its roots, which are thin skinned and may be four inches long by an inch or more in diameter, contain little sugar and almost no starch. The carbohydrate stored in them is virtually all in the indigestible form of inulin, and yields little that is nourishing to either man or domestic animals. For this reason, too, the pleasant-tasting roots can be converted into delicious pickles, relishes, and other dietary preparations for diabetics, without increasing their intake of sugars.

Giant lobelias (Lobelia bequaerti, *right foreground) grow at 13,000 feet on Mt. Kilimanjaro, Mt. Kenya, and the Ruwenzori range. (E. Aubert de La Rue)*

Inulin is the carbohydrate found also in the roots of Eurasian elecampane *(Inula helenium),* which can be seen wild and in cultivation from Britain to the Himalayan foothills and, from introductions at various times, in North America from Nova Scotia to Minnesota and southward. Its large egg-shaped tubers on the roots are sought for a medicinal confection that retains the natural warm, bitter taste and camphorlike odor. The four-inch flower heads of elecampane have an abundance of golden ray florets, each with a narrow long corolla, around the central disc florets, which change in color from yellow to tan as they age.

"Daisy" to a European usually suggests an almost stemless little plant *(Bellis perennis)* that sends up a few one-inch flower heads on two or three-inch slender stalks at almost any time of year when the weather is well above the freezing point. The numerous yellow disc florets are surrounded by many pink or white ray florets with narrow corollas, backed by a bright purple involucre. Known in Britain also as eye-gowan, March daisy, lawn daisy, and herb Margaret, it has been introduced by Europeans into many parts of Asia and North America, often escaping cultivation but rarely taking over an entire lawn.

Edelweiss (Leontopodium alpinum), *a prize for alpine climbers, tolerates high altitudes among the rocks in the Alps and other mountains of Europe. (L. Gensetter)*

The discovery of a white daisy growing wild in a field tempts some people almost irresistably to follow through the old saying "She loves me, she loves me not, she loves me, . . ." pulling out the ray florets one at a time until all have been discarded. For children, a whole fieldful of white daisies may be enough to start the making of a daisy chain. Usually the flowers are those of ox-eye daisy (or whiteweed, *Chrysanthemum leucanthemum),* which grows erect and often unbranched in its native Eurasia and also over North America, where it has been introduced and spread from Labrador to British Columbia, south to Texas and Florida. Young people are frequently delighted to discover that the name of the most widespread subspecies in Canada and the United States comes trippingly from the tongue, despite the multiplicity of syllables, like the rhyming refrain to be sung around a Maypole: *Chrysanthemum leucanthemum pinnatifidum,* referring to the deep notches along the sides of the leaves.

The Shasta daisy, which matures at a height of about thirty inches rather than thirty-six, often branches profusely, and bears flower heads as much as four inches in diameter, is a hybrid developed by Luther Burbank chiefly from *C. maximum,* a native of the Pyrenees. Europeans are familiar also with shrubby yellow marguerite *(C. frutescens)* from the Canary Islands, whose flower heads include yellow disc florets and white ray florets much like those of the ox-eye and Shasta daisies. Greater variety of color marks those super-daisies of florists' shops, the chrysanthemum hybrids of East Asian origin, whose horticultural varieties include many in which the disc florets are replaced by extra ray florets whose strap-shaped corollas curl and twist. They attract human attention to the gigantic or unnaturally firm flower head, but discourage pollinating insects.

Gardeners enjoy the colorful flowers and highly aromatic foliage of several chrysanthemums native to Asia, which are now raised commercially to get flower heads that can be dried and powdered, yielding the insecticide pyrethrum. "Persian insect powder" from *C. coccineum* and *C. anethifolium,* and Dalmatian "insect powder" from *C. cinerariaefolium* and *C. marschalli* are now important crops in Japan, Kenya, and California. Pyrethrum powder enters easily the breathing tubes of insects, and poisons them effectively at concentrations that are harmless to plants and higher animals. Only its cost keeps it from competing seriously with synthetic insecticides that are more dangerous.

As though in exchange for white daisies from the Old World, the plains of America have provided gardeners everywhere with yellow daisies, such as the golden ox-eye (or false sunflower, *Heliopsis helianthoides)* and the various coneflowers *(Rudbeckia).* The golden ox-eye has opposite leaves, which distinguishes it from a true sunflower, and the yellow ray florets produce seeds, whereas those of both sunflower and coneflowers are sterile. Coneflowers get their name from the conspicuously convex cluster of disc florets, which are usually dark brown and provide the nectar for visiting insects. In the western United States and Canada, one, *R. occidentalis,* lacks ray florets altogether but holds its inch-high clusters of dark disc florets so contrastingly against the sky that bees of many kinds swarm to it. The eastern black-eyed Susan *(R. hirta),* which grows to a height of only about three feet in open dry meadows and pasture lands, bears twenty to forty orange-yellow ray corollas each as much as two inches long around the crowded conic group of dark-brown disc florets. The tips of the ray corollas reflect strongly the ultraviolet part of sunlight, which is so stimulating to the compound eyes of honeybees. The insects detect the circles of ultraviolet spots from considerable distance and descend to alight at the center of each, where nectar and pollen await them.

The coneflower *R. laciniata,* which has a cluster of disc florets shaped like a gumdrop bearing greenish-yellow tubular corollas at the center of long yellow ray florets, grows abundantly in thickets over a home area extending from Arizona to Manitoba and eastward to Florida and Quebec. It provided gardeners with a favorite horticultural variety known as golden-glow, in which ray florets almost completely replace the fertile disc florets and produce a head that may be nearly spherical. Golden-glow has become one of the tall showy composites to cultivate as a backdrop in gardens. We saw thousands of them used in this way all over Britain and Scandinavia during the summer of the Shakespeare Festival. Surely some of the European visitors to Ann Hathaway's garden in Stratford-on-Avon noticed the floral anachronism unwittingly introduced by those who refurbished it. In place of the Old World plants that must have grown there in the late 1500's when William Shakespeare and his Ann walked the curving paths, were imports from the Americas: Brazilian scarlet salvia, "French" marigolds and zinnias and cosmos and dahlias (all originally from Mexico), clumps of tall goldenrods and of black-eyed Susans, backed by solid stands of golden-glow. The golden-glow even showed a speckling of the same blood-red aphids (plant lice) that infest the wild progenitor on American soil. None of these plants were among those listed by Shakespeare's contemporary, John Gerard (1545–1612), as growing in his London garden.

The "winking Mary-buds" of Shakespeare's *Cymbeline* are the two-inch flower heads of the pot-marigold *(Calendula officinalis),* native to southern Europe. Horticultural varieties are often raised to decorate flower gardens, but whole fieldsful of them are cultivated in Europe as a potherb and fodder for cattle. In the early morning or late evening, or during a cloudy day, a person can pass such a field without seeing a single blossom. The sun fortunately came out in time to show us acres of pot-marigold in Denmark, and to let us see that the pale yellow ray flowers change by the hour to a deep orange as they age. When each head closes for the night or under the threat of rain, the green bracts of the involucre hide almost all of the color.

Many annuals among the composites of the New World are now enjoyed in flower gardens everywhere. "French" marigolds *(Tagetes patula)* represents a genus with members native all the way from the American Southwest to Argentina; the distinc-

tively fragrant foliage is usually divided pinnately into a dozen or more segments. Cosmos *(Cosmos bipinnatus)* often has leaves so lacy in their twice pinnate subdivision that they scarcely cast a shadow in the hot sun that brings out the best features of the three-inch flower heads, each with a yellow central disc and about eight broad strap-shaped corollas from ray florets in white or pink or red. Zinnias (mostly *Zinnia elegans)* bear thick, smooth-edged, opposite leaves on stiffly erect stems; their solitary terminal flowers sometimes expand to a diameter of four inches, ranging in color from scarlet and purple through pink, orange and yellow to white, and attracting both butterflies and hummingbirds by day, hawkmoths and owlet moths (noctuids) by night as pollinators. Sometimes the goldfinches attack zinnia heads that have passed their prime, tearing away at the green involucral bracts to reach the ripening seeds in the outermost florets.

Gardeners who choose to cultivate the huge flower heads on horticultural varieties of dahlias *(Dahlia pinnata)* are usually prepared for the annual routine of digging up the heavy roots each autumn before frosts spread into the soil. After all stems have been

On New Zealand's South Island, the large mountain daisy (Celmisia coriacea) *produces thick leathery leaves and, when the snow melts, flowers. (New Zealand Information Service)*

In Pakistan, the giant sunflower (Helianthus annuus) *from the Great Plains of North America is appreciated for its edible seeds. (M. Woodbridge Williams)*

severed, the roots must be stored in sand that is kept neither too wet nor too dry, until they can be planted again in the garden after spring is well established. People who lack the facilities or the patience for protecting the roots of garden composites in this way often prefer the hardier gaillardias (such as *Gaillardia aristata),* which are native to the American plains from Manitoba into Mexico. Despite the handsome flower heads, which are often four inches across, the gaillardias of Texas are commonly regarded merely as roadside weeds and sprawling denizens of open land, called blanket-flowers. Elsewhere, in gardens, the same flowers are greatly appreciated.

Smaller daisy-like heads are borne by many of the 1300 different members of the huge genus *Senecio* —one of the largest among flowering plants. For home and greenhouse culture, the florists' "cineraria" *(S. cruentus)* from the Canary Islands is particularly beautiful, and has been developed into many different colors. Smaller golden flowers appear outdoors, without attention, on the golden ragwort *(S. aureus)* which thrives both on moist ground and in stony pastures over the eastern half of North America, and has now been introduced to European gardens. Golden ragwort starts each season with a few new heart-shaped leaves that could be mistaken for those of violets. Then its tough fibrous roots send up a

slender angular stem bearing alternate, elongated leaves almost as divided as those of a dandelion. Finally the stem branches like a candelabra, and displays its many separate clusters of brownish-orange disc florets surrounded by a dozen or less narrow orange-yellow rays. Until the flowers open, the plant might be suspected of being merely an American version of groundsel *(S. vulgaris)* of Europe, now widespread as a weed, which lacks ray florets altogether.

Giant groundsel *(S. keniodendron)* is extraordinarily different in attaining a height of twenty feet or more, like a gigantic cabbage on a trunk like that of a palm tree, growing on the high misty slopes of Africa's Ruwenzori Range, Mt. Kilimanjaro, and Mt. Kenya. At the other extreme is German ivy *(S. scandens* with ray florets and *S. mikanioides* without), much used in hanging baskets because the slender twining stems produce pale green triangular or five- to seven-pointed leaves and occasional clusters of yellow flower heads.

Several composites have held a respected place in medicine, although few of them continue in as high esteem. Achilles is supposed to have found a healing power in the fragrant yarrow *(Achillea millefolium),* and some people still gather this weed of Eurasia in its homelands and in North America where it was introduced long ago. They dry its leaves, which are twice-divided and so finely toothed as to have a lacy appearance, and its flower heads, each about one-third of an inch in diameter in flat-topped compound clusters of pinkish white. But physicians question the efficacy of applying the plant to wounds, as Achilles is claimed to have done for soldiers injured in the siege of Troy.

Tansy (or bitter buttons, *Tanacetum vulgare)* of European fields has yielded an ethereal oil that can be used carefully as a vermifuge, following a practice begun in the Middle Ages. Excess dosage with it is usually fatal. But wherever western civilization has spread in the temperate world, tansy has gone along to become an occasional crop or a persistent weed. Usually its stem rises to a height of about three feet and then branches repeatedly in supporting the yellow, button-shaped flower heads, each half an inch across with most or all florets having tubular corollas.

Early in the present century, the use of a bitter extract from Eurasian wormwood *(Artemisia absinthium)* became a criminal offense in many countries where previously it had been added to a strong alcoholic liquor called absinthe. The extract, supplemented by several additional flavorings including anise, caused addiction, leading to increasing use and personal deterioration. The liquor is still sold, but without the wormwood ingredient. The plant itself, which produces inconspicuous flowers, is but one of a genus containing some two hundred species, including Asiatic moxa *(A. moxa)* and the common sagebrush *(A. tridentata)* of North American arid plains. In China and Japan, cones one-quarter of an inch wide made of compressed dry leaves of moxa are used in the ancient practice of moxibustion; placed on the body of a sick person over the special sites listed in the lore of acupuncture, they are ignited and burned down to the skin, producing a small blister that leaves a scar. Believers in moxibustion claim that the agents causing arthritis, headache, colic, and other malfunctions escape from the body through the blisters or are somehow destroyed by the treatment.

In the first known book of materia medica, written by the Greek physician Pedanius Dioscorides in the 1st century A.D., the word ambrosia—food of the gods—was applied to an imported herb from North Africa. No one knows why, but the name has been adopted scientifically for the plant and for fourteen other species in the same genus *Ambrosia* from the New World. They are the hated ragweeds which, unlike most composites, rely on the wind to carry their abundant pollen and cause innumerable cases of intense suffering classed as "hay fever." Most of them are, as the great Asa Gray remarked, "coarse homely" herbs, with inconspicuous greenish flowers, the staminate heads in terminal spikes and the pistillate heads often lower down in the axils of the leaves. The commonest American ragweed *(A. artemisiifolia)* has become naturalized in Europe, where it is known as Roman wormwood. Two others have gained a roothold on the mainland of Eurasia and can be expected to spread: the perennial western ragweed *(A. psilostachya)* of dry prairies, and the giant ragweed (or buffalo-weed, *A. trifida)* which sometimes attains a height of eighteen feet in its single year of growth. All ragweeds seem to fruit prolifically, and their hard little seeds can survive for at least five years, needing only to be in contact with wet soil to establish themselves. That more of them do not grow attests to their popularity as food for seed-eating birds, such as quail and sparrows, and for small mammals, including field mice.

We often wish that more animals ate the fruits of bur marigolds *(Bidens)*, the 240 different kinds of which are widely distributed over the world. Some advertise their presence with daisy-like flower heads around which are a few glistening white ray florets,

The balsamroot (Balsamorhiza sagittata) *of western North America gets its name from the fragrance in its underground stems. (U.S.D.A.)*

helping attract butterflies to the golden disc florets at the center. In other species, the ray florets are tiny or absent. Always, however, a flower head transforms rapidly into an all-too-effective agent of seed dispersal. Every floret contributes a flat dry fruit with two or more barbed prongs pointing radially outward from the center of the head (the end of the flower stalk). At the slightest touch against the fur of a passing animal or a person's clothing, the fruits catch hold and dig in. They make their way right through the wool of a sheep and irritate its skin, sometimes seriously. They jab through a sweater sleeve or a sock. The only compensation we find is that, in tropical America, some of the most spectacular of butterflies—the heliconiids, such as the yellow-striped black zebra butterfly of Florida—come from caterpillars that eat only the foliage of bur marigolds. Rather than have all *Bidens* exterminated and lose the wonder of seeing these insects on their magically glimmering wings, we'll grumblingly put up with pulling stick-tights, beggar-ticks, or devil's-pitchforks from our clothing wherever we go through the damp fields.

We can even say a good word for the burdocks *(Arctium)* of temperate Eurasia, most of whose six species are now widespread in North America as well. Some of them were introduced deliberately by

colonists from Europe who wished to follow their old custom of digging the roots, peeling these and the largest stems, boiling and eating the clean firm tissue as a vegetable. Wherever this tradition is followed, burdock is no problem. It becomes a noxious weed, and a nuisance to owners of long-haired dogs and sheep, chiefly where the plant is allowed to grow unmolested on neglected land. Its lower leaves are coarse, as much as a foot in length and breadth, but the upper ones remain smaller, particularly around the groups of flower heads toward the tips of the outstretched branches. The individual heads resemble little thistle heads, with only tubular florets, the corollas white or purple, surrounded by an almost spherical involucre. Each of the many involucral bracts is slender and ends in a sharp, strong hook. These hooks catch on clothing or the fur of passing animals firmly enough to tear loose the whole ripening flower head, helping it ride away with its seeds still enclosed, to be scratched off and dropped far from the parent plant. Using these hooks, a person needs no pin to attach a burdock flower head in full color to his lapel. Children often gather burdock heads and mass them together into castles and imitation statuary.

Thistles are prickly, spiny herbs, whose seeds are lifted from the ripened flower heads by the wind tugging at terminal tufts of "thistledown." These plumed seeds ride the breeze for miles before settling where they may germinate, letting one plant become parent to thousands over a great area. All of the florets are tubular in the globe thistle *(Echinops sphaerocephalus)* of Eurasia, the bull-thistle *(Cirsium vulgare)* of Eurasia and North Africa, the Scotch thistle (or cotton-thistle, *Onopordum acanthum)* of Europe, and the Lady's-thistle *(Silybum marianum)* of Mediterranean coasts. Some of the outer florets are enlarged and somewhat raylike in star-thistles *(Centaurea)* and blessed-thistle *(Cnicus benedictus)* of Eurasia. So varied are the composites, however, that several members of these and related genera

Left above: On the Hawaiian island of Maui, the Haleakala silversword begins production of its one tall stem of daisylike flowers after adding a few silvery leaves yearly for two decades or more. It dies and topples (left) once its seeds are ripe. (Both by Lorus and Margery Milne) Right: Giant groundsels (Senecio keniodendron) *at Lac Vert, high on the Ruwenzori Mountains, produce daisy-like flowers atop twenty-foot stems. (Bernard Pierre)*

Small pointed flowers radiate from the top of globe thistles (Echinops), *native from southern Europe to Japan. (A. W. Ambler: National Audubon)*

hold favored roles in the world of men. The Scotch thistle is the national flower of Scotland, and the prickle-less cornflower (or bachelor's-button, *Centaurea cyanus)* of Europe has been chosen to be the floral emblem of Germany. Still another thistle *(Cynara scolymus)* is cultivated extensively in southern France, in the southern United States and around Monterey in California for its giant buds; it is globe-artichoke, one horticultural variety of which is only slightly spiny and has thick, juicy, flavor-filled bracts composing the involucre. These heads are three to four inches in diameter and about the same dimension in height.

THE LIGULIFLOROUS COMPOSITES

Most members of this subfamily are like the thistles in having wind-borne seeds. Most, in fact, are hawk-weeds *(Hieracium)*—one of the largest genera of flowering plants, with more than two thousand species recognized. Most are also native to Europe and Asia, although many have been spread from there to the New World, South Africa, Australia and New

Zealand, either deliberately or as accidental impurities among shipments of commodities.

Only in Europe is sow thistle *(Sonchus oleraceus)* popular as a food. There the young stems and leaves are gathered, boiled in salty water to remove the bitter latex, and the "greens" served hot as a potherb while the cooking water is discarded. Elsewhere sow thistle is a weed that thrives in croplands, gardens and lawns if not destroyed regularly. From waste corners new generations are always ready to start out, as red or brown dry fruits each borne by its dirty white parachute of fine hairs. Every plant seems able to produce dozens of flower heads with pale yellow corollas on all the florets, fifty or more to the head, yielding as many fruits by late summer or early autumn.

As though this efficient mode of dispersal were not enough to insure the future of each species, many of them show additional versatility in reproduction. If no insect arrives with pollen of the right kind, the stigmatic portion of the pistil in each floret curls doubly toward the tube of fused anthers and picks up pollen—insuring seed by self-fertilization. The hawkweeds also send out horizontal "runners" as radiating stems at the tips of which new plants develop and take root. Each, in turn, produces a rosette of drought-defying hairy leaves tight against the ground, and extends a tall stalk at the top of which several heads of yellow or orange-red flowers expand. The sturdier hawkweeds are often known as devil's-paintbrush, or king-devil. Horticulturalists generally claim that the success of hawkweeds is a sign of poor management of the land, and that with proper fertilizer the competing plants will crowd them out. After seeing *Hieracium aurantiacum* invade some of the best-fertilized lawns in New England, we wonder whether the sellers of fertilizer are not promoting for their own benefit an idea of scarcely greater validity than Pliny's: that hawks used these plants to strengthen their eyesight.

In many a lawn all over the temperate world, another of these introduced composites from Europe settles with the traditional lightness of thistledown and takes firm root. It is dandelion (or blowballs, *Taraxacum officinale)*, whose commonest name is an imitation of the French dents-de-lion ("lion's teeth"), referring to the large recurved tooth-shaped lobes along each side of the leaves. European people often gather the leaf rosettes early in the summer and boil them as potherbs. Others collect the golden flowers atop their slender hollow stalks and extract their sweetness as the basis for dandelion wine. From

248

Fleshy bracts surrounding the flower head of true arti-chokes (Cynara scolymus) *are sought by gourmets in Europe and America. (J. C. Allen & Son)*

Espeletia schultzii *is the dominant vegetation on snowy ledges between 10,000 and 14,000 feet up in the Sierra Nevada of California. (Karl Weidmann)*

all of these setbacks the plant recovers, spreading new leaves and sending up more flowers from the stemless top of the thick tap root. A related plant *(T. kok-saghyz)* native to Soviet Kazakstan, near the border of China, was discovered in 1931 to contain a latex from which acceptable rubber could be made.

From the Old World, two of the nine known kinds of chicory *(Cichorium)* have traveled to other areas of the temperate zones with man's deliberate help. Common chicory (or succory, or blue-sailors, *C. intybus)* yields young leaves that can be cut for salad greens, with an only slightly bitter taste. Its roots, dug soon after flowering ceases in autumn, are of wider appeal, to be dried, ground, roasted, and used to heighten the bitterness and color of coffee. Chicory coffee is so popular in northern Europe that great fields of chicory are raised in the Low Countries, Germany, and France, and to some extent in Yorkshire, England, and the southern United States. The sky-blue flowers in flat heads nearly two inches across open in the morning, usually from July until killing frosts in autumn. A low-growing relative *(C. endivia)* has been cultivated in northern Europe and Britain since the 16th century, and more recently in America, but whether it originated in Mediterranean countries or the Far East will probably always remain unknown. Called simply endive (pronounced

on'-deev), its narrow, curled, much-notched leaves can be kept from developing their normal bitterness by shielding them from the sun. Tended in this way, they serve as decorative substitutes for lettuce in winter salads.

Lettuce itself *(Lactuca sativa)* has been cultivated for more than 2500 years, gradually taking its place as the world's most popular salad plant. Probably it originated in Asia Minor. The Romans knew it only as the "looseleaf" variety, for the firm, headed types were not developed until during the Middle Ages. If not harvested, the lettuce plants produce upright stems that branch toward the top, displaying there small yellow heads of flowers that open in the morning and close soon after noon. A dozen or so flat seedlike fruits mature in each head, each with a tuft of fine silky fibers to bear it aloft in the breeze. The generic name refers to the milky juice, which is less evident in the edible species than in the many wild ones, such as prickly lettuce (or compass-plant, *L. scariola)* from across Eurasia (the Canary Islands to Siberia). Prickly lettuce is now naturalized as a weed in North America, serving chiefly for the entertainment of people who discover how often its oblong leaves point alternately north and south, each with its blade turned vertical, one spiny edge up and the other down, like a natural compass.

PART

4

The Lily Legions, to Cattails and Orchids

The Bible says: "It is by their fruits ye shall know them." Plantsmen have looked inside the fruit for details that would help them subdivide the flowering plants. In particular, they have counted the number of seed leaves (cotyledons) that the embryo bears while it waits to be awakened from its dormancy. It may have two, or only one. If one, the plant that grows from the seed will be a "monocot," a member of the Subclass known fully as monocotyledonous angiosperms. It may be a lovely lily, a lowly grass, a lofty palm tree, or a lonely orchid. Yet its style of growth will differ in characteristic ways from that of any hardwood and of most of the plants we call herbs.

These differences show throughout the plant, and have done so since first a monocot left a trace of its existence in the fossil record. That was about half-way back from the present to the time when the first flower on earth unfolded in the sunlight. Probably the earliest monocot was a strange offspring from parents that were kin to buttercups. Certainly they were members of the Order to which buttercups belong, the Ranales. But that first monocot held a magic combination in its inheritance. It evolved in new directions, exploiting new environment. Its underlying symmetry was new—its flowers and fruits parted three ways (or in multiples of three) instead of four or five. In its stem it had no possibility of adding new conducting tubes for water and elaborated food; it could only make full use of all the parts its terminal bud provided. Instead of forming a solid trunk of wood, added to sheath after sheath as dicots do, it kept its conducting tubes in discrete bundles. Often, but not invariably, the veins in its leaves ran parallel, unbranching, all the way from the base to the tip.

What are the dominant plants on a prairie, tolera-

ting best the wild fire that may sweep across when the land lies parched? Grasses—monocots. What plants provide the shade, the fuel, and delicious dates in a desert oasis? Palms—monocots. What plants conceal and feed the muskrat and the nesting ducks in a marsh? Cattails and other monocots. The fifty thousand kinds of monocots living today may well be the wave of the future, the seed plants that inherit the earth.

CHAPTER 28

The Regular Lilies

CUES: *If the monocot plant bears flowers with a regular, six-parted perianth and a compound ovary with three united carpels, it is almost sure to be a member of the Order Liliales. It may be a smelly onion, or a fragrant hyacinth, an ancient dragon-tree, a century plant, or a crocus pushing up through the snow to summon the first bees of springtime.*

The plantsmen of the world have gradually over-come their former reluctance to credit the showy lilies with being an Order of great antiquity. It now seems probable that plants of this type were among the early flowers of the Cretaceous period, contem-poraries of the long-extinct dinosaurs. Most, if not

250

all, of the other monocots may well have sprung from the lily line, in many cases by loss of the floral features that make the lilies so well loved, so widely known, and so successful.

Almost eight thousand different species are grouped in the Order Liliales, with representatives from most parts of the world. A large number of them, both in tropical and temperate (as well as arctic and alpine) regions, live where the winters are too cold and the summers too briefly watered to allow much growth. The plants thrive despite this handicap by storing food reserves in underground parts, and opening their leaves and flowers rapidly in spring. This spectacular growth, matching a short season closely is appreciated by florists and gardeners, who become familiar with the resting stages of the plants. These may be thick horizontal rhizomes (stems), as in asparagus, or swollen tubers, as on yams, or upright short stems (corms), as in gladioli and crocus, or greatly enlarged buds (bulbs), as in onions and hyacinths.

THE LILY FAMILY (Liliaceae)

"Swear not by the moon, the inconstant moon," cried Juliet to her Romeo. But the predictable cyclings of that inconstant satellite determine which of two different lilies will be the Easter lily of the year. Easter, ever since A.D. 325, has been celebrated in the Christian world as early as March 22 and as late as April 25, according to when the first full moon arrives after Spring Equinox. When Easter is late, the decorative white lilies are Madonna lilies (Lilium candidum) of southern Europe, which have been symbols of purity ever since the ancient Greeks attributed the plant's origin to drops of milk falling to earth from the bounteous breasts of Hera—wife and sister of almighty Zeus. When Easter is early, the Madonna lilies have not yet opened, and their place is taken by the white-trumpet lily (or Bermuda lily, L. longiflorum), a native of Japan. In the United States, where floral gifts are popular, the Madonna lily is popular for Mother's Day (the second Sunday in May) and Memorial Day (May 30), both of which fit into the normal flowering season for this handsome plant.

In all of the true lilies (Lilium), the six showy petal-like parts of the perianth form a funnel-shaped or bell-like portion from the open end of which the lobes diverge or even curve back upon themselves to display the inner surface. The T-shaped stamens and central style are about equally long, the stigma

The sisal plant (Agave sisalana) *is raised in plantations in Africa as well as its native Latin America for the tough fibers in its leaves. (Anna Riwkin)*

often not spreading its three parts until after the anthers have split open and displayed their golden pollen for hours. Often the inner surface of the perianth bears decorative markings, such as the six broad yellow stripes of the golden-banded lily of the Orient (L. auratum), or the handsome freckling in the nodding tiger lilies (such as L. tigrinum of Southeast Asia and the turk's-cap, L. superbum, of eastern North America). Erect flowers ranging in color from lemon-yellow to an intense red are produced by some of the "orange lilies" such as the European favorite (L. bulbiferum) and the wood-lilies (L. philadelphicum) of North America. Many of these plants reproduce both by seeds and by small black spherical bulbils that develop in the axils of the leaves, then roll or are carried by animals away from the parent plant. Often a seed or a bulbil that takes root requires a few years to accumulate in its scaly bulb enough reserves of food to raise a sturdy stem with a terminal cluster of large flowers. But thereafter for several successive seasons, the bulb may continue at

full vigor, producing a new upright stem and floral display each season.

Far more precarious is the way of life of seven different kinds of fawn-lily *(Erythronium)*, of which the dog's-tooth-violet is the best known. Like other members of the genus, this little wildflower produces just two smooth and shining leaves each year from its small bulb. Dying back to the bulb each autumn, the plant accumulates food reserves for seven years or more before sending up its first flower stalk with a single nodding blossom. That of the dog's-tooth-violet, native across Europe and temperate Asia to Japan, is a reddish purple, whence comes the generic name from the Greek *erythros* for red. It is somewhat smaller than the golden flowers of the glacier-lily *(E. grandiflorum)* which often carpet the high country of the Rocky Mountains soon after the sun bares the ground by melting the winter's snow. The eastern part of America has its fawn-lilies too, in the yellow adder's-tongue *(E. americanum)*, the white dog's-tooth-violet *(E. albidum)*, and the rarer rosy-pink one *(E. propullans)* found in Minnesota. Seldom does a flower-picker realize how long the plant has been hoarding its reserves before raising its solitary blossom. Yet if a person or an animal removes the two leaves of the year as well as the flower stalk, the plant is usually doomed. From its remaining meager reserves it cannot produce a new pair of leaves quickly enough to get much good from the summer sun before drought arrives, and to survive it must gain energy for a winter and for production of still another pair of leaves the following spring. All of the fawn-lilies are in constant peril from flower-pickers. All but the giant kind *(E. oregonum)* on America's West Coast, which has poisonous bulbs, are in danger too from squirrels that may dig them up for food.

A particularly dangerous poison protects the corm and other parts of the autumn crocus *(Colchicum autumnale)*. It is the alkaloid colchicine, which has found recent use in the study of inheritance and in horticulture because it interferes with the normal ballet of the chromosomes during the nuclear divisions of plant growth. It can kill the plant or, at lower concentrations, lead to abnormal groupings of chromosomes that are inheritable (polyploids). Some of these modified plants are economically valuable

Characteristically South African, the thick-leaved aloes (Aloe *species) grow right to the coast of the Transkei, Republic of South Africa. (Carl Frank)*

because of their greater lushness of foliage, larger flowers, or special resistance to diseases. Autumn crocus is a European representative of a genus found native from the British Isles to Central Asia. John Gerard, the English herbalist, knew it as mede saffron, but to him its style of growth seemed paradoxical. It "bringeth forth leaves in Februarie, seed in May, and floures in September; which is a thing cleane contrarie to all other plants whatsoever, for that they doe first floure, and after seed." The long delay between autumn flowering and spring fruiting by production of a capsule after the three new leaves of the year have made their appearance is due to the very slow growth of the pollen tube, and the equally slow extension of the flower stalk, carrying the capsule up above ground in summer.

Similar, but different poisons are produced by many favorites among the spring flowers that gardeners raise from bulbs. Star-of-Bethlehem *(Ornithogalum umbellatum)* of Mediterranean Europe, but now introduced and naturalized widely in America, and squill *(Scilla)* from the temperate parts of the Old World, become dangerous if frost heaves their small, white, onion-like bulbs out of the soil where children or animals eat them. Neither the common blue-flowered scilla *(S. sibirica)* nor the lavender-colored one *(S. nonscripta,* known in England as a bluebell or a harebell), contain as much poison as the scales on the bulbs of a close relative, red squill *(Urginea maritima)* of Europe. Until recently, red squill extract was the most reliable rat poison known; rats eat it readily, and fail to save themselves (as people and most domesticated animals do) by vomiting up any lethal dose. Now that rats are showing a new immunity to synthetic poisons, a return to use of squill may be necessary.

Even the delightful little lily-of-the-valley *(Convallaria)* contains a dangerous poison in its white underground stems. The cultivated one *(C. majalis)* is native to Europe, but has escaped over much of the temperate world where it was introduced because people admired its one-sided series of fragrant bell-shaped flowers and the perfume they produce. A wild lily-of-the-valley *(C. montana)* graces the woodlands of the Appalachian Mountains in the United States.

Lily-of-the-valley, like *Trillium* and *Asparagus*, belongs to a part of the lily family in which the fruits are fleshy berries rather than dry three-sided capsules full of seeds. *Trillium* bears net-veined leaves in whorls of three, and shows a distinction between the green sepals and white or red petals in

253

Near Palm Springs, California, a reserve safeguards a forest of Joshua trees (Yucca brevifolia), *which flower chiefly in years when rainfall exceeds the average ten inches. (Conzett and Huber)*

we watch the rapid growth of slender arching stalks of Solomon's-seal *(Polygonatum).* For more than ten years these plants in northern New England have begun opening their pendant bell-shaped flowers during the first two weeks in May—on exactly the day when the first ruby-throated hummingbirds arrived from the South, ready to visit the Solomon's-seal and other flowers. The particular plants we watch are of the Eurasian species *(P. officinale),* which is pollinated by hawkmoths in its broad native range. Introduced in American gardens, it follows the same timing as the native species of this circumpolar genus, such as the coarse woodland Solomon's-seal *(P. canaliculatum)* of eastern Canada and the mountain forests as far south as Tennessee. The migrant hummingbirds reach the foothills of Virginia in late March or early April, but there too these members of the lily family are just beginning to bloom. For a hummer that travels all the way with spring into the Province of Quebec, the season must be a continual parade of Solomon's-seals all at the same peak of perfection. By the time the black or dark-blue berries are ripe, the hummingbirds may have raised their families and be headed south again toward winter quarters.

Many of the bulbs that are planted in autumn to provide colorful flowers in spring produce leaves that persist after the blossoms fade, and restore the reserves upon which the following year's bloom depends. By crossing, selection, and carefully nurturing the most attractive varieties, horticulturalists (particularly in Holland) have developed ornamental plants amazingly different from the wild ancestors. The cultivated hyacinths *(Hyacinthus orientalis)* came from a diminutive plant of Asia Minor and Greece, scarcely larger than a scilla. Double hyacinths may be still more showy, but most of them have lost the delightful fragrance for which the plant is so

the perianth. These plants of eastern Asia and North America are among the most characteristic woodland spring flowers, and later hold scarlet or black berries as much as an inch in diameter a foot or more above the forest floor where birds and small mammals eat them and distribute the indigestible seeds. In the three hundred different kinds of *Asparagus,* the leaves are reduced to mere scales with small green side-branches (phylloclads) in the axils. Some of the African species are appreciated for their beauty, and sold as florist's asparagus-fern *(A. plumosus)* or even as houseplants on the stems of which are a few hooked thorns, for which florists call them "smilax" *(A. asparagoides).* The young stems of the European *A. officinale,* cut a few days after they have grown above ground and before hard fibers have developed internally, provide a delicious vegetable when cooked, or green additions to a salad while raw. After the harvesting season closes in spring, the plants must be allowed to grow normally; they attain a height of five to six feet, producing small greenish bell-shaped flowers that are followed by red berries.

Each spring in the flower beds around our home,

Right above: Desert country in the American Southwest, Mexico and Central America supports an assortment of century plants (Agave *species), which terminate their lives when they produce a tall stem with clusters of flowers. (Vinton Richards) Right: Many species of* Yucca *in the American Southwest are called soapwoods or soap plants because the juice of the stem can be worked into a cleansing lather. (James R. Simon) Far right: This near-relative of the belladonna lily* (Amaryllis) *extends its flower stalks from the arid soil of the Peruvian desert, but produces no leaves except after the sporadic rains. (E. S. Ross)*

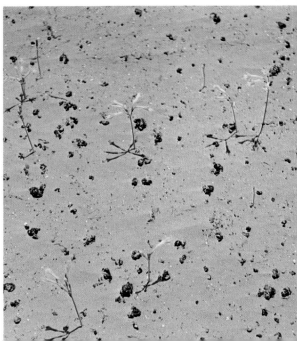

well loved. Tulips *(Tulipa gesneriana)* today are far more diverse and decorative than in the 16th century when they were first introduced from Turkey into the Low Countries of northern Europe. Probably they originated in central Russia and Armenia. Other members of the genus are native to southern Europe, northern Africa, and across Asiatic temperate countries as far as Japan. Some of them closely resemble the hardy, though delicate-appearing, mariposa-lilies *(Calochortus)* of the western United States; several have been adopted for garden cultivation and are known there as "globe-tulips," "butterfly-tulips," or "meadow-tulips." The Mormon pioneers in Utah relied for food upon the edible bulbs of one called the sego-lily *(C. nuttallii)*, found wild from the southern fringe of Canada's prairie provinces into the mountains of New Mexico and California.

Throughout the lily family, no other flower parts adhere to the ovary. But some plantsmen question whether a superior ovary is enough to earn a place in Liliaceae for several genera of plants with strong resemblances to members of kindred families. Except for their superior ovaries, it would be easy to classify in the daffodil family (Amaryllidaceae) the 325 different kinds of onions *(Allium)*, the African love-flowers (or blue-lilies-of-the-Nile, *Agapanthus)*, and the handsome brodiaeas *(Brodiaea)* of temperate South America and the western United States. Each of them produces a bulb, a group of narrow leaves almost like those of grasses, and an upright flower stalk at the top of which is a cluster of blossoms protected at the bud stage by from one to three, thin, leaflike bracts called spathes. Onions are all plants of the Northern Hemisphere, where they are famous for their characteristically pungent odor. Best known are the commercial onion *(A. cepa,* a native of Asia), the garlic *(A. sativum,* of southern Eurasia), the leek *(A. porrum,* of the Near East), and chives *(A. schoenoprasum,* of the Mediterranean countries, today found wild or escaped in Greece and Italy). Probably the Romans introduced the leek into Britain, where it was adopted by the Welsh as a national emblem to be worn in parades on St. David's day.

Far left: After the snow melts from the mountain passes and high valleys in the American West, glacier lilies (Erythronium grandiflorum) *produce leaves and flowers. (James R. Simon) Left: The Canada lily* (Lilium canadense) *flowers during June and July in meadows from eastern Canada to Georgia. (Lorus and Margery Milne)*

The red-and-green kangaroo-paw (Anigozanthos manglesii) *is native to West Australia. (Australian News and Information Bureau)*

Some of the coarsest plants in the lily family might also be placed in the Family Amaryllidaceae next to the century-plants if not for their superior ovaries. These include branching trees of arid regions, which are most unusual among monocots in being able to increase in girth through the activity of a special sheath of cells below the bark, which provides new bundles of conducting tissue and an abundance of pithlike spacing cells. The giants are the dragon-trees *(Dracaena)* of the Old World tropics, particularly a species *(D. draco)* in the Canary Islands. One of these, blown down by a hurricane in 1868, was found to be seventy feet tall and forty-five feet in girth at the base; its age was estimated at six thousand years, but no sure way is known to confirm this figure. From the surface of the leathery leaves of *D. draco,* and from cracks in its sturdy trunk, a dark-red resin ("dragon's blood") has long been harvested. During the 18th century, it was used as a varnish on the best Italian violins. More recently it served, along with a similar product from other kinds of dragon-tree, to protect the zinc plates from acid during the process of photo-engraving.

Visitors to the southwestern United States may see comparable vegetation in the Joshua trees *(Yucca brevifolia),* which sometimes attain a height of forty

feet and a radial spread of twenty. As in dragon-trees, a Joshua tree produces leaves and flowers only in crowded clusters at the ends of its stout branches. Formation of flowers, however, stops growth in that direction and seems to stimulate branching near by in the following year. Others among the thirty species of *Yucca,* all native to the southern parts of North America, are Adam's-needle *(Y. filamentosa)* of the Southeast and Spanish-bayonet *(Y. aloifolia)* of the Southwest, which Texans call "bear grass." All yuccas produce long tapering sharp-pointed leaves, waxy white flowers, and a sticky pollen which is carried from the stamens by an insect partner—the pronuba moth *(Pronuba yuccasella).* The female moth gathers pollen into a ball, carries it to another flower, and there presses it into the cup-shaped stigma of the pistil. Having instinctively insured pollination and fertilization of the many ovules, she lays an egg or two on the ovary. The caterpillars that hatch out devour a few of the developing seeds, but many others mature to reproduce the plant. Where yuccas have been introduced on the West Indian islands and in the Old World, they form no seeds without their partners.

Sunbirds pollinate the two hundred different kinds of *Aloe* found in Africa south of the great deserts. Most of them are native plants in South Africa, but a few grow on mountain slopes near the Equator. The pendant flowers in each cluster are firmly supported by branching stems upon which the birds stand while reaching up their long beaks to get nectar and insects that are deeper into the tubular blossoms than the pollen and stigmatic surfaces. Horticulturalists, who have adapted aloes to ornamental use in temperate gardens, succeeded in producing plants with colors of blossom other than the usual pinkish orange found so uniformly on arid highland of Africa, such as the Great Karoo. The sunbirds attend also the clustered pendant blossoms of the related red-hot-poker plants *(Kniphofia),* native to Madagascar, East Africa and South Africa. Florists generally refer to the decorative cultivated red-hot-pokers as Tritoma, perhaps because *K. tritoma* provided

Left above: Two members of the genus Lilium *are "Easter lilies," depending upon whether the holy day comes early or late in the season. The earlier is the Bermuda lily* (Lilium longiflorum). *(Grant Heilman) Left: Snowdrops* (Galanthus nivalis), *native to southern Europe and Asia Minor, are usually the first showy flowers of the year. (Roche)*

much of the ancestral stock for the many hybrids.

Only the high cost of hand labor in New Zealand prevents a greater use of the valuable hard fibers from leaves of New Zealand "hemp" (or New Zealand "flax," *Phormium tenax),* a plant that could be confused easily with an *Aloe,* a *Yucca,* or some of the century-plants. Its short thick underground stems (rhizomes) produce tufts of heavy leaves, each four to six feet long and two to three inches wide at the base. No other vegetation from the temperate zones yields such strong fibers for the manufacture of twine and rope. But to get the fibers, the mature leaves containing them must be cut individually by hand, the nonfibrous tissues removed by scraping and washing. Dried fibers are arranged in parallel strands, to be packed into bales and exported. Later in the year, flower-bearing stems grow from the tips of the rhizome branches, extending gradually through the tuft of remaining leaves to a height of five to fifteen feet. All parts of the plant above ground die and must be removed in plantations when the fruits are ripe, adding to the labor costs. Attempts to develop profitable fields of *Phormium* in temperate Latin America, where the plant is known as *formio,* have met with indifferent success because of competition from cheaper (though weaker) fibers grown in the tropics.

Bowstring "hemp" is obtained in a similar way, mostly by hand labor, from snake-plant (or mother-in-law's-tongue, *Sansevieria zeylanica* and related species native to Southeast Asia, Australasia, and Africa). The plant is grown extensively for its soft, silky fibers in Australia, South China, Java and India. Elsewhere the sansevierias are appreciated more as ornamentals that thrive without attention outdoors in warm countries and, despite adverse circumstances, in hotel lobbies and homes where the climate is colder. In some horticultural varieties the green leaves are marked crosswise above with darker green bands and have a yellow border. Occasionally a sansevieria produces a tall slender flowering stalk with pale fragrant blossoms on all sides. Seen against the sky it can call to mind the spires of *Yucca* flowers, which Indians of the American Southwest call "candles of God." At other times few people would suspect so close a relationship between the yuccas and the hedges of snake-plants they see growing in the Bahamas or along the French Riviera.

THE DAFFODIL FAMILY (Amaryllidaceae)

Sisal "hemp," for binder twine and other purposes, is but one of the many useful products obtained from various members of the century-plant genus *(Agave),* which has about three hundred species in arid parts of tropical and subtropical America. Half of these plants are native to the highlands of Mexico, where they appear to store reserves of food in their heavy leaves which radiate in all directions from the top of a short buried stem. On plantations where sisal *(A. sisalana),* henequen *(A. fourcroydes),* maguey (or American aloe, *A. americana),* or other commercial species are raised, it is standard practice to harvest the sword-shaped leaves at a rate that allows the total of full-sized ones never to exceed about eight. If ten or more attain their maximum of eight to ten feet in length, and one to two pounds in weight, the plant is likely to send up a sturdy flowering stalk and die. On the rockiest soil, if managed well, each plant may yield twelve to fifteen leaves a year starting at age four or five, and continue at this rate until it is about twenty years old. In Yucatan, sisal and henequen are expected to produce over a span of twenty-five years, in plantations of six hundred to 1200 plants to the acre. For most people, a plant that takes from six to fifteen years undisturbed to flower and die is so old that its date of germination has been forgotten; it is a "century-plant." The same common name is often given to members of the related genus *Furcraea* (or *Fourcroya)* from tropical America, one Brazilian species of which *(F. gigantea)* has been planted extensively on the island of Mauritius and is the source of "Mauritius hemp." Another *(F. macrophylla* from Colombia) yields fique fibers to be made into bags for coffee beans. Both *A. americana* and *F. gigantea* produce flower stalks as much as eighteen inches in diameter at the base, but only those of maguey are commonly cut before the flowers open. A bucket-shaped cavity can be hollowed in the base, and the sweet sap that collects there removed as the raw material for the fermented beer known as pulque or the distilled liquor tequila.

More widely familiar are the members of the amaryllis family that grow from bulbs or corms, producing strap-shaped leaves, and solitary flowers or whole clusters that add beauty to the indoor world of winter or to the garden in spring and early summer. For these artistic purposes the plants have been gathered from almost every continent. They show their ancestral relationships in the flowers by the inferior ovary, and the frequent development of a special cuplike corona from the perianth (forming the tubular part of a daffodil flower) and of a thin bract as a spathe from the stalk that bears the one or more blooms at the top.

The Australian grasstree (or blackboy, Xanthorrhoea *species) develops a foot-wide trunk topped by a shaggy mass of foliage and by flower stalks sometimes fifteen feet high. (W. Serventy)*

Daffodils *(Narcissus pseudonarcissus)* grow wild in much of southern Europe, a region that is the home for most of the forty species in this favorite genus of ornamental spring bulbs. Daffodil flowers are solitary, as are those of the hoop-petticoat *(N. bulbocodium* of Portugal and Spain) in which the corona is larger and more bell-shaped, and those of the pheasant's-eye (or poet's narcissus, *N. poeticus,* of Mediterranean Europe and Asia Minor) whose golden corona is very short—barely more than a thin circular rim around the stamens and pistil, at the base of the flaring six-parted white perianth. Fragrant "bunch

narcissuses" have small coronas too, but usually show a stiff thickening of the rim. The large bright yellow jonquils *(N. jonquilla)* from southern Europe and North Africa have this habit of producing many flowers atop each tall slender stalk, exposing them when the thin spathe there unfolds as though around a single bud. Similar clusters of smaller blooms, usually with a golden corona, appear on the flower stalks of the paper-white narcissus *(N. tazetta alba* from southern Europe), in which the perianth lobes are white, and of the Chinese sacred-lily (or joss-flower, *N. tazetta orientalis,* from across Asia to China and Japan), which has an all-yellow perianth.

The corona forms a showy flaring flimsy cup and bears the six stamens in the forty different kinds of spider-lily *(Hymenocallis)* of subtropical and tropical America. It is an inconspicuous bell in the handsome flowers of the Amazon-lily *(Eucharis grandiflora)* of Colombia and other members of the South American genus. But a corona scarcely can be found in the giant flowers clustered atop floral stems of the fine belladonna lily *(Amaryllis belladonna)* from South Africa's Cape Province, or in the pink-and-white atamasco-lily *(Zephyranthes atamasco)* of rich woodlands in the southeastern United States. Nor is a corona evident in the drooping white solitary flowers of snowdrops *(Galanthus),* of which Europe has provided several different kinds, each capable of rising through the snows of late winter and earliest spring as the first showy flower of the year.

When not in bloom, some members of the amaryllis family blend inconspicuously among the grasses which they resemble. This is true particularly of the one hundred different kinds of stargrasses *(Hypoxis)* native to the Southern Hemisphere, to Southeast Asia and North America. They grow from short buried rhizomes, usually with hairy grasslike leaves, but throughout the spring and early summer may produce slender hairy flower stalks as much as eight inches tall. Atop these a single bud or as many as

Right above: The dragon tree (Dracaena draco) *of Teneriffe, in the Canary Islands, is one of the world's plant curiosities—a branching, tree-sized lily. Resin from the trunk was used as varnish for great Italian violins. (Tropical Films) Right: The glory-lily* (Gloriosa superba), *native to tropical West Africa, climbs on tendrils from the narrow leaves. (E. S. Ross) Far right: Blackboys in eastern Australia are native grasstrees from which rise flower clusters an inch in diameter and four feet tall. (Lorus and Margery Milne)*

seven, each covered densely by soft hairs, may open its six golden lobes to a diameter of as much as an inch—like stars in the grass. A somewhat similar plant in western Australia, known as kangaroo-paws *(Anigozanthos manglesii),* has been chosen as the floral emblem of the state. Its hairy flower stalk is dark red and often three feet tall, bearing on one side near its tip a series of hairy flowers for which the plant is named. As each flower opens, its tubular perianth splits lengthwise below and spreads until the formerly outcurled blue-white tips are all turned up, like the toes of a kangaroo. Below each lobe hangs a golden anther from a stamen.

THE IRIS FAMILY *(Iridaceae)*

The three-part fleur-de-lis, which was used as a decorative design in the crown of Empress Theodora as long ago as A.D. 527, is now assumed to represent the flower of an iris—perhaps of the Florentine iris *(Iris florentia)* whose fragrant white blossom was chosen by Charles V during his reign as King of France (1364–1380) as the national emblem of that country. The dried rhizome of this plant has long been powdered and sold as "orris root," whose fragrance is an acceptable imitation of the floral odor of fresh violets. Others among the two hundred species of *Iris* are native over much of the North Temperate Zone, mostly as plants in wet soil such as marsh edges (both brackish and fresh) and meadow swales. Known in British areas as "flags," these are assumed to be the plants referred to in the King James translation of the biblical story of Exodus, as bordering the Nile River where the infant Moses was concealed in his floating cradle—an ark woven of bulrushes. Irises differ from most other members of the iris family in having three downturned perianth lobes (the "falls") and three upturned lobes (the "standards"), rather than all lobes closely similar. Like all 1500 species in the family, they possess just three stamens in each flower.

Regular flowers are the rule among the 250 different kinds of *Gladiolus* native to the Old World from southern Europe to South Africa, the three fragrant species of *Freesia* from South Africa, the spring

The many varieties of crocuses pushing through the snow in early spring belong to the genus Crocus *native to Mediterranean countries and eastward to Crimea. (Yellow: Grant Heilman; white: Rene Pierre Bille)*

crocuses *(Crocus)* of Mediterranean countries, the dozen types of tiger-flower *(Tigridia)* from Latin America, and the beautiful little blue-eyed-grasses *(Sisyrinchium),* some seventy-five different kinds of which can be found between Canada and Patagonia. Some of the horticultural varieties of *Gladiolus* show a handsome bilateral symmetry, as do most of the cultivated hybrids known as "montbretias," derived from species of *Tritonia* native to South Africa. Crocuses *(Crocus vernus)* open their surprisingly large yellow, white or purple flowers close to the ground in the very beginning of the growing season, when almost any sign of spring is welcomed enthusiastically by people and thirsty honeybees. From the pistils of the autumn-blooming yellow crocus *(C. sativus)* of Asia Minor a yellow dye can be prepared. Known as saffron, it was a royal color in early Greek times. Mixed with perfumes, it gave color and fragrance to the floors of public buildings and the water of Roman baths. History records that the streets of Rome were sprinkled with saffron when Nero made his entry into the city. During the Middle Ages, it seems to have disappeared from use in Europe until reintroduced by returning crusaders. Today it may be met in Spanish and Iranian areas giving color to cooked rice.

THE YAM FAMILY *(Dioscoreaceae)*

All but about fifty of the 650 species in this little family are yams *(Dioscorea),* with starchy rhizomes or tubers weighing as much as one hundred pounds and annual twining stems that bear heart-shaped or fiddle-shaped leaves in which the veins form a network unusual among monocots. Although most of these different kinds of yams come from tropical America, the species that are cultivated for food are native to the Old World. One of the best *(D. esculenta)* is grown by the women in shady swamps and marshy patches on the South Sea islands, in Southeast Asia, and on the subcontinent of India. The Chinese yam *(D. batatas),* which is appreciated for food in the Orient, has been introduced into America and escaped from cultivation, but is grown mostly as an ornamental; its stem of the year may reach a length of thirty feet, and its perennial tubers a length of two feet. The white yam *(D. alata),* a native to the South Sea islands and India, is often raised in the southeastern United States for feeding livestock. A Hawaiian species *(D. bulbifera),* called the "air potato" because it produces large, edible, aerial tubers, can be raised in southernmost Florida and the Gulf of Mexico where frost is rare. All of these yams form small greenish, bell-shaped flowers with three or six stamens or an inferior three-winged pistil (or both), ripening into membranous capsules. True yams, unlike the softer types of sweet potato which are often called yams in the United States, contain steroids from which cortisone and sex hormones can be manufactured. The same constituents have been found in the bizarre South African plant known as elephant's-foot (or Hottentot bread, *Testudinaria elephantipes),* of which the enormous starchy rhizome protrudes from the desert soil, protected from desiccation by hexagonal corky plates, extending annually (or after a rainy period) vinelike stems with leaves and flowers.

THE RUSHES (Family Juncaceae)

When we try to find a short cut across a wet meadow or the corner of a marsh, and attempt to keep our feet dry by stepping from one tussock of vegetation to the next, we generally rely on hummocks produced by rushes *(Juncus),* of which about 225 different kinds grow in such places, in ditches, and along paths, with representatives on all continents. Many attain a height of four feet from a short creeping rhizome and spreading fibrous roots. On the upright stems, small scales represent the leaves. Near the top, clusters of small flowers develop, each with an inconspicuous six-parted perianth, three or six stamens, and a pistil with a superior ovary that matures into a three-valved capsule. These floral features distinguish the rushes easily from the sedges, grasses, reeds, cattails, and bulrushes among which they commonly grow.

The tussocks of rushes provide hiding places and nesting sites for many kinds of waterfowl. Small birds and mammals of the marshlands eat the hard, seedlike fruits. Muskrats and moose feed on the coarser roots and rhizomes. Even the trails the animals make often remain evident for years because the low-growing path rushes continue to thrive where other vegetation was trampled time after time. People, too, have found uses for rushes. "Matting" in Japan and other parts of the Orient is often made from the upright stems of rushes, woven into floor coverings and room dividers. Basketwork and even chair seats may be constructed from the hard stems. In other regions, people dry short lengths of stem, peel away the outer tissues, and let the central pith serve as a wick in open oil lamps and in tallow candles. The fuel rises by capillarity so rapidly

through the air spaces within the pith that "rush lights" are often burned to give cheap and fairly strong illumination at outdoor gatherings after dark.

CHAPTER 29

Plants That Attract Waterfowl

CUES: *If a monocot plant produces thick horizontal stems (rhizomes) in the muddy bottom of a swamp or estuary, or even fibrous roots there, and bears flowers in which the carpels are separate and the perianth parts resemble sepals or petals, it is probably a member of the Order Helobiales. It may be an eelgrass, an arrowhead, a water-celery, or waterweed.*

Ducks and geese get so much of their nourishment from the foliage, the buried rhizomes and the fruits of these plants that the vegetation and waterfowl seem to go together. Certainly the birds settle and feed wherever the plants are numerous. Probably the waterfowl transport the seeds, either in mud sticking to their feet or by failing to digest all that they swallow. Some of the plants produce a fleshy covering over an indigestible stony layer that protects the seed, like a diminutive plum. Others yield only hard little nutlets (achenes) in abundance, one or more from each flower.

Although this is one of the small orders of plants, with less than four hundred species, its members contribute so much to the welfare of waterfowl and marine turtles that naturalists everywhere come to appreciate it.

EELGRASS AND ITS KIN (Family Zosteraceae)

When Julius Caesar took his cavalry as well as his army into North Africa in 46 B.C., he was faced with

Bear grass, a member of the lily family, appears progressively farther up the mountain slopes in Glacier National Park, Montana, and other parts of the American Northwest as spring advances. (Josef Muench)

the problem of finding food for the horses. History records that he had his men gather from the shallow water along the Mediterranean shores large quantities of a grasslike plant and wash it in fresh water for the animals to eat. It was eelgrass (or grass-wrack, *Zostera,* probably *Z. marina),* which still grows there. It is found also in estuaries and lagoons of both the Northern and Southern Hemispheres where it is protected from the violent waves of storms and where the salinity is less than that of open ocean. Its narrow green leaves often attain a length of three feet, immersed completely by every high tide but yielding to each movement of the water, remaining attached securely to the creeping rhizome in the mud. Eelgrass appears to reproduce exclusively by vegetative means if the salinity is more than half that of the open sea. Farther up the estuaries, strange flowers appear on it in season. They lack a perianth, and are crowded in two rows along the midrib on one side of a narrow leaflike support (spadix) which is almost hidden within the sheathlike base of a leaf (spathe). Staminate flowers have a single large stamen, from which threadlike pollen is extruded. It is caught by two bristle-like stigmas projecting from the pistillate flowers. Later the barrel-shaped fruits mature, each as much as a quarter inch in length, to be distributed by the flow and ebb of tides.

Until the late 1930's, no one realized how lucky Caesar had been to find eelgrass so abundant. Now it is known to vary spectacularly in abundance. About thrice each century it dies off abruptly, suddenly susceptible to a parasitic slime mold *(Labyrinthula)* that earlier had caused only a chronic, low-grade infection. These facts were discovered as a result of a die-off in the early 1930's along the Atlantic coast of North America, largely because New Englanders began missing their favorite waterfowl for dinner—the little goose known as the American brant. The numbers of this bird had decreased to a small fraction of that in former years when eelgrass was plentiful, because eelgrass provides eighty per cent of a brant's diet. Shellfishermen too complained that their business was ruined. No longer could clams and oysters filter from the shallow coastal water the abundant microscopic plants

The giant arrowhead (Sagittaria latifolia) *varies in the shape of its leaves, partly according to the depth of water in which it grows. The stems provided a starchy food for American Indians. (E. Javorsky)*

as food, for these now had few eelgrass leaves on which to spread and reproduce as a thin film in the light. Eventually the cause of the change, which took place all over the world in less than a decade, was traced to a series of dry years. With less rain on land, less water in the rivers, less dilution of the sea that washed into the estuaries, the eelgrass showed less resistance to the parasitic slime mold.

Nearer the Equator, sea turtles and sea cows (manatees) hunt out related plants in coastal salt water and brackish estuaries. Botanists who named these salt-tolerant kinds of immersed flowering plants have dipped into Greek mythology for *Posidonia* (from Poseidon, the sea god) and *Cymodocea* (from Cymodoce, a sea nymph). One of the two kinds of *Posidonia* grows around Australian coasts, and the other near the straits of Gibraltar, both on the Atlantic coast and the Mediterranean coast. Manatee-grass *(C. manatorum)* is common along the north coast of South America and around the Gulf of Mexico to southern Florida, matching fairly well the distribution of sea cows.

Pondweeds *(Potamogeton),* found only in fresh water, greatly outnumber the species that tolerate salt around them. Some pondweeds extend oval leaves on long petioles, letting them float in the surface film. Others hold their foliage completely immersed. Most valuable of them for waterfowl is the widespread sago pondweed *(P. pectinatus),* whose repeatedly branching stems are almost threadlike and bear leaves so narrow as to suggest mere bristles. Its fruits mature at the time of autumn migration, and provide more food for ducks than most other kinds of vegetation at that time. The achenes are commonly still held into air on the stalks that raise the inconspicuous spikes of flowers where wind could distribute their pollen. Each of the compact spikes consists of many tiny flowers, but only the staminate ones suggest blossoms. Each of them displays four thin sepal-like parts, spreading symmetrically from the four anthers of the short stamens; this imitation perianth is comparable to the anther lobes of a ditch-weed. The pistillate flowers of pondweeds lack even this ornamentation, bearing four separate carpels, each with a tiny beak to represent the pollen-catching stigma.

THE ARROWHEAD FAMILY *(Alismataceae)*

Few plants suggest their names so strongly as do the arrowheads *(Sagittaria),* which grow along the edge of a marsh in wet mud. Each leaf on a tall slender

petiole is shaped strongly like an arrow point. But farther out into the water the same plants may produce lance-shaped leaves or narrow, almost grass-like blades identical in shape with those they spread in the water itself. Once aware of the relation between depth of water and form of leaf, a naturalist can look out from shore at the arrowheads and guess fairly well how gradual or steep is the slope of the muddy bottom. Arrowheads produce separate stems with whorls of flowers, each blossom with three white petals and three green sepals around more than six stamens and / or more than six separate carpels. Waterfowl eat the rhizomes of many different species of arrowhead, giving rise to the alternative names of duck potato and swamp potato. In North America, where the Indians used to dig arrowhead rhizomes for food, an introduced species from Eurasia, *S. sagittifolia,* is now cultivated locally in the San Joaquin and Sacramento valleys of California by the Chinese who raise market vegetables there. Only its modern name is new there—tule potato —for the arrowhead grows in the irrigated fields to a height of three to four feet, just as it does around marsh edges from Japan to Ireland. Nor is this the largest species that seems likely to escape from cultivation and become naturalized. The coarsest of all, *S. montividensis,* was introduced as an ornamental in California from England, to which its seeds had been taken from Argentina; it is native to South America on both sides of the Andes as far north as Brazil and Peru, where its leaves attain a height of six feet and its purple-marked white flowers a diameter of three inches.

Far less conspicuous are the half dozen different kinds of waterplantain *(Alisma),* the largest of which produce oval, pointed leaves in a rosette as much as two feet across. In both the Eurasian waterplantain *(A. plantago-aquatica)* and the most widespread North American kind *(A. triviale,* often called mud-plantain), the flowering stalk rises nearly twenty inches high before branching in successive whorls of small branchlets, which again branch in the same way before ending in small perfect flowers with three

Left above: Perennial arrowgrass (Triglochin *species) of the rush family grows to eighteen inches high in marshes of all continents, endangering cattle and sheep with its cyanides. (U.S.D.A) Left: Eelgrass* (Zostera marina) *at low tide at Tomales Bay, California, indicates that the water is neither entirely saline nor fresh. (M. Woodbridge Williams)*

one-quarter-inch white (or rose-colored) petals and three sepals of the same length.

THE FROG'S-BIT FAMILY (Hydrocharitaceae)

Plants of this family have become popular all over the world among hobbyists who raise fish in aquaria. The plants provide shelter for small fishes, add oxygen to the water, and decorate the tank with a semblance of the natural conditions in a pond. Few of these features might be predicted from knowing why botanists group together the various genera and species: the flowers have their perianth parts arising from the sides of the pistil (making the ovary inferior) and, although pollination occurs in air, the leathery or berry-like fruits mature under water.

Frog's bit (Hydrocharis from Eurasia and Limnobium from America) generally floats on the water surface, extending circular leaves or proliferating by runners at the tips of which new rosettes of foliage develop. On the water surface, too, the flowers expand inconspicuously. The staminate type appear in threes on long stalks from a single spathelike leaf, whereas the pistillates are solitary on a short stalk from a two-leaf spathe. As they ripen, the fruits sag into the water and there become many-seeded leathery berries. They may be bite-size for a frog, but too poor an imitation of an insect to appeal to an adult amphibian.

Water-soldier (Stratiotes aloides) of Europe spreads similar rosettes of bayonet-shaped leaves rather stiffly just below the surface of the pond or ditch water where the plant drifts freely until midsummer. Then many of the leaves break into air and new ones are added around a short flower stalk. If the water is deep enough while the fruits are ripening, the whole plant sinks down to the bottom and remains there until spring when the seeds are released. Generally this saves the water-soldier from being frozen in the ice that roofs the pond in winter.

Tapegrass (or water-celery, Vallisneria) grows rooted to the bottom in little tufts of leaves which, in ponds and streams to six feet deep, may be three feet long and an inch broad at the base. Tapegrass leaves can be distinguished easily from those of true grasses by a faint network of branching veins rather than parallel unbranched veins running from base to tip. Tapegrass flowers prove to be solitary pistillate ones if they are exposed by a three-part spathe that opens at the end of a long slender stalk reaching to the water surface. The staminate flowers are in compact clusters, on short stalks close to the roots, but break off while still in the bud stage and float to the surface where they open. Once pollinated the pistillate flowers are pulled below the water film again by a spiral curling of the stalk; usually the fruits mature long before winter ice coats the water. Ducks in migration tip to reach the fruits, the winter buds, and underwater portions of the rhizomes. Fishes and muskrats seek these edible portions too. No other aquatic plant seems to provide such a wealth of food for the larger water creatures, or to grow so reliably both in places fed by springs of crystal purity and in gutters through coastal marshes where the salinity rises often to a quarter of that in the open ocean. Fortunately, tapegrass is common in European waters and in the eastern and southern parts of North America where waterfowl gather for nesting and wintering. Farther south, and in the full salinity of coastal lagoons around islands of the South Pacific, a related plant known as turtle-grass (Thalassia testudinum) is often the only flowering plant to be found among the seaweeds growing close to shore.

Ducks also feed readily on the soft leafy stems and, when available, the small oblong fruits of waterweed (or water-thyme, or ditch-moss, Elodea), of which eight different kinds are native to the New World. These plants grow submerged, rooting when they touch a muddy bottom, with clear-green flaccid leaves in whorls of three or four. The whorls arise at moderate intervals in deeper water and on older stems, more crowded together where the light is intense, and on new growth. Each leaf has a midrib but no obvious veins, and is mostly only two cells thick. They tolerate partial shade and also occasional exposure to brackish water.

Waterweeds thrive in aquaria, making them popular with fish culturists. But if the hobbyist discards living plants of surplus Elodea into the nearest ditch—or even into the community sewer—the waterweed may soon begin to choke a whole waterway. One species (E. canadensis) that is common in quiet streams and ponds all across Canada and south to North Carolina, Utah, and California, was introduced accidentally into Ireland about 1836 and soon became a pest. More recently it appeared on the European continent and in England, once reaching such abundance in the Cam River at Cambridge that the annual punting races had to be postponed until the foreign vegetation was cleared away.

So far, only pistillate representatives of E. canadensis have escaped in Europe, and only staminate plants of the coarse South American E. densa have yet arrived in eastern North America. No fruits are

formed, but vegetative reproduction has sufficed. In aquaria, the staminate flowers of *E. densa* rise above the water into air and open from a membranous spathe in small but handsome clusters. Each flower spreads widely with three green sepals, three broad white petals half an inch in length, and as many as nine stamens united by their filaments into a short tube.

Sexual reproduction does occur in still another species, *E. nuttallii,* found where it is native in the northern and eastern United States and adjacent Canada. Ducks enjoy its fruits, which develop even where the plants are growing in tidal estuaries with moderate salinity. Its flowers are inconspicuous, however, the pistillate ones small and floating in the surface film but still attached by a slender stalk. The staminate flowers often lack petals altogether; they break free while still in the bud stage, and rise to the surface before opening. Small insects still find them and attend to pollination.

CHAPTER 30

The Cattails, Burreeds and Screwpines

CUES: *If a monocot plant produces flowers in which the perianth is no more than a few scales or bristles, and the carpels (numbering one or more) are separate and borne by no true spadix, it is almost sure to be a member of the Order Pandanales. It*

Left above: The screwpine (Pandanus utilis) *of the East Indies and Australian coasts takes its name from the spiral arrangement of its leaves. (D. T. Smithers: National Audubon) Left: Cattails* (Typha *species) produce two types of flowers. The staminate ones near the tip of the stalk drop off, while the lower pistillate ones produce fruits. (Wilhelm Schacht)*

may be a cattail or a burreed in a marsh, or a woody screwpine along a tropical or subtropical coast.

Before botanists became convinced that the plants in this Order show simplification through loss rather than as representatives of a primitive style of growth, they regarded the Pandanales as the simplest of monocots. Now it is generally believed that the 432 different species are the survivors of an ancestral line that branched off from the lily stock and progressively lost the showy parts of the flower while depending ever less upon insects for pollination.

THE CATTAIL FAMILY (Typhaceae)

Over most of the world, the conspicuously tall grasslike vegetation of marshes and shallow lakes proves to consist of cattails (or reed-mace, *Typha*), of which only a dozen species are known. The "common cattail" (*T. latifolia*) is found native across Eurasia, in North Africa, and in North America from Alaska to Newfoundland, south into Mexico. From a heavy rhizome in the mud, erect stems rise jointless into air, bearing pale green (or gray-green) leaves less than an inch broad yet sometimes reaching ten feet high. The stem continues to extend and develops at its tip a cylindrical compact cluster of flowers, the staminate beyond the pistillate ones. The individual flowers are so crowded together that it is difficult to see which two to five stamens belong to one blossom, or that the carpels concealed among fine brown radiating hairs are separate—one to each pistillate flower. Wind attends to pollination, and the staminate flowers usually drop off, leaving only the stalk on which they grew as a spiky extension beyond the thickening cylindrical cluster of ripening nutlets (achenes). At first, these form a handsome spike as much as eight inches long and one inch in diameter, smooth and velvety to the touch. But as the fruits ripen and the winter storms tear at the spike, it begins to break up. By early spring the individual nutlets have been carried off by the wind, each pulled along by some of the hairs still attached to its base.

Few animals seem to depend upon cattail fruits as food, and fewer still get nourishment from the fibrous foliage or the massive rhizomes in the soggy mud. Sometimes the carp and muskrats work together, the fish exposing the rhizomes by sucking away the overlying sediments and the muskrats chewing on the plant parts thus exposed. More often, cattail leaves provide merely a shelter for animals that choose to live in a marsh, despite the scarcity of food there. Muskrats nip off the long leaves and build houses with them. Redwing blackbirds and marsh wrens find concealment for their nests. From these sanctuaries the animals can radiate when hungry, for it is seldom far to more productive land or water beyond the dense stands of cattails.

THE BURREEDS (Family Sparganiaceae)

In cool and temperate marshes and shallow lakes, the vegetation of the Northern Hemisphere and of Australasia often seems more open because it is almost a solid stand of burreeds (*Sparganium*). From a creeping rhizome in the mud, these plants rise as hard, branching stems bearing narrow grasslike leaves and globular clusters of flowers in which the staminate ones occupy the uppermost part of each cluster. Each staminate flower includes a bristly perianth and from three to six stamens; after pollination it shrivels and provides more space in the cluster for the expanding seeds which develop one to a pistillate flower, protected by a bony shell. All of the twenty different kinds of burreed provide shelter for waterfowl and muskrats. They feed on its fruits and on young rhizomes that they can reach in the muddy bottom. Deer eat the exposed parts of the plants, and moose often pull up the buried portions as well. Yet the burreeds generally reproduce fast enough to compensate for all of these attacks, and serve importantly in anchoring the soil on flood plains of rivers and wave-beaten shores of shallow lakes.

THE SCREWPINES (Family Pandanaceae)

At Brighton and Plymouth and Penzance, all along the south coast of England to Land's End, some of the "palms" that lend a tropical charm to the shore resorts are actually palms. The others are screwpines (*Pandanus*), which are far more woody and unlike palms in branching repeatedly before spreading four-ranked clusters of tough fibrous leaves from the many tips. Each leaf clasps the stem at its base, then tapers gradually to a point, with a strong keel below matched by a groove above, making it an open V in cross section. Leaf scars provide a close series of rounded ridges encircling each bare stem and trunk. Often a large number of strong prop roots come out a few feet above the ground and form a sort of skirt around the base of the tree, sometimes replacing the trunk entirely and seeming to raise the plant on sturdy stilts.

We found screwpines growing as far north as Inverewe Gardens near Poolewe on the Irish Sea, where the Scottish Highlands are tempered by the warm waters of the Gulf Stream. At the latitude of central Labrador and the Aleutian Islands—farther north from the Equator than the tip of Tierra del Fuego is south of it—this seemed a long way from the tropical and subtropical homelands of screwpines, which are native to the Old World from Africa through Indonesia to Australia. Each tree is either staminate or pistillate, but in each case the flowers are densely clustered. The fruits suggest a pendant pineapple, and are similarly the composite product of many flowers each of which contributes one fleshy part with a central armored seed. At least one kind, from the Nicobar-breadfruit *(P. leram)* of the Andaman Islands in the Bay of Bengal, is edible, providing a starchy food that is enjoyed locally. On the remote island of Mauritius, another species (called vacoas, *P. utilis)* provides fiber from the leaves, used in making bags. Most commonly grown in greenhouses, and outdoors as an ornamental where the winter weather is mild, is a species from Polynesia *(P. veitchii)* in which the prop roots and branching stems are particularly well developed, attracting attention from many people who might not otherwise notice the stranger from the tropics.

CHAPTER 31

The Graceful Palms

CUES: *If the monocot plant is a woody vine or a tree with large leaves that are palmately notched or pinnately compound, each with a petiole broadly clasping the stem, and if the flowers appear in clusters from one side of a large spathelike bract, it is certain to be a member of the Order Palmales. It may clamber over other vegetation, as do the rattan palms, or be a graceful tree 150 feet tall with a crown of giant leaves at the top, as in the royal palms and date palms.*

All of the more than 1500 different species in the Order Palmales have a place in the one family Palmaceae (or Arecaceae). The great Swedish botanist Carl von Linné referred to palms as *Principes*— "Princes of the Plant World." No other family of monocots includes so many handsome kinds of trees. Yet the tree trunk in each instance arises in the normal monocot way, entirely from primary tissues produced by the terminal bud. The secret of such a heavy trunk is in the giant bud. For several years, each seedling expands its root system and spreads ever-larger leaves from ground level while the bud of the stem is attaining its full size. Thereafter the central column rises gradually, its bud at the top, hidden deeply among the bases of leaves in the crown of the tree.

With rare exceptions, palms have no way to add conducting tubes within the unbranched trunk, and they continue for life with approximately the same number of leaves ("fronds") by using the same tubes for new leaves as old ones are discarded. In the bud stage, each leaf is tightly pleated. Those of "feather palms" expand into a series of separate, usually reedlike leaflets from the two sides of a sturdy midrib—a continuation of the strong petiole. In "fishtail palms," the leaflets are fanshaped or even divided still more. Among "fan palms," the single blade displays a handsome pattern of radiating veins, which diverge from the end of the petiole in two levels that match the former pleating. From vein to vein the green tissue of the leaf blade rises and falls alternately until, toward the margin, it flattens out and may be deeply dissected between veins.

The date palm *(Phoenix dactylifera)* is a feather palm. It has been cultivated in western Asia and North Africa for at least five thousand years, and is no longer known in the wild condition. In irrigated orchards and isolated oases around natural wells in the desert, date palms rise majestically to a height of as much as one hundred feet, each tree capable of yielding one hundred pounds of dates annually for fully a century. Since each ripe date weighs less than half an ounce, this means at least 3500 of the fruits maturing to a length of about an inch, suspended in several profusely branched clusters in the shade of the spreading leaves. Productive orchards are tended today all the way from the Canary Islands

The California fan palm (Washingtonia filifera) *conceals its slender trunk amid the pendant fronds that have died. (Hubert A. Lowman)*

to Pakistan and India, with about eighty per cent of the world crop coming from Iraq. Date palms were planted in Latin America during the 18th century by Spanish missionaries, and descendants of some of these trees are still to be found beside missions in Mexico. But in the New World, commercial date orchards are maintained only in California and southern Arizona, where irrigation water can be provided and the air is sufficiently dry and hot.

No other fruit tree produces so generously with so little water. The gain from a given amount of irrigation can be increased still more if the natural pollination by wind from staminate to pistillate trees is replaced by hand labor. All but a few of the trees in an orchard can then be fruit-bearing pistillate ones. Each staminate tree provides an abundance of pollen, which can be shaken over the pistillate flowers while fresh or even saved for a year or more in a bag to be used as needed. By the time each fruit is ripe, its firm sticky pulp around the slender stony seed may be more than fifty per cent sugar (sucrose). Dried still more in the hot sun, the fruit is effectively preserved from attack by molds and becomes a convenient form of nourishment for man and domestic animals, as well as the principal export from the casual agriculture of arid lands between fifteen and thirty degrees north latitude. The Arabs and many of their neighbors with a different ancestry have learned to fortify the negligible proteins and fats of date fruits with cheeses and other products from milk of camels, goats, donkeys, and horses. The dishes prepared according to local custom may not be palatable to people from distant parts of the world, but they do provide a reasonable balance of nutrients, satisfying the needs of human inhabitants along the fringe of the great deserts.

Date palms whose fruit is of inferior quality and others among the dozen kinds of *Phoenix* from North Africa and tropical Asia are often tapped for the

Far left above: The nikau palm (Rhopalostylis sapida) *is the only member of this distinguished plant family native to New Zealand. Left above: Cubans call this native tree a petticoat palm* (Copernicia torreana) *from the way its dead leaves remain around its base. (Both by Lorus and Margery Milne) Left: The valuable date palm* (Phoenix dactylifera), *characteristic of oases in North Africa and the Near East, is a feather palm yielding thatching materials as well as a fruit and raw materials from which sugar, wine, mats and hats are made. (Bill Stackhouse)*

sweet sap that is on its way into flower clusters. As soon as the cluster expands, it is cut off and a suitable container hung under the tip of the severed stalk. As much as a gallon of liquid can be collected daily over a period of weeks or even months, commonly as much as fourteen per cent sugar. With dried palm leaves as fuel, the sap is boiled down to crystallize the sugar. The residual molasses can be fermented to become palm wine, or be distilled after fermentation to obtain alcohol, or be allowed to progress to the stage of palm vinegar. In India and the eastern tropics of the Old World, an estimated 100,000 tons of palm sugar, known as jaggery, are produced and consumed locally each year, often by barter. If intensive cultivation of palms for sugar were attempted, it would probably be possible in a few years to produce from these trees more sugar than from all the cane and sugar beets now raised.

Sugar and wine are made also from the sap of several unrelated palms. Those most famous for these products in the Indomalayan area include the stemless nipa palm *(Nipa fruticans),* a feather palm that thrives along tidal streams of the East Indies and Philippines, and the taller gomuti palm *(Arenga saccharifera)* with similar fronds on drier land. The fishtail palms *(Cyarota)* of the same region are equally productive, particularly one called the toddy palm (or jaggery tree, *C. urens*). From the nipa and fishtail palms the native people gather an edible starchy pith, and also valuable fibers known as kittul, used for making special brushes with which to raise the pile on velvet and other fabrics. The popularity of palm wine has led botanists to give the species name *vinifera* ("wine-bearing") to some fan palms too: the wine palm of West Africa *(Raphia vinifera),* and the Chilean wine palm *(Mauritia vinifera).* The former is among twenty-two species of a genus represented both in West Africa and South America, all of them yielding also strong fibers that can be removed from their petioles: piassava from the African wine palm and raffia from *R. ruffia* of Madagascar. Similar fibers, called buriti or muriti, come from the petioles of the stately Chilean wine palms which, along with fifteen other species of *Mauritia,* form magnificent groves on the savannas of Brazil. Nor will an old Hindu song let any hearer forget that sugar and wine are among the 801 valuable products from the palmyra palm *(Borassus flabelliformis),* a fan palm whose name seems to have no relation to the village of Palmyra on the northern edge of the Syrian Desert; instead, this is a "palmy" palm—perhaps a "palm of palms."

Granular starch from the pith of palms is sago, used to make puddings in most parts of the world, and when ground into sago flour, also to stiffen textiles by "starching" them. Most of the sago in international commerce comes from the feather palms of genus *Metroxylon,* native to India and Malaysia, in which the fruit is strangely covered by overlapping scales remaining after other parts of the flower have dropped off. The name sago is given also to the dry granular starch from the gomuti, palmyra, and toddy palms of India, from the flour palm *(Phoenix farinifera)* of Malacca, and in the West Indies, even from the feathery cabbage palm *(Roystonea oleracea),* which is often the commonest native palm all the way up the island chain from the Guianas of South America to Florida. The starch is stored mostly in pith cells of the mature trunk. The name "cabbage" refers to a much more wasteful use of this and other palms: by cutting down a whole tree and peeling away the bases of all the open leaves in its crown, the crisp delicious tissues of the terminal bud can be reached as the ingredients for "millionaire's salad" or cooked "hearts of cabbage palm." Raw they remind us of the sweetest celery; cooked, they suggest cabbage in appearance but not in delectable flavor. But we feel guilty whenever we meet these delicacies on the table, for the total amount of "cabbage" in a palm bud is scarcely more than the ten pounds or so that a fully expanded leaf will weigh. To kill a tree for so little hurts our consciences.

Unlike the cabbage palm, the old dead leaves of which merely droop in a shaggy mass around the trunk, the roystoneas known as royal palms shed their fronds cleanly. They tower toward the sky for 100 to 125 feet, as slate-gray columns crowned by a giant rosette of feathery fifteen-foot leaves. Unlike the trunks of dicot trees, these show no gradual taper, decreasing in diameter toward the top. Instead, the column of a royal palm usually varies considerably, now thicker, now more slender, recording how much the terminal bud was swollen with rain from wet years and dry as each level of the trunk was produced.

Cuba has chosen one royal palm *(R. regia)* as its national tree. A closely related one *(R. elata)* is native to southernmost Florida, where it was once widespread over the Keys and westward to Cape Sable. For a while the continued existence of this handsome palm was threatened by people who felled the trees for "cabbage" and timber, or who dug up the palms to transplant them for landscape purposes,

or who set grass fires that were disastrous. Now a delightful grove has been preserved near the headquarters of the Everglades National Park. And nurserymen have discovered that seedlings grow rapidly, with a ready market. Until the trees are fifteen to twenty years old, however, and have raised their terminal buds well above the ground, they are vulnerable to the frosty weather that occasionally reaches as far south as Miami. No beauty is left in an avenue of royal palms that have died of the cold, but a corridor lined on both sides by living trees is a joy to see.

Feather palms with smooth, slender gray trunks in Indomalaysia and on islands of the South Pacific usually prove to be members of *Areca,* and commonly are betelnut palms *(A. catechu),* which are cultivated for their seeds. Perhaps 300 million people in the Old World enjoy chewing betelnut, and prepare it or buy it already dried. The egg-sized fruits of the palm are harvested just before they ripen. The fibrous husk is torn off, exposing a mottled seed, which is boiled, sliced, and dried in the sun. For chewing, a small piece of the dark brown material is wrapped in a leaf of the betel pepper *(Piper betle),* along with a pellet of lime and perhaps a bit of an aromatic spice, such as cardamon or turmeric. The mixture stimulates the flow of saliva and colors the liquid a brick-red, often temporarily staining the tongue, teeth, gums and lips an orange-brown. Betelnut chewers spit out the excess saliva, and seem to gain mild stimulation from the chewing. The small amounts swallowed may aid in digestion, and possibly give some protection against parasitic worms. The chief alkaloid of betelnuts (arecoline) has found some use as a vermifuge in veterinary medicine.

In West Africa, somewhat shorter and more sturdy feather palms are known as oil palms *(Elaeis guineensis),* found native within three hundred miles of the South Atlantic Ocean from Gambia to Portuguese West Africa. Mature trees bear several clusters of fruits each year, averaging about four thousand fruits weighing together perhaps sixty pounds. Each fruit is a fibrous, plumlike object between one and two inches long and as much as an inch in diameter, its flesh between thirty and seventy per cent an extractable palm-pulp oil, and its seeds yielding approximately fifty per cent of a different palm-kernel oil. The pulp oil more closely resembles olive oil, and has found use in such diverse operations as the manufacture of tin plate, of cosmetics and dentifrices, of margarines and salad dressings, of fuels

The juice from seeds of the assai palms (Euterpe oleracea) *of Brazil is often thickened with cassava starch to make a creamy drink. (E. Aubert de La Rue)*

Coconuts have floated ashore and seeded themselves on so many tropical islands that no one is sure where this feather palm originated. (Anna Riwkin)

and lubricants. Palm-kernel oil finds its greatest market in the soap industry, with glycerine an important byproduct. In Indomalaysia and some parts of Latin America, where oil palm plantations have been developed, horticultural strains of the palm in which the oily pulp is particularly thick and the seeds very small are favored because a better price can be had for pulp oil than kernel oil.

So far, no oil palms have competed seriously with coconut palms for the market in vegetable oils. Coconuts *(Cocos nucifera)* are among man's oldest crops, and today provide about a fifth of all the oils and fats in international trade. More than a thousand other uses have been catalogued for various parts of the tree, making it more of a "tropical jewel" than any other plant. Yet the trees themselves have a particularly unkempt, wind-torn appearance. Generally they lean at an angle, then curve upward and taper slowly to a crown of leaves perhaps one hundred feet above the ground. Each of the ten to fifteen feathery fronds may be twenty feet long. As each one ages, dies, and crashes to the ground, it leaves another corrugation partly encircling the

rough trunk; and a new leaf, pointing skyward like a spear, unfolds to take its place.

Partly because coconut fruits are known to float long distances on water and then germinate where storms throw them high on an ocean beach, and partly because tropical people have adopted the tree as the source of so much good in their lives, it is impossible today to learn where coconut palms originated. Sir Francis Drake encountered coconuts in the Cape Verde Islands surrounded by the Atlantic Ocean off the bulge of Africa, during his visit there in 1577. He noted in his logbook that within the shell of the seed was "a kinde of substance very white, no less goode and sweete than almonds." Captain James Cook, with the help of two able naturalists (Joseph Banks and Daniel Solander) on his voyage around the world in 1768–1771, reported coconut trees growing on most of the islands he visited in the South Pacific. The coconuts may have preceded him from South America, where all other members of the genus *Cocos* are native, floating and drifting to remote bits of land (such as Tahiti) as did the experimental raft *Kon-Tiki* in 1947. Coconuts

277

may have been brought eastward from Africa, instead, by the people who first colonized the South Pacific. The availability of coconuts might well have made possible the travels of daring canoers from island to unknown island. Coconuts in their husks are natural canteens. If a dozen or so are tossed into a canoe before departure, they keep fresh and uncontaminated within themselves a supply of drinkable water, as well as nourishment. If the canoe is upset accidentally, the coconuts float, and can be collected again before the thirsty voyagers proceed.

On many South Sea islands, tradition holds that coconut trees will grow well only where they can hear the sounds of the sea and the sounds of human voices. It is traditional, too, to plant a coconut tree when a baby is born and to judge the age of that individual according to the growth of the tree. After about forty years on a tropical beach, the tree is likely to die, partly of malnutrition in coral sand with too little fresh water reaching its roots. It is replaced quickly with a new seedling coconut. A person who survives the second tree is then about eighty years old, and a third may be planted in its stead with a brave show of optimism. In a plantation, where the trees shelter one another from the wind and the owners supply fertilizer, a coconut palm may bear fruit from the time it is ten years old until it is sixty or eighty or one hundred years old.

Coconut palms open new butter-yellow spathes to display their clusters of small flowers all through the year. An abundant nectar rewards bees that visit, and delights the beekeepers later in the concentrated form of palm honey. Twelve months pass between the opening of each small flower and the ripening of the coconut. Yet so continuous is the crop that a mature palm may produce between 300 and 450 fruits each year. If left to ripen fully, a four- or five-pound nut tumbles to the ground almost every day, dropping often from a height of as much as one hundred feet. No sensible person builds his thatched dwelling under the fruiting crown of a tree, or takes a nap in its shade where a nut can strike.

The thick fibrous husk, which is so important in floating the ripe fruits through tropical seas, develops slowly. While it is green and comparatively thin, the shell of the familiar "nut" inside is soft. Actually, the

Partly covered by dunes on the coast of Venezuela near Maracaibo, these coconut palms (Cocos nucifera) *are still near the sea—the conditions in which they are said to grow best. (Karl Weidman)*

A coconut palm may produce 450 fruits a year, each carrying "milk" in its fibrous husk as its own supply of water. (Anna Riwkin)

"nut" is one enormous seed—among the largest known. At first it is full of a translucent jelly, which is spoonable and delicious. Later the jelly liquefies into the clear "milk" of green coconuts—perhaps the most refreshing drink in the tropics. As the seed ripens, its husk turns brown and protects it from animals. The shell of the seed becomes flinty, and within it the nourishment of the milk (a liquid endosperm) is transferred and built into an ever-thickening layer of "flesh." At the same time, pure air (free of molds and bacteria) is released within the nut, and the liquid will slosh around if the fruit is shaken. In a ripe coconut, little milk remains.

The late Dr. David Fairchild, plant explorer extraordinary and expert on palms of all kinds, showed us how to choose a coconut at the best stage for milk. He literally unscrewed one from a tree he had planted on the Kampong in Coconut Grove, Florida (site of his delightful book, *The World Grows Round My*

Door), and whacked off the stem end with a big knife. Carefully he pared around a small hole opened into the seed's interior, preparing a sanitary surface against which to press our lips while tipping up the fruit and drinking its contents. Later, in Latin America, we found that local people favored certain trees above others as a source of drinking coconuts *(pipas)*. In the West Indies, by contrast, any seaside coconut tree seems equally suitable. Negro boys climb the trees barehanded and barefooted, carrying the end of a rope to which a handsaw is attached. Once in the crown of a tree, a boy pulls up his rope and saw, ties the free end to a whole cluster of coconuts in the drinking condition, amputates the stalk, and lowers the cluster on the rope to a friend below. On horse-drawn carts the fruits go to town, to street corners and market places where native people buy them cheaply. The pedlar who leads the horse uses his knife in exactly the same way Dr. Fairchild showed us, preparing each fruit freshly for a waiting, critical customer.

About seven months after pollination, a coconut is ready for drinking. Left on the tree for two months more, its white flesh builds up to maximum thickness, and the seed is ready for harvesting if its goodness is to be used in a factory producing sweetened, desiccated coconut. If, however, coconut oils are the goal, the fruit is left in place through the twelfth or thirteenth month or is merely gathered when it falls to the ground of its own. Even then, the coconuts may be stacked for a week or more to let the oil-bearing cells ripen further. After the fruits are husked by skilled men, the seeds are cut expertly into two with a knife and left to dry. The flesh curls away from the shell fragments, and is separated completely for further drying on cloths or racks to become saleable copra. After a processing plant has expressed the oil from copra, and sent it on its way toward the manufacture of soap, shampoos, margarine, or other products, the press cake is sold to feed cattle.

More than three billion coconuts are opened every year. For this reason, any nut that is unusual is likely to be discovered, no matter how rare its special

Left above: When the seed inside a coconut awakens, a root grows out through one of three thin spots at the stem end, carrying with it a bud. (Lorus and Margery Milne) Left: The branching of the doum palm (Hyphaene thebaica) *of southern Egypt and East Africa often gives the tree a special grace. Its fruit has a gingerbread flavor. (E. Aubert de La Rue)*

The carnauba palm (Copernicia cerifera) of Brazil produces the hardest natural commercial wax, with the highest melting point. (E. Aubert de La Rue)

feature may be. One of these rare events has excited mankind for longer than written history extends: at long intervals, a coconut is found to contain a pearl. Usually it is a perfect sphere, as much as half an inch in diameter, glistening a creamy white and showing under a magnifier a delicately pebbled surface. So extraordinary are these coconut pearls that the mode of their formation remains undiscovered. Some people believe that a pearl forms only in a coconut that, for unknown reasons, lacks the three

ordinary "eyes" through which the seedling emerges. Oriental princes have prized coconut pearls so highly that the world supply has been effectively treasured in the Far East. Few occidental people ever see this tropical jewel, for even the big museums seldom have a coconut pearl for display.

Although a coconut seed has three "eyes" through its shell, the embryo plant extends itself through only one of them. This happens after a whole coconut has lain on the ground for week after week, until humid air penetrates and awakens the dormant seed. As the pure white root grows out at the stem end of the husk, the fibrous covering splits apart, making space for the green scroll that is the first leaf, rolled into a compact bud. From the husk the root and leaf emerge

The Chinese fan palm (Livistona chinensis) *is a member of a genus found in Indomalaysia and eastern Australia. (J. H. Gerard: National Audubon)*

California fan palms (Washingtonia filifera) *are native also to adjacent parts of Mexico. (Gladys Diesing: National Audubon)*

almost simultaneously, the root turning quickly downward and securing a firm hold on the soil. Rapidly the bud unrolls and the green leaf begins making food. Slowly the husk disintegrates and adds a little humus to the soil.

The fibers of the husk, like those of the tree trunk, are known as coir (rhymes with foyer). We have the equivalent of more coir than one husk contains on the porch just outside our front door, and another at the back. Each is a heavy-duty mat made from coconut fibers, originating (according to the label) in India. It is the equivalent of a flat brush an inch thick, more than a foot in one direction and two in the other, and an effective means to reduce the amount of mud and dirt from shoes before entering the house. Longer coir fibers are made into bigger brushes and heavy ropes. Seamen rely on them, for coir remains almost undamaged by salt water, although hot dry sun soon makes the fibers brittle. Short fibers are often converted into coir dust, sometimes called coconut "peat," for use by horticultural-

ists around the roots of plants. Dry coir, in the husk or out, burns readily and, in areas where coconuts are raised for copra, the fires used to dry the crop are kept going solely on husks and dead tree trunks.

The hard shells surrounding the fleshy endosperm of coconut seeds can be converted into some of the finest charcoal and used for filtering toxic materials from gases. This use leapt into importance during World War I, when soldiers began encountering poison gas from the enemy lines. The cannisters of the gas masks with which the men were hastily furnished contained coconut shell charcoal granules, and all of the gas inhaled had to travel past the poison-absorbing material. Recently, finer granules of the same material have been packed into filter cigarettes in the hope that this action would remove cancer-producing substances from the tobacco smoke.

In primitive societies, virtually every part of a coconut tree has several uses. Coconut shells serve as bowls and scoops, and can be carved into usable spoons. Long fibers from the leaf petioles can be twisted into strong string, and used to lash the fronds into an overlapping thatch on a framework of split petioles, as a roof or wall that keeps out even the heaviest tropical rain. A roof of this kind still admits air and protects the people who live under it from the intense heat of the sun. The leaflets may be woven into floor mats, or thin partitions, or baskets of many shapes and uses, or hats, or brooms, or torches to brighten the night. On Guam the natives feed coconut meat to land crabs, which they regard as a delicacy. Domestic animals, too, get a daily ration of this nutritious material and, in turn, add variety to human meals in which coconut flesh appears prepared in a hundred different ways. Coconut milk remains the purest and most available drinking water. It can be let sour to a vinegar, for use on crisp bits of palm bud salvaged when a live tree must be felled. Even the outer part of a coconut palm trunk is worth separating from the fibrous pith inside; it can be split lengthwise to yield strips for flooring or framing a native hut, or be cut into panels that will take a polish, known then as "porcupine wood." We have a bird feeder made from a coconut shell.

The porcupines among palms are found in tropical American rain forests. Black palms *(Astrocaryum)* produce long sharp black spines on each leaf petiole and seem armored all the way up the trunk by stiff spinelike projections as much as four inches long, which quickly discourage any animal that might try to climb the tree. The trunk spines are actually the remnants of vascular strands, each supported by stiffening tissue that pulled free from the petiole of a falling leaf and remained in place on the trunk. Similar strands of greater length, called tucuma fiber (from *A. tucuma),* can be salvaged from the pith of the tree, and are an export from Brazil. If a black palm trunk is scraped, its outer surface is astonishingly hard and smooth. The woody material can be used as pilings upon which to build houses in swamplands where floods are frequent, or be split lengthwise into flooring material. We visited an Indian family in the wilds of Darien province, Republic of Panamá, that lived in a thatched house made entirely of local black palm pieces. To reach the ground-floor level, we scrambled up a leaning length of black palm trunk which had been freed of spines and notched to form steps along one side. On a floor that was almost as flat and polished as though made of fitted oak boards, we stood perhaps eight feet above the soggy mud below. The palm trunks that supported the house continued upward,

to a framework under the thatching of black palm leaves. We could see some of their petioles still armed with spines. Hammocks were slung from one upright post to the next, and between them we could look out in any direction through the wall-less structure into the surrounding rain forest from which these people gathered everything they needed. Even the slender black cord around the waist of each adult, which supported a short length of cloth for modesty's sake, was of tucuma fibers laid together by hand into a circlet of the correct girth.

Feather palms in the New World include a few still stranger than the black palms. In the rain forests from Costa Rica to Brazil are stilt palms *(Iriartea)* which grow tall and slender in the rain-soaked mud. At an early age, each produces a complete conical array of down-slanting adventitious roots from the trunk, rising perhaps four to six feet above the soil. These are the stilts that take the place of buttresses, preventing the tree from toppling in the oozy ground. Often the central trunk rots away in the center of the skirt of outspread aerial roots, leaving them as the only support for the tree above. In the Old World, palms grow through the rain forests as woody vines, clambering over other vegetation, sometimes to lengths of five hundred feet or more. Those of the large genus *Calamus* are harvested in Indonesia, their stems split lengthwise and sold as rattan for woven wooden furniture and chair seats, or cut into suitable lengths of attractive shape and called Malacca canes, to be used as walking sticks. In the forests these palms are true lianas, holding their position by means of their recurved leaf bases, the four- to seven-inch feathery leaves arising singly at intervals along the stem, each armed with hooklike spines.

The fan palms have their distinctive members too. The doum palm (or gingerbread tree, *Hyphaene thebaica)* of Egypt and the Sudan is but one of about thirty species in this genus found in Africa, Madagascar, and India, all of which show the unusual ability to branch several times, each division of the trunk bearing its own crown of leaves. The fruit of the doum palm has the flavor of gingerbread. Carnauba wax, exported from Brazil for the manufacture of candles, shoe polish, floor wax and other purposes, is scraped from the severed, flailed leaves of the wax palm *(Copernicia cerifera);* of all commercial natural waxes, carnauba is the hardest, with the highest melting point. (Sometimes a substitute for it is offered, made from a feather palm of the northern Andes, *Ceroxylon andicola,* which has the double distinction of growing higher on mountains—to 13,450 feet elevation—than any other palm and attaining individual heights of two hundred feet; it is legitimately called a wax palm too.) The petticoat palm of Cuba, named for the way its old leaves hang down around its trunk, is *Copernicia torreana.*

One of the fan palms remained a mystery for centuries after its giant fruits were first discovered cast ashore by storms in the Indian Ocean. It grows naturally only far northeast of Madagascar on the Seychelles Islands, where few ships stop. Its fruits became famous as "coco-de-mer," each in its husk weighing up to forty pounds, containing a single two-lobed seed much like a deformed coconut, and the largest seed in the world. Fully five years are needed for the parent tree, which is pistillate, to mature a cluster of these tremendous fruits; the tree itself must be at least thirty years old before it bears at all. Thereafter the Seychelles nut palm (or double coconut, *Lodoicea seychellarum)* continues to produce a few seeds each year. At the same time, it rises to a height of ninety feet or more, crowned by a great head of fan-shaped leaves each measuring twenty-five feet from trunk to tip. Unlike other palms, the Seychelles nut palm develops a socket-like bowl around the base of the trunk. This socket is so hard and weatherproof that it commonly remains intact for a century or more after all traces of the tree itself have rotted away. Fortunately, there is no magic about the Seychelles Islands in producing double coconuts. In many other tropical parts of the world the same palm trees have now been introduced. In each they are producing either pollen or fruits, the latter just as much museum pieces as though they had grown in their remote native area.

The giants among fan palms from Ceylon through the East Indies to Australia are the half-dozen members of the genus *Corypha,* derived from the Greek word for peak or summit—the acme of beauty among palms. The talipot palm *(C. umbraculifera)* is literally an "umbrella-carrier." Its large leaves can be used to ward off rain. Between showers, fans woven from leaf strips can help people tolerate the summer heat. In India, the substitute for writing paper known as olla consists of sheets cut from talipot palm leaves, flattened and dried to permanent form; they take ink readily. In the Philippines, makers of hats find use for a fine fiber called buntal, removed from unopened leaves of this palm. And the trunk of the tree, which grows from sixty to one hundred feet tall, contains a sago-like starch known simply as talipot.

Southernmost Europe and parts of the United States with comparable weather are on the fringe of natural distribution for fan palms. Only one, the dwarf palm *(Chamaerops humilis)* is native to the Mediterranean shores of Europe; both it and the other species in the same genus *(C. macrocarpa* from the African coasts of the same sea) are the source of black fibers known as African hair, used as a substitute for horsehair in old-style upholstery of furniture. Southern California and southwestern Arizona have two of the known species of *Washingtonia,* the third living in adjacent Mexico; all of them are tall trees. Those in Palm Canyon, close to Palm Springs, California, give to the canyon in the Indian Reservation there the appearance of an Arabian oasis. And in the southeastern United States, from North Carolina southward, are many different palms known as palmettos. Some, such as the cabbage palmetto *(Sabal palmetto),* attain a height of eighty feet on the slightly elevated, somewhat drier "hammock" lands of the Florida Everglades.

Probably no other plant of Florida's vast marshes and swamp country aided the Seminole tribe of Indians so much when they took refuge in this inaccessible sanctuary. For these hungry people, it made little difference whether the "hearts of cabbage palm" they got from the terminal buds came from feather palms or palmettos. The fan-shaped leaves made good thatching material. Cabbage palmetto produces edible fruits in clusters of small rounded blackish drupes each with a single armored seed. Domestic pigs thrive on them. And the trunks of the cabbage palmetto could be used for building stockades, fences, corduroy roads through the swamplands, and wharf pilings along both inland waterways and inlets of the sea. The tree even withstands occasional fires, holding its characteristically rounded head against the sky, the tips of the frayed fan-shaped leaves fringelike and drooping. Except for a distance of eight or ten feet below the crown, the trunk is rough, bare of leaves, and resistant to damage from either heat or ax. The topmost region is more likely to be studded with "boot-straps," which are the remains of petioles after the rest of the leaves have broken free and tumbled to the ground. The tree's greatest danger in a fire may be from the heat generated as its own dead leaves burn in a heap around its base. A far greater danger today is from real-estate developers, whose bulldozers are knocking down and burying cabbage palmettos by the square mile. We wonder where, when this source of supply is gone, people will get the unopened palm leaves they buy as religious symbols to carry on Palm Sunday.

It would be easy to be deceived into thinking that young palmettos of the same kind were growing up in every vacant area, for the same type of leaf can be seen in neglected pastures all the way from the Carolinas into east Texas and well down into Florida. But these are a very different palm, the saw palmetto (or scrub-palmetto, *Serenoa repens*). Rarely does it grow erect. More commonly its heavy trunk twists along the ground, the lop-sided crown rising irregularly as stiff, nearly circular leaves, each deeply cut, from petioles so spiny that the word sawtooth describes them perfectly. The flowers, however, attract honeybees and provide most of the nectar that goes into palm honey. The small black fruits once helped keep Indians from starving; now birds eat most of them. Fibers from the leaves can be made into brushes, or the leaves themselves can be shipped to Europe—as many are to Germany before Christmas time—to be made into artificial palms to decorate crèches. Even the most weedlike of the palms gains importance if a good enough market can be found to pay for the hand labor of harvesting the plant.

Known as the hurricane palm or the ceriman (Monstera deliciosa), *this attractive climber, native to the American tropics, bears delicious fruit. (Werner Stoy: Camera Hawaii)*

CHAPTER 32

The Spathe-Bearers

CUES: *If the monocot plant bears its tiny flowers in a compact cluster around a fleshy stalk, particularly if the stalk (the spadix) is partly surrounded by an eye-catching modified leaf (the spathe), and its leaves are not folded lengthwise like those of a palm, it is likely to be a member of the Order Arales. It may be a calla lily, a skunk cabbage, a cultivated taro plant, a floating duckweed, or a famous member of Sumatra's flora producing the largest known flower cluster—fifteen feet high, with a spathe four feet in diameter cupping a vertical spadix eight-and-one-half feet tall.*

Almost all of the nearly 1600 different kinds of plants in this Order are denizens of tropical rain forests, or humid temperate woodlands, or wet ground close to a marsh or swamp. Those that float on the water surface include among them the smallest of all known flowering plants, their parts so greatly reduced that stems, leaves, and most flower parts are missing altogether.

THE ARUM FAMILY (Araceae)

The true arums *(Arum)* include only about a dozen species, native to southern and central Europe, but since these were the most familiar to early botanists, all of the more exotic members of the family acquired the same general name or were called "aroids" (arum-like). Cuckoopint (or cuckoopintle, *A. maculatum*), often known in Britain as lords-and-ladies, has a whitish rhizome from which arrow-shaped leaves with net venation rise on long petioles in early spring, signalling the advance of the season all the way from North Africa into southern Scandinavia

285

and central Germany. Soon after the leaves expand, new stalks rise up, each topped by an upright white or purple spathe that opens like a giant single petal to expose the top of a bright yellow or purple spadix. The flowers, however, remain hidden from view where the spathe encloses the lower half of the finger-shaped spadix. They emit a fetid odor, which attracts carrion flies and other insects. These press through an obstacle course of downpointing stiff hairs that arise from the inner surface of the spathe. Finding their escape route blocked by the hairs, they mill around over the stamens until these open and coat the insects with pollen. Only then do the stiff hairs wither, opening the prison, and freeing the pollinators. Many of them get caught promptly in another cuckoopint, where the stigmas are ready but the stamens are not yet open. Later in the season, the spathes drop off, exposing a knob-shaped cluster of brilliant red berries which contain so much calcium oxalate in needle-like crystals that they are poisonous.

The presence of oxalate crystals and associated toxic proteins in plants of the arum family is so widespread that extreme caution is advisable in tasting the leaves, stems, rhizomes or fruits of any of them. Dumb cane *(Dieffenbachia)* from tropical America, which is often grown as a decorative house plant, gets its name from the prompt irritation and swelling of the tongue that develops if a person chews a piece of a leaf. Dieffenbachias produce upright stems up to six feet tall, marked symmetrically with conspicuous leaf scars, and large variegated leaves shaped like those of a banana plant, each with a short petiole.

All across Eurasia and North America in cool bogs and around pond margins in shallow water, water arum (or arum lily, *Calla palustris)* is noticed because of the glistening white spathe on a foot-high stalk, among handsome dark green heart-shaped leaves on long petioles, which arise from the same rhizome in the muddy bottom. The spread spathe is often mistaken for a flower, whereas the true flowers are green and clustered around the knob-shaped spadix. The lower flowers usually have a central pistil surrounded by six stamens, while upper flowers produce stamens only. The "Calla lily" of florists is a South African relative *(Zantedeschia).* The cultivated one *(Z. aethiopica),* which produces a large white spathe and leaves shaped like arrowheads, grows in wet meadows from thick starchy rhizomes. In South Africa it is regarded as a weed, and dug up to feed pigs. Neither of these aroids traps insects even temporarily, as does the cuckoopint.

In eastern North America, from Massachusetts southward, golden club *(Orontium aquaticum)* comes into bloom in early spring, often raising its pointed oval leaves out of the water film at the same time that slender brownish stalks grow upward, each with the topmost inch or two a yellow spadix of tiny flowers that have no obvious spathe associated with them. Even water snails join the small insects that crawl over the flowers and attend to pollination. A spathe seems equally hard to find on sweetflag (or flagroot, *Acorus calamus)* which grows and flowers later in the same places, as well as over many other parts of North America, Eurasia and North Africa. Actually, in sweetflag, the spathe is there but takes the form of an elongated flat green projection beyond the sideways-turned green spadix, resembling one of the plant's narrow sword-shaped leaves more than a floral appendage. Sweetflag produces many leaves and leaflike stalks with flower clusters from the same large rhizome in the mud. People have sought rhizomes of this plant for thousands of years, to dry the starchy tissues and then grind them into a fragrant powder called calamus. Use of sweetflag rhizomes to make incense for burning on special occasions goes back at least to the time of King Tutankhamen, for dried material of this kind was among the treasure discovered beside the sarcophagus of the Egyptian boy-king. Introduction of incense into the rituals of Judaism and Christianity came much later. Babylonians, and afterward the Greeks, used sweetflag rhizomes as a source of mild medicines. In India and Ceylon, calamus powder is still relied upon as an insecticide. And in many a land where sweetflag grows, children discover the pungent, pleasant flavor of these large clean-looking stems they can dig from the mud of pond margins. The name sweetflag reflects this, and also the parallel veined leaves which resemble those of iris, reeds and other monocots far more than those of most members of the arum family. Aroids generally have a midrib in each leaf, with branch veins on both sides, often filled in between by net venation.

Most aroids, in fact, are denizens of the rain forests in tropical America where they grow as seedlings in the dense shade of tier upon tier of higher vegetation. Many of them reach the light by climbing the tree trunks, becoming bigger plants as they ascend, often changing their character spectacularly. We met this first in Panamá, where a thready vine grew up the smooth bark of a giant tree so tall, so covered by epiphytes that we could not identify it. From the raw infertile mud at the foot of the tree we traced the vine upward. Six inches above the ground its leaves began and continued, at about two inch intervals, each heart-shaped and conforming to the bark as though it had been ironed on. At three feet above ground level, the stem was a little thicker and we could see minute extensions from it reaching into the texture of the bark, probably as adventitious clinging roots that collected no nourishment from the support. The leaves grew progressively bigger until, at perhaps eight feet above the soil, they were three inches across instead of barely one. About ten feet higher still, the stem was fully a quarter of an inch in diameter and the slightly larger leaves had short petioles that held them clearly away from the bark. With our field glasses we studied the vine's progress up the tree, its anchoring roots thicker, its stem enlarging to half an inch through, and then an inch or more. The petioles grew longer, and the leaf blades tilted more, letting us see their undersides. At thirty feet above the ground, there were a few notches in the edge of each leaf, and at forty feet a natural oval hole between side veins. Sixty feet up the stem of the vine curled over the lowest limb of the tree, and there produced a dozen leaves we recognized from their perforations and slotted margins as belonging to the ceriman *(Monstera,* perhaps *M. deliciosa),* often called the hurricane palm. Among the dense vegetation where these monstrous plants grow, no real wind can ever reach them. The openings in their huge leaves must have some other significance. From the high horizontal part of the *Monstera* stem, a dozen roots had grown down all the way to the soil, each of them as thick as a lead pencil, presumably getting dissolved substances needed in trace amounts by the foliage so far from where we stood.

When one of these big vines is cut down and chopped into short lengths, each can be grown as a separate plant in moderate light or even full sun if plenty of water is supplied. It retains its ability to produce giant leaves, with petioles several feet long and perforated, slotted blades three to four feet across. The horizontal stem seems able to give rise also to stalks bearing a great cluster of flowers around

Right above: Skunk cabbage (Symplocarpus foetidus) *of Eastern Asia and eastern North America pushes up through marshy or low ground in early spring and unfurls huge green leaves. (Lorus and Margery Milne) Right: Jack-in-the-pulpit* (Arisaema triphyllum) *of eastern North America is a spring wildflower that produces red berries in the summer. (Esther Heacock)*

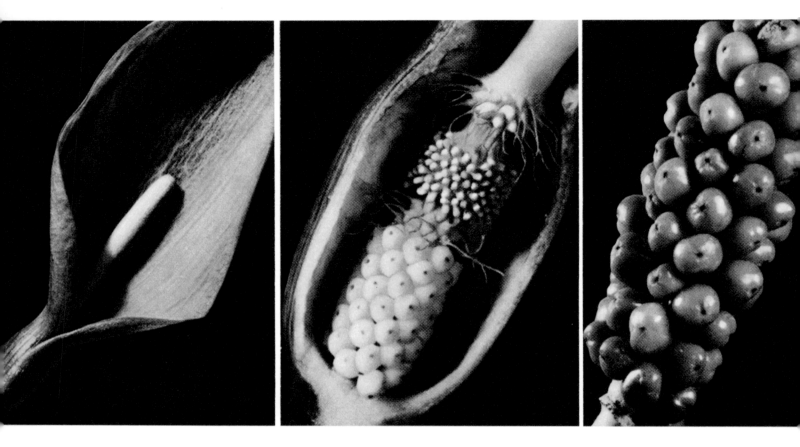

Within the leaflike spathe of an Arum *is the cylindrical cluster of flowers, called the spadix* (left). *The stamens are slightly farther from the supporting stalk than the pistils* (center) *from which the fruit develop* (right). *(Conzett and Huber)*

a heavy spadix, partly surrounded by a thin yellow spathe. If pollinated, the ovaries mature to become components of a compound fruit which somewhat suggests that of a pineapple plant, although it is crowned with no tuft of stiff green leaves. A piece of a ripe one, chilled and served with sliced bananas, is a dessert to remember forever—hence *deliciosa*.

A similar manner of growth is met among many of the 230 species of *Philodendron,* and some of the five hundred different kinds of *Anthurium,* all from tropical America, and often cultivated to give an illusion of the tropics in homes farther from the Equator. Most of the cultivated species of *Anthurium* are ones in which the spathe is large, flat, bright red, and provides an almost unbelievable background to the slender spadix with its tiny flowers. A red spathe

is not necessary to draw pollinating insects to the flower clusters in their native haunts. We recall an *Anthurium* in Costa Rica which we discovered only because it was attracting a steady stream of brilliant metallic bees. Through a shaft of sunlight that penetrated the edge of the rain forest, their bodies glinted in flashing green as they flew in, each insect to crawl excitedly for a few moments over the pollen-gilded spadix before being displaced by another bee. The pale green spathe blended inconspicuously with the leafy background.

In these, as in many other aroids, the heart-shaped leaves on long petioles are better known than the flower clusters, which are often inconspicuous and appear later in the season when the foliage hides them from casual view. It is for leaves, not for floral display, that people set out the frost-tender rhizomes of *Caladium*—perhaps the horticultural varieties with variegated patterns in red, yellow, and pale green that have been developed from the twenty different wild species of the genus found in rain forests of tropical America. Giant leaves of the same shape come from similar rhizomes of *Colocasia,* sold by florists as elephant's-ear. But of the eight different kinds native to the wet shady areas of Indomalaysia, the most important to mankind is certainly dasheen *(C. esculenta)* and an almost flowerless variety called taro *(C. esculenta antiquorum)*. More than 150 million people in Southeast Asia and on islands in the South Pacific rely upon starchy foods prepared from rhizomes of these plants for their principal nourishment.

The swollen rhizomes of dasheen and taro grow vertically and are clad in a few scaly leaves, which makes them corms rather than tubers. They can be harvested and stored for a few months in a dormant condition, ready to be peeled, scraped or shredded, washed thoroughly to free them of poisonous oxalates, and then cooked. Hawaiians ferment a paste made from taro rhizomes and call the edible product poi. No reliable estimate of the total amount of dasheen and taro produced has ever been reached because most of these foods are consumed in the tropical countries where they are grown. Nutritionists know, however, that dasheen and taro correspond to unrelated cassava in being inadequate to maintain health without extensive supplements of protein and fats. Where these plants, rather than cereal grains or potatoes, provide the principal carbohydrates in human diets, illness and death from protein deficiency are most prevalent.

Two of America's wildflowers in the arum family have become famous because they open their cowl-shaped spathes weeks or months before their leaves expand for the growing season. Along the Pacific coast from British Columbia to California grows the western skunk cabbage *(Lysichiton camstschatcense)*, while in wet places from Quebec to Manitoba and south to upland Georgia and Tennessee this harbinger of spring is the eastern skunk cabbage *(Symplocarpus foetidus)*, a member of a genus found also in eastern Asia. So early in the season, the only insects active may be flies that have hibernated. But the fetid odor of the flower clusters attracts the flies in numbers. They enter the dark cavities shielded from the light by purple-streaked green spathes, and walk over the flowers studding the knob-shaped spadix. Each little flower has four sepals, an equal number of stamens opposite them, and a central pistil with a four-angled style tipped by a small stigma. Late in the summer, after the large pointed oval leaves have expanded fully, the spathe shrivels, revealing a cluster of dark reddish berries.

In the rain forests of Sumatra, a related aroid— the krubi *(Amorphophallus titanum)*—produces the largest floral cluster known. This giant is one of ninety different species of the genus found in tropical Asia and, like the others, sends up spathe and spadix before the foliage of the season opens. In the krubi, the tip of the post-sized spadix attains a height of fifteen feet, rising from the center of a huge cup-shaped spathe four feet in diameter at the rim. This rim may be eight feet above ground level and slightly more above the zone where the conical structure is attached to the spadix. Encountering so tremendous a display, it is easy to think of it as one flower rather than as a cluster with hundreds coating the lower half of the central spadix. From the true flowers comes a fetid odor not unlike that of skunk cabbage. Flies are attracted in large numbers. But the Asiatic elephants of Sumatra may be the principal pollinators. Explorers have claimed that these large animals visit the spathe cups to drink the rain water they hold, and that pollen travels from one krubi spadix to the next as a golden powder on the brows of thirsty pachyderms.

We like the elephant story, and hope it is true. We think of it when we find a four-inch spathe and spadix in the moist woods wherever the local wildflowers include some of the 110 different kinds of *Arisaema:* Africa, Asia, and North America. In the eastern provinces of Canada and eastern states, several species in this genus are called jack-in-the-pulpit, with the

In Southeast Asia and on islands of the Pacific, the taro plant (Colocasia esculenta antiquorum) *is cultivated for its starchy edible corms. (Anna Riwkin)*

upright spadix as Jack, and the spathe with its rain-shedding tip as the pulpit. The related green dragon *(A. dracontium)* of the southern and southwestern United States produces a more elongated and upright spathe tip that suggests a lizard's tail. American Indians used to dig the rhizomes of arisaemas as "Indian turnips," but to get rid of the oxalates a long series of preparatory steps was necessary. After baking or boiling the rhizomes, they peeled away the rough surface, dried the starchy pulp, pounded it to a flour, heated it again and let it stand exposed to air for days. We wonder how desperate the Indians were for food, that they would go to so much trouble. "Indian turnips" cannot be eaten raw. Merely to bite into a fresh rhizome causes a severe and long-lasting stinging sensation that spreads over the whole lining of the mouth and throat.

The broad range of plant form among aroids includes even a free-floating aquatic member known as water-lettuce *(Pistia stratiotes),* which is widespread in the tropics and cultivated in many parts of the world by fanciers of tropical fish. Its down-hanging roots with their fringing roothairs and its many runners extending horizontally to new little plants all provide havens for small fishes, while the foliage increases the amount of oxygen available in the aquarium water. The plant has escaped cultivation and become a weed in Hawaii.

THE FLOATING MINIATURES
(Family Lemnaceae)

To a botanist, it is easy to visualize ancestral plants similar to water-lettuce growing ever simpler and smaller until all that remained was a stemless leafless "frond" less than half an inch across, floating in the surface film or sinking to the shallow bottom of some pond. This description would fit a water-flaxseed *(Spirodela)* with several dangling roots, or a duckweed *(Lemna)* with a single root, or a water-meal *(Wolffia)* with no root at all. These include the smallest of flowering plants, no more than one fiftieth of an inch across, reproducing vegetatively by formation of new "fronds" from the edges of old ones, and flowering occasionally with a tiny spathe around a single short stamen or a solitary pistil. In *Wolffia,* a staminate and a pistillate flower appear simultaneously, bursting out of the top of the "frond." In the other genera, the spathes are hidden in the edge of the fronds and the flowers are exposed right at water level. About two dozen different species of these plants occur on fresh waters all over the tropi-cal and temperate world. Where winter coats the ponds with ice, the duckweeds and their kin sink regularly to the bottom in autumn and rise again after the water grows warmer and the sun more intense in spring. Only the most observant naturalists find these plants flowering between late June and early August. Ducks, geese, pheasants, muskrats, beaver, and other animals feed on the green flakes of vegetation whenever they can reach them.

CHAPTER 33

The Pineapple and Plants Like It

CUES: *If the monocot plant has flowers that are regular or nearly so, and if, in the three carpels that are united to form the pistil, the seeds develop a mealy endosperm as the food reserve for the seedling, it is sure to be a member of Order Farinales. It may be a wandering Jew, a Spanish moss, a pineapple, or a water-hyacinth.*

The 2500 different kinds of plants in this Order show strong resemblances to some of the lilies on one hand and to wetlands vegetation such as arrow-head *(Sagittaria,* Order Helobiales) on the other. From the lilies they are distinguished chiefly by the nature of the reserve food in the seeds, which among

Spathe-bearers. Right above: The water-arum (Calla palustris) grows in cold bogs and marshes on all sides of the North Pole, and as far south as Pennsylvania in America and as Switzerland in Europe. (Steve McCutcheon) Right: Golden club (Orontium aquaticum) grows from a horizontal stem in the muddy or sandy bottom in shallow freshwaters of eastern North America. Far right: Central American rain forests are often brightened by the flaring spathe of the flamingo flower (Anthurium scherzerianum)— a member of the arum family—and the blossoms of big Cattleya orchids. (Both by Lorus and Margery Milne)

lilies have a fleshy endosperm. From plants in Order Helobiales they differ most in their united carpels, and in having far more endosperm in each seed. As in both of these other orders, the ovary is usually superior.

THE SPIDERWORTS (Family Commelinaceae)

From the soft, jointed stems of a spiderwort *(Trades-cantia),* a mucilaginous material can be pulled out as fine as a spiderweb, and it will harden to a thread with just a few minutes' exposure to the air. These plants of warm and temperate parts of the Americas have a hairy, sticky stem with grasslike leaves clasping it at intervals. All summer long they produce irregular clusters of flowers that open in the early morning, the three large petals symmetrically disposed around six stamens and a central pistil. But by mid-afternoon, the petals have curled and contracted into glutinous drops, which give the plant its other name of Job's tears.

One of the commonest of houseplants, wandering Jew *(Zebrina pendula)* from Mexico and Central America, produces similar blossoms of smaller size. Often they develop on cuttings grown in a jar of tap water on a window sill, even before adventitious roots develop and tempt the housewife to pot her plant where its soft stems can droop and display the variegated leaves, each striped lengthwise with white or yellow alternating with green. If examined carefully, a flower of wandering Jew is seen to have its pale purple petals joined to form a tube at the base, whereas those of a spiderwort are completely separate from one another.

Once familiar with these plants of flower garden and windowsill, a person quickly recognizes as a wild relative the two hundred different kinds of day-flower *(Commelina),* particularly the Asiatic species *(C. communis),* which has become a widespread

Far left: Perching bromeliads add color to the trunk and limbs of a prickly bucare tree (Erythrina poeppigiana). *Left above: Members of the pineapple family that perch high among the branches of forest trees in tropical America include about eighty species of* Vriesia. *They hold about a gallon of water in the rosette of leaves. (Both by Karl Weidmann) Left: Taking away only the light from the tree upon which they perch, bromeliads are often called "air plants." Because they hold so much rain water, they are also referred to as "tank epiphytes." (Clark Ross)*

The water-hyacinth (Eichhornia crassipes) *of tropical America floats because of gas trapped in the bases of the leaves. Introduced into Florida waterways, it has become a pest. (E. Javorsky)*

weed in ditches, roadsides and damp corners. It is one of the few flowers with a pure blue color. But only its upper two petals are large, the third quite small, and hardly showing out of the pair of green bracts that fold together around the clustered flowers. Each day one flower opens, and then closes again. Yet so many buds are hidden between the same pair of green bracts that the appearance of a new blossom each morning, rather than the same one again, is easily overlooked.

Clusters of flowers, rather than individual blossoms, draw attention to a stiff-leaved herb of the West Indies, known as Moses-in-the-bulrushes *(Rhoeo discolor)* or oyster plant. Fitting among the bases of the straight, purplish leaves, where they radiate toward the sky in all directions, the flower clusters develop between a pair of large bracts suggesting the floating ark built for the infant Moses or the shells of an oyster. The plant grows easily on poor

Fields of cultivated pineapple (Ananas sativus), *each fruit the product of a whole cluster of flowers, ripen in the sun on the Hawaiian Islands. (Werner Stoy: Camera Hawaii)*

soil despite occasional wettings with salt-water spray, and has been introduced all around the world in tropical and subtropical gardens, often as a broad border for large flower beds.

THE PINEAPPLE FAMILY (Bromeliaceae)

All but one of the 1500 species in this family are plants of the Western Hemisphere, where they are mostly short-stemmed plants with rosettes of stiff leaves. Representatives of many genera grow as epiphytes on horizontal tree limbs in the rain forests of tropical America, a majority of these plants holding gallons of water in tanklike bases of the foliage rosettes and adding literally tons of weight to the trees that support them. Frogs and dragonflies, mosquitoes and snails raise their families in these pondlets high above the ground. Other bromeliads produce dense thickets of saw-edged leaves between the bases of the trees in the rain forest, making human progress

on foot virtually impossible unless the plants are hacked to pieces in cutting a trail. Bromeliads thrive in the open under desert conditions from Florida around the Gulf of Mexico into Central America, and still others achieve the proportions of century plants in the Andes, even above timberline. Flower spikes of *Puya raimondii* attain a height of forty feet.

The flowers of bromeliads are commonly borne in distinctive heads, each in the axil of a colorful bract. So handsome and unusual are these plants that bromeliad fanciers cultivate more than two dozen genera with about the same type of care accorded orchids from the same tropical countries. Visitors to the southeastern United States encounter Spanish moss *(Tillandsia usneoides)* hanging in long gray festoons from live oaks, other trees, and telephone wires; this plant captures all its required moisture and nutrients from dust among fine hairs that coat its slender stems and leaves, and has no roots at all. The small yellow flowers and slender hairy fruits are generally overlooked. Other species among the four hundred in *Tillandsia* are conspicuous epiphytes known as "air plants," seen on bald cypress and many forest trees in Florida and southward as far as Chile.

Pineapples are the fruit of just one of the five species of *Ananas (A. sativus)* found from Paraguay to Mexico. The small seedy ancestral type of fruit had found favor among the American Indians long before Columbus discovered the New World. By the time he met these fruits in 1493 on the island of Guadeloupe, they were known all the way from their native southern Brazil and Paraguay into Central America and up the West Indian island chain. Spanish and Portuguese colonizers introduced the plants into their colonies in Africa. By 1548 they were being raised in India and the Dutch East Indies. Yet it was in English greenhouses, where the fruits were being raised to supply a larger market than imports could match, that the new horticultural varieties without seeds and with larger fruits were developed. The improved stock was reintroduced into the Americas, the Azores, Africa, India, Malaya and Australia. Those upon which the Hawaiian pineapple industry got its start came from England by way of Australia.

The purple flowers of a pineapple develop in a cylindrical head a short way back of the tip of an upright stalk. The bracts in whose axils the flowers appear, the ovaries of all the pistils in a cluster, the pedicels upon which the flowers are borne, and the fibrous upright stalk that holds them (and continues to a terminal cluster of stiff small leaves) all fuse into one sweet, juicy mass containing up to fifteen per cent of sugar. Since there are no seeds, the plants must be propagated from basal suckers, or from the crown cut from the top of a fruit, or from side branches that sometimes arise just below it. Production is often mechanized, with pollination eliminated through use of plant hormones to induce fruit formation, and powerful trucks with conveyor belts on outriggers to load the ripe pineapples picked by swift-moving men armed with sharp knives. The annual shipments from Hawaii to the continental United States alone now exceed 200,000 tons of fresh and canned fruit and nearly as much prepared as canned or frozen juice.

THE PICKERELWEEDS (Family Pontederiaceae)

The twenty-eight members of this little family are distinctive in having all six lobes of the perianth petal-like, not just three and the others sepal-like. They are plants of pond margins or actually float free, buoyed up by air chambers within the swollen petioles of the leaves in each rosette. Pickerelweed *(Pontederia)* grows conspicuously around the edge of small bodies of fresh water in which pickerel fish may live; it is an American genus of tropical and temperate regions. The fresh-looking bright green leaves are lance- or heart-shaped, on tall petioles, from creeping rhizomes in the muddy bottom. The purple flowers are clustered around the top two or three inches of a tall spadix, with a small bractlike spathe some distance down the stalk from the flowers.

The flowers are much larger, more handsome, and tend toward a bilateral symmetry in water-hyacinth *(Eichornia crassipes),* a floating representative of this tropical American genus. In ponds and slow streams of Florida, Australia and Java, where it has been introduced, it interferes with navigation and drainage by multiplying rapidly and clogging the water surface. Sea cows (manatees) eat it in its native streams and keep it under control there, but other kinds of wildlife seem to get little from it. Floridians call it a "million-dollar weed" because they have

Right above: In the Andes of Ecuador, a bromeliad (Puya raimondii) *with foliage like that of an* Agave *sends up a tall flower cluster. (Rolf Blomberg)   Right: In the Cordillera Real of Ecuador, a large bromeliad known as achupalla* (Pouzzetia *species) lives at 13,000 feet, the upper limit of the paramos. (E. Aubert de La Rue)*

spent many millions of dollars trying to eradicate it. Even farther from the Equator, where it is killed almost completely by frost each winter, it spreads with spectacular speed both by vegetative division of the parent plant and by means of inconspicuous seeds from the small capsules that ripen after the flowers fade.

CHAPTER 34

The Bountiful Grasses and Sedges

CUES: *If the monocot plant produces a cylindrical or three-sided stem with conspicuous nodes at which only one leaf arises, and if the base of the leaf sheathes the stem for some distance before angling off to become the blade, and if the individual flowers are small, lack a perianth, but rise in the axils of dry chaffy scales and are grouped into simple or compound clusters, it is almost sure to be a member of Order Graminales. It may be a bulrush, a sedge, a bamboo, a grass, a sugar cane, or a maize plant.*

Although the 8500 different kinds of vegetation sharing the features of this Order represent only a small fraction of the variety to be found among flowering plants, they definitely outnumber as individuals all other kinds that produce seeds. Part of their success arises through their outstanding ability to remain dormant for months or years, either as seeds or mature plants, while the weather around them is too cold or too dry for growth and reproduction. This has allowed them to colonize the world's arid lands and to support there not only their own diversification but also an incredible wealth of grazing and seed-eating animals. At the same time, they have freed themselves from the need for pollinators, relying instead upon the wind or upon self-fertilization to set their seeds. Uncountable populations of sedges and grasses follow their special way of life in the marshes, forests, savannas, plains and deserts of the tropics, and beyond the forests in the temperate and arctic lands, and between treeline and the ice-fields on lofty mountain peaks.

The flowers of these plants are extremely simple and similar, forcing botanists to use for classification details in the arrangement of the flowers (florets) in clusters, features of the fruits or seeds, and characteristics of the stems and leaves. The simplicity is believed to be through reduction and loss of unessential parts as the sedges and grasses evolved from lilylike ancestors.

THE SEDGES (Family Cyperaceae)

Usually a member of this family can be recognized by touch from the three-sided shape of the solid stems. Ordinarily the leaf bases form closed sheaths around the stems, the blades grasslike and diverging in three ranks. In each flower cluster, the individual florets rise in the axil of an overlapping bract, with no more than tiny scales or bristles to represent sepals and petals, customarily with three stamens, and a one-chambered, one-seeded superior ovary bearing a style that is deeply either two- or three-cleft.

As early as 2400 B.C., the people of northern Egypt found that a lasting material on which to write could be made from a coarse plant growing along the muddy margins of the Nile. They began cultivating the paper reed *(Cyperus papyrus)*, and continued to do so in the delta of the great river until the 5th or 6th century when substitutes (including vellum from sheepskin) took its place. Today, the paper reed is extinct as a wild plant in northern Egypt. It can still be found native in southeastern Europe, Asia Minor, southern Egypt, the Sudan, and Ethiopia, and introduced as an ornamental of special interest in many other warm parts of the world. It grows to a height of fifteen feet, all its leaves springing from the base, where its thick triangular stem grows horizontally in the mud. Its tall flowering stalks slant upward steeply and terminate in a rocket-burst of drooping branches, each bearing dozens of small spikelets, each spikelet a compact two-sided cluster of tiny florets protruding from flattened bracts.

Fruit heads on pampas grass (Cortaderia argentea) grow so abundantly over the Argentine pampas as to convert it into a "rolling sea of silver." (Harvey Caplin)

We have the word of Theophrastus, the "father of botany" (370–286 B.C.), that the flowering heads could be used only for making garlands with which to decorate the shrines of the gods. But the rhizomes could be dug and dried for fuel, the pith of the stems eaten raw or cooked as a food, and lengthwise strips cut from the outer parts of the stems made into paper, cloth, mats, sails, sandals for priests, and even boats. Indeed, the "ark of bulrushes" in which the infant Moses was hidden "among the flags near the river" is believed to have been made of paper reed, and is translated in this way in the King James Bible.

A much smaller relative of the paper reed is the yellow nut-grass *(C. esculentus),* found wild in tropical Africa, and from tropical America north to the Maritime Provinces of Canada and westward to Washington state. It spreads easily into agricultural land and, in the United States, is regarded by farmers as a serious weed. At the same time, it is one of the favorite foods of waterfowl such as mallard ducks, individual birds having been known to contain in their crops as many as three hundred of the small walnut-shaped tubers borne by the plant on horizontal, twisting stems just beneath the surface of muddy bottoms in shallow water. In West Africa, a local subspecies *(C. esculentus sativus)* is cultivated for human food, and produces crowded tubers on short stems at the rate of three tons to the acre. It is known as chufa, earth-almond, or tigernut, and grows now in the southeastern United States where it was introduced two centuries ago as a familiar food for imported Negro slaves. Their name for the West African subspecies is often transferred to the wild American form. Chufa was taken also to Europe, and there found people who were interested in it as a new food. But in these foreign lands, true chufa rarely flowers—even side by side with the wild local

In arctic tundra and in cold bogs at lower latitudes the flowers of cottongrass (Eriophorum species) *extend conspicuous heads of white hairs. (Richard Harrington)*

form *(C. esculentus esculentus)* while it is blooming profusely.

The name "bulrush" is now reserved for the two hundred different species of *Scirpus,* most of which are marsh plants or grow along the margins of ponds and streams. Bulrushes anchor loose soil and aid in the slow natural conversion of shallow water to land suitable for trees or agricultural crops. Waterfowl eat bulrush fruits, and show almost as strong a liking as muskrats do for the stout scaly rhizomes that form interlocking mats below the water surface. In western North America, two different bulrushes that grow in extensive marshy areas are known as tule grass *(S. acutus* and *S. lacustris),* and the marshes as tules. In the high Andes, where Lake Titicaca lies

Left above: Sea lymegrass (Elymus arenarius) *is well adapted to binding the shifting sand dunes along exposed coasts. It is native to Eurasia, and often grows eight feet tall. (Ingmar Holmasen) Far left: Rye grass* (Secale cereale), *an annual from Eurasia, is more important in Europe than America as a source of flour for breadmaking. It is little used in Asia. (Julius Behnke) Left: Feathery plumes wave fifteen feet high above the fields of sugar cane* (Saccharum offinarum) *in warm countries throughout the world. Soon after, the canes are cut, stripped of leaves, and crushed to extract the sweet juice. (Weldon King)*

along the border between Bolivia and Peru, the Indians collect the upright stems of a local bulrush *(S. totara)* and from these fashion their fishing canoes —known generally as "reed boats." These and other bulrushes often attain a height of eight feet, each of their virtually leafless upright stems crowned by a compound cluster of flowers.

Just by running a finger gently along the edge of a stem, it is easy to distinguish the sawgrasses (or twig-rushes, *Cladium),* which have sharp teeth, from the bulrushes, which are smooth. Differences in their florets and fruits are more fundamental. European sawgrass *(C. mariscus)* is confined to that continent and adjacent parts of Asia and Africa. Now it is regarded as a weed. But the prehistoric people who built the Swiss lake dwellings appear to have had many important uses for the plant, for sawgrass mats and other articles are abundant among the treasures dug up by archeologists. Far more widespread is Jamaican sawgrass *(C. jamaicense),* which produces coarse stiff leaves three to nine feet long, forming dense thickets in marshes of the West Indies, North and South America, eastern Asia and the South Pacific islands, Madagascar, and Africa south of the great deserts. Its saw edges cut at skin and clothing, making these wetlands almost impenetrable.

Utterly different in appearance are the tufts of cottongrass (or bog-cotton, *Eriophorum)* which grow in wet moors and bogs across the North Temperate Zone and into the Arctic. Many of the twenty different species are circumpolar. All are recognizable from the cottonlike tufts of white silky bristles that project beyond the flowers in numerous clusters, each at the end of a slender stalk about a foot in length.

A similarly low habit of growth is usual among the thousand species of true sedge *(Carex),* most of which grow in tufts and tussocks on poorly drained land at almost any latitude or altitude. Members of this genus differ from most others in the family in that they bear their staminate and pistillate florets in

Left: Sedges (Cyperus *species) on the muddy shores of the lower Amazon near Macapa, Brazil, capture sediment and help extend the land. (E. Aubert de La Rue) Right above: Among the few plants that survive in the Great Sandy Desert of Saudi Arabia is the sedge* Cyperus conglomuratus, *known as Al-'Andab. (ARAMCO) Right: Paper was made as early as 2400* B.C. *in Egypt from stalks of the tall common sedge* (Cyperus papyrus) *growing along the Nile. (Conzett and Huber)*

Tall woody grasses, such as Arundo conspicua, *grow on hillsides in New Zealand, known by their native Maori names. (New Zealand Information Service)*

ducts" is a prayer that would appeal to almost two billion rice-eaters in whose diet bread has no place. It would match the custom of Africans whose staple is mealies made of maize, and of Masai tribesmen who rely upon milk and blood from cattle that eat grasses.

Grasses differ from sedges in having cylindrical stems, which are usually hollow straws except at the solid nodes where leaves arise. Each leaf ordinarily has a long sheath, slit along one side, clasping the stem above the node, and a narrow trough-like blade. In many kinds of grasses, the leaf blades curl their sides together in dry weather, reducing the loss of water from their upper surfaces. Elongation of the stem, branching, and production of extra roots all occur at nodes.

Like sedge flowers, those of grasses are called florets, and develop only in clusters—usually in compound clusters. As a cluster expands, pairs of dry chaffy bracts (glumes) separate a little and expose the elongating spikelets, each bearing from one to fifty florets, depending upon the kind of grass. Normally, a floret has two distinctive bracts of its own (the lemma and palea), each somewhat resembling a glume. The inner parts of the floret are exposed, often for only an hour or less each day, when the two bracts are forced apart by the swelling of two or more small rounded bodies called lodicules, found close to the base of the single pistil deep inside. The stamens arise between the lodicules, and consist of very slender filaments and long anthers that generally flop out into the breeze when the bracts spread apart. Usually a grass flower has just three stamens; bamboos are unusual in having six, or as many as one hundred stamens per flower. The pistil usually bears two divergent styles and two long feathery stigmas that extend between the two bracts and capture pollen from the wind; only one seed develops.

Grass pollen appears particularly well adapted to wind distribution, being completely smooth on the outside—never pitted and sculptured like the pollen of other plants. But a great many kinds of grasses rely little upon the wind bringing the pollen they need. Instead, each floret pollinates itself. In wheat, for example, fully a third of the pollen falls from the anthers onto the ripe stigmatic surfaces before the bracts separate and expose the stamens to the wind. However, if pollen from another plant of the same species does arrive in time, it often extends its pollen tubes to the ovules so much faster than the pollen from the same flower that cross-fertilization takes place.

separate parts of the spiky clusters, and produce around the ovary a special, thin, sac-like enclosure (the perigynium) which is retained around the single nutlet, helping it float or be carried by the wind.

Very few of the true sedges are conspicuous enough to be noticed unless they are in flower and their golden stamens wave in the sunlight. The Japanese *C. morrowii* and the New Zealand *C. comans* are sometimes grown as ornamentals in greenhouses or as potted plants for the house. Sedges of all kinds probably serve man best when allowed to grow as a mat holding down the soil, aiding in the natural processes of land building and erosion control, and providing food for birds, muskrats, and other small animals. In the Arctic particularly, they afford some degree of privacy for nesting waterfowl.

THE BOUNTIFUL GRASSES *(Family Gramineae)*

More than the plants of any other family, the grasses contribute food and wealth to mankind and nourish the domestic animals upon which so much of civilization depends. "Give us this day our daily grass pro-

Grasses are the dominant plants on the broad prairies and steppes of the world. They compete with dicotyledonous trees for the savannas and forest edges. In all but the driest deserts, a few grasses manage to survive and reproduce often enough to hold a place. At high latitudes and high altitudes, they are often the only flowering plants. Recently in Alaska and the Canadian Arctic, where fires have destroyed the slow-growing lichens upon which caribou depend, grasses have spread permanent carpets; the caribou must go elsewhere for food, or dwindle in numbers to match their altered range. In all of these places, the grasses prevail because of their tolerance for occasional fires. Burned to ground level, they spring up again from their fibrous roots and concealed horizontal stems, or from dry fruits that have escaped the flames—largely because of their extreme abundance. Grasses recover too from occasional visits by grazing animals in great numbers, and support nomadic herds so well that the last sixty million years have become in many parts of the world the time of grasses and hoofed mammals—particularly those that chew the cud.

1. THE BAMBOO TRIBE (Bambuseae)

The coarsest and most treelike of the grasses are the canes (Arundinaria) of northern Australia and of warm moist regions in Asia and the Americas, and the similar bamboos, which have representatives in these areas and in tropical Africa as well. Canes and bamboos, as we see them, are upright sturdy branches from underground horizontal rhizomes which bind the soil together and send down great numbers of fibrous roots. Each upright branch produces a series of lesser side branches from the axils of the leaves, which are peculiar among grasses in having a petiole-like constriction between the sheath and the blade. The sheath remains for weeks or months clasping the stem, while the blade drops off at the end of the growing season. Spikelike clusters of flowers spring from the axils of leaves on the side branches or near the tops of the main stems. Each flower has three lodicules (or six, in some bamboos). This feature, and the presence of six or more stamens per floret in many bamboos, leads botanists to regard these plants as perhaps the most lily-like of all in the grass family. Some bamboos are equally unusual among grasses in producing armored nutlike fruits, or fleshy berries with a single seed. In the Old World, the melon-bamboo (Melocanna) develops edible fruits that are pear-shaped, and as much as four inches

long. The melon-bamboo is actually viviparous for, if its fruits are not picked, they remain attached until the seed has germinated, using nourishment from the fleshy covering. After its roots and leaves are exposed and ready to take over, the young plant and shriveled fruit are dropped together to the ground.

Indomalaysia has the tallest of all bamboos (Dendrocalamus giganteus), which attains a height of 120 feet. Its young vertical branches from the rhizome often grow as rapidly as fifteen inches a day. Its tremendous stems, like those of many among the seventy-five species of Bambusa in the Old World, prove immensely valuable for building materials in the construction of homes, bridges and fairly large ships. If the solid cross partitions at the nodes are burned out with a red-hot rod thrust in from one end, the bamboo stem becomes a fine pipe for an aqueduct. Short lengths, with partitions intact, serve as containers. For these and hundreds of other uses, the coarse Bambusa vulgaris of Madagascar and tropical Asia is still cultivated widely. Short lengths of rhizome that are thrust into the soil quickly extend vertical stems, supporting bean vines and other climbers, such as crops of yams. If a field set out in this way is neglected for a few years, the bamboos take over and produce a dense forest. A sample of this kind has been left on the island of Jamaica, where a well-traveled road passes through "bamboo walk," all of it escaped B. vulgaris. A bamboo thicket at full luxuriance is one of the most impenetrable barriers known, for the stems are heavily impregnated with silica and quickly dull the sharpest cutting tool with which a traveler attempts to hack a trail.

A canebrake of Arundinaria gigantea, the "southern cane" found in the United States from Virginia to Ohio and southward, is often equally impassable. This is the "wild bamboo" that attains a height of thirty feet if left to grow in a suitable place. It is often cut to make fishing poles and shorter lengths for furniture. Its young stalks, still unsilicified, are enjoyed as fodder by cattle. Still younger "shoots" are harvested for use in Oriental dishes for people, and sold cooked in cans as bamboo shoots. Comparable parts of almost all bamboos find local use, both among human residents and some of the most spectacular animals in the world. Mountain gorillas of the eastern Congo depend largely for food upon the tender young bamboos (Arundinaria and others) of the mixed forests in which they roam. The giant pandas of western China, which are close relatives of raccoons, feed almost exclusively on soft stems and fresh foliage of Bambusa and Dendrocalamus.

Only the historical accidents of animal distribution seem to have left without a parallel creature the considerable bamboo thickets of the American tropics. We thought of this more than once while exploring the tangles of New World bamboos along the Sierra del Muerto in Costa Rica toward Panamá, where some of the seventy species of *Chusquea* and thirty of *Guadua* rise from the mountain slopes at high elevations. These tangles are strongly reminiscent of Africa's gorilla country. In Latin America, the introduced *B. vulgaris* is no more useful than the native *G. angustifolia,* a thorny species that grows to be eighty or ninety feet tall. Other local kinds are more suitable for cattle fodder or paper pulp.

By comparison with the canes and bamboos, most other grasses seem lowly and ephemeral; their leaf blades are not shed from a persistent sheath, and in their flowers the lodicules are less conspicuous, either two in number or lacking altogether. Quite uniformly, the ovary wall becomes fused to the thin "seed coat," as is true in few among the canes and bamboos. Such a fruit is known colloquially as a "grain," and to botanists as a caryopsis. Other than grasses, few plants produce fruits of this type. Fine details of floret clusters and their associated bracts provide distinctions that botanists find significant for separating the grasses into a dozen different tribes.

2. THE FESCUE TRIBE (Festuceae)

In the fescue tribe, the spikelets that bear the florets break off above the glumes and apart between the ripening fruits. Most members of the tribe are meadow grasses of temperate and cool regions, many of them important in pastures and for harvesting as hay. Outstanding for forage are some European fescues *(Festuca);* the smooth brome grass *(Bromus inermis)* native to Siberia, much of China, and northern Europe; Kentucky bluegrass *(Poa pratensis,* introduced from Eurasia although apparently native from Labrador to Alaska), and some of the lovegrasses *(Eragrostis)* of the North Temperate Zone. In Ethiopia, *E. abyssinica* is known as teff, and raised extensively as a cereal grain for local consumption; of the common cereals in human diets, only wheat seems superior to teff for its higher protein content.

More conspicuous members of the fescue tribe are the pampas grasses *(Gynerium* and *Cortaderia)* of South America and the cosmopolitan reeds *(Phragmites communis)* of wetlands and stream borders. In pampas country, tall hedges along rivers and drainage ditches are commonly *G. argenteum,* but the one introduced widely as an ornamental is *C. argentea* from Argentina and Brazil. All of these grasses attain a height of ten to twelve feet, and display their clustered flowers in handsome, tall, waving plumes fifteen to thirty inches long and as much as nine inches across. The flowers of the reeds appear more feathery, perhaps because they seldom produce seeds. For this reason, reeds contribute chiefly shelter to wildlife, whereas pampas grasses yield edible grains through much of each winter season. Reeds, however, have greater value in flood control because their buried rhizomes link together and resist uprooting more effectively than those of related plants.

3. THE BARLEY TRIBE (Hordeae)

The barley tribe consists of grasses in which the flower cluster is a compact symmetrical spike. It often breaks apart at maturity to shed the spikelets, each with one grain, or two, or several, depending upon the species. From four to six grains per spikelet seems customary in the upheld spikes of quack grass (or witch-grass, *Agropyron repens),* now a cosmopolitan weed with Eurasian forebears, and a pest alike in croplands and lawns. Its creeping, ivory-colored rhizomes persist for years in the soil, its gray-green leaves continue to spread during summer's drought, and its wiry fruiting branches defy the lawnmover, developing in July after preferred grasses have ceased to grow vigorously without continual watering. By contrast, the valuable grasses in this tribe are Eurasian annuals with fewer and larger fruits in compact heads: barley *(Hordeum),* wheat *(Triticum),* and rye *(Secale cereale).*

Barley may well be man's oldest cereal crop plant. Apparently the Egyptians were raising it in 5000 B.C., the Mesopotamians in 3500, the Stone-Age peoples of northwestern Europe (including the Swiss lake-dwellers) about 3000, and the Chinese by 2000 B.C. Recent research points to a probable mixture in barley's ancestors between wild plants from Ethiopia and others from southwestern Asia. Through selection, the form of the fruiting head was improved, to become more regular, until each notch in the terminal spike came to contain on opposite sides either three spikelets with a single floret apiece ("six-rowed barley," *H. vulgare)* or one spikelet ("two-rowed barley," *H. distichum).* The heads resemble those of wheat, with a "beard" of long stiff bristly extensions from the spikelets extending four to six inches beyond the end of the spike. Barley, however, contains much less gluten than wheat and cannot be made into a porous bread. Today, more than half of the three billion bushels harvested annually are fed to livestock, particularly pigs and fowl. Another major fraction is made into porridge, or used to give body to soups and stews, or ground to flour and baked into flatbread. In Mohammedan areas of North Africa and western Asia, barley for porridge and flatbreads retains the same popularity it held in biblical Palestine, in classical Greece, and throughout the Roman Empire. Elsewhere, it has been replaced to a greater extent by wheat. On a world basis, about ten per cent of the barley crop is used for making malt for the brewing and distilling industries; in western Europe and the United States, the proportion often exceeds twenty-five per cent. This role depends on the fact that whole barley sprouts readily in water and the young seedlings are rich in the starch-splitting enzyme diastase. If the germinated grains (green malt) are killed by drying and crushing, the product (malt) will convert to sugar not only the remaining starch in the barley but also the starch in other crushed grains added to the brew. Yeasts then have sugar to convert to alcohol, whether in the production of beer or of distilled liquors.

About a fifth of the cultivated land in the world is now devoted to wheat. This is roughly four times the area used for barley, and twice as much as for rice. Yet until the 20th century, when improved wheats were developed and better agricultural methods introduced, the yields were unspectacular and the number of people provided with food far less. Wheats for cereal grains have been cultivated in Asia Minor and Iraq since about 5000 B.C., but no single ancestor can be found. Instead, the several types of modern wheat appear to be descended from successful crosses among wild species of true wheats *(Triticum)* and goatgrasses *(Aegilops)* and perhaps of *Agropyron* as well, all from semi-arid lands of Eurasia. Wheats, in fact, require less water to bear fruit heavily than any other cereal raised in quantity by man. They also contain more protein. Selection, however, has been directed chiefly toward improving the yield per acre, early ripening, resistance to frost or to diseases such as rusts, and ease of threshing out the grains. The spikelets in the compact heads bear two or more florets each, and after self-pollination and ripening, two oblong grains that free themselves from the

The long bristles from heads of ripening barley (Hordeum vulgare) *all extend about equally from the stem. (Grant Heilman)*

Among the most widely cultivated of cereals in cool climates, oats (Avena sativa) *ripen in loose heads. (Grant Heilman)*

Many varieties of sorghum (Sorghum vulgare) *have been developed from the wild Guinea corn of Africa. (Jesse Lunger: National Audubon)*

enclosing scales but do not fall out until struck. Most important today are the macaroni wheat *(T. durum),* which seems to have originated in both Ethiopia and the Mediterranean region, and bread wheat *(T. vulgare),* for which no wild ancestors are known. Bread wheat, which contains more gluten than other strains, probably arose among cultivated fields and was developed by agriculturalists but never showed the ability to persist in competition with other grasses. It is as dependent upon man as he is upon the grain it yields.

Rye is the hardiest of the common cereals, and the most tolerant of poor, sandy soils. It has the tallest and strongest stem (straw), often attaining a height of six to eight feet, compared to four feet in wheat and three in barley. Its bristly beard on flowering and fruiting heads spreads out at an angle to the stem, perhaps helping the florets (usually two on each spikelet) capture pollen from the wind; cross-pollination is usual. Rye is used principally as a food

for livestock, and to a lesser extent for making a tough, porous, dark-colored bread, and as the source of starch and some flavor for distilling rye whiskey.

4. THE OAT TRIBE (Aveneae)

The oat tribe consists of grasses in which the chaffy bracts (glumes) at the base of each spikelet are so large that they tend to hide the florets (two to a spikelet) and the fruits as these mature. Commonly the spikelets are borne in an open cluster, as in the cultivated oats *(Avena sativa),* the ancestors of which seem to have been domesticated as recently as 2500 B.C., in southern Russia, the Near East and North Africa. Probably the total harvest of oats today, chiefly in moist temperate regions, is close to equaling corn (maize) as the world's third most important cereal—after wheat and rice. In many places, however, the grain actually raised does not reach commercial channels, but is used instead locally as food for livestock. It rivals wheat in nutritional features and, in its proteins, offers a balance of those amino acids required for human health better than any other cultivated cereal. The Scotsmen who breakfast on oatmeal porridge and add groats (oat grains) to other traditional dishes, including haggis, gain greatly from an introduced grass that seems ideally suited to their climate.

Wild members of the oat tribe include some perennials that grow in tufts, often in almost pure stands on inhospitable land. Poverty-grass (or Junegrass, *Danthonia spicata*) has a circumpolar distribution, extending as far south in America as Oregon, New Mexico, and Florida, always on exhausted soil, whether it be clay or sand or even gravel. Other members of *Danthonia* are chiefly South African, where they include the Bushman grass *(D. suffrescens)* which colonizes the crests of desert dunes. In Australia, where nearly a third of the country is arid grasslands studded with mulga scrub *(Acacia aneura),* "mulga grass" is usually *D. racemosa.* In New Zealand, where still other danthonias are native to the poorest soil and driest country, they are often interspersed with the related hairgrass *(Deschampsia caespitosa),* which is not quite cosmopolitan although it grows wild also in Tasmania, on African mountains, across northern Eurasia, and south from arctic America to New Jersey, Ohio, and California.

5. THE BENTGRASS TRIBE (Agrostideae)

Timothy grass *(Phleum pratense)* belongs among the large group in the bentgrass tribe. In America during the days of vehicles and farm equipment drawn by horses, timothy was the favorite and leading crop for hay. With the advent of combustion engines and decline of horses, its popularity waned. A native to Eurasia, it was called Herd's grass by New Englanders in memory of John Herd, who found it in 1700 growing near the Piscataqua River at Portsmouth, New Hampshire, apparently its first landfall in the New World. In a letter dated July 16, 1747, written by Benjamin Franklin to Jared Elliot, is the earliest known use of the name timothy for it. Franklin identified Herd's grass as "mere timothy," perhaps a reference to Timothy Hansen, the man credited with introducing the immigrant grass from New England to Maryland. In America today, as in much of Eurasia, timothy grows as a roadside weed, raising on a slender extension of each upright stem a compact cylindrical flowering head two to four inches tall and one-quarter of an inch in diameter, from which

purple stamens project before they open and expose their golden pollen.

If timothy grass cannot be used as fuel for a tractor or automobile, at least one of its relatives *(Stipa tenacissima,* known as esparto) has been harvested in quantity as a fast-burning fuel to give power in railway locomotives and steam-electric power plants in North Africa! This wild, coarse grass has long held a place of importance along the Barbary Coast, for weaving into sandals, carpets, hats, and bags, for making brooms and rope for the Spanish Navy, and as a stock feed for camels, goats and sheep. Hand-pulled from the arid soil, it is still hauled in enormous loads by camels to the ports. There it may be cleaned of a useful wax, not much inferior to carnauba wax, and then shipped to Great Britain to be made into wrapping paper. A close relative is bunchgrass *(S. ichu),* which is the principal food for livestock on the high plains of Bolivia above ten thousand feet elevation—the altoplano between the mountain ranges southeast of Lake Titicaca. These living conditions are not too unlike those where the triple-awn grasses *(Aristida)* are found in the mulga scrubland of Australia, on the fringes of the Kalahari Desert in southern Africa and of the Sahara in North Africa, and on the driest plains of the United States. The ability to curl every leaf and avoid water loss that is characteristic of these plants is highly developed in marram grass (or beachgrass, *Ammophila),* found binding the sand along the shores of America and Europe, but not in the bentgrasses *(Agrostis)* and reedgrasses *(Calamagrostis)* of pastures, golf courses and lawns in temperate and cool countries.

6. THE CANARY GRASS TRIBE (Phalarideae)

The shining fruits sold as "canary seed" for caged birds of sparrow size come from an annual grass native to the Canary Islands but now escaped in most parts of the world where people keep small birds as pets. The canary grass *(Phalaris canariensis)* has loose, rough leaves but produces a distinctive flowering head atop a slender smooth stem. The cluster of florets, one at the tip of each spikelet (beyond two sterile florets), crowd together into a mass about an inch long and one-half inch in diameter, shaped like a tulip bud. Flour from ground canary seed is made into "weaver's glue," which is used to size cotton fabrics, giving them a slight stiffness and a feeling of being new. A related reed-grass *(P. arundinacea)* of Eurasia and North America grows wild as a perennial in meadows and swales; a horticultural variety

The long stiff bristles of the flower cluster of broom sorghum (Sorghum vulgare technicus) are gathered for sale to industry. (Jesse Lunger: National Audubon)

with striped leaves is cultivated as "ribbon grass."

Meadows and swales, both brackish and fresh, in the cooler parts of Eurasia and North America provide a favored habitat for holy grass (or vanilla-grass, or Indian-grass, *Hierochloë odorata),* which comes into flower in late spring. Its vanilla-like odor is so pleasant that people who are close to the land tend to take advantage of it. In northern Europe, the holy grass is gathered to be strewn before church doors on saint's days, perfuming the air and the churchgoers who walk over it. In America, Indian women and children used to gather this grass and

weave its slightly dried stems into fragrant baskets that kept emitting their characteristic odor for months. Colonists collected the flower heads, which are loose and spreading, to dry them and stuff them into bed pillows, or into sachet bags to be placed between linens in closets and dresser drawers.

7. THE GRAMA TRIBE (Chlorideae)

In the days when New England was still a frontier, the central plains of North America from central Canada to Mexico and from the Rockies to just west of the Appalachian Mountains were a vast grassland with a wealth of buffalo grass *(Buchloë dactyloides)* and grama grasses *(Bouteloua).* Upon their green growth and drying hay, incredible populations of nomadic bison and pronghorns lived. The prairie wolves that picked off the weak, the defective, and the old animals spaced out their meals of bison and pronghorn by catching prairie dogs and gophers venturing from deep burrows under the grass roots. Now over much of the area, these grasses and animals are gone, replaced by agricultural crops and livestock from distant lands. In places too arid for wheat and too poor for ranch cattle in large numbers, the buffalo grass and grama grasses still persist, often mixed with immigrants such as Rhodes grass *(Chloris gayana)* from South Africa and other species of the genus from Southeast Asia, Australia, or South America. They are often called "windmill grasses" because their flowering and fruiting clusters tend to splay out in branches with spikelets along only one side—a distinctive feature of all members of the tribe. This pattern is well known in the dogtooth grasses *(Cynodon)* of Australian grasslands, and in the European species *(C. dactylon)* now naturalized and become a weed over much of North America, where it is known as Bermuda grass or scutch-grass. Bermuda grass is a perennial in warm climates, where it tolerates close grazing and spreads rapidly despite hot sun. From Virginia northward it is killed by winter cold, and grows as a summer annual.

Similar one-sided sprays of flowers and fruits develop on the marsh-grasses (or cord-grasses, *Spartina)* that grow as coarse perennials in salt marshes, fresh-water marshes, and alkaline sloughs along coasts and as far inland in Europe as the Mediterranean coast, in North and South America, and on remote islands in the Southern Hemisphere. One American species *(S. alterniflora)* offers a useful marker for sharp-eyed operators of small boats. It grows along coasts from Newfoundland to Florida and Texas between the line of mean sea level and that of the highest predicted tides for each region. By noticing the zone of marsh occupied by this grass, the observer can often decide intelligently whether to beach his boat or anchor it, because he can tell how far the tidal change will go. Inadvertently introduced into Europe, this grass has hybridized with a near relative *(S. maritima)* to produce an aggressive plant now spreading widely. The European *S. maritima,* like the American salt-meadow grass *(S. patens),* has long contributed forage known as "saltwater hay" as a cheap food for cattle.

8. THE ZOYSIA TRIBE (Zoysieae)

Among the most successful introductions into parts of the world where grassy lawns are appreciated, are several perennial grasses from the Far East belonging to the genus *Zoysia.* Japanese lawn grass *(Z. japonica)* from Japan and Korea is coarse, and tolerates even the cold winters of Canada. Manila grass *(Z. matrella)* from the Philippines requires a Mediterranean climate, with little frost. Least tolerant is Mascarene grass *(Z. tenuifolia)* from Mauritius and other islands in the Indian Ocean, which produces extremely fine blades on its leaves. All develop a strong turf of interlocking rhizomes that tend to block invasion by weeds and maintain a resilient carpet of green along highways, in parks, on golf courses and other recreational areas, or around private homes.

9. THE RICE TRIBE (Oryzeae)

Rice has been the prime food of the Orient since about 2400 B.C. At present it is the principal source of nourishment for about two-thirds of the world's people, in a culture where each adult who can afford it will eat between two hundred and four hundred pounds of rice a year—most of it simply boiled for a minimum of time. Paradoxically, rice is the most popular but not the most abundant cereal. It is the poorest in protein, both quantitatively and qualitatively, of all the grains used for human food. Only the people whose principal food is cassava *(Manihot)* or taro *(Colocasia)* suffer more from nutritional deficiencies than those who depend on rice. But where water and cheap labor are abundant and there is no fuel to cook a cereal product more than rice requires, rice is virtually the only possible crop that can support a large population. Fewer tons of rice are raised than of wheat, partly due to inefficient methods and partly to a smaller area of wetlands available with the proper temperature range and rainfall. That so many people live on rice means that most of them barely survive on the quantities they can grow or purchase. Famine is inevitable among them whenever the rains are too few to keep the paddy fields full of water until the grain is ripe, or when any other calamity prevents the harvesting of the all-important rice crop.

Cultivated rice *(Oryza sativa)* has become, like wheat, dependent upon human care and unable to grow wild in competition with native vegetation. Seed grain is usually broadcast or, to save time, germinated in bamboo containers and set out by hand in irrigated fields when it is four or five inches tall. Each seed produces a clump of upright stems with slightly rough leaves almost completely sheathing

Indomalaysian bamboo (Dendrocalamus), *which grows as much as fifteen inches daily, is valuable in construction of houses and bridges, and for use as tight containers and long pipes.* (Walter Dawn: National Audubon)

the internodes. At the top of each stem, a loose tassel-like cluster of flowers develops, the small florets one to a spikelet, self-pollinating themselves from six stamens apiece. The long slender grains become hard with starch, and remain within their surrounding bracts until the fruiting heads are cut, dried, and threshed—often by simple pounding with blunt poles in a pail-sized cavity. The grain coats are brown and contain most of the vitamins and proteins the plant provides. But in many parts of the world, these nourishing coats are polished away to reveal white rice that is far less suitable for food. Processers may modify them further by covering each grain with a thin film of sugar and talc, to keep it from sticking to its neighbors while cooking.

Wild rice (or water-oats, *Zizania)* are tall aquatic annual grasses of eastern Asia and North America, where they provide luxury fruits for waterfowl. The florets, one to a spikelet, are either staminate with six stamens or pistillate and produce slender, brown-

Green-striped yellow bamboo (Bambusa multiplex, *var.* alphonse) *from southern China provides forage for cattle.* (John Gerard: National Audubon)

coated grains the Indians used to harvest by bending the fruiting heads over a canoe and striking them repeatedly. A pound of wild rice costs twenty to thirty times as much as an equal quantity of cultivated rice. Cooked as a vegetable it has infinitely more flavor and much more protein and vitamins.

10. THE MILLET TRIBE (Paniceae)

Millets have long been known as the "poor man's cereal," often the principal food of people in the East and of Africa who are unable to afford rice. Millets grow on poor soil where the rainfall is too scanty for rice. Often the seed is broadcast in spring, the growing plants receiving little or no cultivation. Harvested with sickles, the crop is carried to threshing grounds where women tread on the severed fruiting heads and winnow the product to let the breeze carry away the hulls. Under these conditions no substitute crop will provide as much food. Millet grains actually stand between wheat and rice in protein content. Although the multitudes who eat millet by necessity often long for rice as a "better" grain, they already have the better cereal. Like rice, millets are nonglutenous and can be made into only a flatbread. Commonly they are eaten as porridge, or as cooked sprouted grain, or let ferment to make a beer such as the kaffir beer of southern Africa. In western Europe and America, millets are raised in small amounts as forage crops or as winter food for wild birds. Packaged seeds for pet birds commonly include millets.

The word "millet" is applied to many different plants from which small grains can be gathered. Proso millet (or bread millet, *Panicum miliaceum)* is probably the one that was raised by the Swiss lake-dwellers and in China, perhaps prior to the domestication of wheat. Today it is grown extensively in China, Manchuria and eastern Russia, its grain ripening sixty to eighty days after sowing. In America it is cultivated to a limited extent as a forage crop and for bird seed. Little millet *(P. miliare)* is more popular as a food for people in India. Both of these crop plants are panic-grasses, members of the largest genus in the family, with about four hundred species widely distributed in temperate and tropical regions, many of them important forage plants on the pampas and campos of South America. Like other plants of the millet tribe, they produce spikelets with two florets each, the terminal one with both pistil and stamens, the inner one staminate or neuter.

Tallest of the millets is pearl millet *(Pennisetum*

glaucum), which is a rainy season crop in the Sudan and parts of India. In Nigeria and other areas of West Africa, an early millet *(P. typhoideum)* is often substituted for it. Both are close relatives of elephant grass *(P. purpureum),* which spreads over large areas of savanna country and forms tall-grass prairies in East Africa, southward to beyond the Limpopo River.

Elephant grass is often "higher than an elephant's eye," as the popular song puts it, requiring the pachyderms to raise themselves on their hind legs in the circus-act stance to see over it. Antelopes do the same, and we suspect recognize one another by just their distinctive horns and heads when only this portion of each animal is visible above the grass. The need to keep members of a herd together in tall grass may well have forced antelopes to evolve these prominent features. We feel distinctly handicapped and somewhat apprehensive while driving a small car along a narrow road through elephant grass, knowing that it conceals elephants, herds of antelopes, lions and lesser animals that may suddenly cross right in front of us. The road seems a canyon and the grass a forest wall.

In China and the Near East, foxtail millet *(Setaria italica,* which probably originated in India) is cultivated today as a drought-resistant crop to nourish people. In western Europe and North America, several different horticultural strains of this plant are raised for hay on land too dry to be comparably productive with other grasses. At the other extreme is Japanese millet (or barnyard grass, *Echinochloa crusgalli),* often known as bhasti in the Far East where it is cultivated; it grows well in moist soils and shallow marshes. In America it is the wild millet familiar to sportsmen, who know that ducks, muskrats, upland game birds, and many song birds are attracted to it for the plentiful hard little fruits it drops. They remain protected within the hardened bracts (palea and lemma) of the florets, neither germinating nor deteriorating for months—even in water.

We notice the same longevity in the fruits of crabgrass *(Digitaria sanguinalis).* This European plant reached America long ago as an impurity in seeds, and is now widespread as a weed. Its sprawling stems put down adventitious roots at any node that comes into contact with the soil. Sometimes we wonder if we should give up trying to grow other grasses in the lawn around our home and, instead, raise crabgrass as is done in Poland and some parts of Germany. There it not only provides forage for domestic animals but also fruits that can be hand-picked and cooked in milk like sago. Europeans claim that crabgrass is highly nutritious for man, but only in the Southern States have Americans put the weed to use—as food for cattle. The related acha *(D. exilis),* probably domesticated in the Sudan many centuries ago, is cultivated as a food crop in northern Nigeria and westward along the fringes of the great deserts in Africa.

Sandburs (or burgrasses, *Cenchrus)* from the southeastern United States and tropical America are noxious weeds that have spread despite the irritation they cause. Growing in dry waste places, on sandy soil even close to the sea, and on exhausted land, these plants sprawl until their fruits are nearly ripe. Then the stem tips turn upward, each supporting from eight to twenty short spikelets in the form of a deciduous bur. The two to six florets in a spikelet may have produced fruits, but these are hidden among modified bracts that extend needle-sharp stiff prickles in all directions. They jab into the feet and legs of passing animals, into socks and even leather shoes. One *(C. pauciflorus)* from Mexico and Texas has escaped in Maine around woolen mills, carried as an almost inextricable object picked up by a sheep. These and other sandbur fruits often work their way through a sheep's coat and cause serious irritation of its skin. The burs of other species have spread into the West Indies, Malaysia, Hawaii, and islands equally remote. They have reached Canada, southern California, Europe, and the Far East. Everywhere by late summer they are ready to cause acute pain and to benefit from free transportation, however reluctantly provided.

11. THE SORGHUM TRIBE (Andropogoneae)

Members of this tribe bear two florets in each spikelet, only the terminal one producing fruit as well as pollen. Most are tropical grasses. However, the one hundred and eighty different kinds of beardgrasses (or bluestems, *Andropogon)* include perennial species that contribute some of the most important native hay on the American prairies, some of the best forage in the mulga scrubland of Australia, and food for wild animals in grasslands still nearer the Equator. The oilgrasses *(Cymbopogon)* from the Old World tropics include the source of citronella oil *(C. nardus* from East Asia), of lemon-grass oil *(C. citratus,* sweet rush, of India), and ginger-grass oil *(C. martinii* of the East Indies)—all used in perfumery and to conceal the flavor of unpleasant medicines. Citronella oil used to be popular as a mosquito repellent.

From the obviously grasslike members of this tribe, sugar cane *(Saccharum)* and the various kinds of sorghum *(Sorgum)* differ in having pith-filled, solid stems. Nearly a dozen species of *Saccharum,* none of them with much sugar in their stems, grow wild over a broad area of Asia from India through Malaysia to New Guinea and the Philippines. But the ancestor of cultivated sugar cane *(S. officinarum)* remains unknown. Samples of the plant from Asia reached Mediterranean Europe during the Dark Ages, perhaps as early as A.D. 636, brought by Arab traders. Sugar made from its juice remained an expensive luxury into the 14th century, but thereafter international trade in this flavoring and food increased, based upon plantations established in India and the East Indies. Two centuries later, the culture of the plant—still almost exclusively by vegetative propagation—spread to Africa and tropical America.

Sugar cane is a perennial grass attaining a height of ten to twenty feet, surmounted at maturity by a plumelike tassel or "arrow" bearing hundreds of small spikelets. At this stage, the leaves are already dying and drying. They can be burned off, without significant damage to the juicy stalks, before these are harvested, either by laborers armed with long sharp knives or by machines. Crushed by the crudest or most advanced type of machinery, the canes yield a dark brown opaque juice that is ten to twelve per cent sugar, slightly acid, and mildly laxative. The fibrous residue is called *bagasse*. It can be dried to become a fuel for the steam engines driving the crushers in the sugar mill, or to evaporate the water from the juice after the solution has been treated to neutralize its acids, filtered to remove suspended matter, mordanted to precipitate nonsugars, and decolorized toward the production of white sugar. Progressively the product can be purified until it is 99.9 per cent sucrose, as the purest substance on the grocery shelves. Alternatively the bagasse can be made into wallboard, or stock feed, or fertilizer. Many of the substances removed in purifying the sugar find economic uses. In less advanced countries, the cane juice is merely concentrated by boiling until it can be cast in wooden molds to become flat sticky cakes eight or ten inches in diameter and two to three inches thick. The dark product is panela or rapadura, and contains enough protein, minerals and other materials in addition to sugars to make it a far more nourishing additive to foods than the highly refined white sugar of progressive civilizations. Many of these nutrients remain in the final liquor from sugar refineries, sold as "black-strap molasses," and used now to supplement cattle feeds more than to improve human diets directly. Connoisseurs of rum, made from fermented cane juice, claim that this alcoholic drink also contains nutrients that are regularly removed in the refining of white sugar.

Sorghum probably originated in equatorial Africa, where it is the leading cereal grain, partly because it is so resistant to heat and drought. In hot dry regions its grain largely replaces corn in feeding cattle. In South Africa, we found both sorghum and corn (maize) being ground into a meal known as "mealies," used for making porridge, bread, cakes, paste, and beer. The principal species is *Sorgum vulgare,* but the differences that have been developed to distinguish the many horticultural varieties are so marked that it is easy to assume each to be a different kind altogether. Guinea corn *(S. vulgare vulgare)* with fruiting heads of only moderate density is cultivated as a cereal in the Mediterranean region. Durra *(S. vulgare durra)* in the Nile delta and in North Africa, kaffir corn *(S. vulgare caffrorum)* of South Africa, and shallu *(S. vulgare roxburghii)* of India all produce heavy heads of fruit in a tight cluster perhaps ten inches high and three in diameter, with thousands of individual seeds. Less productive but still highly valued are feterita *(S. vulgare caudata)* of the Sudan, and kaoliang *(S. vulgare nervosum)* of China. The stiff branches of the flower head, rather than the seeds, are the desirable part of broom corn *(S. vulgare technicus),* whereas the sweet, juicy stems of sweet sorghum *(S. vulgare saccharatum)* yield sorghum molasses, and the whole plant prior to flowering is used for forage where Sudan grass *(S. vulgare sudanensis)* is raised. A related species from southern Europe and western Asia has been introduced into America, where it is known as Johnson grass *(S. halepense),* after a William Johnson who promoted its culture in the United States as forage for cattle before the plant escaped and became a serious weed in cultivated fields.

12. THE MAIZE TRIBE (Maydeae)

Of all the members in the grass family, the most highly specialized are maize (or Indian corn, *Zea mays*) and its few close relatives. Distinctively, they bear their staminate and pistillate flowers on separate spikelets. In some members, all of the staminate spikelets form a "tassel" at the end of the stem or of its branches, while the pistillate spikelets are sunken into a fleshy "cob" in the axil of a leaf, exposing only the tips of their threadlike stigmas as the "silk" beyond the surrounding, leaflike bracts of the "husk." A separate pollen grain, carried from a stamen in a floret of a tassel must reach each strand of "silk" for the individual fruit to develop as a "kernel" on the cob. Because the pistillate spikelets sunken in the cob are regularly paired, the number of rows of kernels is always even: eight, or ten, or twelve, or more, to as many as thirty-six. In other members of the tribe, the staminate spikelets and pistillate spikelets are combined in the same cluster.

The date on which the first Europeans met maize —the most important contribution to man's economy from plants of the Western Hemisphere—is well documented. It was November 5, 1492, when two Spanish explorers sent by Christopher Columbus to investigate the interior of Cuba returned with a report. Translated into English by contemporaries, it told of "a sort of graine they call maize which was well tasted, bak'd, dry'd and made into flour." Later, the Indians were found to be raising this crop from Canada to Chile. Seminomadic tribes grew "Indian corn" (later known merely as corn) as a supplement to the meat the hunters brought in. Or they raided more agricultural tribes and stole corn that was in storage. The mound-builders of the Mississippi Valley and the cliff-dwellers of the American Southwest, the pueblo people, the Aztecs of Central America and the Incas of South America, were all corn-growers and corn-eaters. Abundant harvests of this nutritious cereal allowed the time needed to develop the civilizations the Spanish found in Latin America. Within less than sixty years, the seed grains of maize carried to Europe by Columbus and the Spanish, and to Africa by the Portuguese, allowed this new crop to spread eastward to China, north to Scandinavia, and south to the Cape of Good Hope. Its use spread even faster than that of tobacco from the New World.

Not until 1948 did it become clear that the ancestors of domesticated corn were numerous, and that a ear-type crop cultivated for centuries in South America somehow was crossed with teosinte (Euchlaena mexicana) of Mexico to produce hybrids among which more modern maize appeared. Several characteristics of modern grama-grass (or sesame-grass, Tripsacum) from warm parts of North America can be found also in cultivated corn, suggesting that this too contributed to the evolution in human hands of a superior cereal plant—one that never has had to face real competition from wild local vegetation. Indian corn was as dependent upon the Indians as they were on it. It is a true cultigen, a product of man's culture as well as a support for civilization.

Corn of some kind is now grown in Argentina to forty degrees South latitude, in Canada and the U.S.S.R. to fifty-eight degrees North latitude, in the Andes of Peru to above twelve thousand feet, and around the Caspian Sea below sea level. Only wheat is given more cropland; only wheat and rice support more people. Yet a more variable product would be hard to find. Some of the varieties raised in the Andes of Ecuador produce ears less than an inch in diameter and two inches long. One cultivated in the Jalapa region of Mexico has ears as much as four inches in diameter and twenty-five inches long. Where the summer is short, as in Canada and the Pyrenees, some of the flint corns mature in two months. In the long growing season of northern South America, a different variety takes eleven months to attain full size and ripen its kernels.

Under both haphazard and scientific methods, corn has been developed into half a dozen general types or categories: 1. Pod corn (or cow corn, or husk corn, Z. mays tunicata), in which each kernel on the cob is surrounded by its own membranous bract, as well as by the husk around the whole ear; 2. Sweet corn (Z. mays saccharata), in which the transformation of carbohydrates from sugars to starches is delayed until the corn is "old," allowing people to cook it by boiling or roasting, to can it or freeze it while still "green," its food reserves still sweet and translucent, its fruits susceptible to shrinkage and wrinkling; 3. Flour corn (or soft corn, or squaw corn, Z. mays amylacea), in which the starch in each kernel remains soft and mealy, easily ground or chewed; 4. Dent corn (Z. mays indentata), in which unequal drying of the hard and soft starch portions of the kernel leads to formation of a dimple or a crease at the exposed end; 5. Flint corn (Z. mays indurata), in which the starch is almost all very hard and the kernels retain their shape upon drying; and 6. Pop-

Right above: Bread wheat (Triticum vulgare) *is regarded by many people as the most important cereal grass in the world. These full heads, shown slightly larger than natural size, grew in central Jutland, Denmark. (Lorus and Margery Milne)   Right: Cottongrass* (Eriophorum *species) is a showy sedge that is found wild in cool bogs of the Northern Hemisphere in the arctic and alpine regions of both the Old World and the New. (Werner Schulz)   Far right: More of the world's people depend upon rice* (Oryza sativa) *for food than any other crop. It grows well only in flooded fields. (Lorus and Margery Milne)*

corn *(Z. mays everta)*, in which the hard starch and some water are held within a tough membrane, which ruptures suddenly when heat turns the water to steam. Pod corn is raised chiefly by Indians in the Andes, as they have been doing for thousands of years. Sweet corn remains largely a delicacy of the United States and Canada. Flour corn predominates only in the mountains of Bolivia, Ecuador and Peru, where some strains produce kernels almost an inch in each direction. Dent corn is the principal type cultivated in Iowa, Illinois, Nebraska and adjacent parts of the American "Corn Belt"; most of the corn produced there is of hybrid stock, with spectacular yields. In America, dent corn is now chiefly yellow corn, following the discovery that this color corresponds to a higher content of the precursor of vitamin A (carotene), and that yellow corn is therefor more nourishing. It is used for feeding livestock, especially pigs and cattle, for production of corn starch, corn oil, beer, corn liquor (Bourbon whiskey), and other products. For people in the South who enjoy hominy, grits, corn meal mush, and similar foods, dent corn is also raised in a white variety to match the preference of the buyers. Yellow dent corn, ground coarsely into meal, is the basis for the traditional Johnnycake of eastern Canada. It is also the principal type of corn met in Latin America and much of Africa. Corn bread made from it is too tender to cut into slices, but tortillas baked on a stone *comal* over a wood fire can be a meal in themselves, or a plate on which to spread a thick stew, or an edible tool with which to pick up food and convey it to the mouth.

Flint corn is preferred for cultivation in Canada and some northern states because it germinates more readily than other types in cold soil. It finds favor also among corn growers in tropical lowlands because it is so resistant to attack by weevils. Popcorn, which is produced almost entirely in a few areas of Iowa and Nebraska, has become in the United States a traditional confectionary to enjoy at the movies, a party, or a ball game.

Maize may not be the grass family's final contribution to the foods of mankind. A half-hidden gift may be waiting in the grains of Jobs'-tears *(Coix lachryma-jobi)* or one of the five other members of this little genus from India and China. Varieties of Jobs'-tears

The balisier or wild plantain (Heliconia bihai) *of the banana family grows ten to fifteen feet high in Trinidad, where it is the national emblem. (E. Javorsky)*

are already being raised for human food in marshy areas of eastern Asia and the Philippines, where the seed-sized fruits are known as adlay. These grains prove to contain more protein in proportion to carbohydrate than any other cereal tested. But horticultural improvements will be needed to make them harvestable in commercial quantities, for each ripe fruit is enclosed in a stony bract. For years these enclosed fruits have been collected and sold as beads for rosaries and other ornaments, each bluish-white and shining as though made of porcelain and wet like a giant tear. At flowering time, the bract is open at the end, cupped around and concealing the pistillate flower as well as the base of the stalk that supports the staminate spikelet. After pollination, the staminate spikelet drops off, the bract closes, hiding a grain that could have a tremendous future.

CHAPTER 35

The Bananas and Their Kin

CUES: *If the monocot plant bears flowers with an obvious bilateral symmetry, in which the three carpels are united in the pistil, and the seeds develop endosperm as the food store for the seedling, then the ovary is inferior and the plant belongs to the Order Scitaminales. It may be a banana tree, a bird-of-paradise flower, a ginger, a canna, or a zebra plant.*

The two thousand different members of this Order are denizens of the humid tropics, well represented in both the New World and the Old. From their remote ancestral connection to the lilies, they have become specialized in many ways and now seem closest to the orchids. They differ from orchids in possession of endosperm and in having at least one of the stamens modified to become sterile, as a "staminode" often like a petal.

THE BANANA FAMILY (Musaceae)

While standing under a banana "tree" *(Musa)* that is twenty to forty feet in height, or a traveler's-tree

(*Ravenala madagascariensis*) of comparable height, it is hard to think of them as giant herbs. Yet the true nature of the "trunk" on a banana plant becomes evident when it is felled by a few expert blows with a machete. Although eight to ten inches in diameter, it consists entirely of leaf bases overlapping one another—petioles reaching all the way from the rhizome in the ground to the waving blades each ten or twelve feet long high above. At the very center of these concentric petioles is a slender stalk an inch or two in diameter, continuing upward to a height of perhaps fifteen feet, where it becomes exposed by the spreading petioles and arches over to support the terminal cluster of flowers. One "stem" of bananas per tree is the rule.

The pendant floral cluster begins as a compound bud six inches or more in diameter and slightly longer than broad, shaped like a plumb bob. From its stalk end, one purplish bract after another curls back and upward to expose a dozen or so tubular flowers, each with six yellow petals, five functional stamens and one staminode around the central pistil. Bees visit and pollinate the flowers, each of which produces a banana in the "hand" arising in the axil of the purple bract. Elongation of the central stalk allows the developing bananas to enlarge without interfering with the curling of additional bracts and the development of further hands on the same "stem."

On the great banana plantations established by the United Fruit Company in Latin America and the West Indies, we have watched skilled workmen felling the banana trees on which the fruit had reached the critical stage of growth matching the distance it would travel to a specific market. The green bananas would ripen as they traveled, and must arrive on the fruiterer's stand just a day or two before freckling of the skin would develop, showing them to be ready to eat. While one or two men hacked down the "tree," others held the top with forked poles, ready to lower it swiftly under complete control until the "stem" of heavy fruit could be rested on the padded shoulder of a waiting carrier, who would place it gently on an accompanying truck. With the "tree" itself carried off by another vehicle to the compost heap, the underground rhizome would be allowed to extend another upright branch without interference. Usually just three at a time were permitted in each "stool" from a rhizome: the maturing one with fruit, a younger one that would soon take its place when the harvesters passed, and one still more juvenile— perhaps only a foot or two tall.

Edible bananas all come from plants whose ances-

tors originated in West Africa. Before the beginning of written records, these were prized as "God's gift to man" and introduced in East Africa and India. Alexander the Great met the fruit when his armies invaded the Indian subcontinent, and reported that wise men sat in the shade of banana "trees" and ate bananas. This legend is perpetuated in the scientific name of the banana plants whose fruits are most commonly eaten raw *(M. sapientum)*. A coarser variety, prepared usually by boiling or frying, is known in Latin America as *platanos* ("plantains") instead of *guineos,* and are produced by a taller plant *(M. paradisiaca).* In Ethiopia, the largest of all banana "trees" *(M. ensete)* provides local people with leaves up to twenty feet long, the juicy petioles of which are eaten and the fruit disregarded. Still another East African member of the genus, which has seventy-five different species native to the tropics of the Old World, furnishes the Philippine Islands with their principal export crop: Manila hemp or *abacá,* as tough fibers from the petioles of *M. textilis.*

An irrigated plantation of any *Musa* species has some of the features of an orchard and many of a swamp. Herons and other waterfowl hunt there for frogs. Bats take refuge for the day in the still furled leaves that are in the gradual process of opening. But every banana plant fairly glows with green health, its welfare tended almost daily with measured amounts of fertilizer, or water, or fungicide, or insecticide, the weeds kept low so that they will not waste moisture or harbor pests.

In natural swampy areas beyond the banana plantations in Latin America, wild bananas (or platanillos, *Heliconia*) grow as much as ten feet tall but rarely produce a trunklike column from the long slender petioles of the waving leaves. Their floral bracts arise in an alternating array from the two sides of an upright stalk, often brilliant yellow grading into orange-red, opening to expose a few purple flowers that attract hummingbirds. In some the series of bracts diverge from an upright stalk, while

Right: Of the forty species of Heliconia, *called "wild banana" in their native West Indies and tropical America, several produce pendant clusters of bright flowers. Far right: As the pendant bud of the edible banana* (Musa sapientum) *opens, one big bract bends upward at a time to expose the flowers that can produce a "hand" of bananas. The ripening fruit turn upward still more. (Both by Lorus and Margery Milne)*

in other species the display is a pendant one. In Trinidad, the balisier *(H. bihai)* is cultivated for its beauty and has been chosen as the national flower.

Birds are the chief pollinators for related plants in the Old World, in this case sunbirds which reach their long beaks into the deep groups of petals to sip the nectar and catch minute insects. Only a bird seems strong enough, in fact, to reach the nectar in a bird-of-paradise flower *(Strelitzia)* from South Africa. In a one-sided, elongated cluster, these blossoms open in sequence at intervals of a few days. First the pointed orange sepals separate, two rising almost vertically upward, the other lowering itself away from the equally-long purple petals and extended style-and-stigma. Local people think of this as the "crane flower," the upright sepals the crest of the bird, the lower parts the open beak. The third petal in *Strelitzia* is much smaller and broader. It conceals the nectaries and can be raised only after a bird has brushed its breast feathers against the stigma and rested slightly atop the two longer petals, which part like long doors and allow the five functional stamens to press their pollen against the bird as it reaches its reward. This arrangement makes cross-pollination highly probable.

The traveler's-tree of Madagascar produces an almost palmlike pattern of giant oval leaves, whose petioles fit together at the base into a flat array as regular as a woven basket. Some people claim that under natural conditions, the array is always oriented north and south, providing a traveler with a natural compass. Others suggest that a thirsty man could always get a drink of rain water from the *Ravenala* by cutting through a petiole and reaching the quart or more held by it against the rest of the array. Where the traveler's-tree grows, it might be easier to

Left above: The bird-of-paradise flower (Strelitzia reginae) *from South Africa produces long-stalked leaves like those of a banana. Several flowers rise from each of the boat-shaped bracts that tip the flowering stalks. (Lorus and Margery Milne) Far left: Torch ginger* (Phaeomeria magnifica) *from Indonesia is by far the showiest of the ginger family, and one of the most spectacular plants in the world. Each "torch" is a waxy cone as much as ten inches in diameter. (Josef Muench) Left: Even when none of the two-to-three-inch white flowers are showing from the floral head of Malay ginger* (Costus speciosus), *the plant stands out brilliantly in the rain forest. (E. Javorsky)*

find water elsewhere—and with fewer mosquito wrigglers, frog tadpoles, and other creatures swimming in it!

THE GINGER FAMILY *(Zingiberaceae)*

Indomalaysia is the native home for a majority of the 1400 species in this family. To many people, their spicy contributions continue to be an important resource from among the mysteries of the Far East. Ginger itself comes from the fleshy rhizomes of *Zingiber officinale,* a perennial herbaceous plant that grows in reedlike fashion to a height of three or four feet, with alternate narrow leaves. No longer found wild, it is assumed to have been discovered in tropical Asia and adopted by early man. Arab traders found a market for it in classical Greece and Rome, without disclosing its origin. In India it has had a place in cookery and medicine for thousands of years. Generally the fleshy, irregular rhizomes are washed and dried; they remain starchy, impregnated with a volatile oil that gives the spicy flavor and a resin from which the pungent "heat" arises. If the fresh rhizome is washed, scraped, and preserved in sugar syrup, it becomes the delicate preserve known as candied ginger, now exported from both China and the West Indies.

From the washed and desiccated rhizomes of a related plant *(Curcuma longa)* native to the Oriental tropics and cultivated extensively in India and China comes the flavorful dyestuff known as turmeric. Along with ginger and the powdered dry leaves of the shrub *Murraya,* turmeric provides the distinctive character in curry sauces which, in turn, add interest to bland dishes made from rice. The piquancy of curry "powder" is often altered slightly by additions of still another product from a plant of the ginger family: cardamom, from the dried fruit and seeds of *Elettaria cardamomum,* a native of India that is much cultivated there, in Ceylon, and in Latin America. Cardamom plants are often raised between the rows of tea or rubber on plantations, as tall coarse herbs with large leaves. Cardamom as a spice finds use also in some kinds of meat sausage, in medicinal preparations, perfumes, and incense.

Among members of the ginger family, the flowers arise either singly in the axils of conspicuous bracts, or in terminal clusters. The three sepals are united into a cup surrounding the bases of an equal number of separate petals, which usually are of a different color. Around the central pistil, a single fertile stamen is flanked by two infertile stamens united to form a petal-like lip—often the most handsome part of the flower. Two more representatives of stamens may be present, as showy staminodes.

Many of the gingers combining floral beauty with tolerance for living conditions indoors or in summer gardens of the temperate zones have been introduced widely by horticulturalists. Among them are graceful species of so-called "wild gingers" *(Costus)* from the tropics of both hemispheres, the shellflower *(Alpinia speciosa)* from the East Indies, and the fragrant ginger-lily (or torchflower, *Hedychium,* usually *H. coronarium,* presumed to have originated in the foothills of the Himalayas).

THE CANNAS *(Family Cannaceae)*

Although only about sixty species of the one genus *Canna* are known in this little family, and all of them come from tropical America, they have been hybridized so extensively by horticulturalists that the decorative plants set out for late summer displays are of no single specific origin. They are called *C. generalis* just to have a name. Each flower has three sepals, three united petals, a petal-like stamen bearing half an anther (the sole source of pollen), from one to five staminodes, and a style that is petal-like too! In Australia, a Central American species *(C. edulis)* is sometimes cultivated for its edible starchy rhizomes, and known as Queensland arrowroot.

THE ARROWROOT FAMILY *(Marantaceae)*

Tradition, more than medical evidence, holds that the starch of certain rhizomes is easier for children to digest than other kinds of starch. To this preferred material the name of arrowroot is given, perpetuating another legend: that West Indian natives used an extract from the rhizome to neutralize the poison from poisoned arrows. West Indian arrowroot—the real original material—comes from *Maranta arundinacea,* a member of a genus found in many parts of tropical America. Substitute starches sold as "arrowroot" have been prepared from many other plants, including *Canna edulis, Curcuma angustifolia* (East Indian arrowroot), and *Solanum tuberosum* (potato tubers). Adulteration of the real arrowroot can be detected by microscopic examination of the starch granules.

Arrowroot *(Maranta)* leaves are somewhat heart-shaped, pointed, and plain green, borne on a zigzag stem clasped by the petioles. The white flowers almost suggest those of a snapdragon, although their structure is more similar to that of a canna. Similar flowers sometimes appear on a favorite houseplant from Brazil, the zebra plant *(Calathea zebrina),* whose large heart-shaped or oval pointed leaves bear chevron stripes of yellow or white alternating with dark lustrous green.

The arrowroot family includes only about 350 different kinds of plants, but in the tropics of both the Old World and the New they show the greatest specialization in floral structure to be found among near relatives of the bananas. Only the orchids and the grasses surpass them in this respect among monocots.

CHAPTER 36

The Spectacular Orchids

CUES: *If the monocot plant bears flowers with a definite perianth, with the three carpels united into an inferior ovary, which matures as a capsule containing an immense number of minute seeds, and if these seeds contain little or no endosperm as a food supply for the seedling, it is a member of the Order Orchidales. It may be a lady's-slipper, a vanilla vine, a handsome Cattleya, or a dove flower.*

Of all the plants that have developed a partnership with insects, the orchids show the greatest specializations. With subtle odors or strange structure, many of them limit their pollinators to a single species of insect, or just one sex of that species. In some, the flower provides a combination of fragrance and texture that attracts the males of certain small wasps, and releases in their nervous coordination the movements that ordinarily accompany mating with a female. On the surface of the orchid, these movements gather pollen or distribute it in exactly the

Yellow lady's-slipper orchids (Cypripedium calceolus *varieties) flower from May to July in rich mixed woodlands and mossy swamps in Europe, Asia and North America. (Gottscho-Schleisner Inc.)*

places that are important to the success of the plant. In other orchids, such as the waxflower *(Angraecum sesquipedale)* of Madagascar, only a single species of hawkmoth in the area is rewarded for visiting the flower and transferring pollen; this one has a "tongue" long enough to reach the nectar the orchid secretes at the end of a spur on the bottom petal—a spur (nectary) over a foot long.

These features of orchids interested Charles Darwin so much that he drew together his own observations and all those he could find in the scientific literature into a book *(On the Various Contrivances by which Orchids are Fertilized by Insects,* 1862, London). It proved so popular, and led to discovery of so many more details, that a second edition was needed (1877, London). In the intervening years, Darwin wrote an article in which he tried to organize all the information he had on the subject in a form that naturalists would find useful and stimulating to research. It appeared in the respected *Annals and Magazine of Natural History* (1867) entitled "Notes on the fertilization of orchids."

Despite this dependence upon particular insects for pollination, orchids have been able to colonize a great variety of different parts of the world and, in each, to diversify spectacularly. More than 15,000 species of orchids are known. In the humid tropics they live on the ground, and as epiphytes upon the bark and outstretched limbs of giant trees. In temperate and arctic lands they are terrestrial, but find places to thrive in Alaska, Greenland, Siberia, and even above timberline on mountains. Most orchids get all their nourishment from the air, the soil moisture, the direct rain, and light, carrying on photosynthesis like ordinary green plants. The epiphytic kinds often exhibit swollen storage regions called pseudobulbs in their short stems, and extend pendant aerial roots covered by a special layer of moisture-absorbing tissue. A few, such as the coral-roots *(Corallorhiza)* of the Northern Hemisphere, lack chlorophyll altogether and depend upon absorbing organic compounds freed by the decay of nearby vegetation.

The flowers of all these different plants show many features in common, developed apparently by modification of the plainer pattern to be found among lilies and members of the amaryllis family. An

Many an orchid, such as these European Ophrys, *resembles an insect in shape, color and scent, and actually attracts a particular kind to brush against it and transfer its pollen. (Hermann Eisenbeiss)*

Most orchids of the genus Cymbidium *originated in tropical Asia, but fanciers now raise them on almost every continent. (E. Javorsky)*

orchid ordinarily has a six-part perianth, an outer group of three often green and sepal-like, while the inner three are petal-like and one (called the labellum) is larger than the others, often extended in a conspicuous spur toward the flower stalk. Except in the lady's-slippers *(Cypripedium,* which have two functional stamens), only one stamen produces pollen, and it is joined to the style. The pollen grains characteristically stick together in pairs, or fours, or eights, depending on the particular genus of orchids. Often these sticky masses are pressed firmly and suddenly against insect pollinators by the mechanical action of triggers and levers set in operation by the weight of the visitor. In most orchids, only the lateral two stigmatic surfaces capture pollen, and the third is sterile but extends as part of the mechanism that makes cross-pollination more likely. Lady's-slippers are unusual in having all three stigmatic surfaces collectors of pollen.

Lady's-slippers are woodland plants of the North Temperate Zone, visited by queen bumblebees. These heavy insects shoulder their way into the inflated lower petal (labellum) through a slit-shaped opening at the center. They tumble onto the stigmatic surfaces and then pass the paired anthers on their way to nectar and the daylight which they can see through two rear exits. If the inflated petal is thought of as a slipper, the three narrow spreading sepals might be a bow of ribbons holding it to a foot. The sepals are brown in the yellow lady's-slipper (*Cypripedium calceolus*, with a yellow labellum) and the pink lady's-slipper (*C. acaule*, whose pink labellum is usually veined with red), but greenish white in the showy lady's-slipper (*C. reginae* whose white labellum is blotched and streaked with crimson). Other names for these magnificent wildflowers draw attention to the same lower petal: moccasin flower, camel's foot, squirrel's shoes, and whippoorwill shoes.

Virtually all the other orchids possess only a single stamen, and can be grouped legitimately in a huge subfamily, the Monandrae. This is almost the only remnant left of the classification of flowering plants suggested by the great pioneering botanist Carl von Linné. In seeking to bring order out of the earlier chaotic classification of plants, he proposed to group together all with one stamen, all with two stamens, and so on. His scheme worked, but produced too many strange bedfellows. Botanists today rely upon far less obvious features in splitting up the plant kingdom into natural units—categories with a long history of ancestors in common, isolated from those of other categories.

Unlike the lady's-slippers, which bear their flowers singly on tall stalks, most orchids produce blossoms in clusters of a few to several dozen, in various arrangements. The orchids most raised by amateurs and most popular for corsage wear are the forty different species and hundreds of horticultural varieties in the genus *Cattleya*, all originally epiphytes from tropical America. The labellum of a Cattleya forms a rolled tube, projecting around the fertile parts of the flower and flanked above on each side by two other big petals which may measure six inches from side to side. Behind these the sepals spread, each flower part usually a different pastel shade of purple, pink, yellow or white. Colombia has chosen *C. trianae* as its national flower, Costa Rica the Turrialba orchid (*C. turrialba*), and Guatemala the white nun (*C. skinnerii*). Somewhat similar is the national flower of the Republic of Panamá, called the dove flower or Holy Ghost orchid (*Peristeria elata*), in which the labellum resembles a dove of peace with wings upraised, behind a little pulpit.

In the humid tropics of Southeast Asia, northern Australia, and Latin America, epiphytic orchids pro-

duce startling displays of small waxy flowers in bright colors like cascades of butterflies stopped in midair, supported on branching flower stalks that project from the bark and horizontal limbs of trees. The variety is almost overwhelming: one thousand species of *Bulbophyllum* in the Old World tropics, one thousand more of *Dendrobium* in the East Indies and adjacent areas, eight-hundred of *Epidendrum* in the American tropics, where the Spanish call them *pajaritos* ("little birds"). Long-lasting flowers of these kinds and others, many of which have been introduced into Hawaii, are often strung together into wreaths (*leis*) to be worn around the head, or a hat, or the neck, as tokens of welcome, or affection, or gratitude, or goodbye.

Every outdoorsman comes to cherish the orchids met under natural conditions. We think back to inconspicuous ladies-tresses (*Spiranthes*) with their surprisingly intense, delightful fragrance from tiny white flowers on an upright spiralling spike resembling braided green hair. We discovered ladies-tresses first in the Canadian northwoods, and then in southern Sweden where Carl von Linné may have walked two centuries ago. Just the mysterious odor of a peat bog anywhere in the world may be enough to remind us of a day in a remote boggy part of New Jersey, where dozens of different members of the orchid family grew in special luxuriance among insect-eating plants of several kinds.

Near Vera Cruz, Mexico, the manager of a Barclay's Bank helped us locate an orchid we longed to see on its native soil. It is the vinelike vanilla plant (*Vanilla planifrons*). He guided us also to one of the larger companies specializing in the careful curing, grading, and shipment of vanilla fruits, known as

Right above: Each flower on the drooping stalks of the perching orchid Dendrobium fimbriatum, *native to the Himalayas and Southeast Asia, expands to about three inches. Right center: From China and Hainan Island comes the epiphytic orchid* Dendrobium lodigesii, *representing a tremendously large genus found in warm parts of Asia and northern Australia. Right below: From sprawling stems clinging to stones and trees, the orchid* Laelia anceps *extends flowers during the winter from eastern Mexico to Honduras. (All by Werner Schulz) Far right: Many species of* Vanda *orchids have been discovered in Indomalaysia, each perching on some tree, producing fleshy leaves and magnificent clusters of flowers. (Lorus and Margery Milne)*

vanilla "beans" because of their shape. In Latin America, plantations of vanilla orchids are virtually unknown, certainly not on the scale to be found in Madagascar, the Seychelles, Réunion, Java, and Tahiti. But in all these foreign places, pollination must be done by hand labor if there is to be a good crop. Along the low Gulf coast of Mexico and in adjacent parts of Central America, by contrast, native insects attend to pollination. But the vanilla "beans" gathered inexpensively by Indians from wild plants near Vera Cruz cannot be marketed cheaply because of the great amount of skilled hand labor that goes into the ritual of curing, grading, and packing to insure the highest quality.

The procedure is an extremely old one, encountered first by Europeans in the 16th century when the Spanish saw the Aztecs mixing an extract of vanilla with their chocolate beverages. Modern methods show only a few refinements over the ancient ones. For controlled fermentation, the freshly picked unripe "beans" are spread for a time in the morning sun, to warm up and dry slightly. Afterward they are "sweated" in the shade under thick cloths or in large barrels. Before nightfall, they go into airtight boxes to protect them against dampness and chill. During a month or more of treatment, an enzyme that is secreted by hairlike papillae within the narrow confines of the fruit (a capsule), spreads through the fermenting cells of the wall and acts on a glycoside there, converting it into vanillin. When fully cured, a top-grade vanilla "bean" glistens in the sun with minute crystals of vanillin coating its surface. It is then straight, uniformly flat, about eight or nine inches long, three-eighths of an inch wide, one-eighth

of an inch thick, and delightfully fragrant. The best beans are shipped whole, but those of lower grade are often cut into one-inch lengths before packing, or are used in Mexico to make a distinctive *creme de vainilla* liqueur.

Vanillin can be synthesized cheaply from petroleum or from papermill wastes. Dissolved in dilute alcohol, it is sold widely. But no combination of artificial additives seems to make it match the real extract of vanilla "beans." These contribute a blend too subtle to imitate, including odorless vanillic acid, and important traces of essential oils, resins, gums, sugars, and other substances. A cured "bean" contains also a little calcium oxalate.

Vanilla has become a standard ingredient of candies, cakes, perfumes, and many tobacco products. Wherever only one flavor of ice cream is made, that one is sure to be vanilla. Our Mexican friends are proud that their country contributed this prime flavoring to the Western World. But when they call it something resembling "buy-knee'-yuh," they know without being told that the Spanish word *vainilla* is merely the diminutive of the word for a pod. *Vanilla,* the latinized form, now adopted into English and many other languages on every continent, is still an orchid with glossy pointed oval leaves. Its clustered flowers are so inconspicuously yellow-green that they can easily be overlooked by a passing person—or an insect. Each has its tubular labellum suggesting the corona of a daffodil, but backed by two more petals and three sepals. This pattern, and the single stamen joined to the style inside, spells orchid to anyone who delights in the variety shown by this spectacular family of plants.

The orchid Epidendrum cochleatum, *native to Cuba as well as to tropical America from Mexico to Brazil, is virtually ever-blooming. Its flowers, almost four inches long, last many days. (E. Javorsky)*

Index

Asterisks indicate pages containing illustrations

Curcuma, 321, 322
Currants, 97–98, 104*, 113*
Curry bush, 119, 321
Cuscuta, 208
Cushionflowers, 73*
Cushion plant, 186*
Cusparia, 119–120
Cusparia bark, 120
Cusso, 102
Custard-apple, 55
Cutch, 172
Cyarota, 275
Cyathea, 12*
Cycadaceae, 22–26
Cycads, 12, 13, 22–26
Cycas, 18*, 23–26
Cyclamen, 195
Cydonia, 105
Cymbidium, 325*
Cymbopogon, 312
Cymodocea, 267
Cynara, 241, 248, 249*
Cynodon, 309
Cyperaceae, 296–302, 315*
Cyperus, 296, 301*
Cypresses, 30, 41, 43*
Cypripedium, 323*, 236

Dacrydium, 43
Daffodils, 260
Dahlia, 243–244
Daisies, 239, 241–242
Dalbergia, 112
Dammar resins, 122, 156
Dandelion, 248
Danthonia, 307
Darwin, Charles, 42, 223, 325
Dasheen, 289
Datura, 214*, 220
Daucus, 181
Dayflower, 293
Dead man's bells, 221
Deergrass, 170*, 171
Delonix, 110
Delphinium, 51
Dendrobium, 326, 327*
Dendrocalamus, 303, 311*
Deodar, 39
Derris, 112
Deschampsia, 307
Desert-cauliflowers, 82
Devil's-paintbrush, 248
Devilweed, 240
Devonian period, 6–8, 11
deVries, Hugo, 178
Dewberries, 103, 104
Dianthus, 85
Diapensia (family Diapensaceae), 186*
Dicentra, 87
Dicots, 16, 19, 20, 45–249
Dictamnus, 120
Dieffenbachia, 286
Digitalis, 221
Digitaria, 312

Dill, 182–183
Dilly trees, 197
Dionaea, 96
Dioon, 18*, 23, 25–26
Dioscorea, 263
Dioscoreaceae, 263–264
Diospyros, 197
Dipsacaceae, 230
Dipsacus, 230
Dipterocarpaceae, 155–156
Dipterocarpus, 156
Dipteronia, 134
Dischidia, 207
Ditch-moss, 269
Dock, 74*, 78
Dodders, 208
Dodocatheon (family Primulaceae), 192*
Dogbanes, 205
Dog's-tooth-violet, 253
Dogtooth grasses, 309
Dogwoods, 182–183*
Double coconut, 284
Douglas fir, 33
Dove flower, 326
Dracaena, 257, 261*
Dragon-trees, 257, 261*
Drosera, 95*, 96
Droseraceae, 94–96
Drybalanops, 156
Duck potato, 268
Duckweed, 290
Dumb cane, 286
Durian, 148
Durio, 148
Durra, 313
Dutchman's breeches, 87
Dutchman's pipe, 80

Ebenaceae, 197
Ebenales, 196–198
Ebony, 197
Echinochloa, 312
Echinops, 236, 246, 248*
Echium, 211
Edelweiss, 236, 242*
Eelgrass, 267, 268*
Eggplant, 218
Eichornia, 293*, 295
Elaeis, 276
Elderberry, 230
Elecampane, 241
Elemi, 122
Elephant grass, 312
Elephant's-ear, 289
Elephant's-foot, 264
Elephantwood, 127*
Elettaria, 321
Elms, 69–70
Elymus, 298*
Embryo plant, 16, 22
Encephalartos, 24–25
Endive, 249
English ivy, 179–180
English wintergreen, 187
Eospermatopteris, 12
Ephedra, 44
Ephemeral annuals, 20
Epidendrum, 326, 328*

Epidermis, 7, 15
Epigaea, 188
Epigynous, 46
Epilobium, 169*, 177
Episcia, 210*, 224
Ericaceae, 187–190
Erica, 186*, 190
Ericales, 184–190
Eriophorum, 299*, 301, 315*
Eriostemon (family Rutaceae), 114*
Eryngium (family Umbelliferae), 180*
Erythrina (family Leguminosae), 226
Erythronium, 253, 256*
Erythroxylaceae, 117–118
Erythroxylum, 117–118
Eschscholtzia, 89*
Esparto, 17*, 307
Espeletia (family Compositae), 249*
Eucalyptus, 170*, 172*, 174*, 175*, 178–179
Eucharis, 260
Euchlaena, 314
Eugenia, 173
Euonymus, 133
Eupatorium, 236
Euphorbia, 114*, 117*, 123
Euphorbiaceae, 114*, 117*, 123–125
Eurotia, 82
Euterpe, 277*
Evening-primroses, 169*, 177–178
Evergreens, 10*, 11
Eyebright, 228

Fagaceae, 64–69
Fagales, 63–69
Fagopyrum, 77
Fagus, 64, 65*, 66*
Fairchild, David, 279
Fairy thimbles, 221
"False fruits," 180
Farinales, 290–296
Fawn-lilies, 253
Feathergrass, 307
Ferns, 8, 9*, 11, 20
Fertilization, 14, 22
Ferula, 182
Fescues, 15*, 304
Festuca, 15*, 304
Festuceae, 15*, 304
Feterita, 313
Ficus, 67*, 70–72
Fig trees, 66, 67*, 70–72
Filaments, stamen, 14, 115
Filberts, 64
Fique, 259
Firs, 29, 31*, 34*, 37, 38*
Fitzroya, 42
Flacourtiaceae, 157*
Flagroot, 286
"flags," 263
Flamboyant, 110

Flame trees, 222
Flame vine, 222
Flame violets, 210*, 224
Flamingo flower, 288, 291*
Flax, 115
"Flax," New Zealand, 259
Fleur-de-lis, 263
Flopper, 97
Florentine iris, 263
Florets, 239, 296, 302
Flowering plants, 13–20, 45–46
Fly-catcher, 187
Fly-honeysuckle, 229
Foerstia, 6
Forget-me-nots, 211
Forsythia, 200, 204*
Fouquiera, 156, 158*
Fouquieraceae, 156–158*
Four-o'clocks, 85
Foxglove, 221
Fragaria, 104
Frangipani, 202*, 204–205
Frankincense, 121
Franklinia, 150*, 154
Fraxinus, 200
Fried-egg plant, 157*
Frog's bit, 269
Fronds, 12, 23, 272
Fuchsia, 170*, 178
Fumariaceae, 87
Fumitory family, 87
Furcraea, 259

Gaillardia, 244
Galanthus, 258*, 260
Galls, 69
Gamopetalous, 46
Garcinia, 154–155
Gardenia, 228
Garlic, 257
Gaultheria, 189
Gaylussacia, 189
Geiger-tree, 211
Gelsemium, 203
Genlisea, 223
Gentiana, 194*, 203, 206*
Gentianaceae, 194, 198–207
Gentianales, 194*, 198–207
Geraniaceae, 116–117
Geraniales, 115–125
Geranium, 116–117
Gerard, John, 200, 217, 243, 253
German ivy, 244
Gesneria, 223
Gesneriaceae, 210*, 221*, 223–224
Ghostman, 206
Gilia, 211
Gingergrass, 312
Ginger-lily, 322

Gingers, 78*, 80, 320*, 322
Ginkgo, 12, 26*–28
Ginseng, 179, 183*
Glacier-lily, 253, 256*
Gladiolus, 263
Glasswort, 82, 84*
Glechoma, 217
Gleditsia, 109
Globe-artichoke, 248, 249*
Globe thistle, 236, 246, 248*
Glory-lily, 261*
Gloxinia, 221*, 224
Glumes, 302
Glycine, 111
Glycyrrhiza, 112
Glyptostrobus, 40
Gnetales, 43–44
Gnetum, 44
Goatgrasses, 305
Goldenbells, 200, 204*
Golden-chain tree, 108*
Golden club, 286, 291*
Golden-glow, 243
Goldenrods, 239
Gommier tree, 122
Goobers, 112
Gooseberry, 97, 98
Goosefoot family, 81–85
Gordonia, 154
Gorse (furze), 112
Gossypium, 144*, 146
Gourds, 232*, 233–234
"Grain," 304
Grama grasses, 308–309
Graminales, 15*, 17*, 296–317
Gramineae, 15*, 17*, 238*, 297*, 302–317
Granadillas, 150*, 160
Grapefruit, 119
Grapes, 137–138
Grasses, 15*, 16, 17*, 238*, 297*, 302–317
Gravel pink, 188
Gray, Asa, 245
Greasewood, 82
Green dragon, 290
Grevillea, 78
Groats, 307
Ground-cherry, 219
Groundnut, 112
Groundsels, 244, 247*
Guadua, 304
Guaiacum, 118
Guamacho, 161
Guaraná, 135
Guava tree, 174
Guevina, 78
Guinea corn, 313
Gum acacia, 106
Gum arabic, 106
Gum benzoin, 98
Gum guaiacum, 118
Gum trees, 170*, 172*–176
Gunny, 143
Guttiferaceae, 154–155
Gymnosperms, 11–14, 21–44

334